BIG IDEAS MATH®
Modeling Real Life

Grade 2
Common Core Edition

Volume 1

Ron Larson
Laurie Boswell

Erie, Pennsylvania
BigIdeasLearning.com

Big Ideas Learning, LLC
1762 Norcross Road
Erie, PA 16510-3838
USA

For product information and customer support, contact Big Ideas Learning at **1-877-552-7766** or visit us at ***BigIdeasLearning.com***.

Cover Image:
Valdis Torms, bgblue/DigitalVision Vectors/Getty Images

Printed in the U.S.A.

ISBN 13: 978-1-63708-564-6

3 4 5 6 7 8 9 10—25 24 23 22

One Voice from Kindergarten Through Algebra 2

Written by renowned authors, Dr. Ron Larson and Dr. Laurie Boswell, *Big Ideas Math* offers a seamless math pedagogy from elementary through high school. Together, Ron and Laurie provide a consistent voice that encourages students to make connections through cohesive progressions and clear instruction. Since 1992, Ron and Laurie have authored over 50 mathematics programs.

"Each time Laurie and I start working on a new program, we spend time putting ourselves in the position of the reader. How old is the reader? What is the reader's experience with mathematics? The answers to these questions become our writing guides. Our goal is to make the learning targets understandable and to develop these targets in a clear path that leads to student success."

Ron Larson

Ron Larson, Ph.D., is well known as lead author of a comprehensive and widely used mathematics program that ranges from elementary school through college. He holds the distinction of Professor Emeritus from Penn State Erie, The Behrend College, where he taught for nearly 40 years. He received his Ph.D. in mathematics from the University of Colorado. Dr. Larson engages in the latest research and advancements in mathematics education and consistently incorporates key pedagogical elements to ensure focus, coherence, rigor, and student self-reflection.

"My passion and goal in writing is to provide an essential resource for exploring and making sense of mathematics. Our program is guided by research around the learning and teaching of mathematics in the hopes of improving the achievement of all students. May this be a successful year for you!"

Laurie Boswell, Ed.D., is the former Head of School at Riverside School in Lyndonville, Vermont. In addition to authoring textbooks, she provides mathematics consulting and embedded coaching sessions. Dr. Boswell received her Ed.D. from the University of Vermont in 2010. She is a recipient of the Presidential Award for Excellence in Mathematics Teaching and later served as president of CPAM. Laurie has taught math to students at all levels, elementary through college. In addition, Laurie has served on the NCTM Board of Directors and as a Regional Director for NCSM. Along with Ron, Laurie has co-authored numerous math programs and has become a popular national speaker.

Contributors, Reviewers, and Research

Big Ideas Learning would like to express our gratitude to the mathematics education and instruction experts who served as our advisory panel, contributing specialists, and reviewers during the writing of *Big Ideas Math: Modeling Real Life*. Their input was an invaluable asset during the development of this program.

Contributing Specialists and Reviewers

- **Sophie Murphy**, Ph.D. Candidate, Melbourne School of Education, Melbourne, Australia
  Learning Targets and Success Criteria Specialist and Visible Learning Reviewer
- **Linda Hall**, Mathematics Educational Consultant, Edmond, OK
  Advisory Panel
- **Michael McDowell**, Ed.D., Superintendent, Ross, CA
  Project-Based Learning Specialist
- **Kelly Byrne**, Math Supervisor and Coordinator of Data Analysis, Downingtown, PA
  Advisory Panel
- **Jean Carwin**, Math Specialist/TOSA, Snohomish, WA
  Advisory Panel
- **Nancy Siddens**, Independent Language Teaching Consultant, Las Cruces, NM
  English Language Learner Specialist
- **Kristen Karbon**, Curriculum and Assessment Coordinator, Troy, MI
  Advisory Panel
- **Kery Obradovich**, K–8 Math/Science Coordinator, Northbrook, IL
  Advisory Panel
- **Jennifer Rollins**, Math Curriculum Content Specialist, Golden, CO
  Advisory Panel
- **Becky Walker**, Ph.D., School Improvement Services Director, Green Bay, WI
  Advisory Panel and Content Reviewer
- **Deborah Donovan**, Mathematics Consultant, Lexington, SC
  Content Reviewer
- **Tom Muchlinski**, Ph.D., Mathematics Consultant, Plymouth, MN
  Content Reviewer and Teaching Edition Contributor
- **Mary Goetz**, Elementary School Teacher, Troy, MI
  Content Reviewer
- **Nanci N. Smith**, Ph.D., International Curriculum and Instruction Consultant, Peoria, AZ
  Teaching Edition Contributor
- **Robyn Seifert-Decker**, Mathematics Consultant, Grand Haven, MI
  Teaching Edition Contributor
- **Bonnie Spence**, Mathematics Education Specialist, Missoula, MT
  Teaching Edition Contributor
- **Suzy Gagnon**, Adjunct Instructor, University of New Hampshire, Portsmouth, NH
  Teaching Edition Contributor
- **Art Johnson**, Ed.D., Professor of Mathematics Education, Warwick, RI
  Teaching Edition Contributor
- **Anthony Smith**, Ph.D., Associate Professor, Associate Dean, University of Washington Bothell, Seattle, WA
  Reading and Writing Reviewer
- **Brianna Raygor**, Music Teacher, Fridley, MN
  Music Reviewer
- **Nicole Dimich Vagle**, Educator, Author, and Consultant, Hopkins, MN
  Assessment Reviewer
- **Janet Graham**, District Math Specialist, Manassas, VA
  Response to Intervention and Differentiated Instruction Reviewer
- **Sharon Huber**, Director of Elementary Mathematics, Chesapeake, VA
  Universal Design for Learning Reviewer

Student Reviewers

- T.J. Morin
- Alayna Morin
- Ethan Bauer
- Emery Bauer
- Emma Gaeta
- Ryan Gaeta
- Benjamin SanFrotello
- Bailey SanFrotello
- Samantha Grygier
- Robert Grygier IV
- Jacob Grygier
- Jessica Urso
- Ike Patton
- Jake Lobaugh
- Adam Fried
- Caroline Naser
- Charlotte Naser

Research

Ron Larson and Laurie Boswell used the latest in educational research, along with the body of knowledge collected from expert mathematics instructors, to develop the *Modeling Real Life* series. The pedagogical approach used in this program follows the best practices outlined in the most prominent and widely accepted educational research, including:

- *Visible Learning*, John Hattie © 2009
- *Visible Learning for Teachers*
  John Hattie © 2012
- *Visible Learning for Mathematics*
  John Hattie © 2017
- *Principles to Actions: Ensuring Mathematical Success for All*
  NCTM © 2014
- *Adding It Up: Helping Children Learn Mathematics*
  National Research Council © 2001
- *Mathematical Mindsets: Unleashing Students' Potential through Creative Math, Inspiring Messages and Innovative Teaching*
  Jo Boaler © 2015
- *What Works in Schools: Translating Research into Action*
  Robert Marzano © 2003
- *Classroom Instruction That Works: Research-Based Strategies for Increasing Student Achievement*
  Marzano, Pickering, and Pollock © 2001
- *Principles and Standards for School Mathematics*
  NCTM © 2000
- *Rigorous PBL by Design: Three Shifts for Developing Confident and Competent Learners*
  Michael McDowell © 2017
- Common Core State Standards for Mathematics
  National Governors Association Center for Best Practices and Council of Chief State School Officers © 2010
- *Universal Design for Learning Guidelines*
  CAST © 2011
- Rigor/Relevance Framework®
  International Center for Leadership in Education
- *Understanding by Design*
  Grant Wiggins and Jay McTighe © 2005
- Achieve, ACT, and The College Board
- *Elementary and Middle School Mathematics: Teaching Developmentally*
  John A. Van de Walle and Karen S. Karp © 2015
- *Evaluating the Quality of Learning: The SOLO Taxonomy*
  John B. Biggs & Kevin F. Collis © 1982
- *Unlocking Formative Assessment: Practical Strategies for Enhancing Students' Learning in the Primary and Intermediate Classroom*
  Shirley Clarke, Helen Timperley, and John Hattie © 2004
- *Formative Assessment in the Secondary Classroom*
  Shirley Clarke © 2005
- *Improving Student Achievement: A Practical Guide to Assessment for Learning*
  Toni Glasson © 2009

Focus and Coherence from

Instructional Design

A single authorship team from Kindergarten through Algebra 2 results in a logical progression of focused topics with meaningful coherence from course to course.

FOCUS

A focused program dedicates lessons, activities, and assessments to grade-level standards while simultaneously supporting and engaging you in the major work of the course.

The **Learning Targets** in your book and the **Success Criteria** in the Teaching Edition focus the learning for each lesson into manageable chunks, with clear teaching text and examples.

Learning Target: Write related addition and subtraction equations to complete a fact family.

Laurie's Notes

Preparing to Teach

Students have heard about time and the language of time. Most students do not understand time or know how to tell time on an analog clock. In this lesson, students are introduced to telling time to the hour. They learn about the hour hand and telling time as o'clock.

Laurie's Notes, located in the Teaching Edition, prepare your teacher for the math concepts in each chapter and lesson and make connections to the threads of major topics for the course.

Think and Grow
4 + 7 = 11
addend
addend
sum
7 + 4 = 11
Changing the order of the addends does not change the sum.
The expressions 4 + 7 and 7 + 4 are both equal to 11.

a Single Authorship Team

COHERENCE

A single authorship team built a coherent program that has intentional progression of content within each grade and between grade levels. You will build new understanding on foundations from prior grades and connect concepts throughout the course.

The authors developed content that progresses from prior chapters and grades to future ones. In addition to charts like this one, Laurie's Notes give your teacher insights about where you have come from and where you are going in your learning progression.

Through the Grades		
Kindergarten	**Grade 1**	**Grade 2**
• Represent addition and subtraction with various models and strategies. • Solve addition and subtraction word problems within 10. • Fluently add and subtract within 5.	• Solve addition and subtraction word problems within 20. • Fluently add and subtract within 10. • Determine the unknown number to complete addition and subtraction equations.	• Solve addition and subtraction word problems within 100. • Solve word problems involving length and money. • Solve one- and two-step word problems. • Fluently add and subtract within 20.

One author team thoughtfully wrote each course, creating a seamless progression of content from Kindergarten to Algebra 2.

	Grade K	Grade 1	Grade 2	Grade 3	Grade 4	Grade 5	Grade 6	
Number and Quantity	Number and Operations – Base Ten				Number and Operations – Base Ten		The Number System	
	Work with numbers 11–19 to gain foundations for place value. *Chapter 8*	Extend the counting sequence. Use place value and properties of operations to add and subtract. *Chapters 6–9*	Use place value and properties of operations to add and subtract. *Chapters 2–10, 14*	Use place value and properties of operations to perform multi-digit arithmetic. *Chapters 7–9, 12*	Generalize place value understanding for multi-digit whole numbers. Use place value and properties of operations to perform multi-digit arithmetic. *Chapters 1–5*	Understand the place value system. Perform operations with multi-digit whole numbers and with decimals to hundredths. *Chapters 1, 3–7*	Perform operations with multi-digit numbers and find common factors and multiples. *Chapter 1* Divide fractions by fractions. *Chapter 2* Extend understanding of numbers to the rational number system. *Chapter 8*	Perfor ration *Chapt*
				Num. and Oper. – Fractions	Number and Operations – Fractions		Ratios and Proportional Relation	
				Understand fractions as numbers. *Chapters 10, 11, 14*	Extend understanding of fraction equivalence and ordering. Build fractions from unit ... mal notation ... d compare	Add, subtract, multiply, and divide fractions. *Chapters 6, 8–11*	Use ratios to solve problems. *Chapters 3, 4*	Use pr to solv *Chapt*

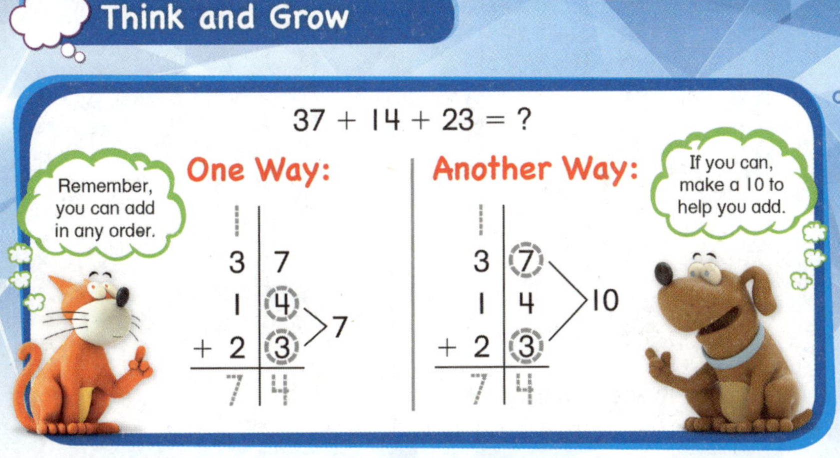

Think and Grow
37 + 14 + 23 = ?
One Way:
Remember, you can add in any order.
Another Way:
If you can, make a 10 to help you add.

Throughout each course, lessons build on prior learning as new concepts are introduced. Here you are reminded of rules and strategies that you already know to help solve the addition problem.

Rigor in Math: A Balanced Approach

Instructional Design

The authors wrote each chapter and every lesson to provide a meaningful balance of rigorous instruction.

RIGOR

A rigorous program provides a balance of three important building blocks.

- **Conceptual Understanding**
  Discovering why
- **Procedural Fluency**
  Learning how
- **Application**
  Knowing when to apply

Conceptual Understanding
You have the opportunity to develop foundational concepts central to the *Learning Target* in each *Explore and Grow* by experimenting with new concepts, talking with peers, and asking questions.

Conceptual Thinking
Conceptual questions ask you to think deeply.

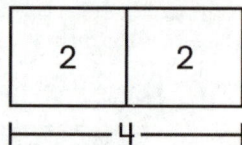

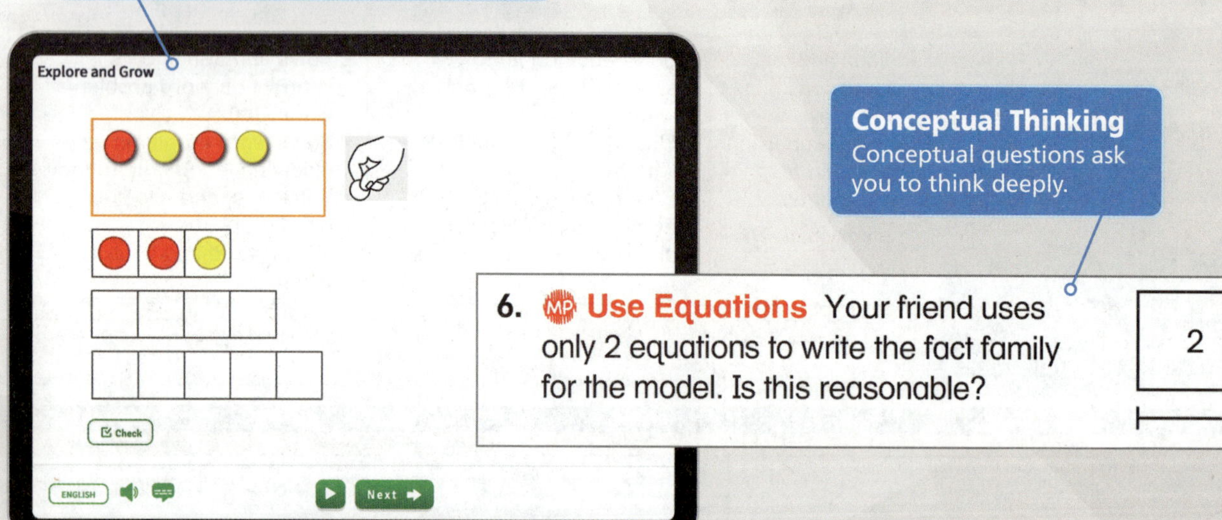

6. MP Use Equations Your friend uses only 2 equations to write the fact family for the model. Is this reasonable?

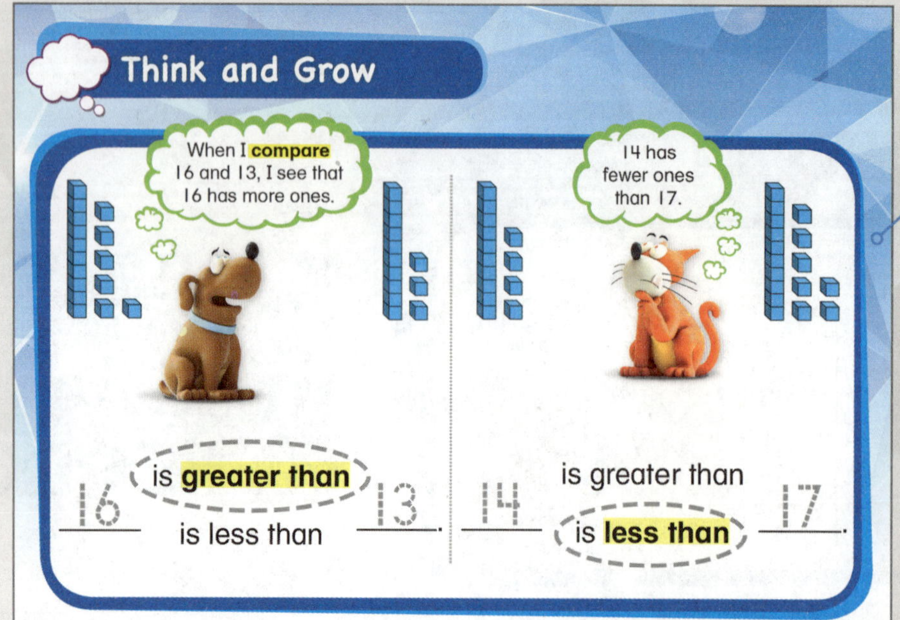

Think and Grow
When I compare 16 and 13, I see that 16 has more ones.
14 has fewer ones than 17.
16
is greater than
is less than
13
14
is greater than
is less than
17

Procedural Fluency
Solidify learning with clear, stepped-out teaching in *Think and Grow* examples.

Then shift conceptual understanding into procedural fluency with *Show and Grow*, *Apply and Grow*, *Practice*, and *Review & Refresh*.

Subtract Numbers within 20

- What do bees make?
- How many bees do you see? 7 of them fly away. How many bees are left?

Chapter Learning Target:
Understand subtraction strategies.
Chapter Success Criteria:
- I can identify counting back strategies.
- I can describe subtraction equations.
- I can explain the subtraction strategy I used.
- I can compare addition and subtraction strategies.

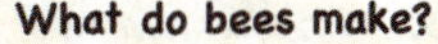

Connecting to Real Life

Begin every chapter thinking about the world around you. Then apply what you learn in the chapter with a related *Performance Task*.

Name ________________

Performance Task 5

1. You keep track of the number of honeybees and bumblebees you see.

Day	Honeybees
Monday	12
Tuesday	6
Wednesday	13

Day	Bumblebees
Monday	5
Tuesday	14
Wednesday	

a. How many more honeybees did you see on Monday than on Tuesday?

____ more honeybees

Daily Application Practice

Modeling Real Life, *Dig Deeper*, and other non-routine problems help you apply surface-level skills to gain a deeper understanding. These problems lead to independent problem-solving.

15. MP **Modeling Real Life** Your magic book has 163 tricks. Your friend's magic book has 100 more tricks than yours. How many tricks does your friend's magic book have?

_____ tricks

16. **DIG DEEPER!** You have 624 songs. Newton has 100 fewer than you. Descartes has 10 more than Newton. How many songs does Descartes have?

_____ songs

Problem-Solving Plan

Walk through the Problem-Solving Plan, featured in many *Think and Grow* examples, to help you make sense of problems with confidence.

You find 19 objects in a scavenger hunt. You find 13 fewer objects than your friend. How many objects does your friend find?

Circle what you know. Underline what you need to find.

Solve:

Use a model to help organize the information.

Friend: 32

You: 19 | 13

Write and solve an addition problem.

$$\begin{array}{r} 19 \\ +\ 13 \\ \hline 32 \end{array}$$

32 objects

THE PROBLEM-SOLVING PLAN

1. **Understand the Problem**
   Think about what the problem is asking. Circle what you know and underline what you need to find.
2. **Make a Plan**
   Plan your solution pathway before jumping in to solve. Identify any relationships and decide on a problem-solving strategy.
3. **Solve and Check**
   As you solve the problem, be sure to evaluate your progress and check your answers. Throughout the problem-solving process, you must continually ask, "Does this make sense?" and be willing to change course if necessary.

Embedded Mathematical Practices

Encouraging Mathematical Mindsets

Developing proficiency in the **Mathematical Practices** is about becoming a mathematical thinker. Learn to ask why, and to reason and communicate with others as you learn. Use this guide to develop proficiency with the mathematical practices.

1

One way to **Make Sense of Problems and Persevere in Solving Them** is to use the Problem-Solving Plan. Take time to analyze the given information and what the problem is asking to help you plan a solution pathway.

Look for labels such as:

- Find Entry Points
- Analyze a Problem
- Interpret a Solution
- Make a Plan
- Use a Similar Problem
- Check Your Work

There are 33 students on a bus. 10 more get on. How many students are on the bus now?

Addition equation:

MP **Check Your Work** When adding 10, should the digit in the tens place or the ones place change?

___ students

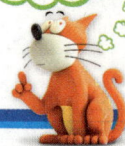

5. MP **Analyze a Problem** Use the numbers shown to write two addition equations.

8 10 2

___ + ___ = ___

___ + ___ = ___

2

Reason Abstractly when you explore an example using numbers and models to represent the problem. Other times, **Reason Quantitatively** when you see relationships in numbers or models and draw conclusions about the problem.

7. MP **Reasoning** The minute hand points to the 7. What number will it point to in 10 minutes?

Look for labels such as:

- Reasoning
- Number Sense
- Use Equations
- Use Expressions

3. MP **Number Sense** Which numbers can you subtract from 55 without regrouping?

15 49 33 24

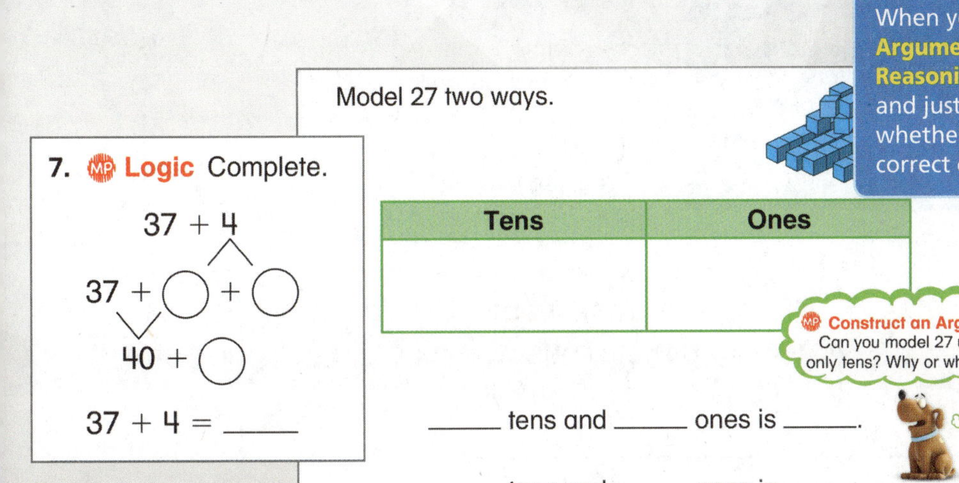

7. Logic Complete.
37 + 4
37 + ◯ + ◯
40 + ◯
37 + 4 = ____
Model 27 two ways.
Tens
Ones
Construct an Argument
Can you model 27 using only tens? Why or why not?
____ tens and ____ ones is ____.
____ tens and ____ ones is ____.

When you **Construct Viable Arguments and Critique the Reasoning of Others**, you make and justify conclusions and decide whether others' arguments are correct or flawed.

3

Look for labels such as:

- Construct an Argument
- You Be the Teacher
- Logic
- Make a Conjecture
- Justify a Result
- Compare Arguments

7. **Graph Data** Complete the weather chart to show an equal number of sunny days and rainy days. Write an equation to show how many sunny days and rainy days there are in all.

SUN	MON	TUE	WED	THU	FRI	SAT

___ + ___ = ___

Think and Grow: Modeling Real Life

Will the scissors fit inside a pencil case that is 7 color tiles long?

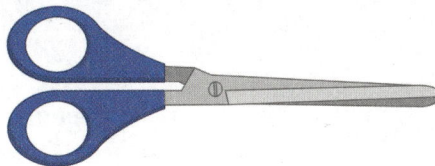

Circle: Yes No

Tell how you know:

Does It Make Sense? To fit inside, should the scissors be shorter or longer than the case?

4

To **Model with Mathematics**, apply the math you learned to a real-life problem and interpret mathematical results in the context of the situation.

Look for labels such as:

- Modeling Real Life
- Graph Data
- Analyze a Relationship
- Does It Make Sense?

BUILDING TO FULL UNDERSTANDING

Throughout each course, you have opportunities to demonstrate specific aspects of the mathematical practices. Labels throughout the book indicate gateways to those aspects. Collectively, these opportunities will lead to a full understanding of each mathematical practice. Developing these mindsets and habits will give meaning to the mathematics you learn.

5

To **Use Appropriate Tools Strategically**, you need to know what tools are available and think about how each tool might help you solve a mathematical problem. When you choose a tool to use, remember that it may have limitations.

Look for labels such as:
- Choose Tools
- Use Math Tools
- Use Technology

8. MP **Choose Tools** Would you measure the length of a bus with a centimeter ruler or a meter stick? Why?

MP Use Math Tools
How can you use a drawing to help organize the information given?

11. DIG DEEPER! There are 63 people in a theater, 21 people in the lobby, and 10 people in the parking lot. How many more people are in the theater than in both the lobby and the parking lot?

_____ more people

6

When you **Attend to Precision**, you are developing a habit of being careful in how you talk about concepts, label work, and write answers.

Look for labels such as:
- Precision
- Communicate Clearly
- Maintain Accuracy

7. DIG DEEPER! Complete the model and the equation to match.

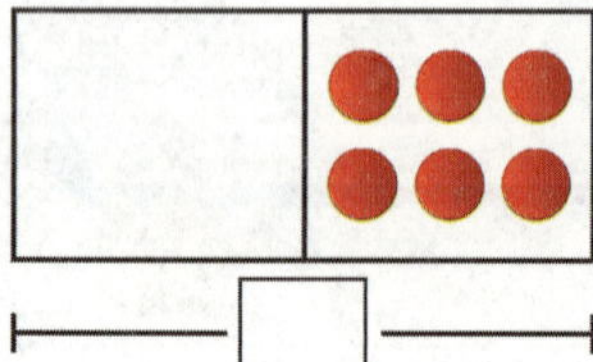

___ + ___ = 8

MP Communicate Clearly
In the model, what shows the addends? the sum?

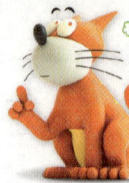

5. MP **Precision** Which picture shows the correct way to measure the straw?

6. MP **Patterns** Find the sums. Think: What do you notice?

$4 + 5 =$ ____

$4 + 4 =$ ____

$5 + 5 =$ ____

	Tens	Ones
	☐	
	3	8
+	2	4

$38 + 24 =$ ____

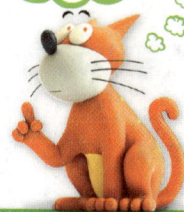

MP **Structure** What step did you use to find 38 + 24 that you would not use to find 31 + 24? Why?

7

Look For and Make Use of Structure by looking closely to see structure within a mathematical statement, or stepping back for an overview to see how individual parts make one single object.

Look for labels such as:
- Structure
- Patterns

8. MP **Repeated Reasoning** What other shape has the same number of surfaces, vertices, and edges as a rectangular prism? How is that shape different from a rectangular prism?

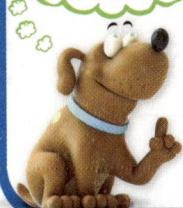

MP **Find a Rule** When you add or subtract 1, what is true about the sum or difference?

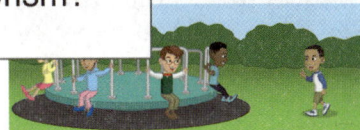

4 + 1 = 5

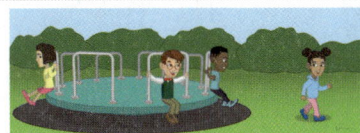

4 − 1 = 3

8

When you **Look For and Express Regularity in Repeated Reasoning**, you can notice patterns and make generalizations. Remember to keep in mind the goal of a problem, which will help you evaluate reasonableness of answers along the way.

Look for labels such as:
- Repeated Reasoning
- Find a Rule

Visible Learning Through Learning Targets,

Making Learning Visible

Knowing the learning intention of a chapter or lesson helps you focus on the purpose of an activity, rather than simply completing it in isolation. This program supports visible learning through the consistent use of Learning Targets and Success Criteria to help you become successful.

Every chapter shows a **Learning Target** and four related **Success Criteria**. These are incorporated throughout the chapter content to help guide you in your learning.

Every lesson shows a **Learning Target** that is purposefully integrated into each carefully written lesson.

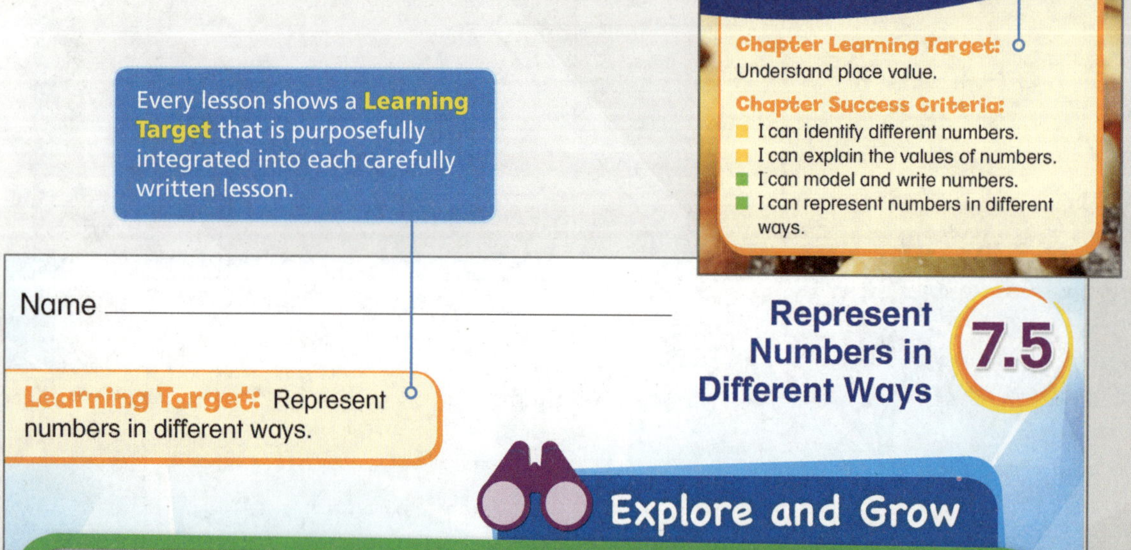

Chapter Learning Target:
Understand place value.
Chapter Success Criteria:
I can identify different numbers.
I can explain the values of numbers.
I can model and write numbers.
I can represent numbers in different ways.
Name
Represent Numbers in Different Ways
7.5
Learning Target: Represent numbers in different ways.
Explore and Grow

Access the **Learning Target** and **Success Criteria** on every page of the Dynamic Student Edition.

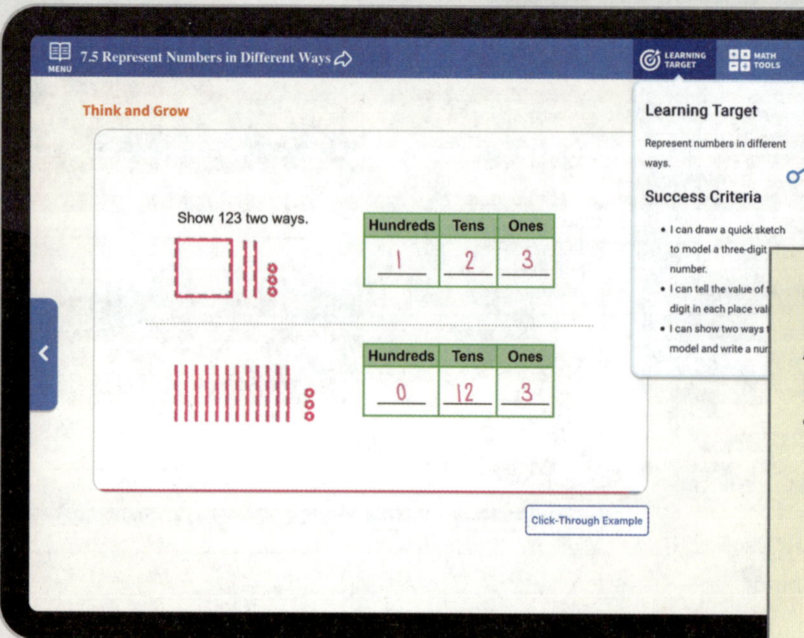

QUESTIONS FOR LEARNING

As you progress through a lesson, you should be able to answer the following questions.

- What am I learning?
- Why am I learning this?
- Where am I in my learning?
- How will I know when I have learned it?
- Where am I going next?

Success Criteria, and Self-Assessment

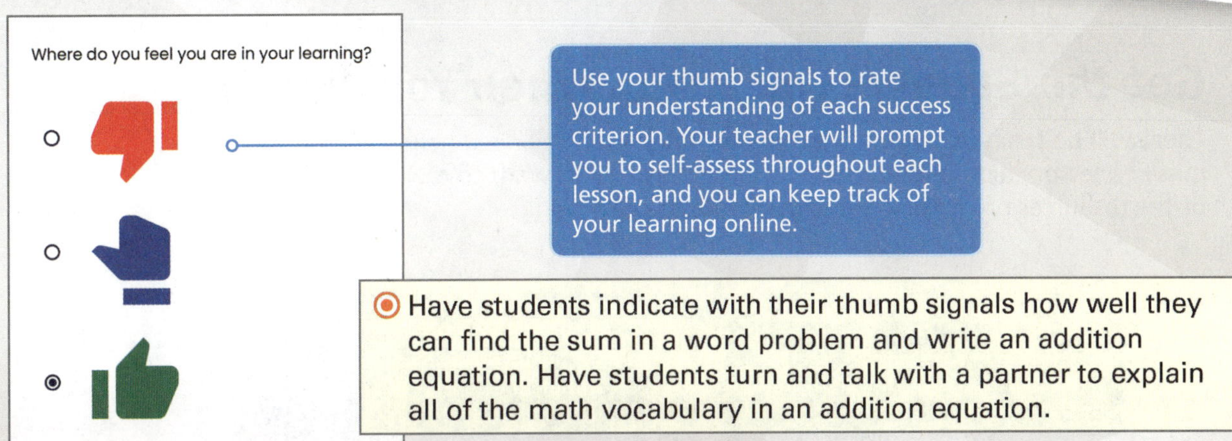

Where do you feel you are in your learning?

Use your thumb signals to rate your understanding of each success criterion. Your teacher will prompt you to self-assess throughout each lesson, and you can keep track of your learning online.

Have students indicate with their thumb signals how well they can find the sum in a word problem and write an addition equation. Have students turn and talk with a partner to explain all of the math vocabulary in an addition equation.

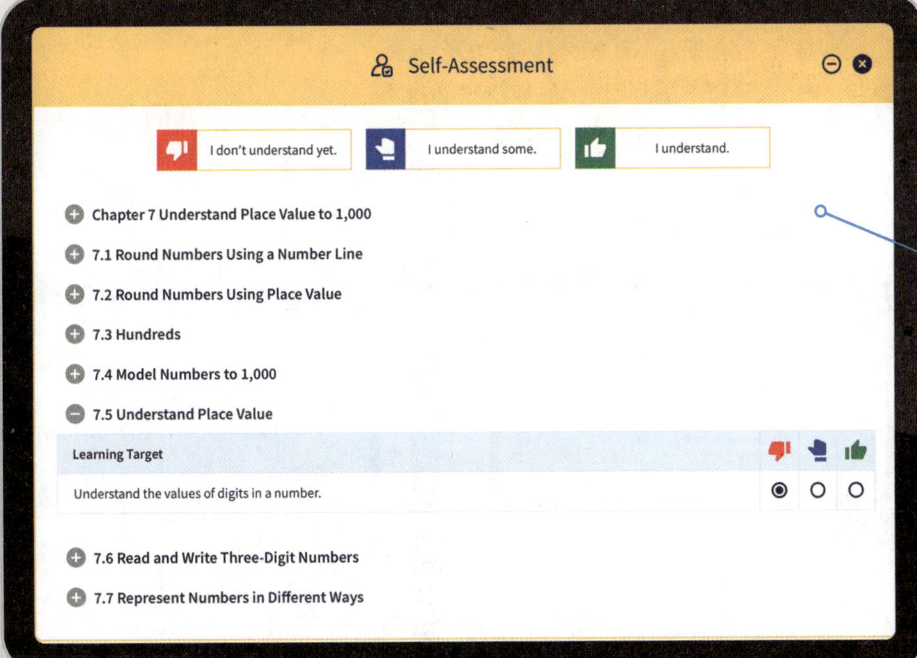

Self-Assessments are included throughout every lesson, and in the **Chapter Review**, to help you take ownership of your learning and think about where to go next.

Ensuring Positive Outcomes

John Hattie's *Visible Learning* research consistently shows that using Learning Targets and Success Criteria can result in two years' growth in one year, ensuring positive outcomes for your learning and achievement.

Sophie Murphy, M.Ed., wrote the chapter-level Learning Targets and Success Criteria for this program. Sophie is currently completing her Ph.D. at the University of Melbourne in Australia with Professor John Hattie as her leading supervisor. Sophie completed her Master's thesis with Professor John Hattie in 2015. Sophie has over 20 years of experience as a teacher and school leader in private and public school settings in Australia.

Strategic Support for Online Learning

Get the Support You Need, When You Need It

There will be times throughout this course when you may need help. Whether you missed a lesson, did not understand the content, or just want to review, take advantage of the resources provided in the *Dynamic Student Edition*.

Use the **Self-Assessment** tool to keep track of your understanding of the lesson's Learning Target and Success Criteria.

Choose **Math Tools** to engage with pattern blocks, digital number lines, linking cubes, and other tools to explore and understand math concepts.

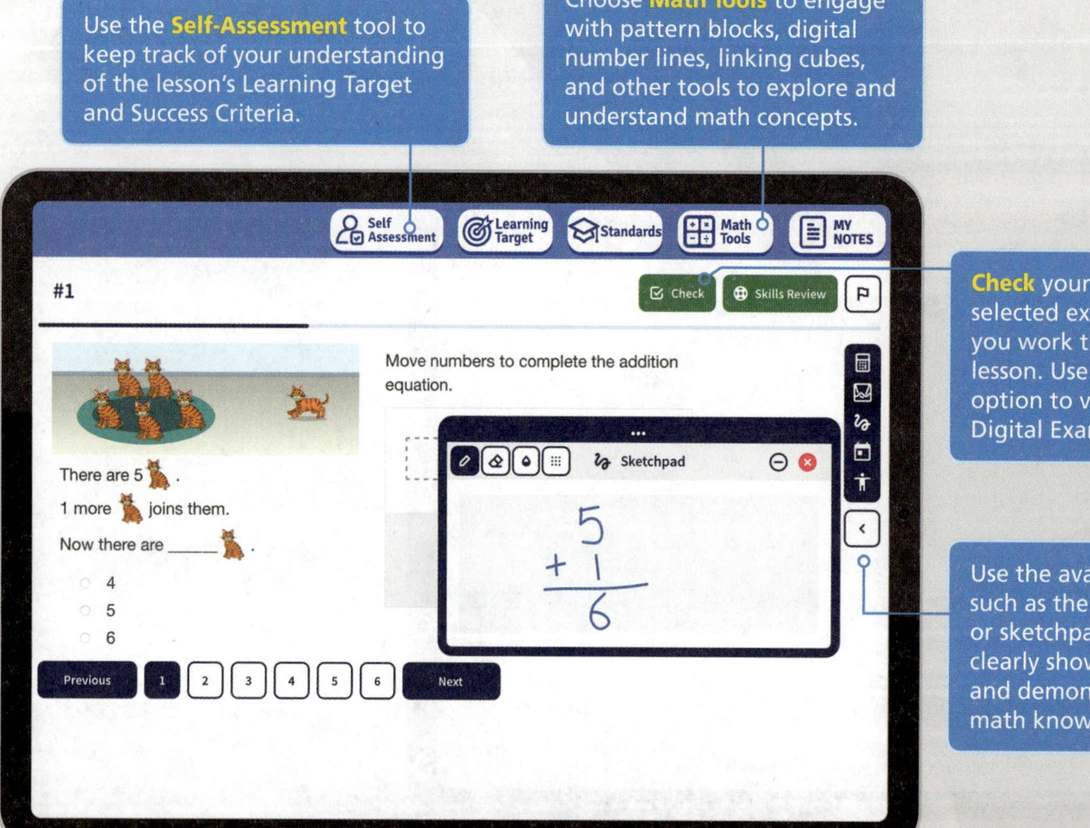

Check your answers to selected exercises as you work through the lesson. Use the **Help** option to view the Digital Example videos.

Use the available **tools**, such as the calculator or sketchpad, to help clearly show your work and demonstrate your math knowledge.

USE THESE QR CODES TO EXPLORE ADDITIONAL RESOURCES

Multi-Language Glossary
View definitions and examples of vocabulary words

Skills Trainer
Practice previously learned skills

Interactive Tools
Visualize mathematical concepts

Skills Review Handbook
A collection of review topics

Learning with Newton and Descartes

Who are Newton and Descartes?

Newton and Descartes are helpful math assistants who appear throughout your math book! They encourage you to think deeply about concepts and develop strong mathematical mindsets with Mathematical Practice questions.

MP Check Your Work
How can you use the addition facts to check that the differences are correct?

MP Precision
Which unit of measure did you use in your answer? Why?

Newton & Descartes's Math Musicals

Math Musicals offer an engaging connection between math, literature, and music! Newton and Descartes team up in these educational stories and songs to bring mathematics to life!

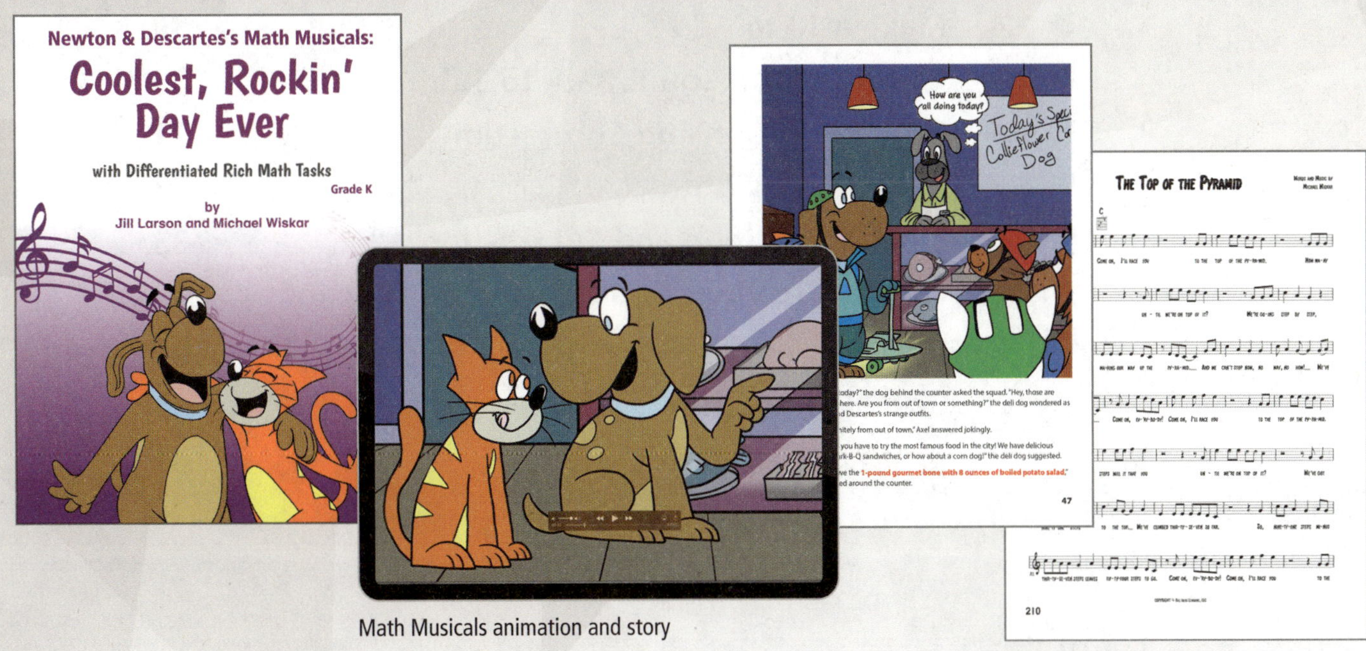

Math Musicals animation and story

Sheet Music

1 Numbers and Arrays

Vocabulary ... 2
■ 1.1 Even and Odd Numbers ... 3
■ 1.2 Model Even and Odd Numbers ... 9
■ 1.3 Equal Groups ... 15
■ 1.4 Use Arrays ... 21
■ 1.5 Make Arrays ... 27
Performance Task: Art Supplies ... 33
Game: Array Flip and Find ... 34
Chapter Practice ... 35

Fluency and Strategies within 20

Vocabulary ... 40
■ 2.1 Add in Any Order ... 41
■ 2.2 Use Doubles ... 47
■ 2.3 Add Three Numbers ... 53
■ 2.4 Make a 10 to Add ... 59
■ 2.5 Count On and Count Back to Subtract ... 65
■ 2.6 Relate Addition and Subtraction ... 71
■ 2.7 Get to 10 to Subtract ... 77
■ 2.8 Practice Addition and Subtraction ... 83
■ 2.9 Problem Solving: Addition and Subtraction ... 89
Performance Task: Library Books ... 95
Game: Joey Jump ... 96
Chapter Practice ... 97

■ Major Topic
■ Supporting Topic
■ Additional Topic

Addition to 100 Strategies

Vocabulary ... 102
- 3.1 Add Tens Using a Number Line ... 103
- 3.2 Add Tens and Ones Using a Number Line ... 109
- 3.3 Use Place Value to Add ... 115
- 3.4 Decompose to Add Tens and Ones ... 121
- 3.5 Use Compensation to Add ... 127
- 3.6 Practice Addition Strategies ... 133
- 3.7 Problem Solving: Addition ... 139

Performance Task: Amusement Park ... 145
Game: Three in a Row: Addition ... 146
Chapter Practice ... 147

Fluently Add within 100

Vocabulary ... 152
- 4.1 Use Partial Sums to Add ... 153
- 4.2 More Partial Sums ... 159
- 4.3 Regroup to Add ... 165
- 4.4 Add Two-Digit Numbers ... 171
- 4.5 Practice Adding Two-Digit Numbers ... 177
- 4.6 Add Up to 3 Two-Digit Numbers ... 183
- 4.7 More Problem Solving: Addition ... 189

Performance Task: Swimming ... 195
Game: Solve and Cover: Addition ... 196
Chapter Practice ... 197
Cumulative Practice ... 201

Let's learn how to fluently add within 100!

Subtraction to 100 Strategies

Vocabulary 206

■ 5.1 Subtract Tens Using a Number Line 207

■ 5.2 Subtract Tens and Ones Using a Number Line 213

■ 5.3 Use Addition to Subtract 219

■ 5.4 Decompose to Subtract 225

■ 5.5 Decompose to Subtract Tens and Ones 231

■ 5.6 Use Compensation to Subtract 237

■ 5.7 Practice Subtraction Strategies 243

■ 5.8 Problem Solving: Subtraction 249

Performance Task: Egg Incubator 255

Game: Three in a Row: Subtraction 256

Chapter Practice 257

Fluently Subtract within 100

Vocabulary 262

■ 6.1 Model and Regroup to Subtract 263

■ 6.2 Use Models to Subtract a One-Digit Number from a Two-Digit Number 269

■ 6.3 Use Models to Subtract Two-Digit Numbers 275

■ 6.4 Subtract from a Two-Digit Number 281

■ 6.5 Use Addition to Check Subtraction 287

■ 6.6 Practice Two-Digit Subtraction 293

■ 6.7 More Problem Solving: Subtraction 299

Performance Task: Paper Snowflakes 305

Game: Solve and Cover: Subtraction 306

Chapter Practice 307

■ Major Topic
■ Supporting Topic
■ Additional Topic

Understand Place Value to 1,000

Vocabulary 312
- 7.1 Hundreds 313
- 7.2 Model Numbers to 1,000 319
- 7.3 Understand Place Value 325
- 7.4 Write Three-Digit Numbers 331
- 7.5 Represent Numbers in Different Ways 337

Performance Task: Trail Mix 343
Game: Naming Numbers Flip and Find 344
Chapter Practice 345

Count and Compare Numbers to 1,000

Vocabulary 350
- 8.1 Count to 120 in Different Ways 351
- 8.2 Count to 1,000 in Different Ways 357
- 8.3 Place Value Patterns 363
- 8.4 Find More or Less 369
- 8.5 Compare Numbers Using Symbols 375
- 8.6 Compare Numbers Using a Number Line 381

Performance Task: Fish 387
Game: Number Boss 388
Chapter Practice 389
Cumulative Practice 393

Let's learn how to count and compare numbers to 1,000!

9

Add Numbers within 1,000

Vocabulary ... 398

9.1 Add 10 and 100 ... 399

9.2 Use a Number Line to Add Hundreds and Tens ... 405

9.3 Use a Number Line to Add Three-Digit Numbers ... 411

9.4 Use Compensation to Add Three-Digit Numbers ... 417

9.5 Use Partial Sums to Add Three-Digit Numbers ... 423

9.6 Use Models to Add Three-Digit Numbers ... 429

9.7 Add Three-Digit Numbers ... 435

9.8 Add Up to 4 Two-Digit Numbers ... 441

9.9 Explain Addition Strategies ... 447

Performance Task: Robots ... 453

Game: Three in a Row: Three-Digit Addition ... 454

Chapter Practice ... 455

Three in a Row: Three-Digit Addition

To Play: Players take turns. On your turn, spin both spinners. Add the two numbers and cover the sum. Continue playing until someone gets three in a row.

Subtract Numbers within 1,000

Vocabulary ... 460
- 10.1 Subtract 10 and 100 ... 461
- 10.2 Use a Number Line to Subtract Hundreds and Tens ... 467
- 10.3 Use a Number Line to Subtract Three-Digit Numbers ... 473
- 10.4 Use Compensation to Subtract Three-Digit Numbers ... 479
- 10.5 Use Models to Subtract Three-Digit Numbers ... 485
- 10.6 Subtract Three-Digit Numbers ... 491
- 10.7 Subtract from Numbers That Contain Zeros ... 497
- 10.8 Use Addition to Subtract ... 503
- 10.9 Explain Subtraction Strategies ... 509

Performance Task: Race Cars ... 515
Game: Greatest and Least ... 516
Chapter Practice ... 517

11

Measure and Estimate Lengths

Vocabulary ... 522
- 11.1 Measure Lengths in Centimeters ... 523
- 11.2 Measure Objects Using Metric Length Units ... 529
- 11.3 Estimate Lengths in Metric Units ... 535
- 11.4 Measure Lengths in Inches ... 541
- 11.5 Measure Objects Using Customary Length Units ... 547
- 11.6 Estimate Lengths in Customary Units ... 553
- 11.7 Measure Objects Using Different Length Units ... 559
- 11.8 Measure and Compare Lengths ... 565

Performance Task: Gardening ... 571
Game: Spin and Cover ... 572
Chapter Practice ... 573

Let's learn how to measure and estimate lengths!

Solve Length Problems

Vocabulary 578

■ 12.1 Use a Number Line to Add and Subtract Lengths 579

■ 12.2 Problem Solving: Length 585

■ 12.3 Problem Solving: Missing Measurement 591

■ 12.4 Practice Measurement Problems 597

Performance Task: Musical Instruments 603

Game: Draw and Cover 604

Chapter Practice 605

Cumulative Practice 607

Represent and Interpret Data

Vocabulary 612

■ 13.1 Sort and Organize Data 613

■ 13.2 Read and Interpret Picture Graphs 619

■ 13.3 Make Picture Graphs 625

■ 13.4 Read and Interpret Bar Graphs 631

■ 13.5 Make Bar Graphs 637

■ 13.6 Make Line Plots 643

■ 13.7 Measure Objects and Make Line Plots 649

Performance Task: Art Supplies 655

Game: Spin and Graph 656

Chapter Practice 657

■ Major Topic
■ Supporting Topic
■ Additional Topic

Money and Time

Vocabulary 662
- 14.1 Find Total Values of Coins 663
- 14.2 Order to Find Total Values of Coins 669
- 14.3 Show Money Amounts in Different Ways 675
- 14.4 Make One Dollar 681
- 14.5 Make Change from One Dollar 687
- 14.6 Find Total Values of Bills 693
- 14.7 Problem Solving: Money 699
- 14.8 Tell Time to the Nearest Five Minutes 705
- 14.9 Tell Time Before and After the Hour 711
- 14.10 Relate A.M. and P.M. 717

Performance Task: Public Transportation 723
Game: Flip and Find 724
Chapter Practice 725

Identify and Partition Shapes

Vocabulary 730
- 15.1 Describe Two-Dimensional Shapes 731
- 15.2 Identify Angles of Polygons 737
- 15.3 Draw Polygons 743
- 15.4 Identify and Draw Cubes 749
- 15.5 Compose Rectangles 755
- 15.6 Identify Two, Three, or Four Equal Shares 761
- 15.7 Partition Shapes into Equal Shares 767
- 15.8 Analyze Equal Shares of the Same Shape 773

Performance Task: Suncatchers 779
Game: Three in a Row: Equal Shares 780
Chapter Practice 781
Cumulative Practice 785

Glossary A1
Index A13
Reference Sheet A23

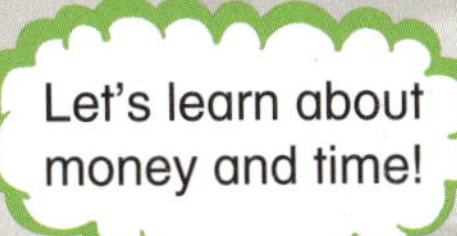

Let's learn about money and time!

1 Numbers and Arrays

- What types of art supplies do you like to use? What can you create with those supplies?
- There are 5 jars of paint in each row. How many jars of paint are there in all?

Chapter Learning Target:
Understand numbers and arrays.

Chapter Success Criteria:
- I can identify odd and even numbers.
- I can explain whether a number is even or odd.
- I can create an array.
- I can write equations.

Name ____________________

Vocabulary

Review Words
plus sign
equal sign

Organize It

Use the review words to complete the graphic organizer.

$$4 + 4 = 8$$

Define It

Use your vocabulary cards to identify the word.

1.    

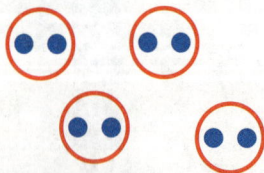

2.  

3.  

Chapter 1 Vocabulary Cards

array

column

equal groups

equation

even

odd

repeated addition

row

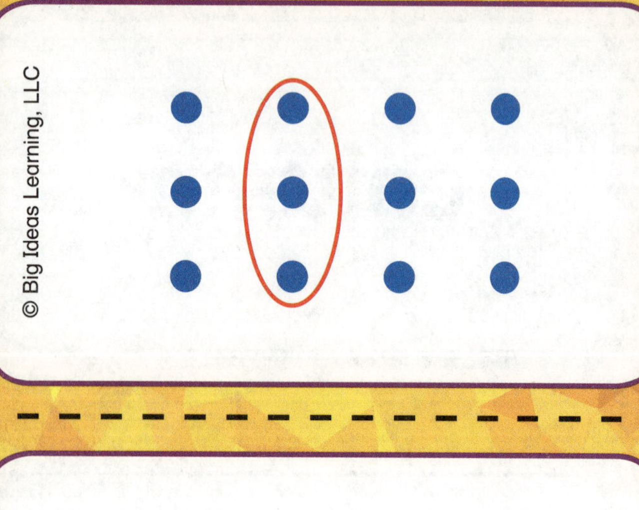

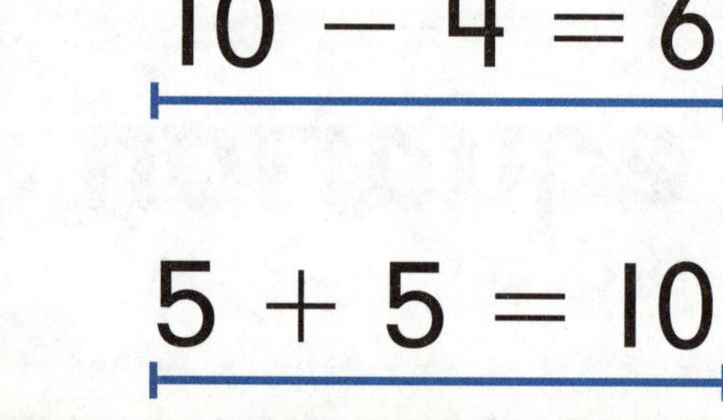

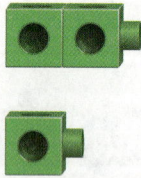

$$10 - 4 = 6$$

$$5 + 5 = 10$$

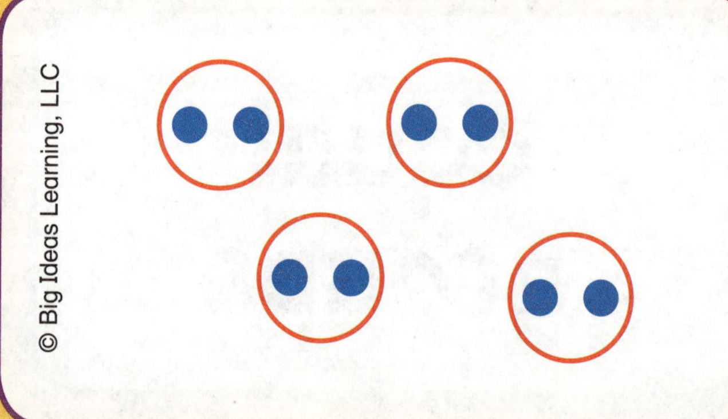

cannot be shown as equal groups

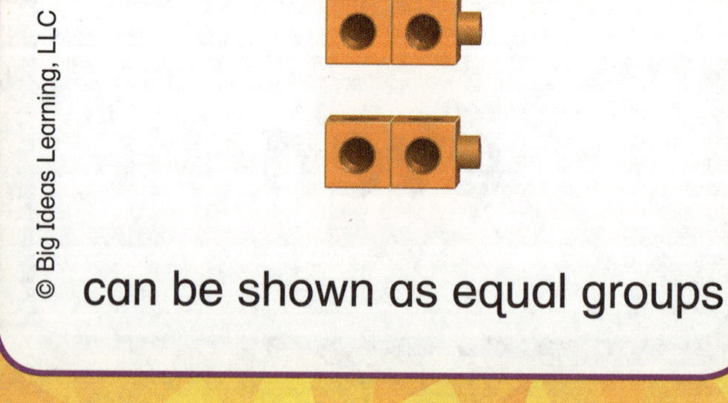

can be shown as equal groups

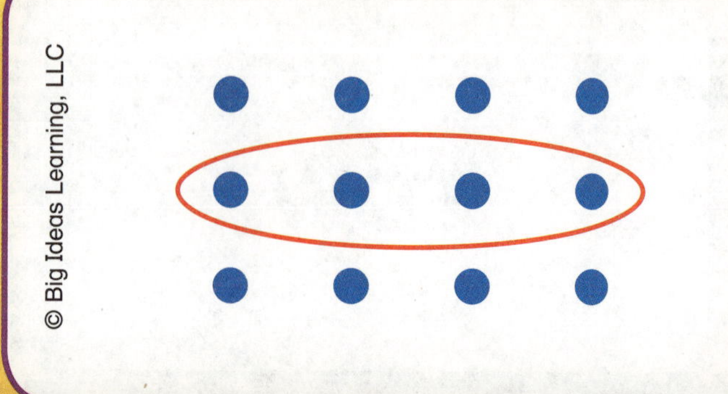

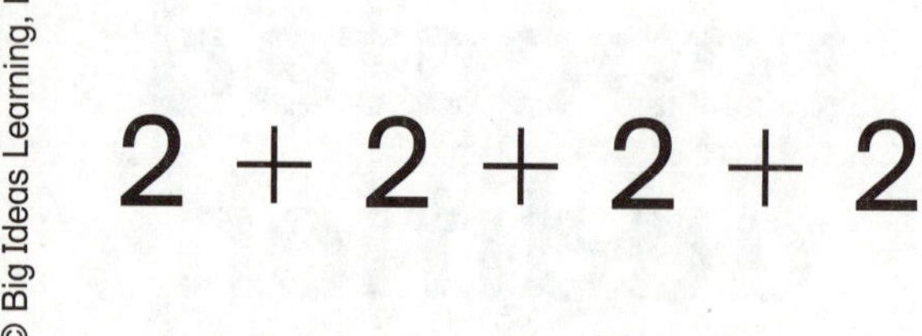

$$2 + 2 + 2 + 2$$

Name ______________________________

Learning Target: Tell whether a number is even or odd.

Use linking cubes to model each story.

There are 6 students in the gym. Does each student have a partner?

There are 5 students in the library. Does each student have a partner?

Analyze a Problem How are your models different?

Think and Grow

An even number can be shown as 2 equal parts.
8
Even
Odd
7
Even
Odd
An odd number cannot be shown as 2 equal parts.

Show and Grow I can do it!

1.

______

Even Odd

2.

______

Even Odd

Color cubes to show the number. Circle *even* or *odd.*

3. 11

Even Odd

4. 16

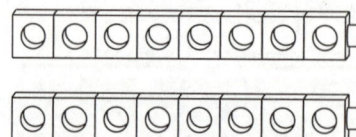

Even Odd

Name ______________________________

Apply and Grow: Practice

Color cubes to show the number. Circle *even* or *odd.*

5. 13

Even Odd

6. 10

Even Odd

Is the number *even* or *odd*?

7. 1

Even Odd

8. 4

Even Odd

9. 18

Even Odd

10. 17

Even Odd

11. 19

Even Odd

12. 20

Even Odd

13.  **Number Sense** Circle *even* or *odd* to describe each group. Then write each number in the correct group.

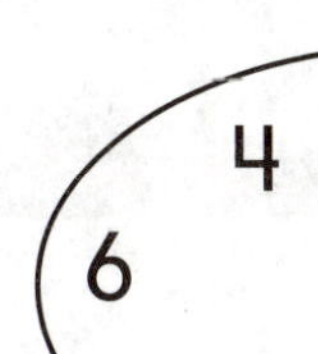

Even Odd

6 4 2 8

Even Odd

3 1 7 5

13 14 15

16 17 18

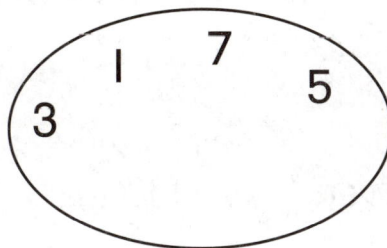

Think and Grow: Modeling Real Life

There is an even number of students in your class. There are more than 16 but fewer than 20 students. How many students are in your class?

______ students

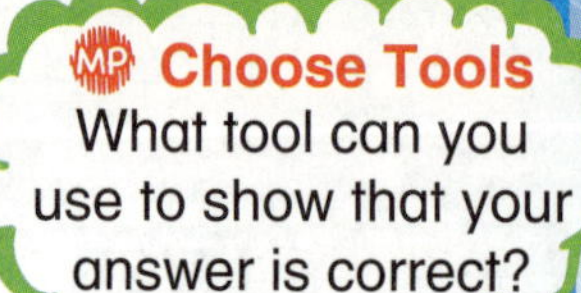

Choose Tools
What tool can you use to show that your answer is correct?

Show how you know:

Show and Grow *I can think deeper!*

14. There is an odd number of cows in a field. There are more than 13 but fewer than 17 cows. How many cows are in the field?

______ cows

15. There are 14 geese on a farm. There are 2 more chickens than geese. Is there an even or odd number of chickens?

Even Odd

Name ___

Learning Target: Tell whether a number is even or odd.

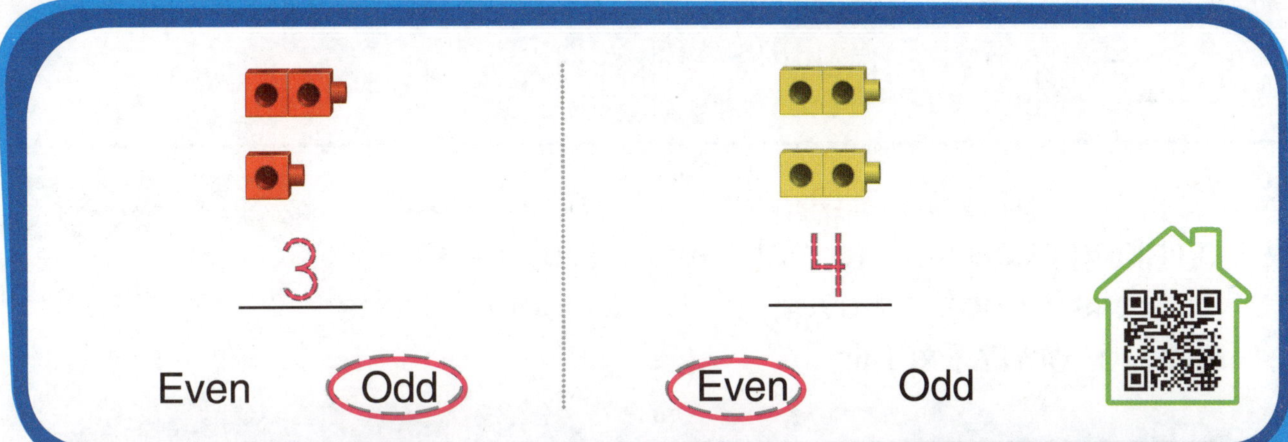

1.

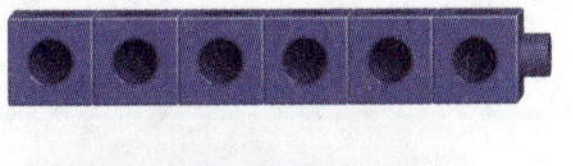

___

Even Odd

2.

___

Even Odd

Color cubes to show the number. Circle *even* or *odd.*

3. 9

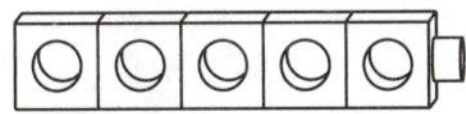

Even Odd

4. 14

Even Odd

5. 18

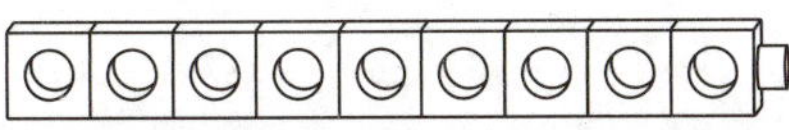

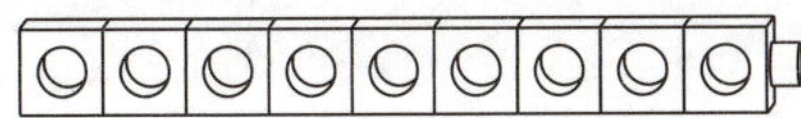

Even Odd

6. 15

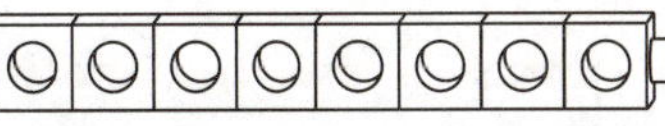

Even Odd

Is the number *even* or *odd*?

7. 2

Even Odd

8. 5

Even Odd

9. **Construct an Argument** You break apart a linking cube train to make two equal parts. There is 1 cube left over. Is the number of cubes *even* or *odd*? Explain.

____

____

10. **Modeling Real Life** There is an even number of eggs in a nest. There are more than 10 but fewer than 14 eggs. How many eggs are in the nest?

______ eggs

11. **DIG DEEPER!** You start at 2 and skip count by an even number. Are the numbers you count *even* or *odd*? How do you know?

____

____

Review & Refresh

12. $6 + 6 =$ ______

13. $9 + 9 =$ ______

Name ______________________________

Model Even and Odd Numbers

1.2

Learning Target: Use an addition equation to model even and odd numbers.

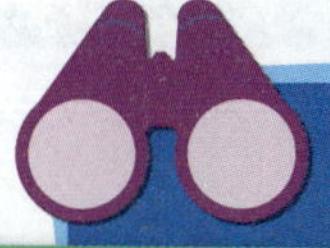

Explore and Grow

Use linking cubes to model each sum. Is the sum *even* or *odd*?

$4 + 4 =$ _____ Even Odd

$5 + 4 =$ _____ Even Odd

Think and Grow

12

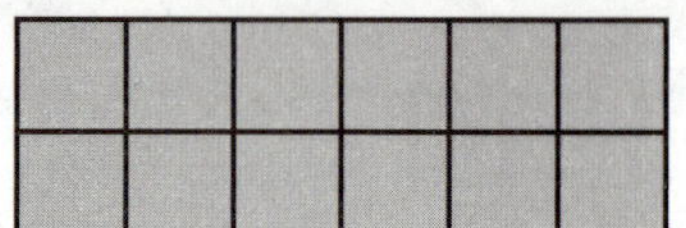

Even Odd

12 = 6 + 6

11

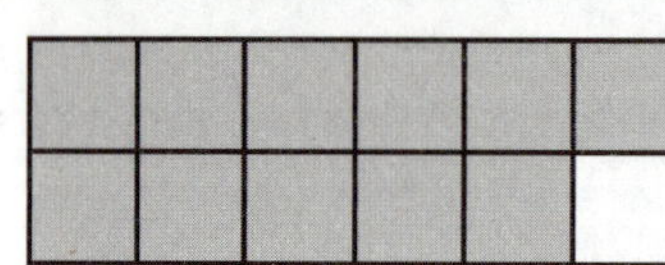

Even Odd

11 = 6 + 5

Remember, 11 = 6 + 5 is called an **equation**.

Show and Grow *I can do it!*

1. 7

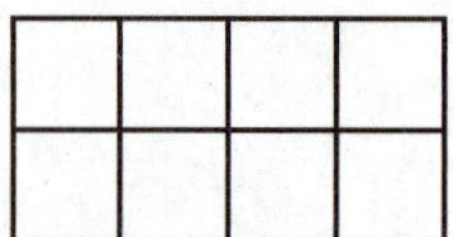

Even Odd

7 = ____ + ____

2. 10

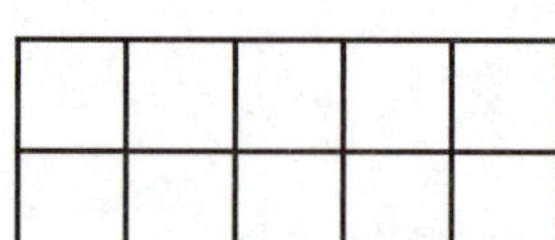

Even Odd

10 = ____ + ____

3. 14

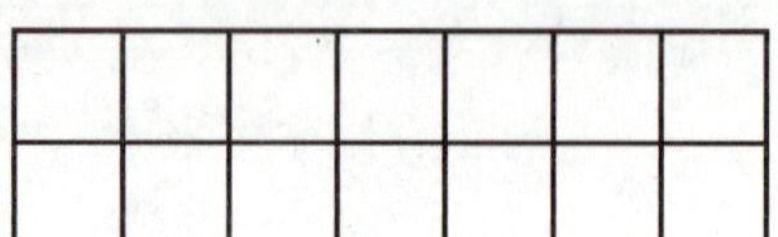

Even Odd

14 = ____ + ____

4. 17

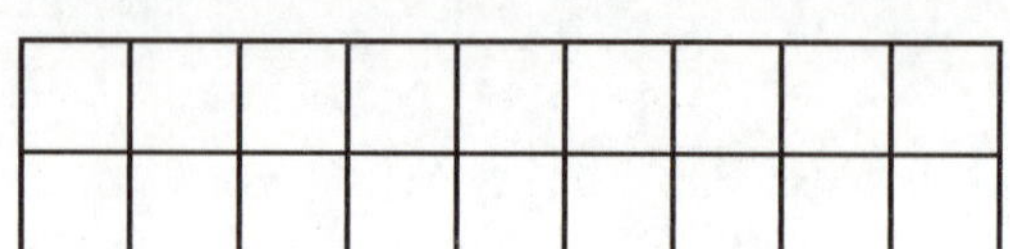

Even Odd

____ + ____ = 17

Name ____________________

Apply and Grow: Practice

5. 18

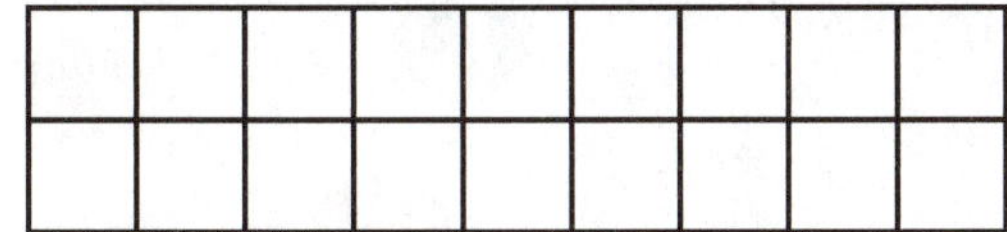

Even Odd

_____ + _____ = 18

6. 13

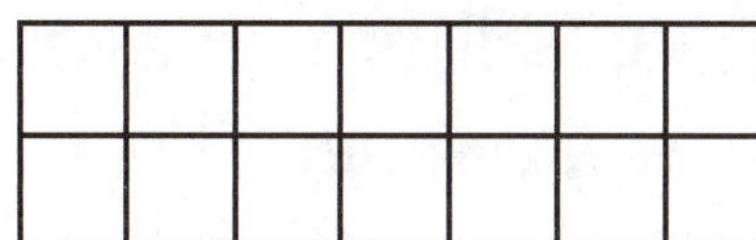

Even Odd

13 = _____ + _____

7. 15

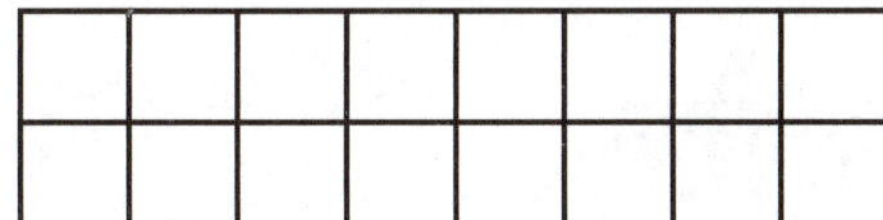

Even Odd

15 = _____ + _____

8. 20

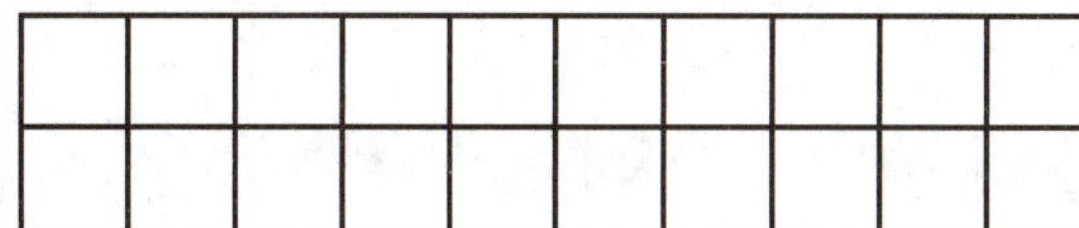

Even Odd

20 = _____ + _____

9. MP **YOU BE THE TEACHER** Descartes uses doubles plus 1 to model an odd number. Is he correct? Explain.

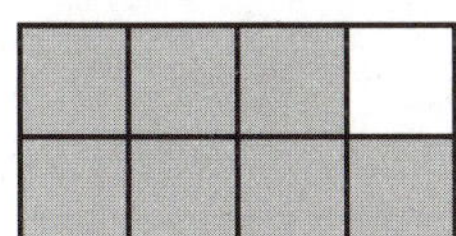

3 + 4 = 7

____

____

____

10. You do 6 sit-ups on Saturday and 7 on Sunday. Do you do an even or odd number of sit-ups in all?

Even Odd

Think and Grow: Modeling Real Life

There is an even number of marbles in one bag and an odd number of marbles in another bag. Is there an even or an odd number of marbles in all?

Which equation could match the story?

$6 + 8 = 14$ $8 + 7 = 15$ $7 + 5 = 12$

There is an ______ number of marbles in all.

Show and Grow *I can think deeper!*

11. Two buckets each have an odd number of seashells. Is there an even or an odd number of seashells in all?

Which equation could match the story?

$9 + 5 = 14$ $7 + 6 = 13$ $10 + 4 = 14$

There is an ______ number of seashells in all.

---

12. **DIG DEEPER!** You have an odd number of flowers. You and your friend have an even number of flowers in all. Does your friend have an even or an odd number of flowers?

Your friend has an ______ number of flowers.

Name ______________________________

Practice 1.2

Learning Target: Use an addition equation to model even and odd numbers.

5

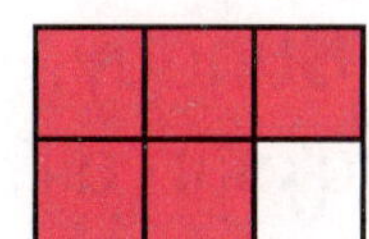

Even   (Odd)

5 = 3 + 2

6

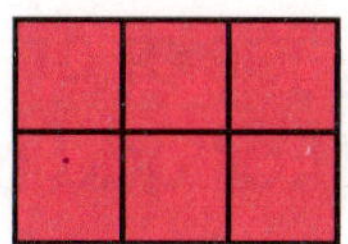

(Even)   Odd

6 = 3 + 3

1. 8

Even   Odd

8 = _____ + _____

2. 17

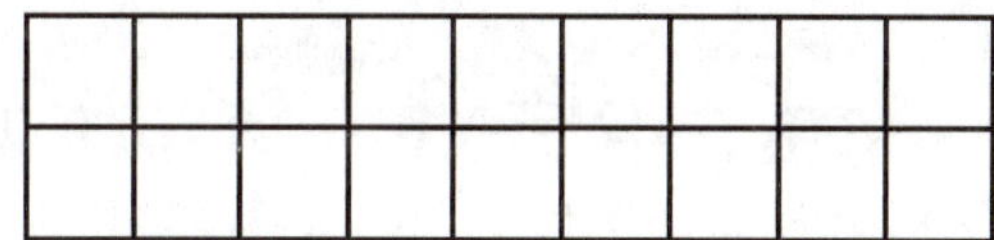

Even   Odd

17 = _____ + _____

3. 9

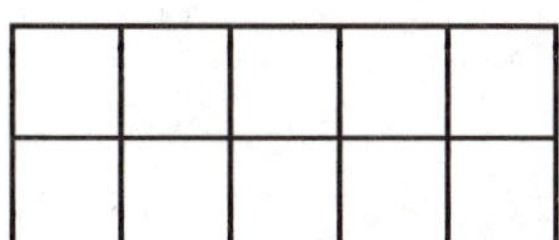

Even   Odd

9 = _____ + _____

4. 16

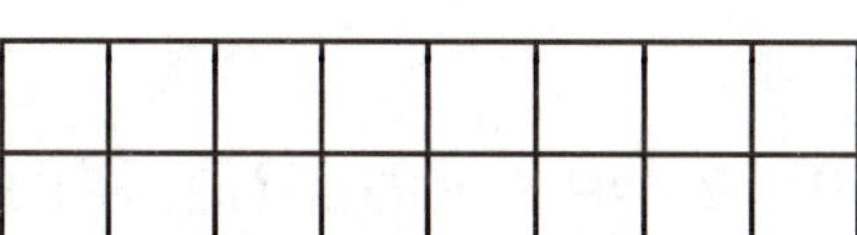

Even   Odd

_____ + _____ = 16

5. **Reasoning** Fill in the blanks using *even* or *odd*.

The sum of two even numbers is ______.

The sum of two odd numbers is ______.

The sum of an even number and an odd number is ______.

6. You do 10 jumping jacks on Saturday and 10 on Sunday. Do you do an even or odd number of jumping jacks in all?

Even Odd

7. **Modeling Real Life** You and your friend each have an even number of googly eyes. Do you and your friend have an even or an odd number of googly eyes in all?

Which equation could match the story?

$3 + 6 = 9$ $4 + 6 = 10$ $5 + 7 = 12$

You have an ______ number of googly eyes in all.

8. **DIG DEEPER!** You hop an even number of times. You and your friend hop an odd number of times in all. Does your friend hop an even or an odd number of times?

Your friend hops an ______ number of times.

Review & Refresh

Circle the shape that shows equal shares.

9.

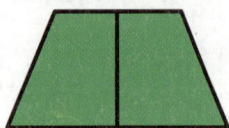

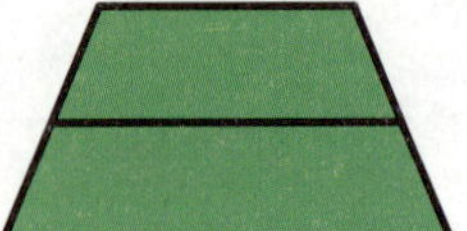

10.

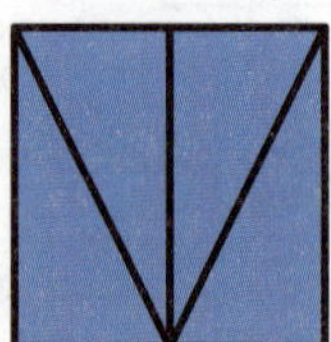

Name ______________________________

Equal Groups

Learning Target: Determine the total number of objects in equal groups.

Explore and Grow

Circle groups of two oranges. Complete the sentence.

_____ groups of 2 is _____.

Think and Grow

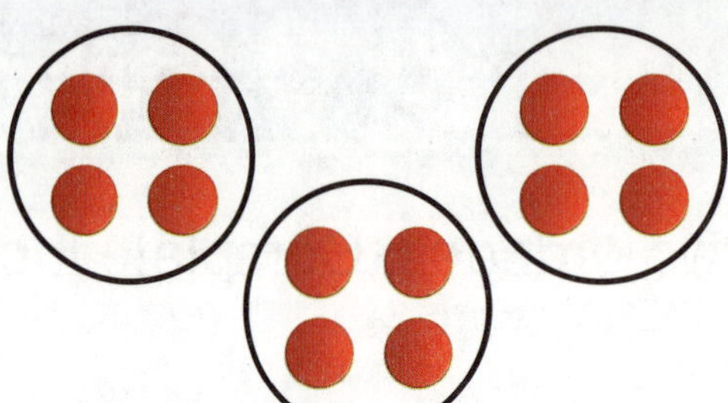

Each group has the same number of counters, so they are **equal groups**.

3 groups of 4

4 + 4 + 4 = 12

Show and Grow *I can do it!*

1. 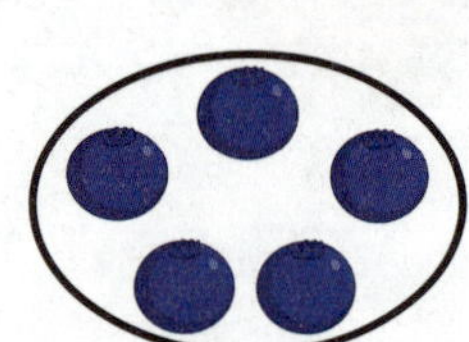 

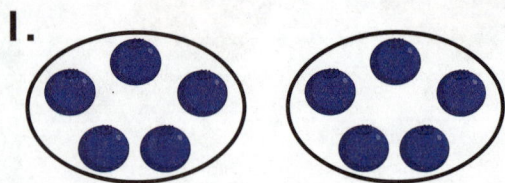

____ groups of ____

____ + ____ = ____

2.  

____ groups of ____

____ + ____ + ____ = ____

3. Circle groups of 3. Write a repeated addition equation.

____ groups of 3

____ + ____ + ____ + ____ + ____ = ____

Name ___________________________________

Apply and Grow: Practice

4. Circle groups of 5. Write a repeated addition equation.

_____ groups of 5

_____ + _____ + _____ = _____

5. Circle groups of 4. Write a repeated addition equation.

_____ groups of 4

_____ + _____ + _____ + _____ = _____

6. MP YOU BE THE TEACHER Newton says he can circle 5 equal groups. Is he correct? Explain.

____

____

Think and Grow: Modeling Real Life

You have 3 boxes. There are 5 pencils in each box. How many pencils are there in all?

Model:

Repeated addition equation:

_____ pencils

Show and Grow *I can think deeper!*

7. You have 5 bags. There are 4 notebooks in each bag. How many notebooks are there in all?

_____ notebooks

8. **DIG DEEPER!** There are 4 boxes. Each box has the same number of glue sticks. There are 16 in all. How many glue sticks are in each box?

_____ glue sticks

9. MP **Justify a Result** Explain how you solved Exercises 7 and 8. What did you do differently?

____

____

Name ________________________

Learning Target: Determine the total number of objects in equal groups.

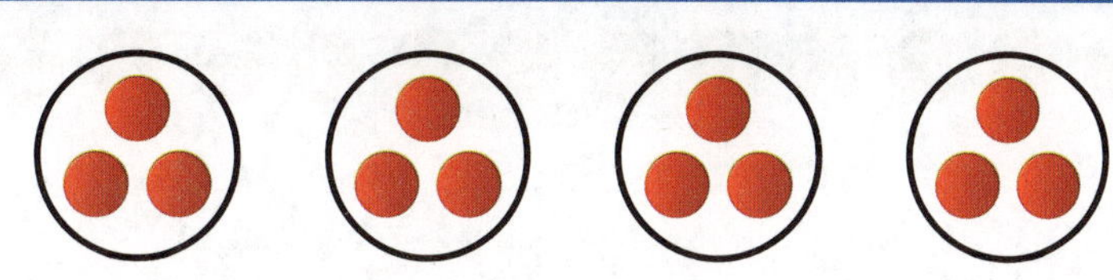

4 groups of 3

3 + 3 + 3 + 3 = 12

1.

____ groups of ____

____ + ____ = ____

2.

____ groups of ____

____ + ____ + ____ = ____

3. Circle groups of 2. Write a repeated addition equation.

____ groups of 2

____ + ____ + ____ + ____ = ____

4. **Structure** Show two different ways to put the buttons in equal groups.

One Way:

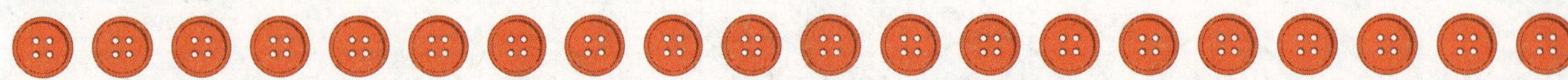

Another Way:

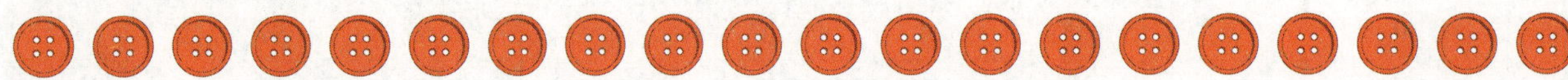

5. **Modeling Real Life** You have 3 jars of paintbrushes. There are 6 paintbrushes in each jar. How many paintbrushes are there in all?

_____ paintbrushes

6. **DIG DEEPER!** A group of 15 people go boating. Your friend says that each boat can carry exactly 6 people. Is she correct? Explain.

____

____

Review & Refresh

7. $62 + 25 =$ _____

8. $83 + 9 =$ _____

Name ________________________________

Use Arrays 1.4

Learning Target: Determine the total number of objects in an array.

Explore and Grow

How many equal groups are there? Write an addition equation to tell how many cars there are in all.

Number of equal groups: ______

Addition equation:

MP Check Your Work
What should the sum of your equation be? How do you know?

Think and Grow

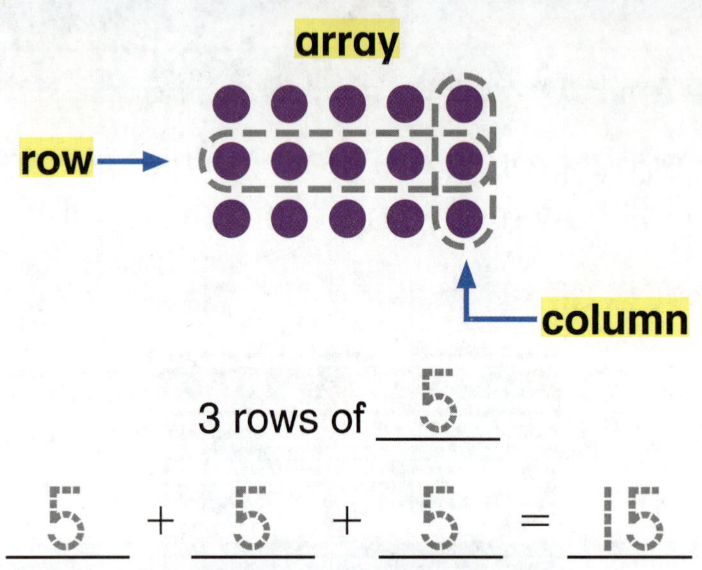

3 rows of 5

5 + 5 + 5 = 15

Show and Grow *I can do it!*

1. 

2 rows of ____

____ + ____ = ____

2. 

3 rows of ____

____ + ____ + ____ = ____

3. 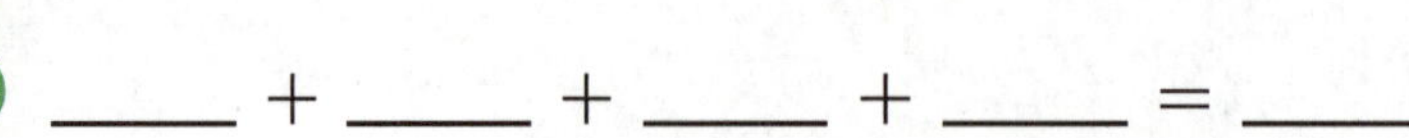

____ rows of ____

____ + ____ + ____ + ____ = ____

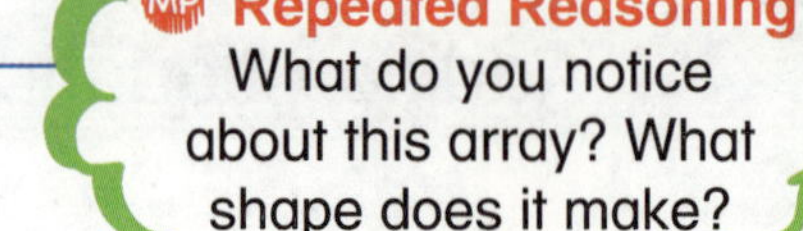

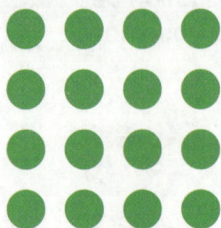

Repeated Reasoning What do you notice about this array? What shape does it make?

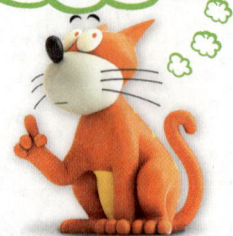

Name ______________________________

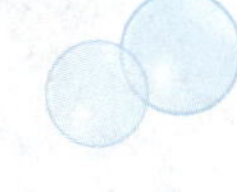

Apply and Grow: Practice

4.

____ rows of ____

____ + ____ = ____

5.

____ rows of ____

____ + ____ + ____ = ____

6.

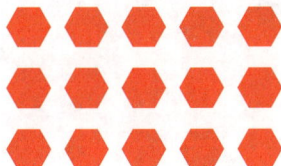

____ rows of ____

____ + ____ + ____ = ____

7.

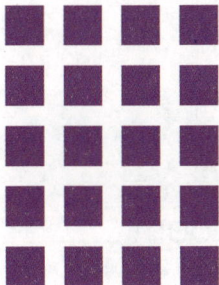

____ rows of ____

____ + ____ + ____ + ____ + ____ = ____

8. MP **Logic** Which arrays show the same number of circles?

____ rows of ____

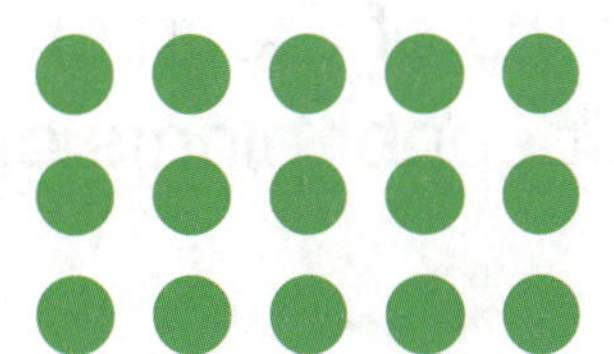

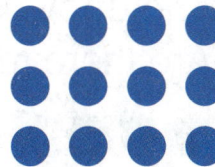

____ rows of ____

____ rows of ____

Think and Grow: Modeling Real Life

The arrays show the desks in two classrooms. Which classroom has more desks?

Classroom A

Classroom B

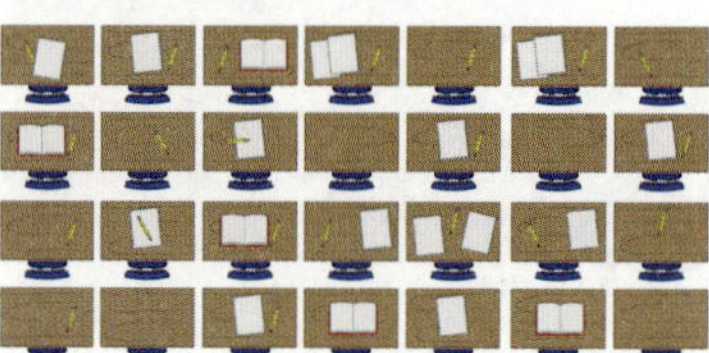

Repeated addition equations:

Classroom A

____ + ____ + ____ + ____ + ____ = ____

Classroom B

____ + ____ + ____ + ____ = ____

Classroom ____

Show and Grow *I can think deeper!*

9. The arrays show gardens of green and yellow pepper plants. Are there more green pepper plants or yellow pepper plants?

____ pepper plants

Name ______________________

Learning Target: Determine the total number of objects in an array.

4 rows of 2

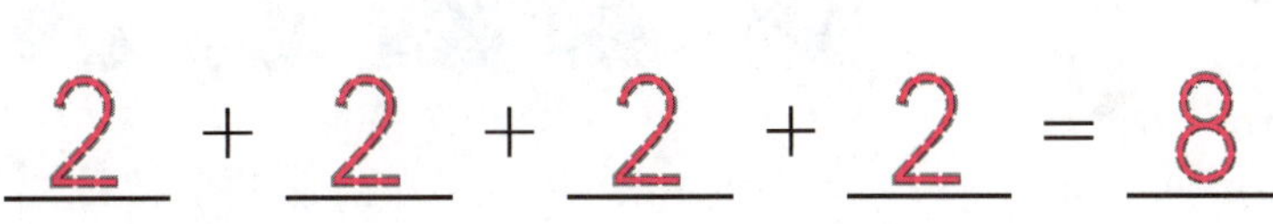

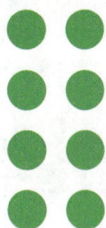

1.

3 rows of ____

____ + ____ + ____ = ____

2.

2 rows of ____

____ + ____ = ____

3.

____ rows of ____

____ + ____ + ____ + ____ = ____

4.

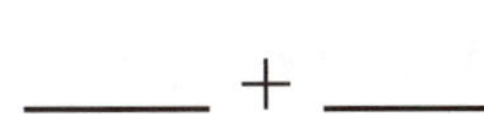

____ rows of ____

____ + ____ + ____ = ____

5. MP **Number Sense** Use the array to complete the equation.

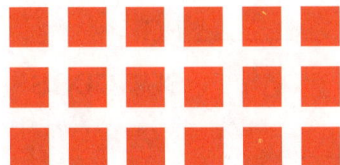

____ + 6 = 12

6. **Modeling Real Life** The arrays show toy cars. Are there more orange cars or blue cars?

_______ cars

7. **DIG DEEPER!** The arrays show a sheet of stickers separated into two pieces. How many rows and columns of stickers did the sheet have before it was separated?

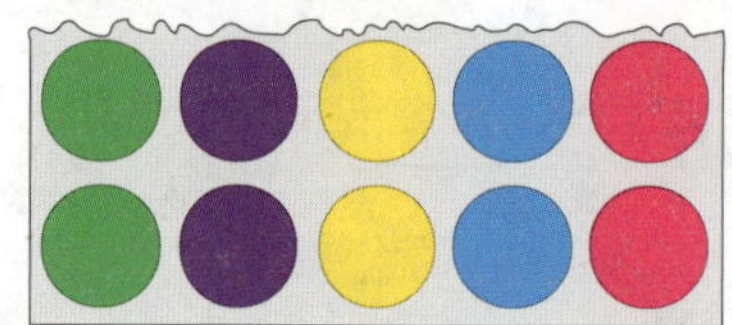

_____ rows and _____ columns

Review & Refresh

8.

_____ flat surfaces

_____ vertices

_____ edges

9.

_____ flat surfaces

_____ vertices

_____ edges

Name ______________________________

Learning Target: Make an array to solve a word problem.

Use counters to model the story. Write an addition equation to match.

There are 4 rows of students. There are 3 students in each row. How many students are there in all?

Addition equation:

Maintain Accuracy How else can the students be arranged?

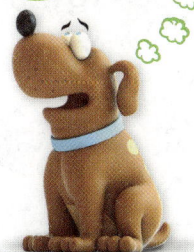

______ students

Think and Grow

A garden has 3 rows of tomato plants. There are 4 tomato plants in each row. How many tomato plants are there in all?

Make an array to model the problem.

Use repeated addition to solve.

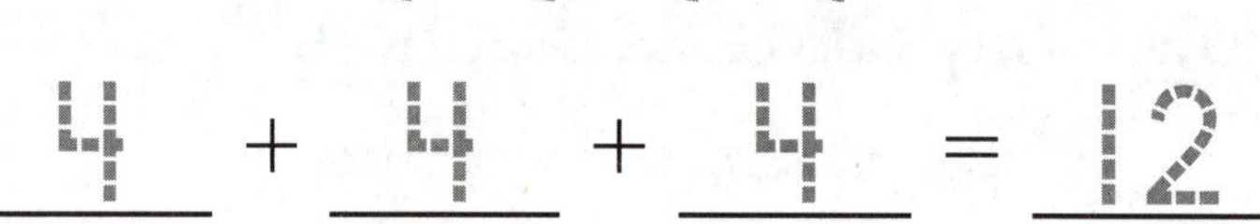
4 + 4 + 4 = 12

12
tomato plants

Show and Grow *I can do it!*

1. A photo album has 3 rows of photos. There are 2 photos in each row. How many photos are there in all?

____ + ____ + ____ = ____

____ photos

2. You have 4 rows of stickers. There are 5 stickers in each row. How many stickers do you have in all?

____ + ____ + ____ + ____ = ____

____ stickers

Name ______________________________

3. An ice cube tray has 5 rows. There are 2 ice cubes in each row. How many ice cubes are there in all?

____ ice cubes

4. A bookcase has 3 shelves. There are 5 stuffed animals on each shelf. How many stuffed animals are there in all?

____ + ____ + ____ = ____

____ stuffed animals

5. A closet has 4 shelves. There are 2 games on each shelf. How many games are there in all?

____ + ____ + ____ + ____ = ____

____ games

6. MP **Structure** Make an array to match the equation.

$5 + 5 + 5 + 5 = 20$

Think and Grow: Modeling Real Life

A marching band has 3 equal rows of drummers. There are 15 drummers in all. How many drummers are in each row?

Model:

Repeated addition equation:

____ + ____ + ____ = ____

____ drummers

Show and Grow *I can think deeper!*

7. A quilt has 4 equal rows of patches. There are 24 patches in all. How many patches are in each row?

____ patches

8. A building has 3 equal rows of windows. There are 18 windows in all. How many columns are there?

____ columns

Name ___________________________

Practice 1.5

Learning Target: Make an array to solve a word problem.

A paint tray has 2 rows. There are 4 paint colors in each row. How many paint colors are there in all?

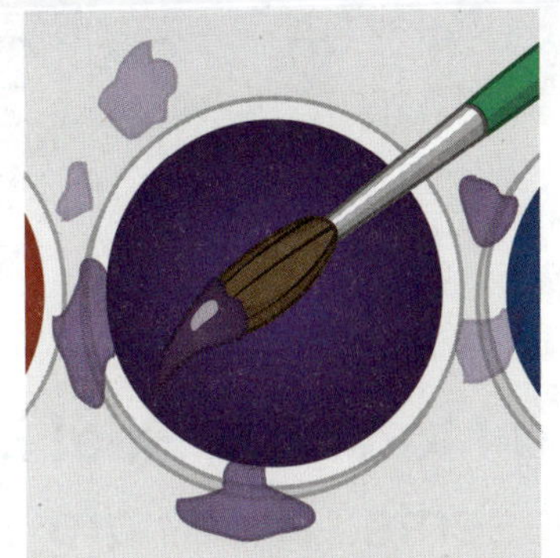

O O O O
O O O O

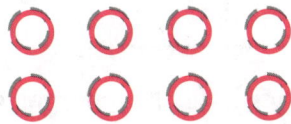

4 + 4 = 8

8 paint colors

1. A parking lot has 3 rows. There are 5 parking spots in each row. How many parking spots are there in all?

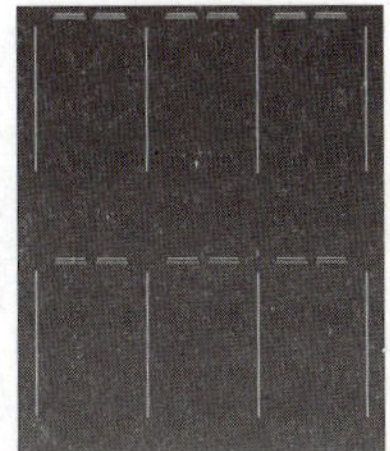

____ + ____ + ____ = ____

____ parking spots

2. A bookcase has 4 shelves. There are 3 books on each shelf. How many books are there in all?

____ + ____ + ____ + ____ = ____

____ books

3. MP **Reasoning** Newton has 10 tokens. Which equations can Newton use to make an array with his tokens?

$2 + 2 + 2 + 2 + 2 = 10$ $\quad$ $7 + 3 = 10$

$2 + 8 = 10$ $\quad$ $5 + 5 = 10$

4. MP **Modeling Real Life** A theater has 4 equal rows of seats. There are 16 seats in all. How many seats are in each row?

_____ seats

5. **DIG DEEPER!** Descartes has 8 rows of 3 counters. He adds 2 rows of counters to the array. Now how many counters does Descartes have in all?

_____ counters

Review & Refresh

6. There are 9 lions in all. How many lions are in the den?

_____ lions

Name ______________________________

Performance Task

1. Your art supplies are packaged in boxes as described below.

Colored Pencils	Markers	Crayons
3 rows 5 in each row	2 rows 7 in each row	4 rows 4 in each row

a. What do you have the most of?

Colored Pencils   Markers   Crayons

b. Do you have an even or an odd number of markers?

Even   Odd

2. a. You have 5 equal rows of paint bottles. You have 20 paint bottles in all. How many paint bottles are in each row?

_____ paint bottles

b. You add another row of paint bottles. How many paint bottles do you have now?

_____ paint bottles

c. Describe another way to arrange the paint bottles you have now.

____

Array Flip and Find

To Play: Place the Array Flip and Find Cards face down in the boxes. Take turns flipping two cards. If your cards show the same total, keep the cards. If your cards show different totals, flip the cards back over. Play until all matches are made.

Name ____________________

Chapter Practice 1

1.1 Even and Odd Numbers

1.

____

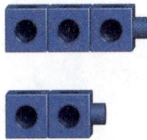

Even Odd

2.

____

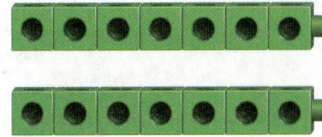

Even Odd

Color cubes to show the number. Circle *even* or *odd.*

3. 12

Even Odd

4. 19

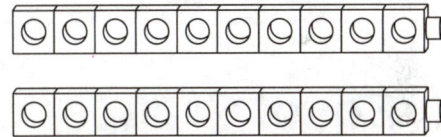

Even Odd

5. **Modeling Real Life** You see an odd number of boats. There are more than 15 but fewer than 19 boats. How many boats do you see?

____ boats

Show how you know:

1.2 Model Even and Odd Numbers

6. 9

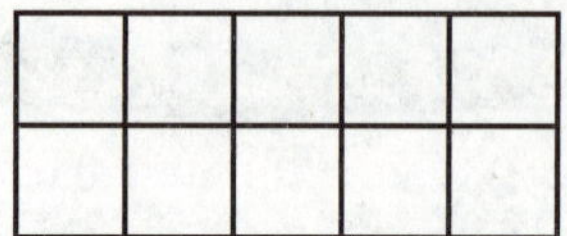

Even Odd

9 = ____ + ____

7. 18

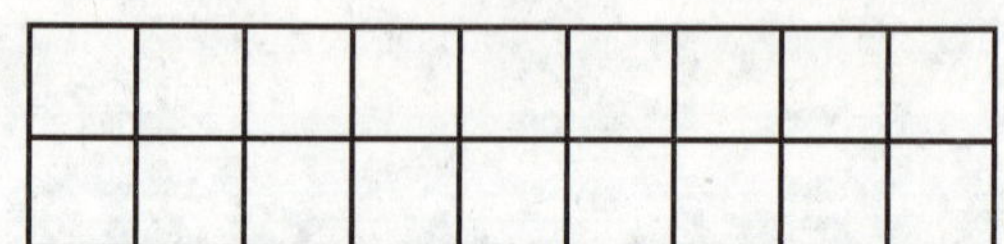

Even Odd

18 = ____ + ____

8. 10

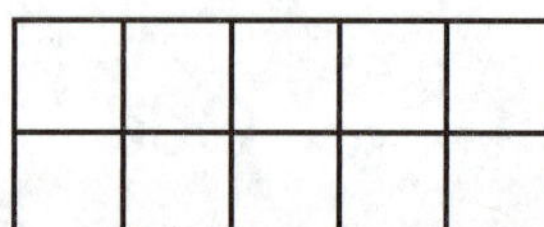

Even Odd

10 = ____ + ____

9. 13

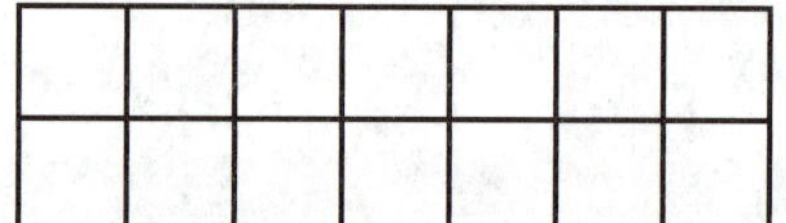

Even Odd

____ + ____ = 13

1.3 Equal Groups

10.

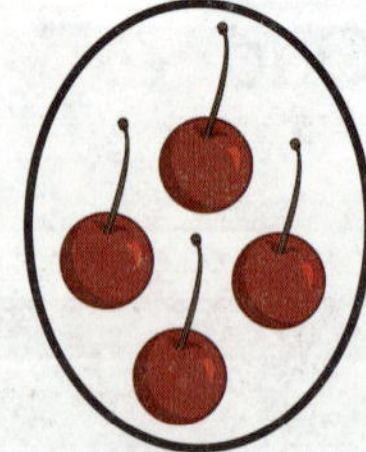

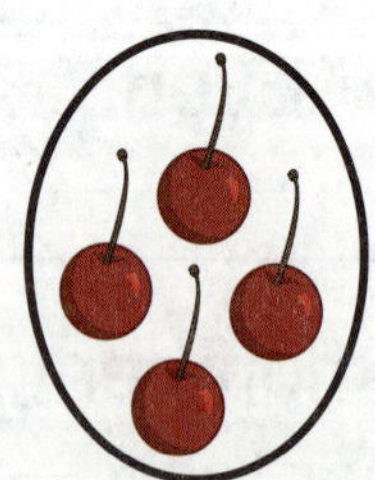

____ groups of ____

____ + ____ = ____

11. Circle groups of 3. Write a repeated addition equation.

____ groups of 3

____ + ____ + ____ + ____ = ____

12. **Structure** Show two different ways to put the balls in equal groups.

One Way:

Another Way:

1.4 Use Arrays

13.

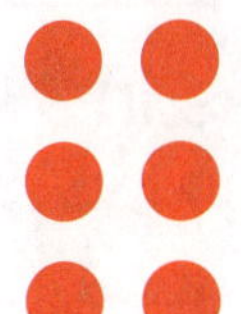

3 rows of ____

____ + ____ + ____ = ____

14.

2 rows of ____

____ + ____ = ____

15.

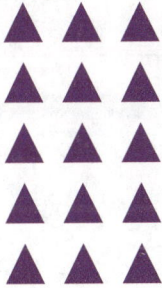

____ rows of ____

____ + ____ + ____ + ____ + ____ = ____

16.

____ rows of ____

____ + ____ + ____ + ____ = ____

1.5 Make Arrays

17. A cupboard has 4 shelves. There are 3 glasses on each shelf. How many glasses are there in all?

____ + ____ + ____ + ____ = ____

____ glasses

18. A bingo card has 5 rows. There are 5 squares in each row. How many squares are there in all?

____ + ____ + ____ + ____ + ____ = ____

____ squares

19. MP **Modeling Real Life** A pet store has 5 equal rows of fish tanks. There are 20 fish tanks in all. How many fish tanks are in each row?

____ fish tanks

2 Fluency and Strategies within 20

- What are your favorite kinds of books?
- You return 12 library books. You have 5 library books left. How many library books did you have to start?

Chapter Learning Target:
Understand strategies.

Chapter Success Criteria:

- I can identify when to use a strategy.
- I can explain a strategy to help solve a problem.
- I can use a strategy to help solve a problem.
- I can reflect on the strategy I used.

Name ______________________________

2 Vocabulary

Review Words

number line
count on
count back

Organize It

Use the review words to complete the graphic organizer.

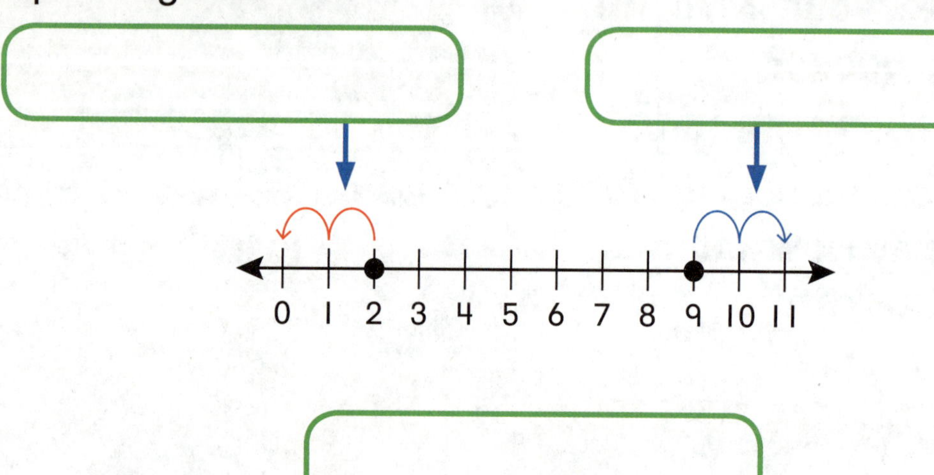

Define It

Use your vocabulary cards to match.

1. addends

2. sum

3. difference

$8 - 3 = 5$

$5 + 3 = 8$

$4 + 3 = 7$

Chapter 2 Vocabulary Cards

addends

difference

doubles minus 1

doubles plus 1

expression

sum

8 − 3 = 5

4 + 3 = 7

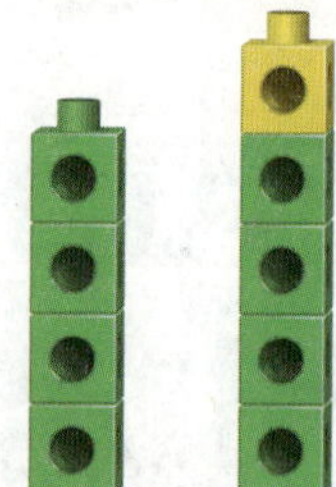

4 + 4 = 8, so 4 + 5 = 9.

4 + 4 = 8, so 4 + 3 = 7.

5 + 3 = 8

4 + 7 7 − 4

Name ______________________________

Add in Any Order 2.1

Learning Target: Add in any order to find a sum.

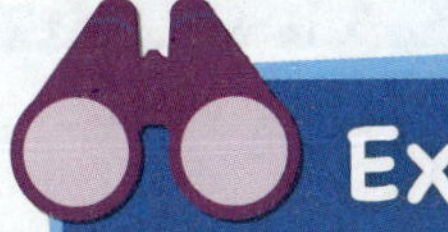

Explore and Grow

Use the table to find the sum. Change the order of the addends. Write the new equation.

+	0	1	2	3	4	5	6	7	8	9	10
0	0	1	2	3	4	5	6	7	8	9	10
1	1	2	3	4	5	6	7	8	9	10	11
2	2	3	4	5	6	7	8	9	10	11	12
3	3	4	5	6	7	8	9	10	11	12	13
4	4	5	6	7	8	9	10	11	12	13	14
5	5	6	7	8	9	10	11	12	13	14	15
6	6	7	8	9	10	11	12	13	14	15	16
7	7	8	9	10	11	12	13	14	15	16	17
8	8	9	10	11	12	13	14	15	16	17	18
9	9	10	11	12	13	14	15	16	17	18	19
10	10	11	12	13	14	15	16	17	18	19	20

$5 + 6 =$ ______ ______ + ______ = ______

$4 + 9 =$ ______ ______ + ______ = ______

Think and Grow

4 + 7 = 11
addend
addend
sum
7 + 4 = 11
Changing the order of the addends does not change the sum.
The expressions 4 + 7 and 7 + 4 are both equal to 11.

Show and Grow *I can do it!*

1. ____ + ____ = ____ ____ + ____ = ____

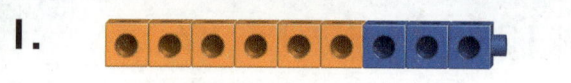

2. ____ + ____ = ____ ____ + ____ = ____

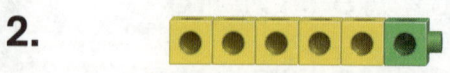

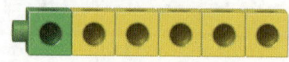

Find the sum. Then change the order of the addends. Write the new equation.

3. 8 + 2 = ____ ____ + ____ = ____

4. 4 + 3 = ____ ____ + ____ = ____

Name ___________________________

Apply and Grow: Practice

Find the sum. Then change the order of the addends. Write the new equation.

5. 5 + 8 = _____   _____ + _____ = _____

6. 7 + 3 = _____   _____ + _____ = _____

7. 6 + 5 = _____   _____ + _____ = _____

8. _____ = 9 + 8   _____ = _____ + _____

9. _____ = 0 + 2   _____ = _____ + _____

10. DIG DEEPER! Which shape completes the equation?

+ =

+ ? =

Think and Grow: Modeling Real Life

You paint 12 shapes. 8 are rectangles. The rest are circles. How many circles do you paint?

Write two equations that describe your shapes:

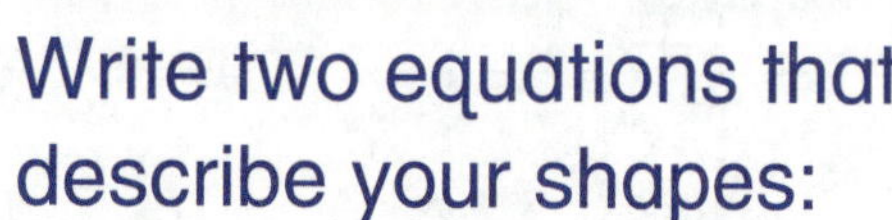

____ + ____ = ____ ____ + ____ = ____

____ circles

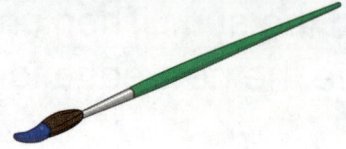

Show and Grow I can think deeper!

11. There are 13 race cars. 6 of them have numbers. The rest do not. How many race cars do *not* have numbers?

Write two equations that describe your cars:

____ + ____ = ____ ____ + ____ = ____

____ cars

Use Math Tools Explain how you can use linking cubes to help solve an equation.

____

____

Name ______________________________

Practice 2.1

Learning Target: Add in any order to find a sum.

5 + 7 = 12

7 + 5 = 12

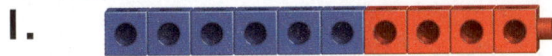

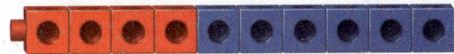

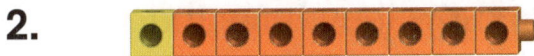

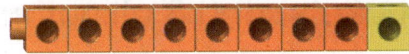

1. _____ + _____ = _____   _____ + _____ = _____

2. _____ + _____ = _____   _____ + _____ = _____

Find the sum. Then change the order of the addends. Write the new equation.

3. 7 + 0 = _____   _____ + _____ = _____

4. 2 + 4 = _____   _____ + _____ = _____

5. _____ = 8 + 7   _____ = _____ + _____

6. _____ = 3 + 8   _____ = _____ + _____

7. **Number Sense** Complete each equation.

$5 + 4 = 4 + \_\_\_\_$ $\qquad$ $0 + 6 = \_\_\_\_ + 0$

$9 + \_\_\_\_ = 2 + 9$ $\qquad$ $\_\_\_\_ + 1 = 1 + 7$

8. **Modeling Real Life** You have 14 blocks. 8 are cubes. The rest are cylinders. How many cylinders do you have?

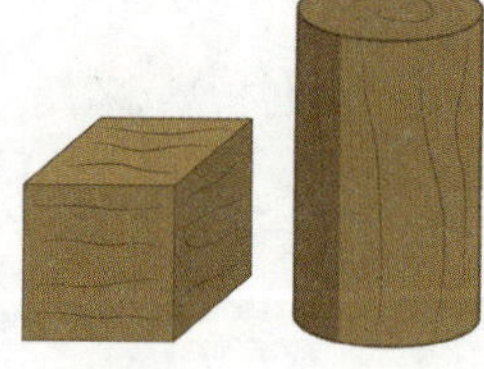

Write two equations that describe your blocks:

____ cylinders

9. **DIG DEEPER!** Newton and Descartes compare their key chain collections. Newton has 3 surfboards, 2 race cars, 5 rockets, and 4 alligators. Descartes has 2 surboards, 5 race cars, 4 rockets, and 3 alligators. How do you know they have the same amount of key chains without adding?

____

____

Review & Refresh

10. Which time does not belong with the other three?

half past 5

half past 6

Name ________________________________

Learning Target: Use the *doubles plus 1* and *doubles minus 1* strategies to find a sum.

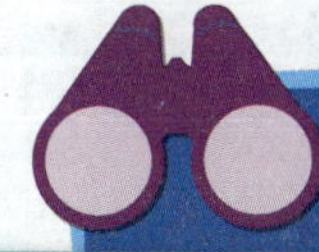

Explore and Grow

Find each sum. How are the equations alike? How are they different?

+	0	1	2	3	4	5	6	7	8	9	10
0	0	1	2	3	4	5	6	7	8	9	10
1	1	2	3	4	5	6	7	8	9	10	11
2	2	3	4	5	6	7	8	9	10	11	12
3	3	4	5	6	7	8	9	10	11	12	13
4	4	5	6	7	8	9	10	11	12	13	14
5	5	6	7	8	9	10	11	12	13	14	15
6	6	7	8	9	10	11	12	13	14	15	16
7	7	8	9	10	11	12	13	14	15	16	17
8	8	9	10	11	12	13	14	15	16	17	18
9	9	10	11	12	13	14	15	16	17	18	19
10	10	11	12	13	14	15	16	17	18	19	20

$6 + 6 =$ ______ $7 + 7 =$ ______

$6 + 7 =$ ______ $7 + 6 =$ ______

Think and Grow

$7 + 8 =$ 15

Double:

7 + 7 = 14

$3 + 2 =$ 5

Double:

3 + 3 = 6

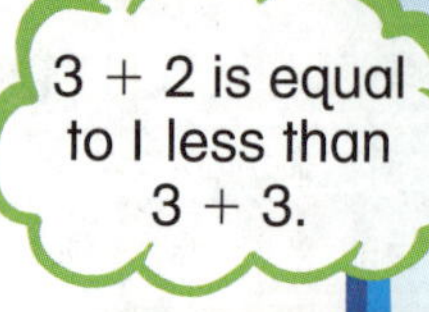

7 + 8 is equal to 7 + 7 and 1 more.

doubles plus 1

doubles minus 1

3 + 2 is equal to 1 less than 3 + 3.

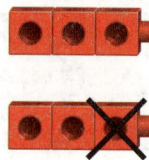

Show and Grow *I can do it!*

Find the sum. Write the double you used.

1. $4 + 5 =$ ____

____ + ____ = ____

2. $7 + 6 =$ ____

____ + ____ = ____

3. $6 + 5 =$ ☐ ☐ + ☐ = ☐

4. $8 + 9 =$ ☐ ☐ + ☐ = ☐

Name ______________________________

Apply and Grow: Practice

Find the sum. Write the double you used.

5.

$$\begin{array}{r} 3 \\ +\ 4 \\ \hline \square \end{array} \qquad \begin{array}{r} \square \\ +\ \square \\ \hline \square \end{array}$$

6.

$$\begin{array}{r} 8 \\ +\ 7 \\ \hline \square \end{array} \qquad \begin{array}{r} \square \\ +\ \square \\ \hline \square \end{array}$$

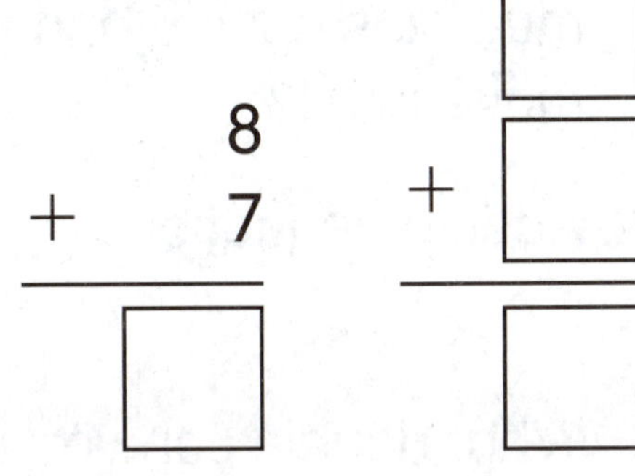

7.

$$\begin{array}{r} 5 \\ +\ 6 \\ \hline \square \end{array} \qquad \begin{array}{r} \square \\ +\ \square \\ \hline \square \end{array}$$

8.

$$\begin{array}{r} 10 \\ +\ 9 \\ \hline \square \end{array} \qquad \begin{array}{r} \square \\ +\ \square \\ \hline \square \end{array}$$

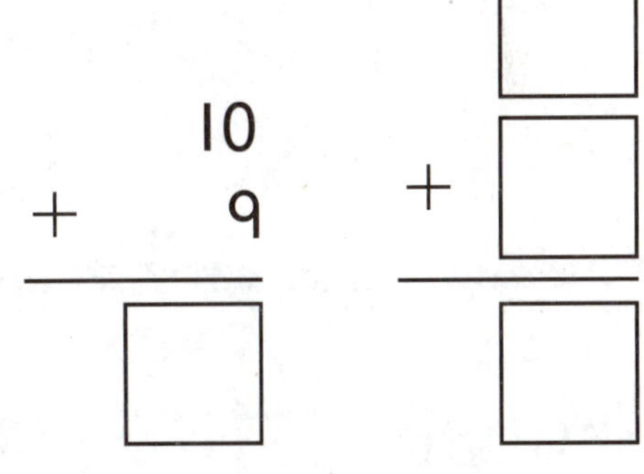

9. _____ = 2 + 3

_____ = _____ + _____

10. _____ = 5 + 4

_____ = _____ + _____

11. _____ = 6 + 7

_____ = _____ + _____

12. _____ = 9 + 8

_____ = _____ + _____

13. **DIG DEEPER!** What double might Newton be thinking?

The sum is greater than 4.
Each addend is less than 5.

_____ + _____ = _____

Think and Grow: Modeling Real Life

You make 9 mud pies. Your friend makes 1 fewer than you. How many mud pies do you and your friend make in all?

Addition equation:

What double can you use?

_____ + _____ = _____

_____ mud pies

Show and Grow *I can think deeper!*

14. You score 6 goals. Your friend scores 1 more than you. How many goals do you and your friend score in all?

_____ goals

15. DIG DEEPER! You and your friend jump in 13 puddles in all. You jump in 7. How many puddles does your friend jump in?

_____ puddles

Name ______________________

Practice 2.2

Learning Target: Use the *doubles plus 1* and *doubles minus 1* strategies to find a sum.

8 + 9 = 17

Double:

8 + 8 = 16

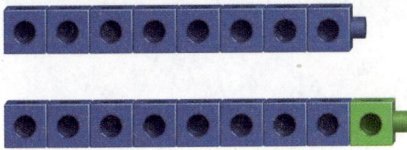

7 + 6 = 13

Double:

7 + 7 = 14

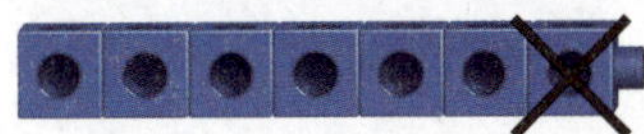

Find the sum. Write the double you used.

1. 4 + 3 = ______

______ + ______ = ______

2. 5 + 6 = ______

______ + ______ = ______

3.

$$\begin{array}{r} 9 \\ +\ 8 \\ \hline \square \end{array} \qquad \begin{array}{r} \square \\ +\ \square \\ \hline \square \end{array}$$

4.

$$\begin{array}{r} 6 \\ +\ 7 \\ \hline \square \end{array} \qquad \begin{array}{r} \square \\ +\ \square \\ \hline \square \end{array}$$

5. ______ = 8 + 7

______ = ______ + ______

6. ______ = 9 + 10

______ = ______ + ______

7.  **Number Sense** Which doubles can you use to find $8 + 9$?

$4 + 4 = 8$ $9 + 9 = 18$ $8 + 8 = 16$

---

8. **Modeling Real Life** You tell 5 jokes. Your friend tells 1 fewer than you. How many jokes do you and your friend tell in all?

______ jokes

---

9. **DIG DEEPER!** Newton and Descartes paint 7 paw prints in all. Descartes paints 1 less than Newton. How many paw prints does Newton paint?

______ paw prints

Review & Refresh

Is the equation true or false?

10. $7 + 8 \stackrel{?}{=} 9 + 6$

______ $\stackrel{?}{=}$ ______

True False

11. $8 - 4 \stackrel{?}{=} 3 + 2$

______ $\stackrel{?}{=}$ ______

True False

Name ______________________

Add Three Numbers 2.3

Learning Target: Add three numbers.

Find the sums.

8 + (2) + (4) = ____
□

(8) + (2) + 4 = ____
□

(8) + 2 + (4) = ____
□

What is the same? What is different?

____

____

____

Think and Grow

You can add any 2 numbers first. The sum is always the same.

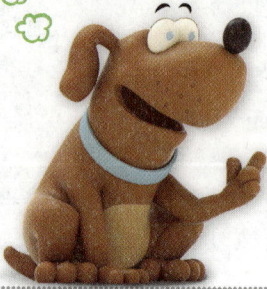

$4 + 6 + 5 = ?$

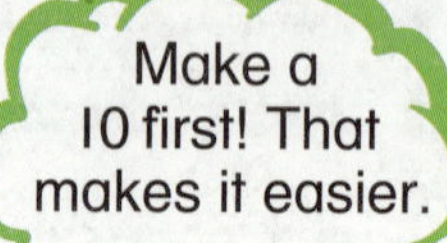

Make a 10 first! That makes it easier.

$4 + 6 + 5 = 15$

10

$4 + 6 + 5 = 15$ (4 + 5 = 9)

$4 + 6 + 5 = 15$ (6 + 5 = 11)

Show and Grow *I can do it!*

Circle two addends to add first. Write their sum. Then find the sum of all three addends.

1. $7 + 3 + 4 =$ ______

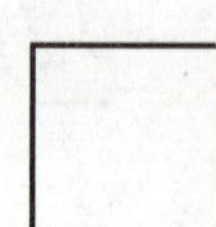

2. $1 + 5 + 3 =$ ______

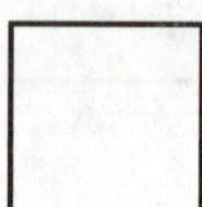

3. $9 + 4 + 4 =$ ______

4. $5 + 2 + 5 =$ ______

Name ______________________________

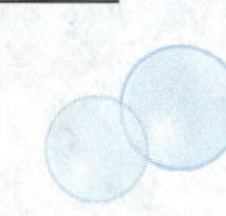

Apply and Grow: Practice

5. 3 + 5 + 5 = ____

6. 9 + 0 + 7 = ____

7. 4 + 2 + 3 = ____

8.
$$\begin{array}{r} 5 \\ 2 \\ +\ 8 \\ \hline \square \end{array}$$

9.
$$\begin{array}{r} 4 \\ 8 \\ +\ 6 \\ \hline \square \end{array}$$

10.
$$\begin{array}{r} 4 \\ 8 \\ +\ 0 \\ \hline \square \end{array}$$

11. 9 + 5 + 6= ____

12.
$$\begin{array}{r} 9 \\ 4 \\ +\ 1 \\ \hline \square \end{array}$$

13. 3 + 7 + 7 = ____

14. MP **Structure** Write the missing addends.

$$\begin{array}{r} 1 \\ \square \\ +\ 5 \\ \hline 10 \end{array} \qquad \begin{array}{r} 9 \\ 9 \\ +\ \square \\ \hline 18 \end{array} \qquad \begin{array}{r} \square \\ 2 \\ +\ 3 \\ \hline 7 \end{array} \qquad \begin{array}{r} 2 \\ \square \\ +\ 4 \\ \hline 11 \end{array}$$

Think and Grow: Modeling Real Life

You have 6 presents. Newton and Descartes each have 4 presents. How many presents are there in all?

Addition equation:

______ presents

Show and Grow *I can think deeper!*

15. You have 8 crayons. Newton and Descartes each have 5 crayons. How many crayons are there in all?

______ crayons

16. You, Newton, and Descartes eat 18 apple slices in all. Newton and Descartes each eat 6 slices. How many apple slices do you eat?

______ apple slices

17. A treasure chest has 20 jewels in all. 7 are blue. 6 are green. The rest are red. How many jewels are red?

______ red jewels

Name ______________________

Practice 2.3

Learning Target: Add three numbers.

2 + 6 + 8 = ?

(2) + 6 + (8) = 16, with 2 and 8 joined to a box showing 10

(2) + (6) + 8 = 16, with 2 and 6 joined to a box showing 8

2 + (6) + (8) = 16, with 6 and 8 joined to a box showing 14

Circle two addends to add first. Write their sum. Then find the sum of all three addends.

1. 2 + 5 + 1 = ____

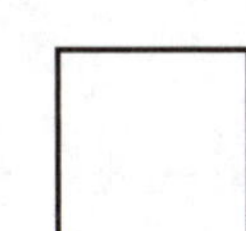

2. 6 + 4 + 4 = ____

3. 0 + 8 + 7 = ____

4.

$$\begin{array}{r} 6 \\ 5 \\ +\ 5 \\ \hline \square \end{array} \quad \square$$

5.

$$\begin{array}{r} 4 \\ 9 \\ +\ 0 \\ \hline \square \end{array} \quad \square$$

6.

$$\begin{array}{r} 3 \\ 3 \\ +\ 3 \\ \hline \square \end{array} \quad \square$$

7. 2 + 8 + 7 = ____

8. 9 + 8 + 1 = ____

9. 8 + 7 + 5 = ____

10. DIG DEEPER! Complete the number puzzle so that each branch has a sum of 20.

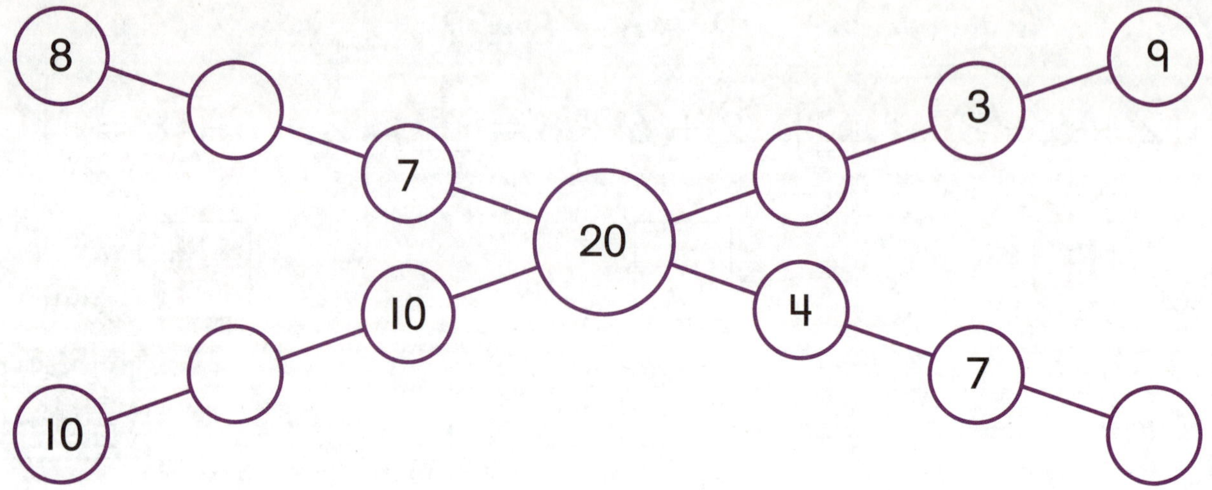

11. **Modeling Real Life** You, Newton, and Descartes have 17 stampers in all. Newton and Descartes each have 6. How many stampers do you have?

_____ stampers

Review & Refresh

12. Make a quick sketch. Complete the sentences.

74

Tens	Ones

_____ tens is _____.

_____ ones is _____.

_____ tens and _____ ones is _____.

Name ______________________________

Learning Target: Use the *make a 10* strategy to add two numbers.

Use counters and the ten frames to find the sum. How can you make a 10 to solve?

$7 + 6 =$ ____

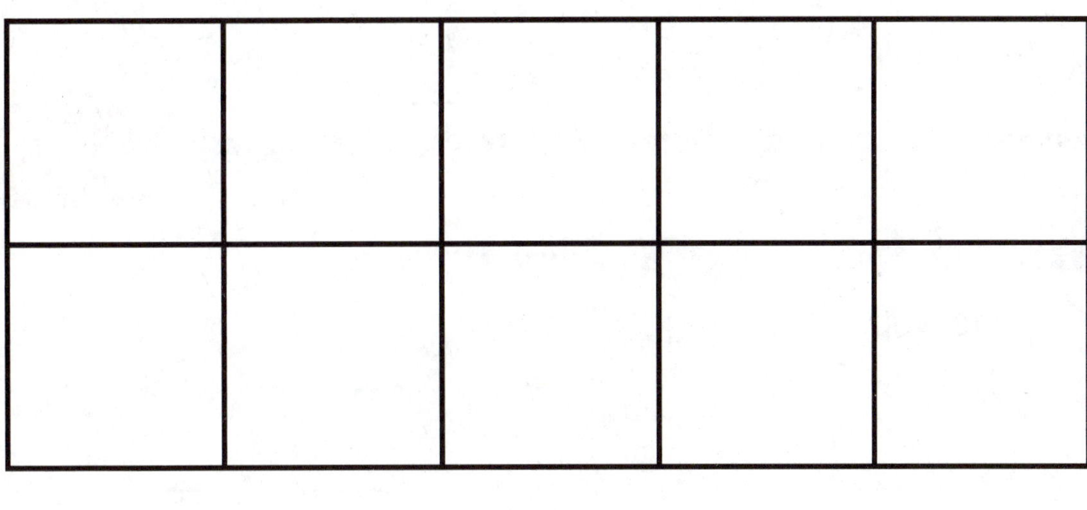

Think and Grow

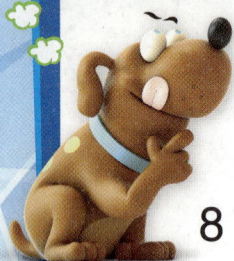

Think of 7 as 2 + 5.

8 + 7 = ?

One Way:

Another Way:

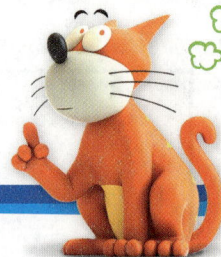

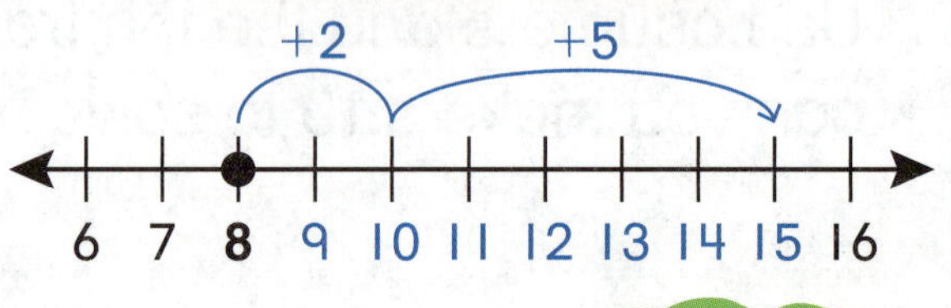

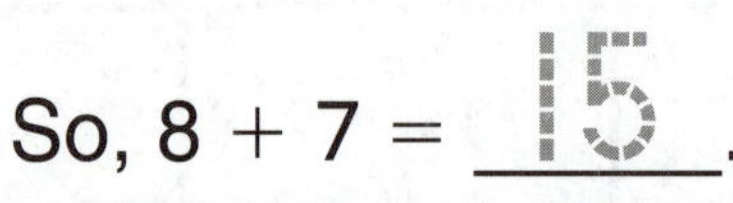

Show and Grow *I can do it!*

Make a 10 to add.

1. 7 + 9 = ?

☐ + ☐ + 9

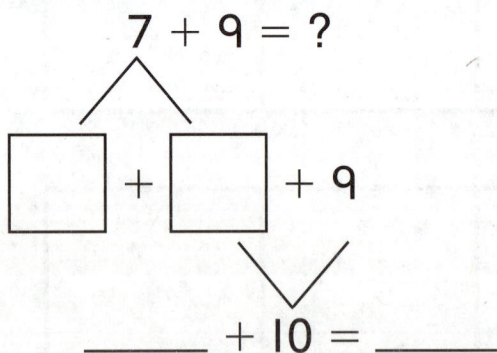

_____ + 10 = _____

So, 7 + 9 = _____.

2. 9 + 5 = ?

9 + ☐ + ☐

10 + _____ = _____

So, 9 + 5 = _____.

3. 6 + 8 = ?

10 + _____ = _____

So, 6 + 8 = _____.

4. 7 + 4 = ?

10 + _____ = _____

So, 7 + 4 = _____.

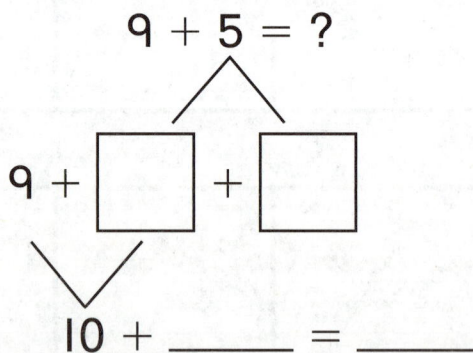

Name ______________________________

Apply and Grow: Practice

Make a 10 to add.

5. 2 + 9 = ?

10 + ______ = ______

So, 2 + 9 = ______.

6. 8 + 4 = ?

10 + ______ = ______

So, 8 + 4 = ______.

7. 9 + 6 = ?

10 + ______ = ______

So, 9 + 6 = ______.

8. 7 + 7 = ?

10 + ______ = ______

So, 7 + 7 = ______.

9. 6 + 5 = ______

10. 8 + 9 = ______

11. 7 + 5 = ______

12. 6 + 6 = ______

13. 9 + 9 = ______

14. 8 + 7 = ______

15. ______ = 4 + 7

16. ______ = 9 + 4

17. ______ = 8 + 8

18. ______ = 6 + 8

19. MP **Number Sense** How can you make a 10 to find 7 + 6?

10 + 2   10 + 3   10 + 4   10 + 5

Think and Grow: Modeling Real Life

There are 13 boys and 4 girls in a line. How many girls must join the line so that the numbers of boys and girls are equal?

Addition equation:

_____ girls

MP Communicate Clearly
How can you use the *make a 10* strategy to solve?

Show and Grow *I can think deeper!*

20. There are 16 seals and 7 whales. How many whales must join them so that the numbers of seals and whales are equal?

_____ whales

21. You and your friend count 15 stars in all. You count 8. How many stars does your friend count?

_____ stars

22. There are 17 fish in a tank. 9 are green. The rest are blue. How many fish are blue?

_____ fish

Name ______________________

Practice 

Learning Target: Use the *make a 10* strategy to add two numbers.

5 + 9 = ?

One Way:

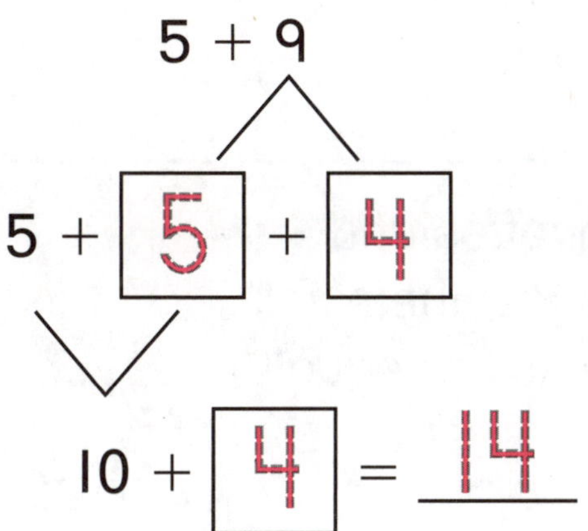

Another Way:

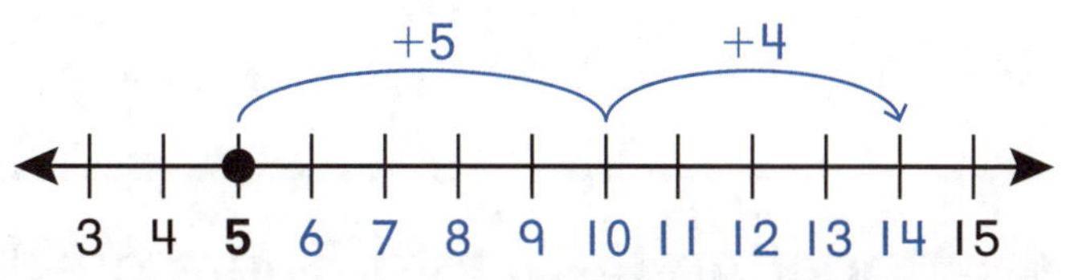

So, 5 + 9 = 14.

Make a 10 to add.

1. 5 + 6 = ?

5 + ☐ + ☐

10 + ______ = ______

So, 5 + 6 = ______.

2. 5 + 8 = ?

☐ + ☐ + 8

______ + 10 = ______

So, 5 + 8 = ______.

3. 7 + 6 = ?

10 + ______ = ______

So, 7 + 6 = ______.

4. 8 + 3 = ?

10 + ______ = ______

So, 8 + 3 = ______.

Make a 10 to add.

5. $3 + 9 =$ ____

6. $8 + 8 =$ ____

7. $7 + 4 =$ ____

8. $4 + 9 =$ ____

9. MP **Number Sense** Complete each equation.

$6 + 7 = 10 +$ ____ $9 + 7 = 10 +$ ____ $8 + 6 =$ ____ $+ 4$

10. MP **Modeling Real Life** There are 12 giraffes and 5 elephants. How many elephants must join them so that the numbers of giraffes and elephants are equal?

____ elephants

11. MP **Modeling Real Life** There are 14 horses on a farm. 7 are brown. The rest are white. How many are white?

____ are white

12. DIG DEEPER! At the library, Newton borrows 8 books and Descartes borrows 4 books. 7 of their books are nonfiction. The rest are fiction. How many fiction books did they borrow together?

____ fiction books

Review & Refresh

Compare.

13. 21 ◯ 22

14. 43 ◯ 34

Name ______________________

Count On and Count Back to Subtract 2.5

Learning Target: Use the *count on* and *count back* strategies to find a difference.

Explore and Grow

Show two ways to find the difference on the number lines.

$13 - 9 =$ _____

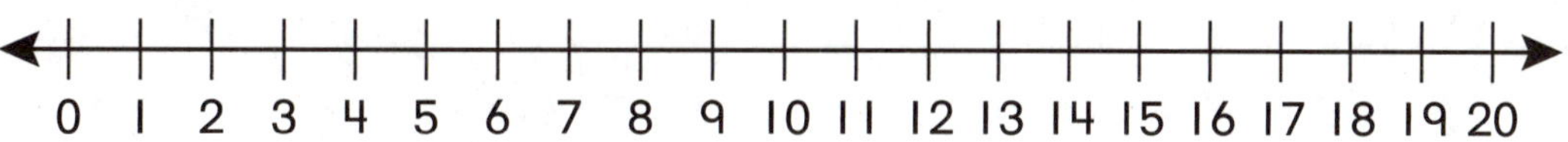

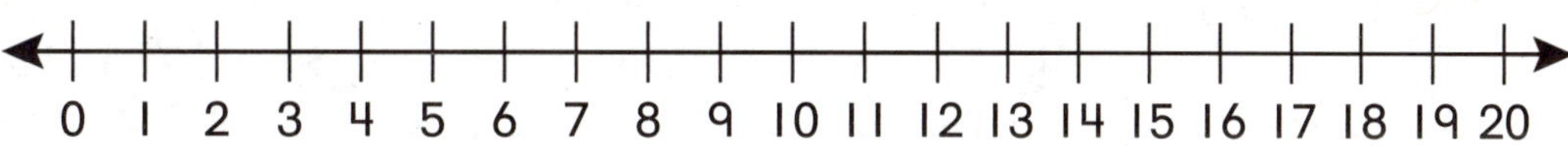

Think and Grow

$12 - 7 = ?$

One Way: Count back to find the **difference**.

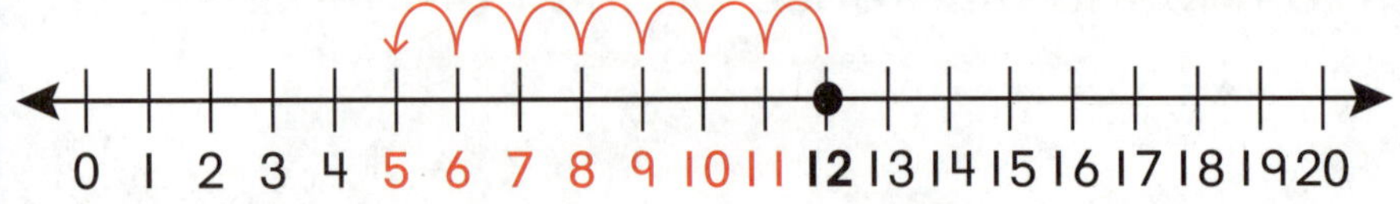

So, $12 - 7 =$ 5.

Another Way: Count on to find the difference.

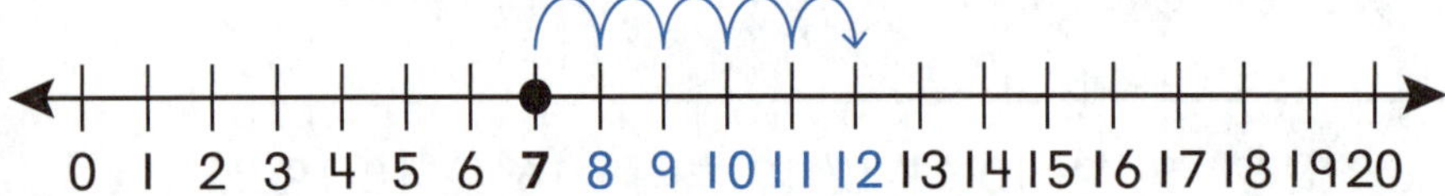

So, $12 - 7 =$ 5.

Show and Grow *I can do it!*

1. $11 - 5 =$ ____

0 1 2 3 4 5 6 7 8 9 10 11 12 13 14 15 16 17 18 19 20

2. $15 - 8 =$ ____

0 1 2 3 4 5 6 7 8 9 10 11 12 13 14 15 16 17 18 19 20

3. $9 - 6 =$ ____

0 1 2 3 4 5 6 7 8 9 10 11 12 13 14 15 16 17 18 19 20

4. $16 - 8 =$ ____

0 1 2 3 4 5 6 7 8 9 10 11 12 13 14 15 16 17 18 19 20

Name ______________________________

Apply and Grow: Practice

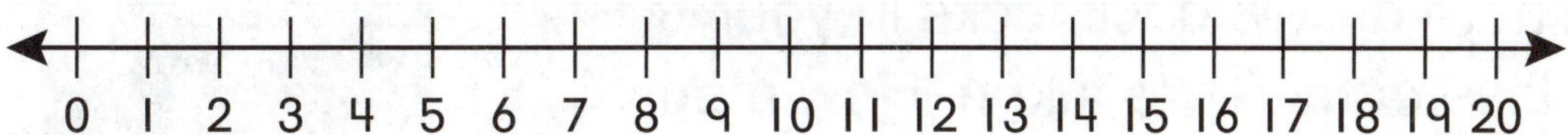

5. 11 − 8 = ____

6. 10 − 6 = ____

7. 14 − 6 = ____

8. 11 − 4 = ____

9. 15 − 9 = ____

10. 16 − 7 = ____

11. 14 − 9 = ____

12. 12 − 4 = ____

13. 10 − 7 = ____

14. 8 − 4 = ☐

15. 11 − 6 = ☐

16. 18 − 9 = ☐

17. ____ = 9 − 2

18. ____ = 13 − 5

19. ____ = 14 − 7

20. **Structure** What strategy did Newton use to solve? How do you know?

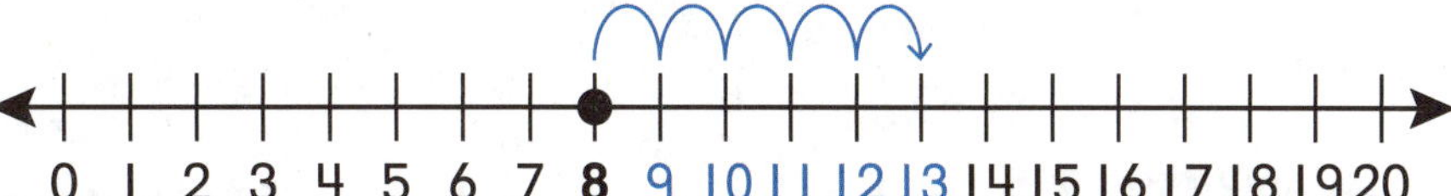

____

____

____

Think and Grow: Modeling Real Life

There are 13 backpacks in your classroom. 9 are taken. How many backpacks are left?

Model:

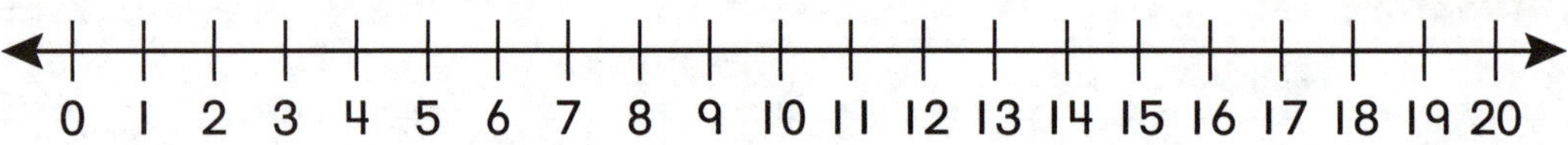

Equation:

_____ backpacks

Show and Grow *I can think deeper!*

21. There are 17 trays in a stack. 7 are used. How many trays are left?

_____ trays

22. DIG DEEPER! Newton wants to download some songs. 8 songs are downloaded. There are 6 songs left. How many songs did Newton want to download?

_____ songs

Name ______________________

Learning Target: Use the *count on* and *count back* strategies to find a difference.

14 − 8 = ?

One Way: Count back.

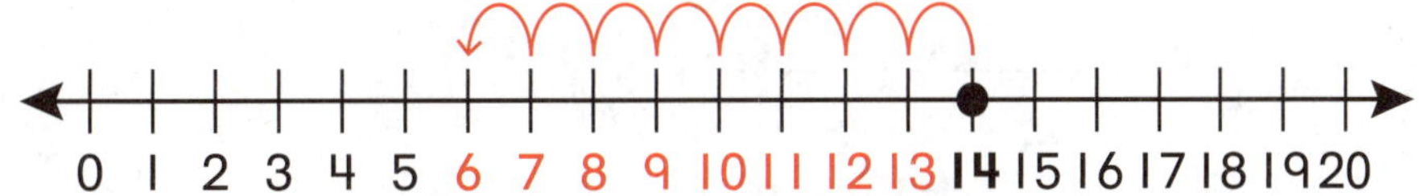

So, 14 − 8 = 6.

Another Way: Count on.

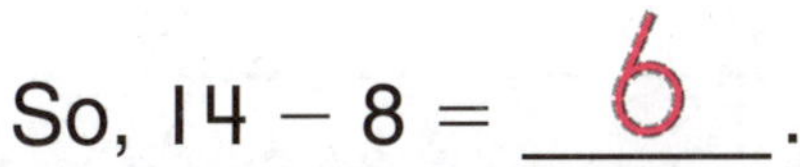

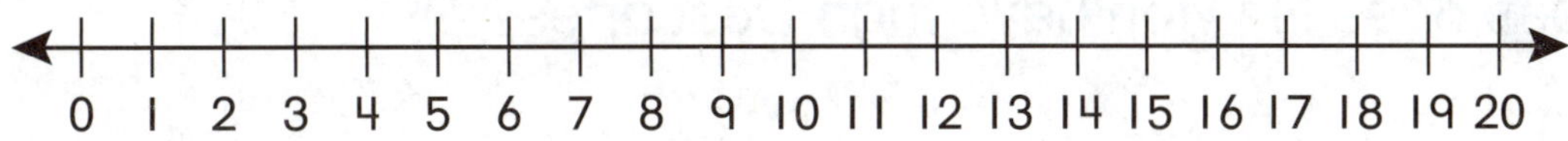

1. 7 − 5 = ____

2. 11 − 7 = ____

3. 12 − 5 = ____

4. 17 − 8 = ____

5. 7 − 2 = ____

6. 16 − 9 = ____

7. 9 − 3 = ☐

8. 13 − 4 = ☐

9. 12 − 6 = ☐

10. ____ = 10 − 8

11. ____ = 8 − 5

12. ____ = 12 − 3

13. DIG DEEPER! Complete the squares so the differences on the outside are correct.

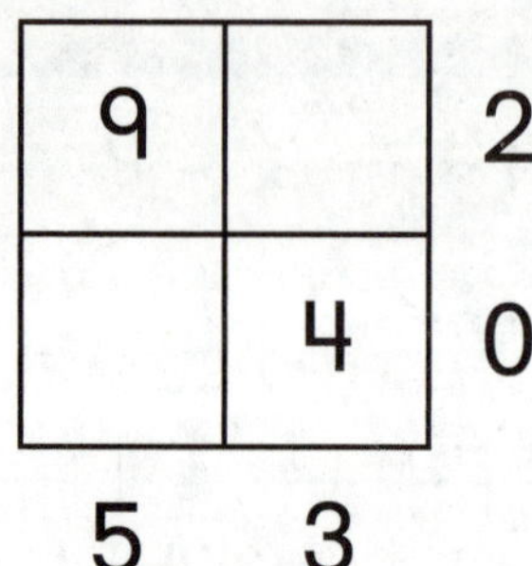

14. Modeling Real Life 15 kids are in line to play four square. 7 of them leave. How many kids are left?

_____ kids

15. Modeling Real Life Newton has 6 pieces of macaroni. Descartes has 15. How many fewer pieces does Newton have than Descartes?

_____ pieces

Review & Refresh

16. Precision Draw more lines to show fourths.

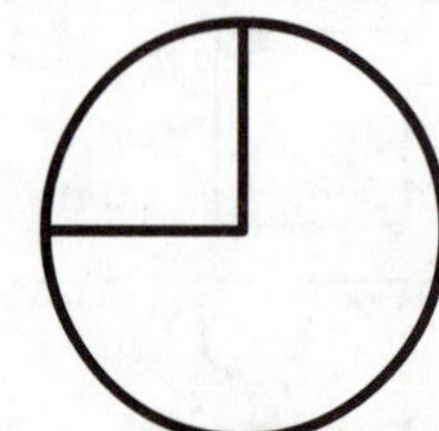

Name ____________________

Relate Addition and Subtraction 2.6

Learning Target: Write related addition and subtraction equations.

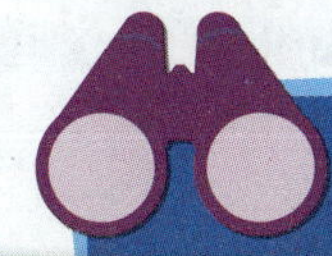

Explore and Grow

Write an addition equation. Complete the part-part-whole model to match. Write a related subtraction equation.

_____ + _____ = _____

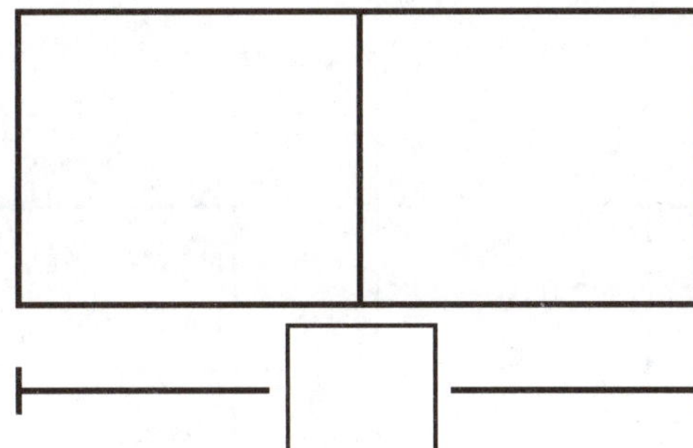

_____ − _____ = _____

Think and Grow

$6 + 9 = \underline{15}$

$15 - 6 = \underline{9}$

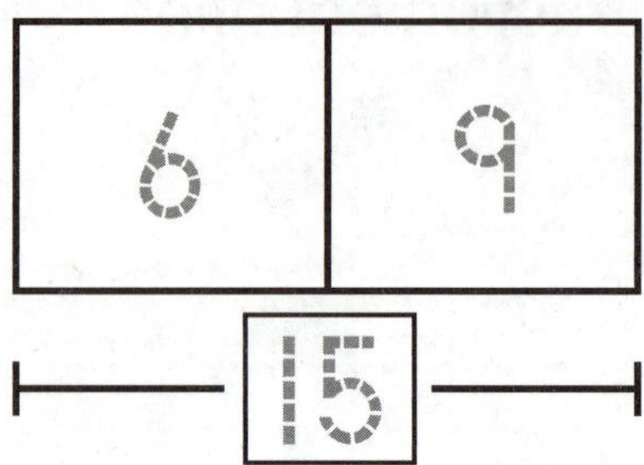

Addition and subtraction equations are related when they have the same parts and whole.

Show and Grow *I can do it!*

1. $5 + 3 = \_\_\_\_$

   $8 - 5 = \_\_\_\_$

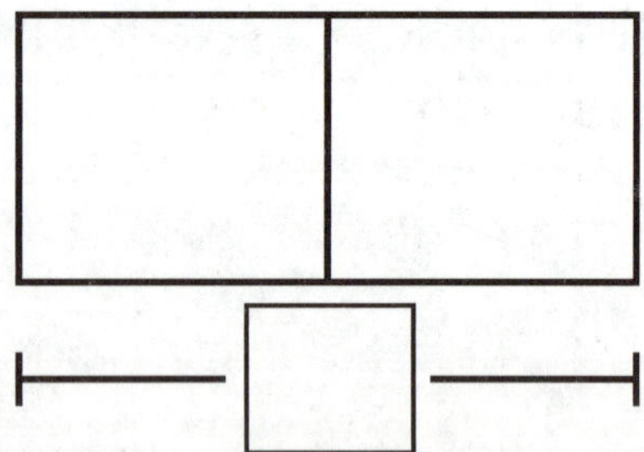

2. $4 + 7 = \_\_\_\_$

   $11 - 4 = \_\_\_\_$

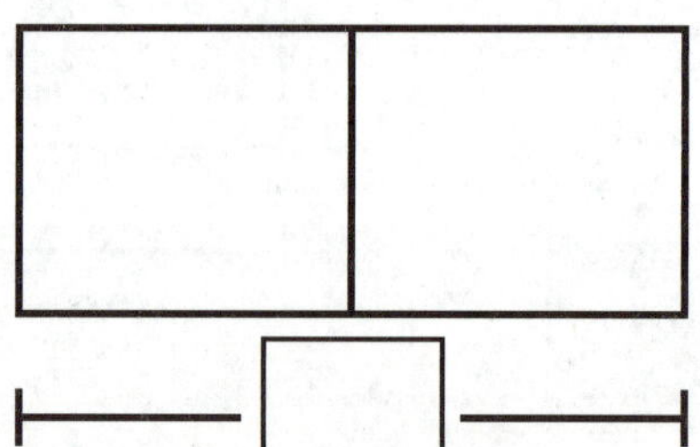

3. $3 + 9 = \_\_\_\_$

   $12 - 3 = \_\_\_\_$

4. $8 + 6 = \_\_\_\_$

   $14 - 8 = \_\_\_\_$

5. $7 + 8 = \_\_\_\_$

   $15 - 7 = \_\_\_\_$

6. $9 + 9 = \_\_\_\_$

   $18 - 9 = \_\_\_\_$

Name ______________________________

Apply and Grow: Practice

7. $4 + 5 =$ ____ $9 - 4 =$ ____	**8.** $5 + 7 =$ ____ $12 - 7 =$ ____	**9.** $8 + 8 =$ ____ $16 - 8 =$ ____
10. $5 + 2 =$ ____ $7 - 2 =$ ____	**11.** $4 + 6 =$ ____ $10 - 4 =$ ____	**12.** $2 + 6 =$ ____ $8 - 2 =$ ____
13. $7 + 7 =$ ____ $14 - 7 =$ ____	**14.** $6 + 5 =$ ____ $11 - 6 =$ ____	**15.** $9 + 6 =$ ____ $15 - 6 =$ ____
16. $3 + 8 =$ ____ $11 - 8 =$ ____ $11 - 3 =$ ____	**17.** $9 + 7 =$ ____ $16 - 9 =$ ____ $16 - 7 =$ ____	**18.** $8 + 5 =$ ____ $13 - 5 =$ ____ $13 - 8 =$ ____

19. MP **Structure** Complete the number bond. Write related addition and subtraction equations.

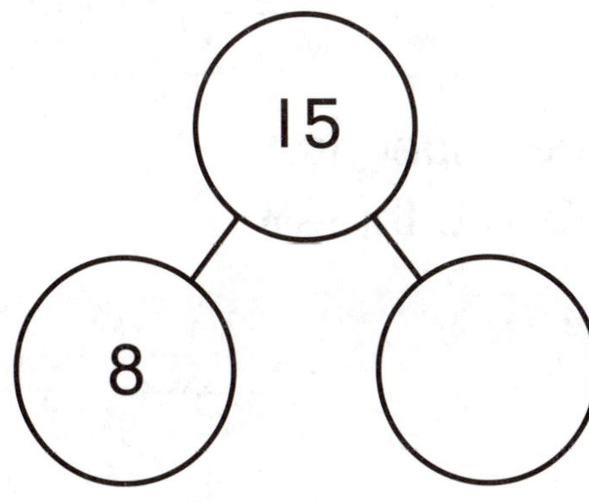

____ + ____ = ____

____ − ____ = ____

____ − ____ = ____

Think and Grow: Modeling Real Life

You have 17 glow sticks. You give away 9 of them. How many glow sticks do you have left?

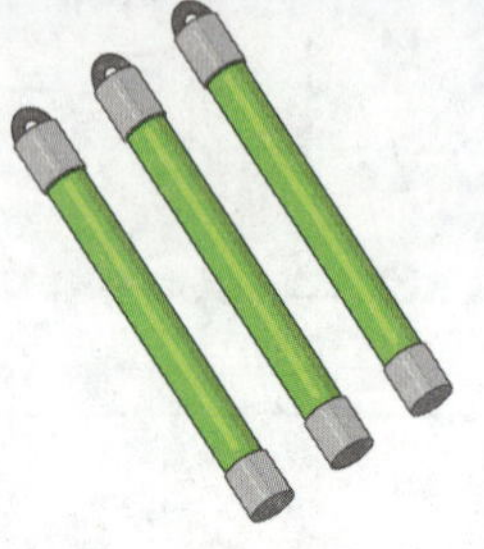

Which addition fact can help you subtract?

17 + 9   9 + 8   9 + 9

Subtraction equation:

_____ glow sticks

Show and Grow I can think deeper!

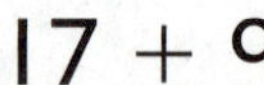

20. A box of sidewalk chalk has 20 pieces. You use 10 of them. How many pieces are *not* used?

_____ pieces

21. There are 7 more butterflies than birds. There are 8 birds. How many butterflies are there?

_____ butterflies

22. A kitchen drawer has 9 fewer forks than spoons. There are 15 spoons. How many forks are there?

_____ forks

Name ____________________

Practice 2.6

Learning Target: Write related addition and subtraction equations.

7 + 8 = 15

15 − 7 = 8

15 − 8 = 7

7	8
15	

1. 5 + 5 = ____

10 − 5 = ____

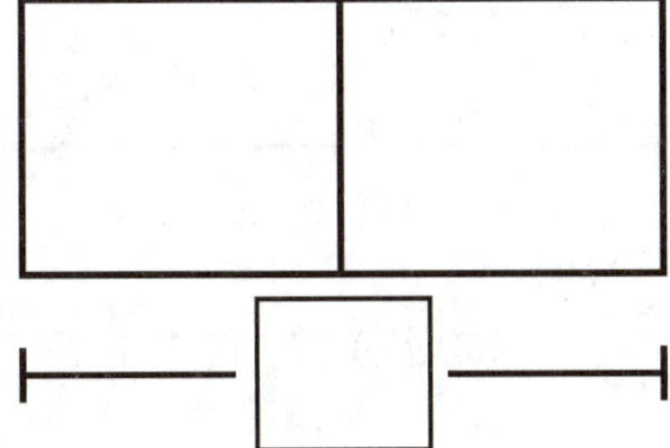

2. 5 + 8 = ____

13 − 8 = ____

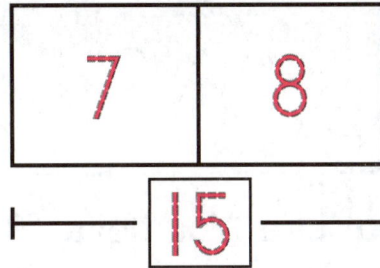

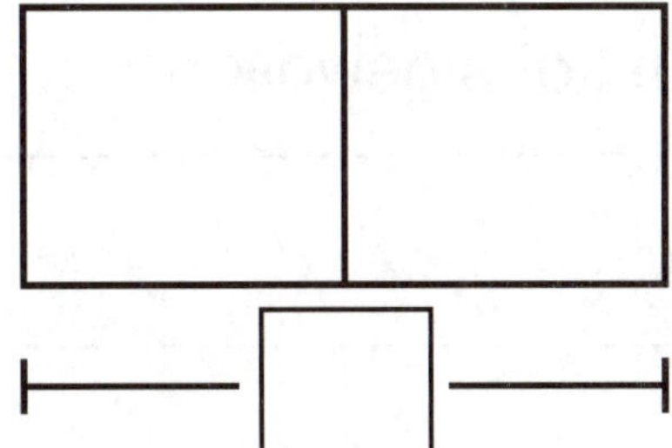

3. 3 + 4 = ____

7 − 3 = ____

4. 8 + 6 = ____

14 − 6 = ____

5. 6 + 6 = ____

12 − 6 = ____

6. 5 + 6 = ____

11 − 6 = ____

11 − 5 = ____

7. 9 + 8 = ____

17 − 9 = ____

17 − 8 = ____

8. 7 + 9 = ____

16 − 9 = ____

16 − 7 = ____

9. **Number Sense** Find the sums. Write a related subtraction equation for each addition equation.

$4 + 9 =$ ____ $7 + 5 =$ ____

____ − ____ = ____ ____ − ____ = ____

10. **Modeling Real Life** You have 13 colors of modeling clay. You use 7 of them to make a sculpture. How many colors are *not* used?

____ colors

11. **DIG DEEPER!** Do the equations $3 + 7 = 10$ and $7 + 3 = 10$ have the same related subtraction equations? Explain.

____

____

Review & Refresh

12. You have 6 bears. Some are brown. The rest are black. You have more brown bears than black bears. How many brown and black bears can you have?

5 brown 1 black 2 brown 4 black

1 brown 5 black 4 brown 2 black

Show how you know:

Name ______________________________

Get to 10 to Subtract 2.7

Learning Target: Use the *get to 10* strategy.

How can you use the number line to find the missing number?

14 − _____ = 10

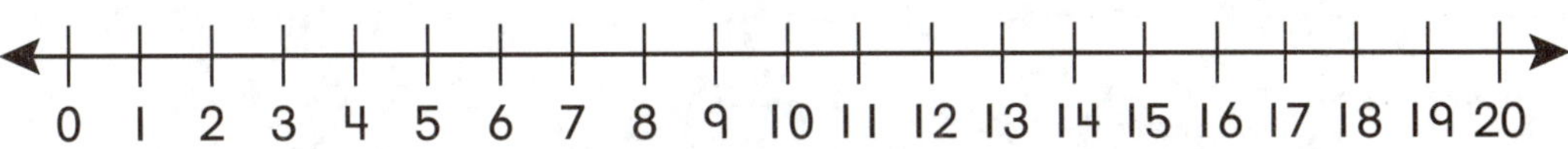

Think and Grow

Start at 15. Subtract 5 to get to 10. Because 7 = 5 + 2, subtract 2 more.

$15 - 7 = ?$

5 + 2

−2 −5

0 1 2 3 4 5 6 7 8 9 10 11 12 13 14 15 16 17 18 19 20

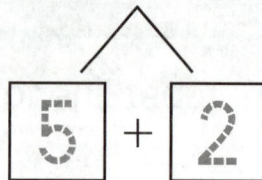

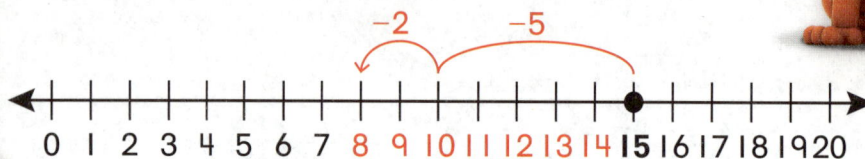

So, $15 - 7 =$ 8.

Show and Grow *I can do it!*

Get to 10 to subtract.

1. $13 - 6 = ?$

☐ + ☐

$10 -$ ______ $=$ ______

So, $13 - 6 =$ ______.

2. $12 - 8 = ?$

☐ + ☐

$10 -$ ______ $=$ ______

So, $12 - 8 =$ ______.

3. $14 - 8 = ?$

$10 -$ ______ $=$ ______

So, $14 - 8 =$ ______.

4. $16 - 7 = ?$

$10 -$ ______ $=$ ______

So, $16 - 7 =$ ______.

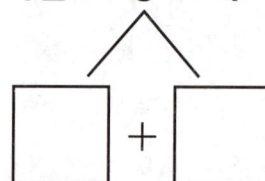

Name ______________________________

Apply and Grow: Practice

Get to 10 to subtract.

5. 12 − 6 = ?

10 − ______ = ______

So, 12 − 6 = ______.

6. 13 − 7 = ?

10 − ______ = ______

So, 13 − 7 = ______.

7. 15 − 9 = ?

10 − ______ = ______

So, 15 − 9 = ______.

8. 14 − 6 = ?

10 − ______ = ______

So, 14 − 6 = ______.

9. 13 − 8 = ______

10. 12 − 4 = ______

11. 17 − 9 = ______

12. 15 − 8 = ______

13. 12 − 7 = ______

14. 13 − 4 = ______

15. ______ = 12 − 3

16. ______ = 16 − 7

17. ______ = 14 − 9

18. ______ = 12 − 9

19. MP **Number Sense** How can you get to 10 to find 13 − 5?

10 − 5 13 − 10 10 − 2 10 − 3

Think and Grow: Modeling Real Life

A first-aid kit has 16 bandages. You use 7 of them. How many bandages are left?

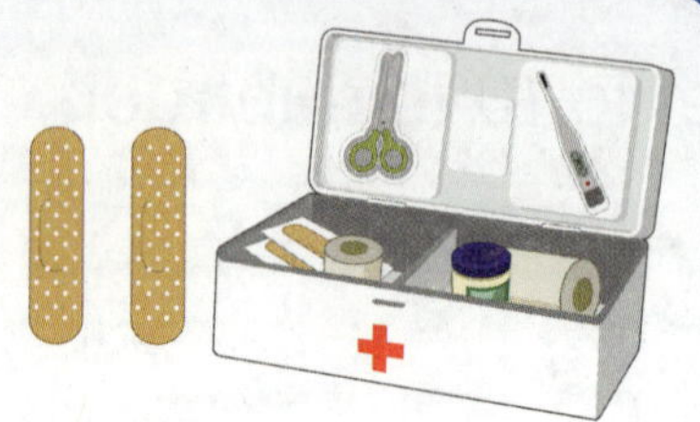

Equation:

_____ bandages

Show and Grow *I can think deeper!*

20. There are 12 elephants at a watering hole. 5 of them leave. How many elephants are left?

_____ elephants

21. DIG DEEPER! There are 17 hot-air balloons on the ground. 5 of them take off at 1:00. 4 more take off at 1:30. How many balloons are still on the ground?

_____ balloons

MP **Justify a Result** Explain how you found the number of balloons still on the ground.

____

____

Name ______________________________

Practice 

Learning Target: Use the *get to 10* strategy.

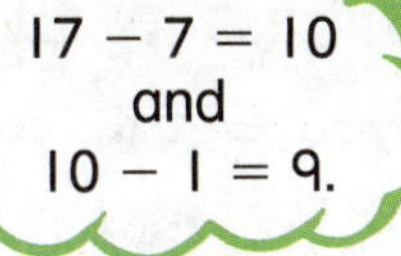

Start at 17. Subtract 7 to make a 10. Because 8 = 7 + 1, subtract 1 more.

17 − 8 = ?

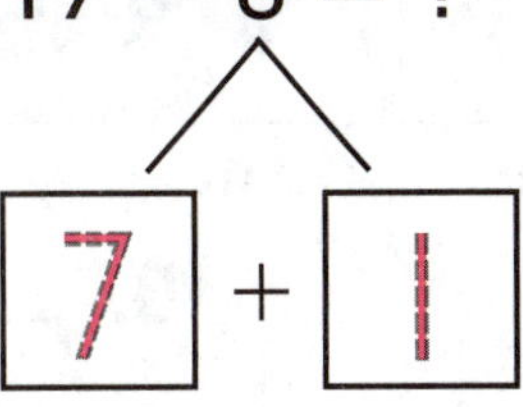

So, 17 − 8 = 9.

Get to 10 to subtract.

1. 12 − 5 = ?

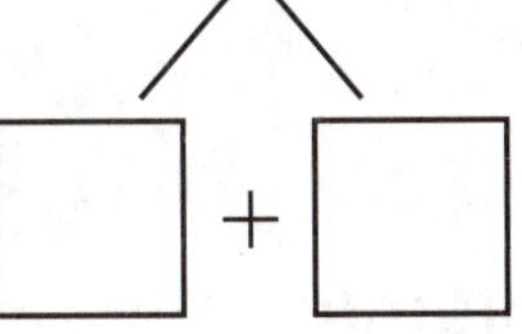

10 − ______ = ______

So, 12 − 5 = ______.

2. 15 − 6 = ?

☐ + ☐

10 − ______ = ______

So, 15 − 6 = ______.

3. 16 − 8 = ?

10 − ______ = ______

So, 16 − 8 = ______.

4. 13 − 9 = ?

10 − ______ = ______

So, 13 − 9 = ______.

Get to 10 to subtract.

5. 14 − 5 = ______

6. 16 − 7 = ______

7. 12 − 8 = ______

8. 13 − 8 = ______

9. ______ = 16 − 9

10. ______ = 14 − 7

11. ______ = 12 − 4

12. ______ = 18 − 9

13. **Number Sense** Complete each equation.

14 − 8 = 10 − ______

15 − 7 = 10 − ______

13 − 6 = ______ − 3

14. **Modeling Real Life** Descartes has 18 items to sell at a garage sale. He sells 9 of them. How many items does he have left?

______ items

15. **DIG DEEPER!** There are 12 penguins. 5 of them leave to find food at 5:00. 3 more leave at 5:30. How many penguins are left?

______ penguins

Review & Refresh

16. 19

Even Odd

17. 12

Even Odd

Name ______________________________

Practice Addition and Subtraction 2.8

Learning Target: Add and subtract within 20.

Explore and Grow

You have 6 yellow buttons and 8 red buttons. Write four equations that describe your buttons.

_____ + _____ = _____

_____ + _____ = _____

_____ − _____ = _____

_____ − _____ = _____

Think and Grow

$6 + 7 = ?$

One Way: Use doubles plus 1.

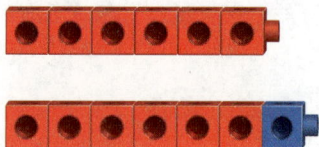

6 + 7 is one more than 6 + 6, or 12 + 1.

Another Way: Make a 10.

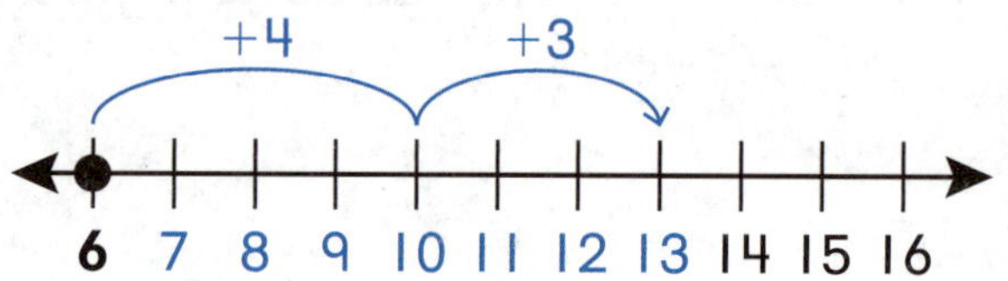

So, 6 + 7 = 13.

$16 - 9 = ?$

One Way: Get to 10.

Another Way: Use a related fact.

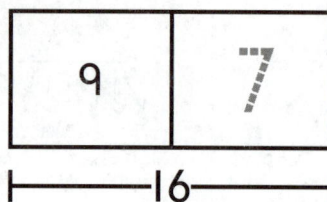

9	7

16

9 + 7 = 16

So, 16 − 9 = 7.

Show and Grow *I can do it!*

1. 3 + 9 = ______
2. 8 − 6 = ______
3. 11 − 4 = ______
4. 7 + 7 = ______
5. 9 + 8 = ______
6. 10 − 7 = ______

Name ____________________

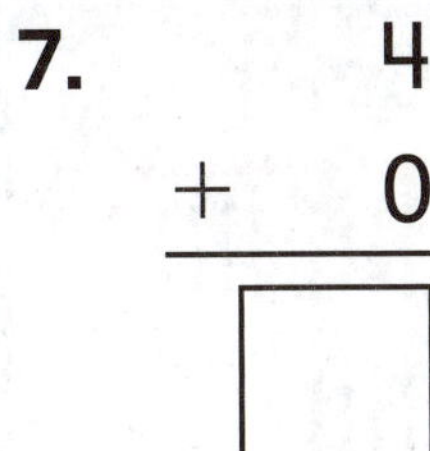

Apply and Grow: Practice

7.	8.	9.	10.
$4 + 0 = \square$	$3 + 7 = \square$	$15 - 7 = \square$	$17 - 8 = \square$

11.	12.	13.	14.
$10 + 10 = \square$	$8 - 0 = \square$	$9 + 2 = \square$	$18 - 9 = \square$

15. ______ = 9 + 1

16. ______ = 4 + 5

17. ______ = 11 − 8

18. ______ = 9 − 5

19. ______ = 7 + 9

20. ______ = 7 − 1

21. ______ = 8 + 4

22. ______ = 14 − 7

23. MP **Repeated Reasoning** Find the missing addend. Explain how you solved.

8 + ______ = 13

____

____

Think and Grow: Modeling Real Life

How many more students have brown hair than blonde hair?

Students' Hair Color	
Brown	卌 卌 ||||
Black	卌 ||||
Blonde	卌 ||

Equation:

_____ students

How many students do *not* have brown hair?

Equation:

_____ students

Show and Grow *I can think deeper!*

24. How many fewer students have hazel eyes than brown eyes?

Students' Eye Color	
Blue	卌 |||
Brown	卌 卌 ||
Hazel	||||

_____ students

How many students do *not* have brown eyes?

_____ students

Name ______________________

Practice 2.8

Learning Target: Add and subtract within 20.

$8 + 8 = ?$

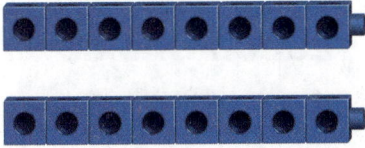

So, $8 + 8 =$ 16.

$12 - 7 = ?$

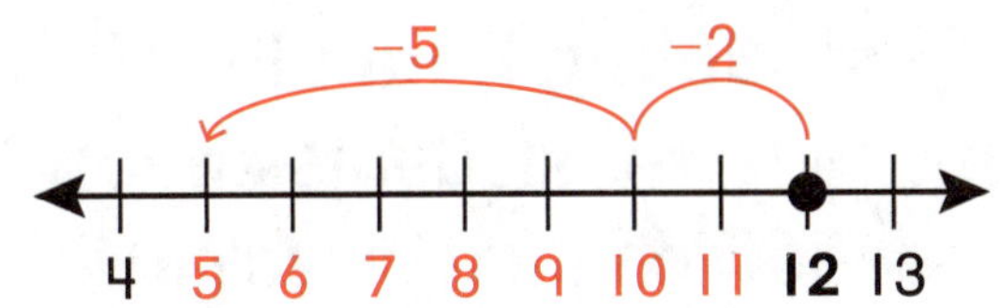

So, $12 - 7 =$ 5.

1. $3 + 5 =$ ______

2. $5 + 7 =$ ______

3. $13 - 6 =$ ______

4. $12 - 8 =$ ______

5. $6 + 0 =$ ______

6. $15 - 8 =$ ______

7. $\begin{array}{r} 5 \\ +\ 1 \\ \hline \square \end{array}$

8. $\begin{array}{r} 17 \\ -\ 9 \\ \hline \square \end{array}$

9. $\begin{array}{r} 8 \\ +\ 7 \\ \hline \square \end{array}$

10. $\begin{array}{r} 10 \\ -\ 1 \\ \hline \square \end{array}$

11. ______ $= 5 + 5$

12. ______ $= 3 - 0$

13. MP **Number Sense** Which expressions have a sum or difference that is greater than 10?

$6 + 6$ $20 - 10$ $14 - 9$ $4 + 7$

14. MP **Modeling Real Life** How many fewer students choose a sandwich than pizza?

Lunch Choice	
Sandwich	𝍸 ||||
Pasta	||||
Pizza	𝍸 𝍸 𝍸

_____ students

How many students do *not* choose pizza?

_____ students

15. DIG DEEPER! Use the tally chart above to write and solve your own word problem.

____

____

Review & Refresh

16. Circle groups of 4. Write a repeated addition equation to match.

_____ groups of 4 _____ + _____ + _____ + _____ = _____

Name ___________________________

Problem Solving: Addition and Subtraction 2.9

Learning Target: Solve addition and subtraction word problems.

Model the story.

You have 5 puzzle pieces. Your friend has 9. How many more pieces does your friend have than you?

Check Your Work How can you use a related fact to make sure your answer is correct?

_____ more pieces

Think and Grow

14 kids are on the bleachers. 5 kids are on the stage. 6 kids are behind the curtain. How many fewer kids are on the stage than on the bleachers?

Circle what you know. Underline what you need to find.

Solve: Kids on bleachers: 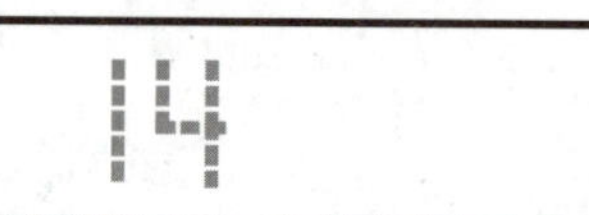 14

Kids on stage:  5 | 9

$14 - 5 = \underline{9}$

$5 + \underline{9} = 14$

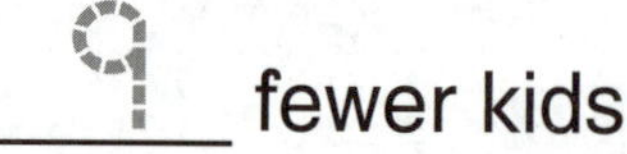

9 fewer kids

You can use addition or subtraction to solve.

Show and Grow *I can do it!*

1. You have 7 more keychains than your friend. You have 15 keychains. How many keychains does your friend have?

You: ______

Friend: ______ | ______

____ ○ ____ = ____

____ keychains

Name ______________________________

Apply and Grow: Practice

2. Some friends are at a community pool. 7 more join them. Now there are 12. How many friends were there to start?

_____ friends

3. Some friends are playing miniature golf. 8 of them leave. There are 6 left. How many friends were there to start?

_____ friends

4. MP YOU BE THE TEACHER Newton has 5 fewer fish than Descartes. Newton has 8 fish. Your friend uses a bar model to find how many fish Descartes has. Is your friend correct? Explain.

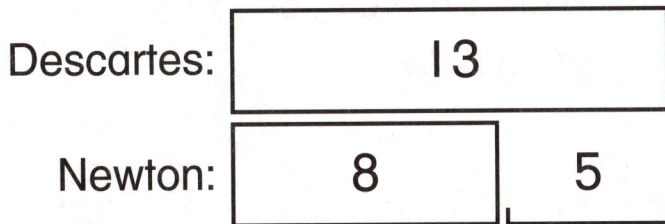

Descartes: | 13 |

Newton: | 8 | 5 |

8 + 5 = 13

13 fish

____
____
____
____

Think and Grow: Modeling Real Life

15 kids play at a park. 6 of them leave. 9 more kids come to the park. How many kids are at the park now?

Step 1:

Step 2:

______ kids

Show and Grow *I can think deeper!*

5. You have 13 baseball cards. You give 5 away. Then you get 4 more. How many baseball cards do you have now?

______ baseball cards

6. **DIG DEEPER!** There are 7 adult lions and some cubs in a pride. The pride has 13 lions in all. 3 more cubs are born. How many cubs are in the pride now?

______ cubs

MP Communicate Clearly Explain how you solved this problem.

____

____

Name ____________________

Learning Target: Solve addition and subtraction word problems.

There are 9 fewer students at the library than at the park.

There are 7 students at the library. There are 6 students at the pool.

How many students are at the park?

Circle what you know. Underline what you need to find.

Solve:

Park: 16

Library: 7 | 9

7 + 9 = 16

16 students

1. You have 3 more movies than your friend. You have 10 movies. Your friend has 5 video games. How many movies does your friend have?

You:

Friend:

____ ◯ ____ = ____

____ movies

2. Some friends are at a skating rink. 6 more join them. Now there are 11. How many friends were there to start?

____ friends

3. **Writing** Find the difference. Write a subtraction problem to match.

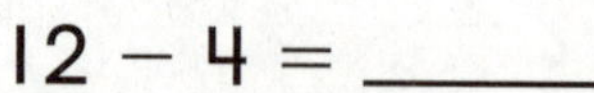

$12 - 4 =$ ______

____

____

____

4. **Modeling Real Life** You make 4 snow angels and Newton makes 5. Descartes makes 3 more snow angels. How many snow angels are there in all?

______ snow angels

5. **Modeling Real Life** Newton has 9 glitter pens. Descartes has 2 fewer than Newton. How many glitter pens do they have in all?

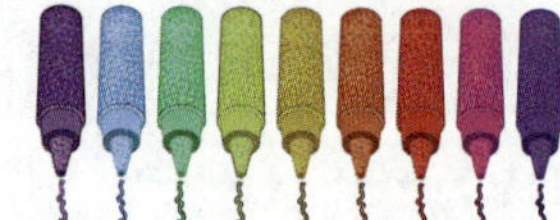

______ glitter pens

Review & Refresh

6. Which two shapes combine to make the shape on the left?

Name ______________________________

Performance Task 2

1. You and your friend check out books from the library as shown in the table.

Type	You	Friend
Science	7	
History	5	8
Adventure		

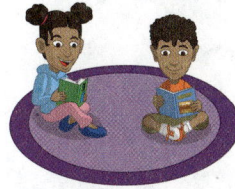

a. You have one more adventure book than science books. How many books do you have in all?

_____ books

b. You and your friend have the same number of books. Your friend has more science books than history books. Your friend has an even number of adventure books. How many science books and adventure books does your friend have?

_____ science books _____ adventure books

c. How many books do you and your friend have in all that are *not* history books?

_____ books

d. You return 3 books on Monday and 6 books on Thursday. How many books do you have left?

_____ books

Joey Jump

To Play: Place your cube on 0. Roll a die to see how many spaces to move. Write an equation that matches on the Joey Jump Add or Subtract Recording Sheet. Continue until you reach the food and then return to the pouch.

Name ____________________

Chapter Practice

2.1 Add in Any Order

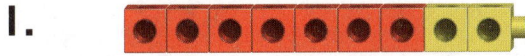

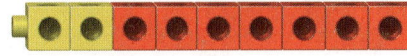

1.

____ + ____ = ____ ____ + ____ = ____

2. MP **Number Sense** Complete each equation.

9 + ____ = 3 + 9 2 + 5 = ____ + 2 9 + 1 = 1 + ____

8 + 0 = ____ + 8 7 + ____ = 8 + 7 ____ + 4 = 4 + 6

2.2 Use Doubles

Find the sum. Write the double you used.

3. 6 + 5 = ____

____ + ____ = ____

4. 8 + 9 = ____

____ + ____ = ____

5.

$$\begin{array}{r} 3 \\ +\ 2 \\ \hline \square \end{array} \qquad \begin{array}{r} \square \\ +\ \square \\ \hline \square \end{array}$$

6.

$$\begin{array}{r} 7 \\ +\ 8 \\ \hline \square \end{array} \qquad \begin{array}{r} \square \\ +\ \square \\ \hline \square \end{array}$$

2.3 Add Three Numbers

7. $6 + 8 + 0 =$ ____

8.
$$\begin{array}{r} 1 \\ 3 \\ +\ 9 \\ \hline \square \end{array}$$

9. $4 + 8 + 8 =$ ____

10. **Structure** Write the missing addends.

$$\begin{array}{r} 5 \\ 7 \\ +\ \square \\ \hline 15 \end{array} \qquad \begin{array}{r} 3 \\ \square \\ +\ 1 \\ \hline 8 \end{array} \qquad \begin{array}{r} \square \\ 0 \\ +\ 6 \\ \hline 12 \end{array} \qquad \begin{array}{r} 4 \\ \square \\ +\ 6 \\ \hline 17 \end{array}$$

2.4 Make a 10 to Add

Make a 10 to add.

11. $9 + 8 = ?$

$9 + \square + \square$

$10 +$ ____ $=$ ____

So, $9 + 8 =$ ____.

12. $7 + 6 = ?$

$7 + \square + \square$

$10 +$ ____ $=$ ____

So, $7 + 6 =$ ____.

13. $9 + 6 =$ ____

14. $4 + 7 =$ ____

2.5 Count On and Count Back to Subtract

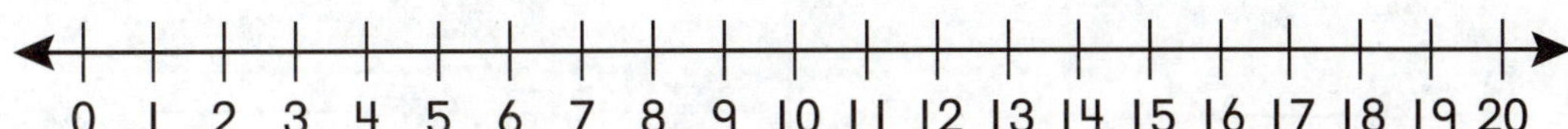

15. 12 − 8 = ____

16. 14 − 5 = ____

17. 17 − 9 = ____

2.6 Relate Addition and Subtraction

18. 7 + 6 = ____

13 − 6 = ____

13 − 7 = ____

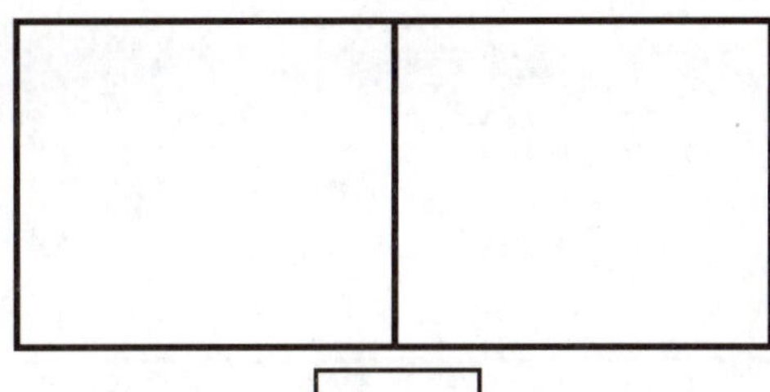

2.7 Get to 10 to Subtract

Get to 10 to subtract.

19. 12 − 4 = ?

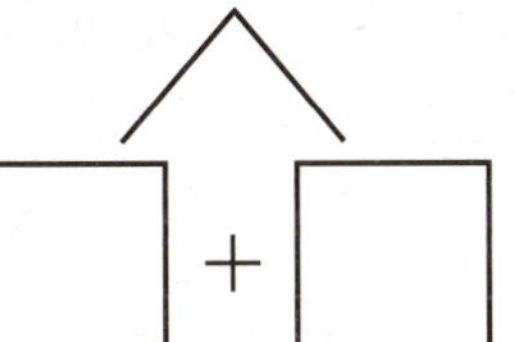

10 − ____ = ____

So, 12 − 4 = ____.

20. 15 − 8 = ?

□ + □

10 − ____ = ____

So, 15 − 8 = ____.

21. 16 − 9 = ____

22. 14 − 7 = ____

2.8 Practice Addition and Subtraction

23. $8 + 3 =$ _____

24. $13 - 7 =$ _____

25. $\begin{array}{r} 9 \\ +\ 6 \\ \hline \square \end{array}$

26. $\begin{array}{r} 15 \\ -\ 7 \\ \hline \square \end{array}$

27. $\begin{array}{r} 9 \\ +\ 9 \\ \hline \square \end{array}$

28. $\begin{array}{r} 12 \\ -\ 6 \\ \hline \square \end{array}$

29. _____ $= 5 + 8$

30. _____ $= 12 - 5$

2.9 Problem Solving: Addition and Subtraction

31. Some friends are playing laser tag. 4 of them leave. There are 8 left. How many friends were there to start?

Circle what you know.

Underline what you need to find.

Solve:

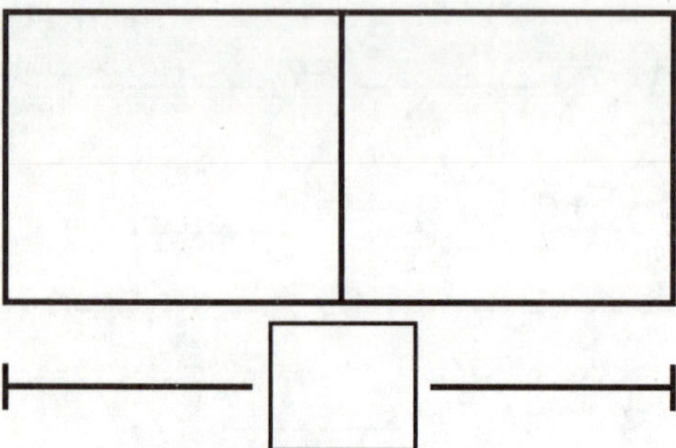

_____ ○ _____ = _____

_____ friends

Addition to 100 Strategies

- Have you ever been to an amusement park? What is your favorite ride?
- There are 25 people on a Ferris wheel. 48 more get on. How many people are on the Ferris wheel now?

Chapter Learning Target:
Understand addition.

Chapter Success Criteria:
- I can identify addition patterns.
- I can explain which strategy I used to write a sum.
- I can write a sum.
- I can solve addition problems.

Name ______________________________

3 Vocabulary

Review Words
ones place
tens place

Organize It

Use the review words to complete the graphic organizer.

73

Define It

Use your vocabulary cards to identify the words.

1.

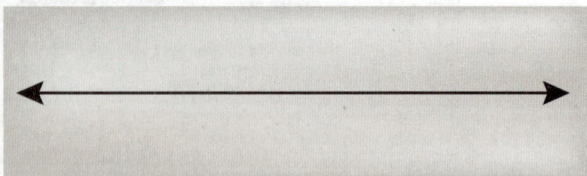

2. A strategy used to make a ten to help add and subtract numbers.

Chapter 3 Vocabulary Cards

compensation

open number line

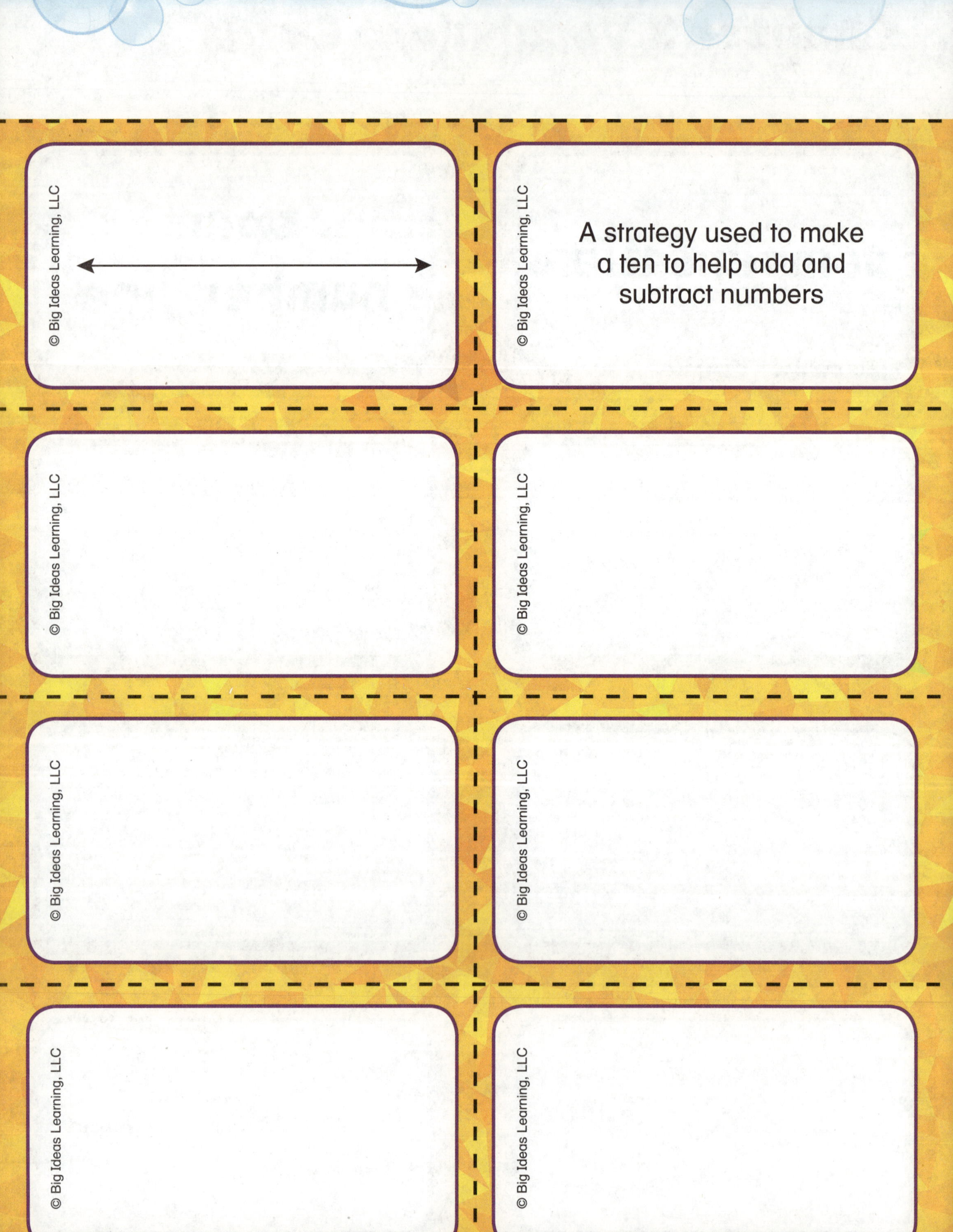
A strategy used to make a ten to help add and subtract numbers

Name ______________________________

Learning Target: Use an open number line to add tens.

Explore and Grow

Color and show how you can use the hundred chart to solve.

27 + 10 = _____ 62 + 30 = _____

1	2	3	4	5	6	7	8	9	10
11	12	13	14	15	16	17	18	19	20
21	22	23	24	25	26	27	28	29	30
31	32	33	34	35	36	37	38	39	40
41	42	43	44	45	46	47	48	49	50
51	52	53	54	55	56	57	58	59	60
61	62	63	64	65	66	67	68	69	70
71	72	73	74	75	76	77	78	79	80
81	82	83	84	85	86	87	88	89	90
91	92	93	94	95	96	97	98	99	100

Think and Grow

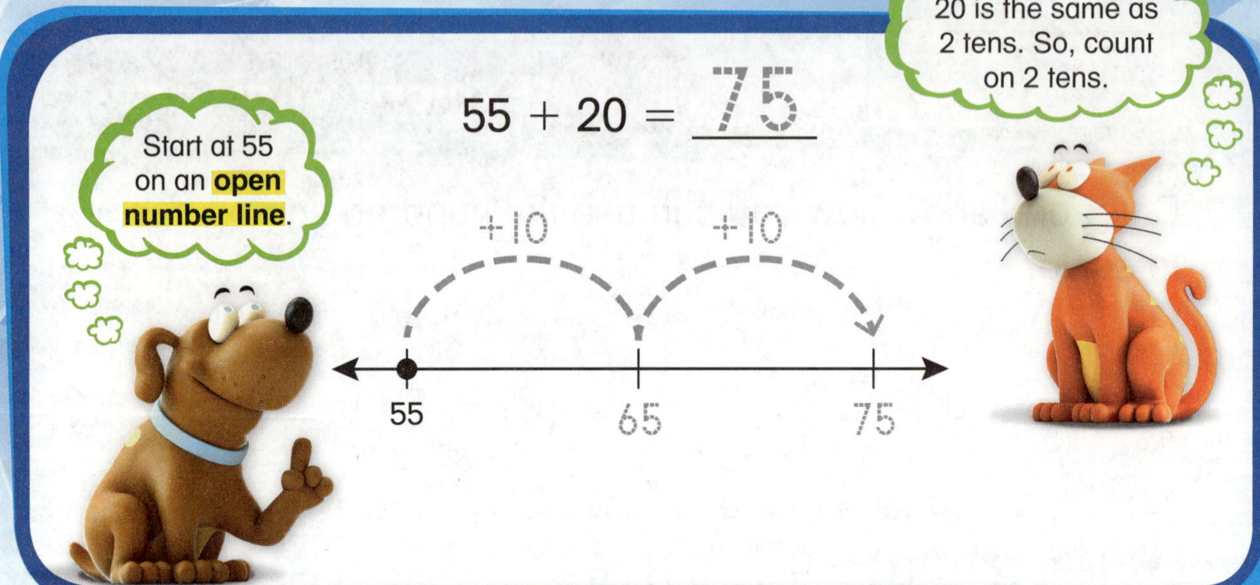

20 is the same as 2 tens. So, count on 2 tens.
55 + 20 = 75
Start at 55 on an **open number line**.
+10
+10
55
65
75

Show and Grow *I can do it!*

1. 70 + 30 = ______

70

2. 38 + 40 = ______

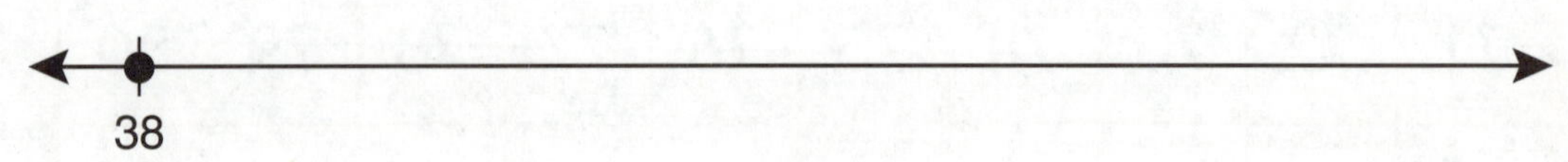

38

3. 22 + 60 = ______

Name ______________________________

Apply and Grow: Practice

4. 60 + 30 = _____

5. 51 + 20 = _____

6. 49 + 50 = _____

7. MP **YOU BE THE TEACHER** Your friend used an open number line to solve 40 + 20. Is your friend correct? Explain.

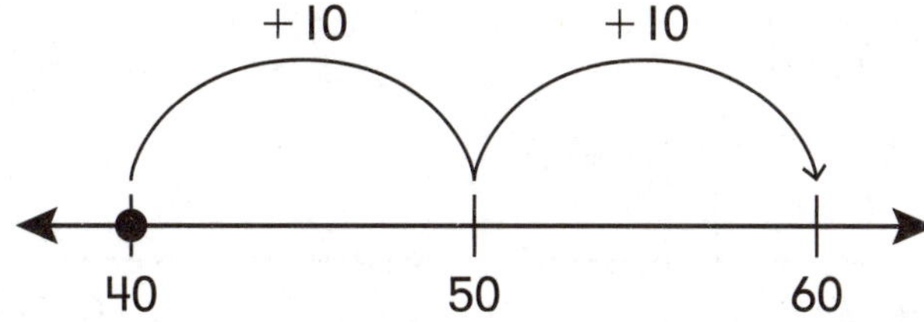

____

____

Think and Grow: Modeling Real Life

You have 66 berries and pick 30 more. Your friend picks 90 berries. Who has more berries?

Addition equation:

Model:

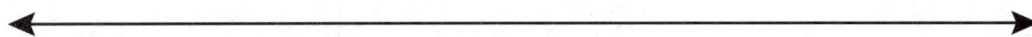

Compare: _____ ◯ _____

Who has more berries?   You   Friend

Show and Grow *I can think deeper!*

8. You have 34 feathers and collect 50 more. Your friend has 85 feathers. Who has more feathers?

You   Friend

9. **DIG DEEPER!** You have 49 stickers. Your friend gives you some more. Now you have 79. How many stickers did your friend give you?

_____ stickers

Name ____________________

Practice 3.1

Learning Target: Use an open number line to add tens.

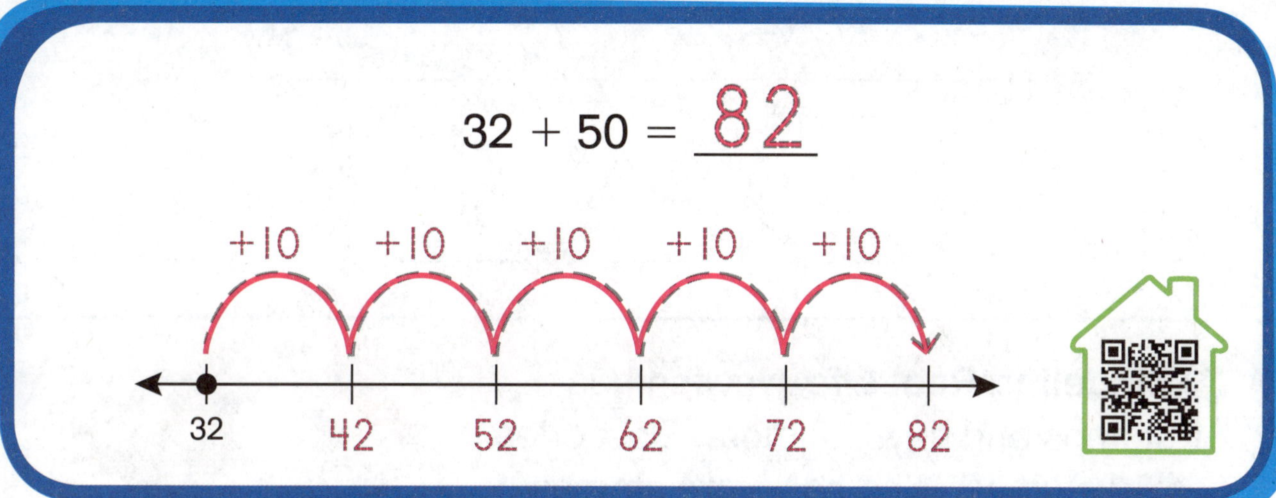

1. 40 + 40 = ____

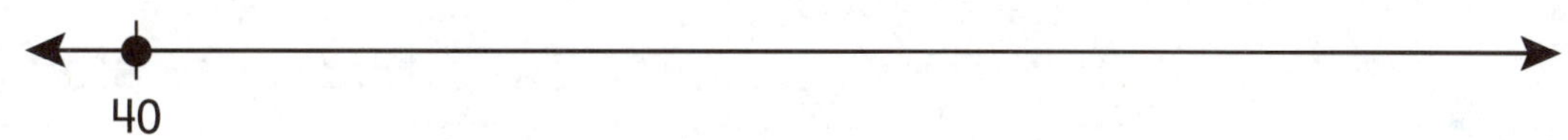

2. 65 + 20 = ____

3. 14 + 60 = ____

4. **Structure** Write an equation that matches the number line.

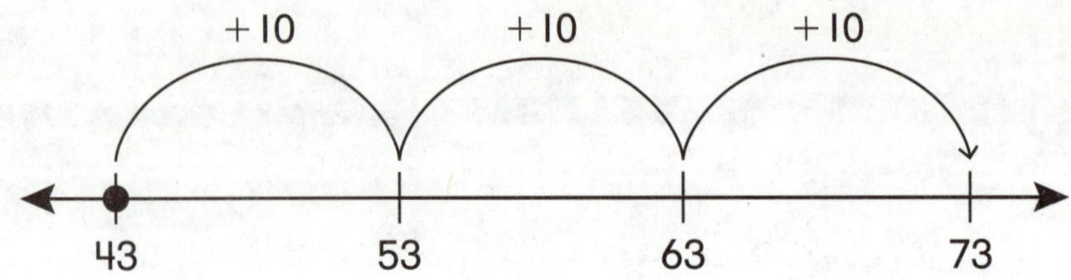

_____ + _____ = _____

5. **Modeling Real Life** Newton has 31 stamps and buys 20 more. Descartes has 50 stamps. Who has more stamps?

__________ has more stamps.

6. **DIG DEEPER!** You have 64 rocks. Your friend gives you some more. Now you have 94 rocks. How many rocks did your friend give you?

_____ rocks

Review & Refresh

Is the number even or odd?

7. 15

Even Odd

8. 8

Even Odd

9. 12

Even Odd

Name ______________________________

Add Tens and Ones Using a Number Line

3.2

Learning Target: Use an open number line to add tens and ones.

Explore and Grow

Color and show how you can use the hundred chart to solve.

13 + 25 = _____

1	2	3	4	5	6	7	8	9	10
11	12	13	14	15	16	17	18	19	20
21	22	23	24	25	26	27	28	29	30
31	32	33	34	35	36	37	38	39	40
41	42	43	44	45	46	47	48	49	50
51	52	53	54	55	56	57	58	59	60
61	62	63	64	65	66	67	68	69	70
71	72	73	74	75	76	77	78	79	80
81	82	83	84	85	86	87	88	89	90
91	92	93	94	95	96	97	98	99	100

Think and Grow

$38 + 23 = \underline{61}$

One Way:

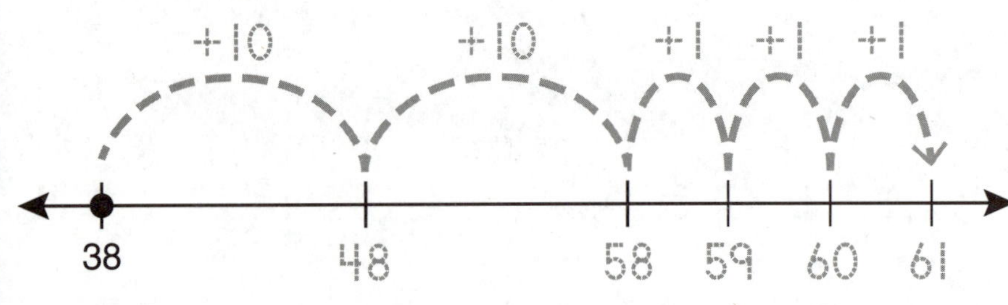

Another Way:

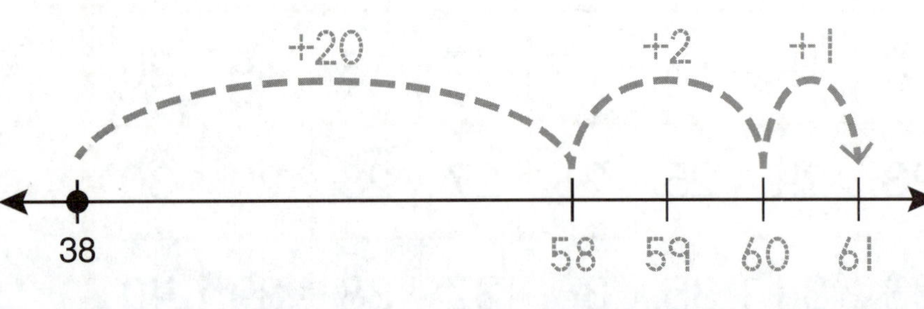

Show and Grow *I can do it!*

1. $69 + 12 =$ ______

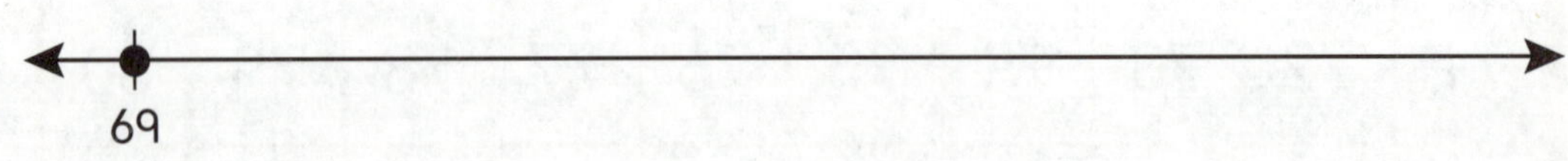

2. $55 + 34 =$ ______

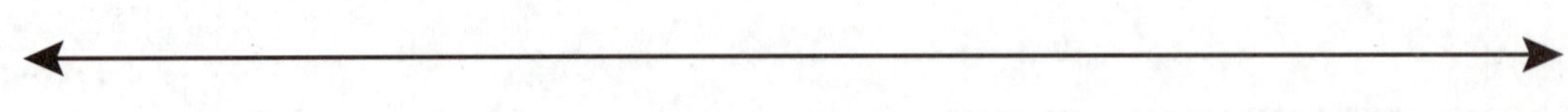

Name ______________________

Apply and Grow: Practice

3. 15 + 32 = ______

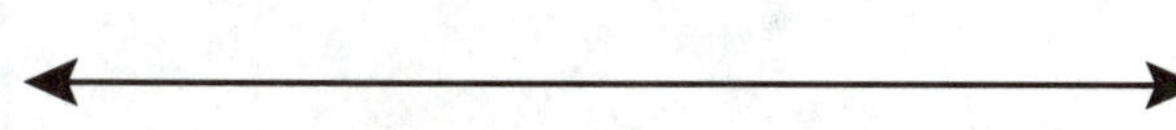

4. 52 + 26 = ______

5. 38 + 41 = ______

6. 65 + 33 = ______

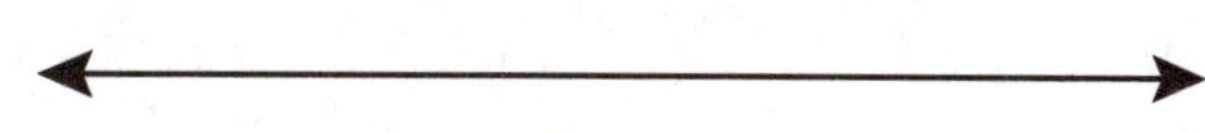

7. MP **Reasoning** Complete the number line and the equation.

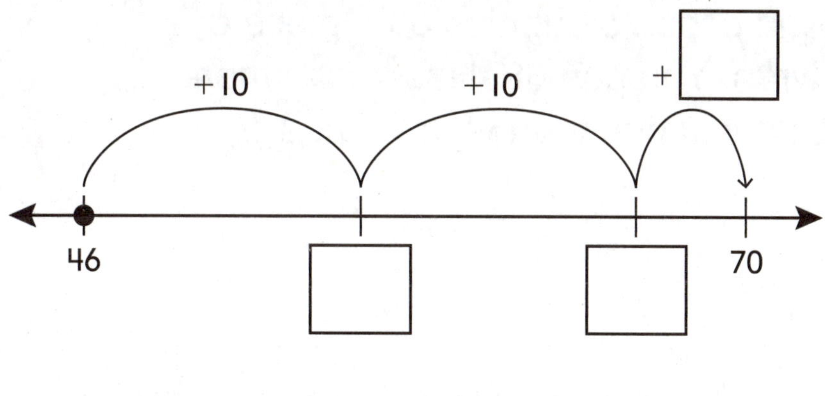

______ + ______ = ______

8. There are 31 tadpoles. Then 19 more join them. How many tadpoles are there now?

______ tadpoles

Think and Grow: Modeling Real Life

Your class plants 21 trees. Your friend's class plants 39. How many more trees does your friend's class plant than your class?

Model:

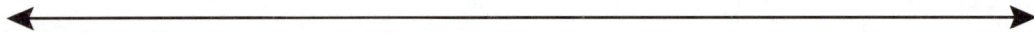

_____ trees

Show and Grow *I can think deeper!*

9. Your friend pops 76 bubbles on a piece of bubble wrap. You pop 88. How many more bubbles do you pop than your friend?

_____ bubbles

10. **DIG DEEPER!** You have 45 bouncy balls. You find some more. Now you have 91. How many bouncy balls did you find?

_____ bouncy balls

Name ______________________

Learning Target: Use an open number line to add tens and ones.

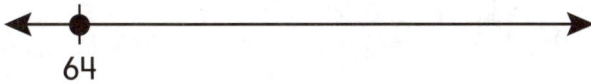

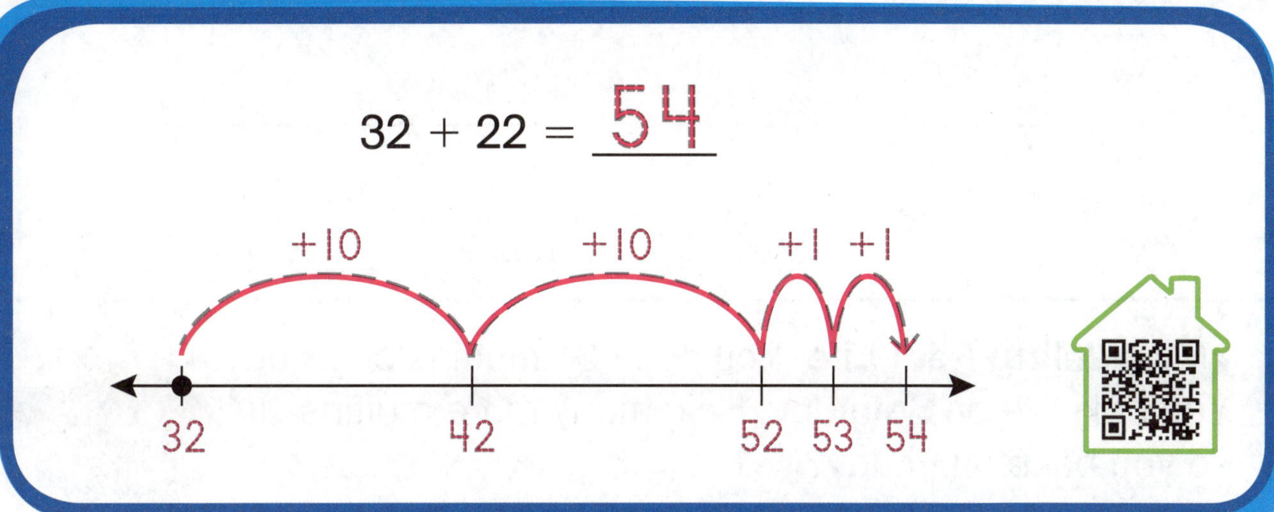

1. 64 + 31 = ______

64

2. 29 + 56 = ______

29

3. 18 + 62 = ______

4. 72 + 11 = ______

5. 53 + 27 = ______

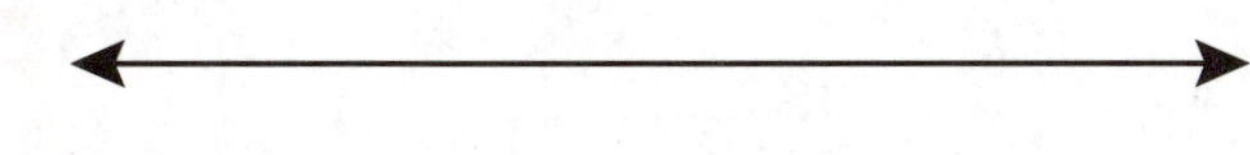

6. 46 + 32 = ______

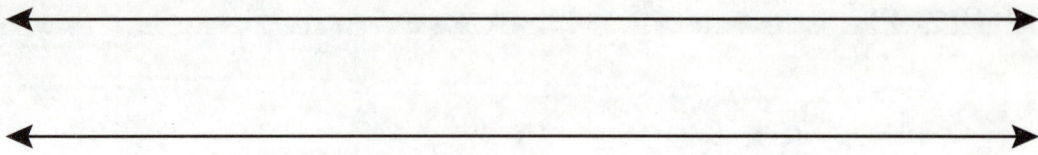

7. 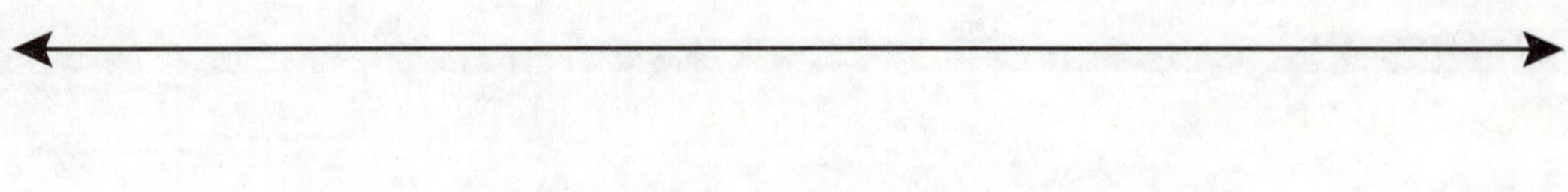 **Structure** Show 27 + 43 two ways.

27 + 43 = ______

8. **Modeling Real Life** You bake 36 muffins on Friday. You bake 24 on Saturday. How many more muffins do you bake on Friday?

______ muffins

9.  Newton has 61 bugs. Then he finds some more. Now he has 78. How many bugs did Newton find?

______ bugs

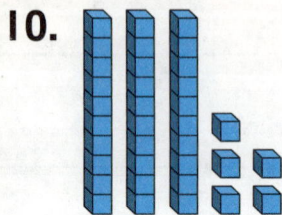

Review & Refresh

10. 

______ tens and ______ ones is ______.

11. 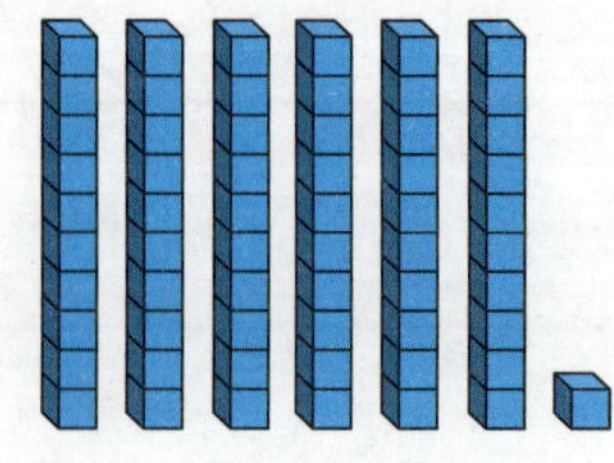

______ tens and ______ ones is ______.

Name ____________________

Use Place Value to Add 3.3

Learning Target: Use place value to add two numbers.

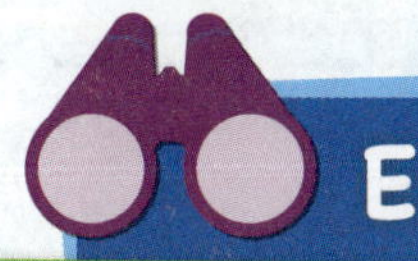

Explore and Grow

How can you use a model to solve?

$$\begin{array}{r} 37 \\ +\ 15 \\ \hline \end{array}$$

Tens	Ones

Think and Grow

Use place value to break apart the addends into tens and ones. Add the tens. Add the ones. Find the whole sum.

46 → 40 + 6

+ 25 → 20 + 5

60 + 11 = 71

Show and Grow *I can do it!*

Use place value to break apart the addends. Then find the sum.

1. 13 → ____ + ____

+ 82 → ____ + ____

____ + ____

= ____

2. 51 → ____ + ____

+ 36 → ____ + ____

____ + ____

= ____

3. 49 → ____ + ____

+ 15 → ____ + ____

____ + ____

= ____

4. 28 → ____ + ____

+ 64 → ____ + ____

____ + ____

= ____

Name ____________________

Apply and Grow: Practice

Use place value to break apart the addends. Then find the sum.

5. 67 → ____ + ____
+21 → ____ + ____
____ + ____
= ____

6. 45 → ____ + ____
+54 → ____ + ____
____ + ____
= ____

7. 72 → ____ + ____
+17 → ____ + ____
____ + ____
= ____

8. 31 → ____ + ____
+15 → ____ + ____
____ + ____
= ____

9. 57 → ____ + ____
+23 → ____ + ____
____ + ____
= ____

10. 26 → ____ + ____
+37 → ____ + ____
____ + ____
= ____

11. MP **Number Sense** Solve. Think: Does the same number make both equations true?

16 + ____ = 27   ____ + 27 = 48

Think and Grow: Modeling Real Life

You use 72 blocks to make a building. Your friend uses 14 more than you. How many blocks does your friend use?

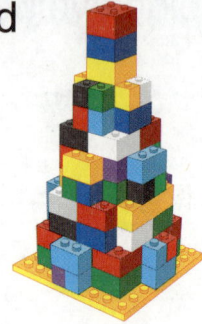

Addition equation:

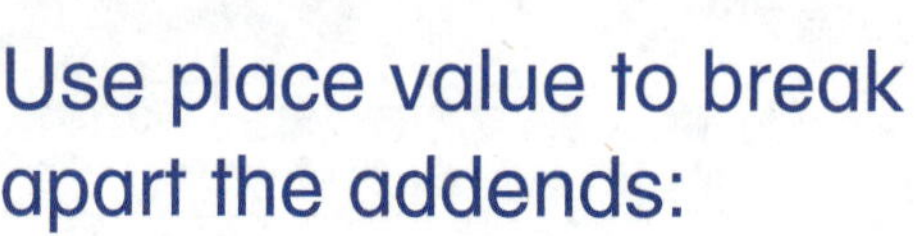

Use place value to break apart the addends: _____ + _____

_____ + _____

Find the sum: _____ + _____ = _____

_____ blocks

Show and Grow *I can think deeper!*

12. Your friend has 57 beads. You have 21 more than your friend. How many beads do you have?

_____ beads

13. You have 68 grapes. 38 are red. The rest are green. How many grapes are green?

_____ green grapes

Name ______________________________

3.3

Learning Target: Use place value to add two numbers.

Use place value to break apart the addends into tens and ones. Add the tens. Add the ones. Find the whole sum.

42 → 40 + 2

+ 31 → 30 + 1

70 + 3 = 73

Use place value to break apart the addends. Then find the sum.

1. 82 → ____ + ____

+ 10 → ____ + ____

____ + ____

= ____

2. 57 → ____ + ____

+ 31 → ____ + ____

____ + ____

= ____

3. 39 → ____ + ____

+ 61 → ____ + ____

____ + ____

= ____

4. 64 → ____ + ____

+ 27 → ____ + ____

____ + ____

= ____

5. **DIG DEEPER!** You buy two packs of pens. You buy 49 pens in all. Which color pens do you buy?

Pen Color	Pens in a Pack
Blue	25
Black	12
Red	24
Green	36

_____ and _____

6. **Modeling Real Life** Newton picks 41 flowers. Descartes picks 28 more than Newton. How many flowers does Descartes pick?

_____ flowers

7. **Modeling Real Life** You have 57 marbles. 36 are yellow. The rest are blue. How many blue marbles do you have?

_____ blue marbles

Review & Refresh

8.

3 rows of _____

_____ + _____ + _____ = _____

9.

2 rows of _____

_____ + _____ = _____

Name ______________________

Decompose to Add Tens and Ones

3.4

Learning Target: Break apart a number to add.

Explore and Grow

Use a model to solve.

$50 + 18 =$ ____

Communicate Clearly Which addend did you break apart to add? Explain.

____

____

____

Think and Grow

Break apart
25 into tens
and ones.

Add the tens to the
first addend. Then
add the ones.

34 + 25 = ?

34 + 20 + 5

54 + 5 = 59

So, 34 + 25 = 59.

Show and Grow *I can do it!*

Use place value to break apart an addend. Then find the sum.

1. 61 + 12 = ?

____ + ____ + ____

____ + ____ = ____

So, 61 + 12 = ____.

2. 74 + 24 = ?

____ + ____ + ____

____ + ____ = ____

So, 74 + 24 = ____.

3. 23 + 44 = ?

____ + ____ + ____

____ + ____ = ____

So, 23 + 44 = ____.

4. 31 + 53 = ?

____ + ____ + ____

____ + ____ = ____

So, 31 + 53 = ____.

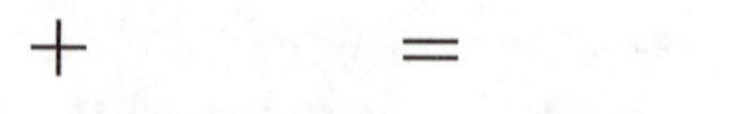

Name ______________________________

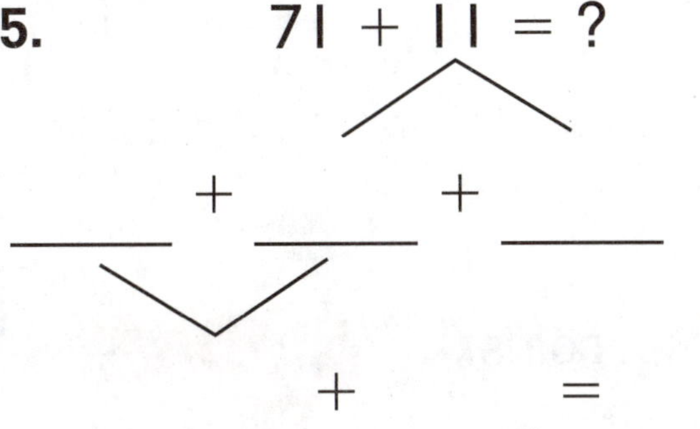

Apply and Grow: Practice

Use place value to break apart an addend. Then find the sum.

5. 71 + 11 = ?

_____ + _____ + _____

_____ + _____ = _____

So, 71 + 11 = _____.

6. 65 + 23 = ?

_____ + _____ + _____

_____ + _____ = _____

So, 65 + 23 = _____.

7. 32 + 47 = ?

_____ + _____ + _____

_____ + _____ = _____

So, 32 + 47 = _____.

8. 25 + 43 = ?

_____ + _____ + _____

_____ + _____ = _____

So, 25 + 43 = _____.

9. 54 + 36 = _____

10. 21 + 61 = _____

11. **Maintain Accuracy** Which expressions have a sum of 72?

52 + 22   41 + 31   11 + 61

51 + 11   47 + 30

Think and Grow: Modeling Real Life

You have 32 coins in a piggy bank. You put in 45 more. How many coins are in the bank now?

Addition equation:

_____ coins

Use Math Tools
How can you use real coins to help solve?

Show and Grow I can think deeper!

12. There are 81 fans at a game. 18 more arrive. How many fans are at the game now?

_____ fans

13. You have 54 songs on a music player. Your friend has 31 more than you. How many songs does your friend have?

_____ songs

Name ___________________________

Practice 3.4

Learning Target: Break apart a number to add.

26 + 42 = ?

26 + 40 + 2

66 + 2 = 68

So, 26 + 42 = 68.

Use place value to break apart an addend. Then find the sum.

1. 53 + 34 = ?

____ + ____ + ____

____ + ____ = ____

So, 53 + 34 = ____.

2. 46 + 13 = ?

____ + ____ + ____

____ + ____ = ____

So, 46 + 13 = ____.

3. 14 + 73 = ?

____ + ____ + ____

____ + ____ = ____

So, 14 + 73 = ____.

4. 31 + 67 = ?

____ + ____ + ____

____ + ____ = ____

So, 31 + 67 = ____.

5. $28 + 61 =$ ______

6. $51 + 41 =$ ______

7. DIG DEEPER! Use the numbers to complete the equation.

4

3

1☐ + ☐5 = ☐6

8. **Modeling Real Life** You see 38 ladybugs. Then you see 21 more. How many ladybugs do you see?

______ ladybugs

9. **Modeling Real Life** You read for 18 minutes and play outside for 35 minutes. How many minutes do you read and play in all?

______ minutes

Review & Refresh

10. Draw a line through the shorter object.

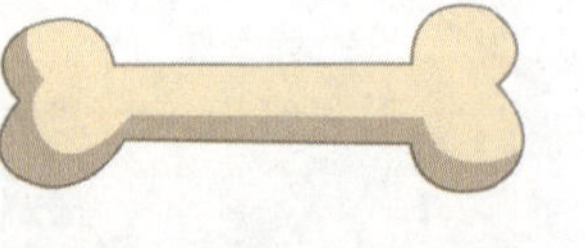

Name ____________________

Learning Target: Use compensation to add.

Use Compensation to Add 3.5

Match the numbers that make a ten.

43	2
75	4
28	7
19	1
56	5

Repeated Reasoning How can making a ten help you add greater numbers?

____

____

____

Think and Grow

23 + 48 = ?

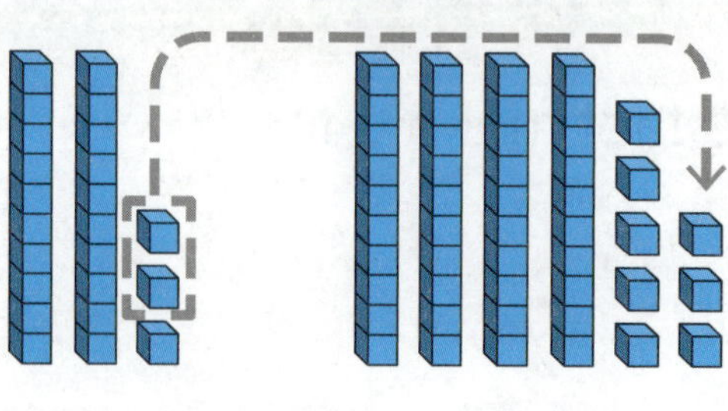

Take ones from one addend to make the other addend a decade number.

23 + 48 = ?

⊖ 2 ⊕ 2

21 + 50 = 71

Show and Grow *I can do it!*

Use compensation to add.

1. 5 + 59 = ?

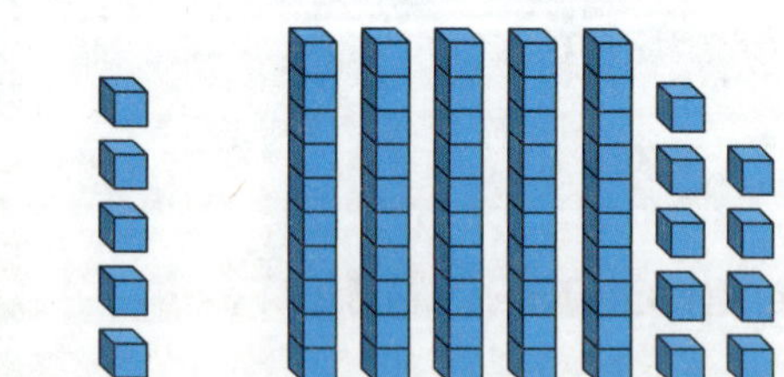

5 + 59 = ?

○ ____ ○ ____

____ + ____ = ____

2. 37 + 16 = ?

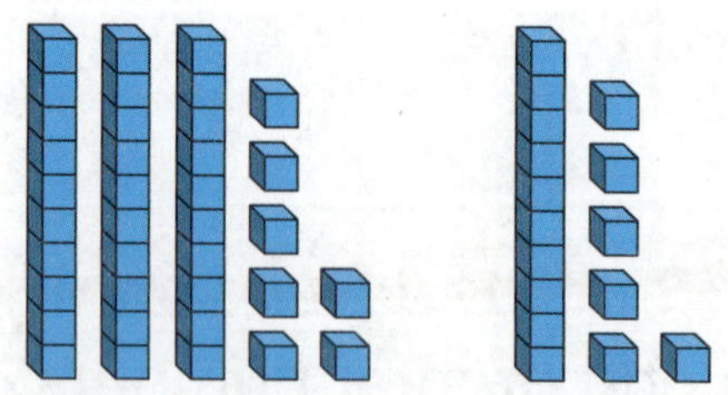

37 + 16 = ?

○ ____ ○ ____

____ + ____ = ____

Name ______________________________

Apply and Grow: Practice

Use compensation to add.

3. 52 + 19 = ?

52 + 19 = ?

○ ____ ○ ____

____ + ____ = ____

4. 43 + 8 = ?

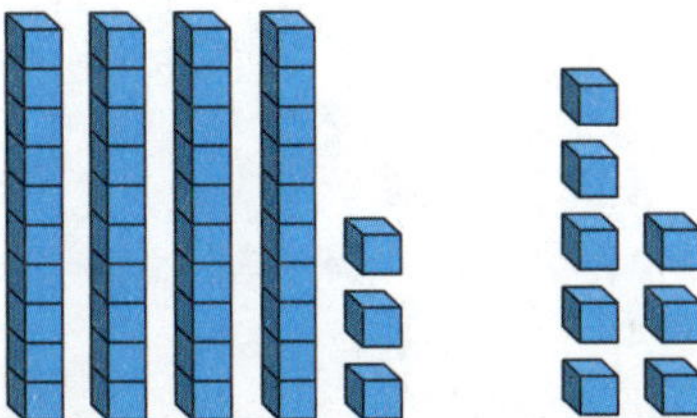

43 + 8 = ?

○ ____ ○ ____

____ + ____ = ____

5. 26 + 35 = ?

○ ____ ○ ____

____ + ____ = ____

6. 68 + 15 = ?

○ ____ ○ ____

____ + ____ = ____

7. MP **Structure** Show two different ways to use compensation to find 25 + 17.

25 + 17 = ?

○ ____ ○ ____

____ + ____ = ____

25 + 17 = ?

○ ____ ○ ____

____ + ____ = ____

Think and Grow: Modeling Real Life

You need 100 tickets for a prize. You have 79 and win 17 more. Do you have enough tickets for a prize?

Addition equation:

Compare: _____ ◯ 100

Yes No

Show and Grow *I can think deeper!*

8. You need to set up 80 chairs. You set up 32. Your friend sets up 49. Do you and your friend set up enough chairs?

Yes No

9. **DIG DEEPER!** You need 50 containers of slime for a party. You have 28. You buy 17 more. How many more containers do you need?

_____ containers

Name ______________________________

Learning Target: Use compensation to add.

55 + 16 = ?

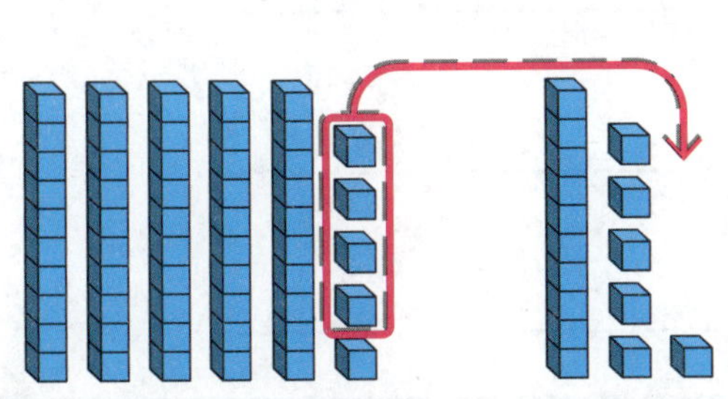

55 + 16 = ?

⊖ 4 ⊕ 4

51 + 20 = 71

Use compensation to add.

1. 46 + 31 = ?

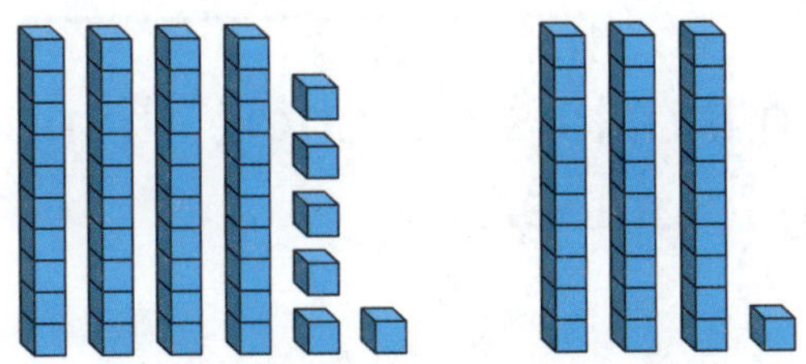

46 + 31 = ?

○ ____ ○ ____

____ + ____ = ____

2. 27 + 15 = ?

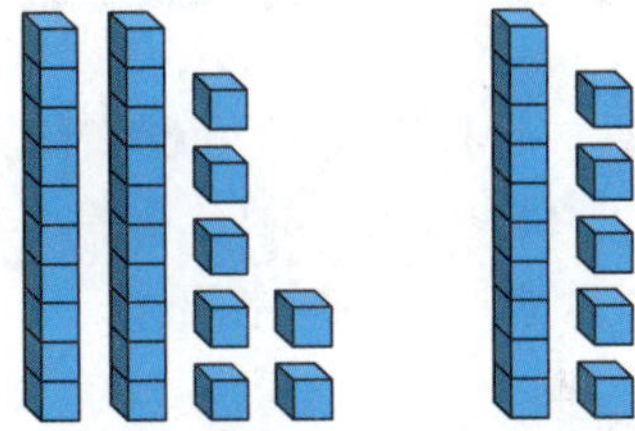

27 + 15 = ?

○ ____ ○ ____

____ + ____ = ____

3. 66 + 34 = ?

○ ____ ○ ____

____ + ____ = ____

4. 56 + 29 = ?

○ ____ ○ ____

____ + ____ = ____

5. **Writing** Explain why you make one addend a decade number when using compensation to add.

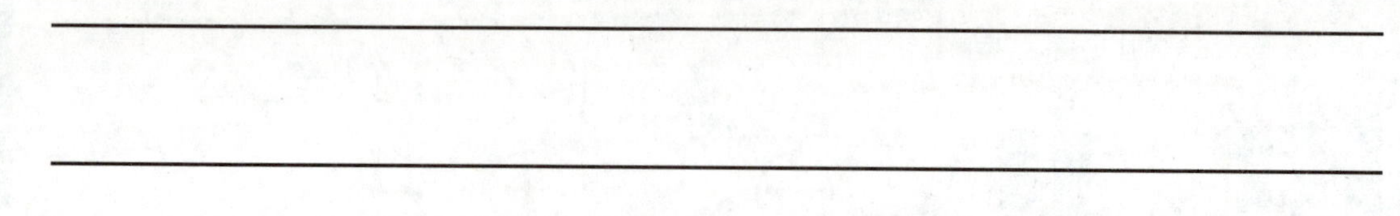

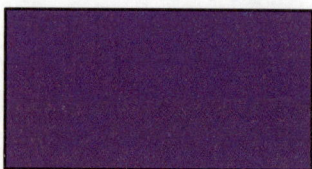

6. **Modeling Real Life** You want to read 50 pages. You read 18 on Monday and 27 on Tuesday. Do you reach your goal?

Yes No

7. **DIG DEEPER!** Write an addition equation that has the same sum as 26 + 67. Both addends are two-digit numbers.

____ + ____ = ____

Review & Refresh

Draw one line to show the parts.

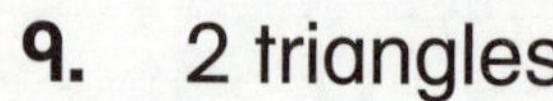

8. 2 squares

9. 2 triangles

Name ______________________________

Learning Target: Choose a strategy to add two numbers.

Explore and Grow

Use any strategy to find the sum.

35 + 41 = ____

MP Compare Arguments Compare your strategy to your partner's strategy. Which strategy makes the most sense to use with these numbers?

____

____

____

Think and Grow

42 + 29 = ?

One Way:

42 → 40 + 2

+ 29 → 20 + 9

60 + 11 = 71

Another Way:

42 + 29 = ?

42 + 20 + 9

62 + 9 = 71

Show and Grow *I can do it!*

1. 50 + 35 = ______

2. 64 + 32 = ______

3. 19 + 26 = ______

4. 78 + 13 = ______

Name ________________________________

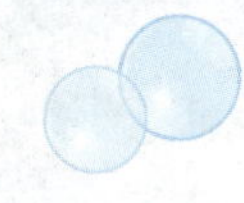

Apply and Grow: Practice

5. $32 + 41 =$ _____

6. $56 + 18 =$ _____

7. $47 + 36 =$ _____

8. $91 + 9 =$ _____

9. _____ $= 67 + 22$

10. _____ $= 51 + 39$

11. MP YOU BE THE TEACHER Your friend breaks apart an addend to solve $24 + 56$. Is your friend correct? Explain.

$24 + 56 = ?$

$24 + 50 + 6$

$74 + 6 = 80$

So, $24 + 56 = 80$.

____

____

____

____

Think and Grow: Modeling Real Life

You collect 23 cans for a food drive. Your friend collects 35 more than you. How many cans does your friend collect?

Addition equation:

_____ cans

Show and Grow *I can think deeper!*

12. You jump rope 67 times today. Tomorrow you want to jump rope 15 more times than you did today. How many times should you jump rope tomorrow?

_____ times

13. Your friend uses 19 fewer nails than you to build a birdhouse. Your friend uses 13 nails. How many nails do you use?

_____ nails

14. The book club has 27 fewer students than the art club. The book club has 24 students. How many students are in the art club?

_____ students

Name ______________________________

Practice 3.6

Learning Target: Choose a strategy to add two numbers.

$37 + 15 = ?$

One Way:

37 → 30 + 7

\+ 15 → 10 + 5

40 + 12 = 52

Another Way:

37 + 15 = ?

⊕ 3 ⊖ 3

40 + 12 = 52

1. $20 + 40 =$ ______

2. $60 + 26 =$ ______

3. $19 + 61 =$ ______

4. $43 + 28 =$ ______

5. ______ $= 45 + 46$

6. ______ $= 33 + 59$

7. **YOU BE THE TEACHER** Your friend uses compensation to solve 28 + 33. Is your friend correct? Explain.

$$\begin{array}{rcrl} 28 & + & 33 & = ? \\ \oplus\ 2 & & \oplus\ 2 & \\ \hline 30 & + & 35 & = 65 \end{array}$$

____

____

____

8. **Modeling Real Life** You have 15 blue crayons and 26 red crayons. How many crayons do you have in all?

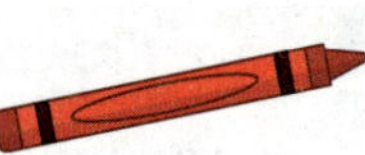

______ crayons

9. **DIG DEEPER!** A city has 27 fewer wooden park benches than metal park benches. There are 24 wooden benches. How many metal benches are there?

______ metal benches

Review & Refresh

10.

Instruments	
Drum	卌
Guitar	卌 IIII
Bell	卌

Is the number of guitars greater than or less than the number of drums?

greater than   less than

Name ____________________

Problem Solving: Addition 3.7

Learning Target: Solve two-step addition problems.

Explore and Grow

Model the story.

Newton has 15 books. Descartes has 22 more.
How many books does Descartes have?

______ books

How many books do Newton and Descartes have in all?

Make a Plan
Which two numbers do you need to add?

______ books

Think and Grow

You have 8 acorns and find 9 more. Your friend has 32 acorns. How many acorns do you and your friend have in all?

Circle what you know. Underline what you need to find.

Solve:

Step 1: Find how many acorns you have.

8 + 9 = 17

Use a double to find the sum. 8 + 9 is equal to 8 + 8 and 1 more.

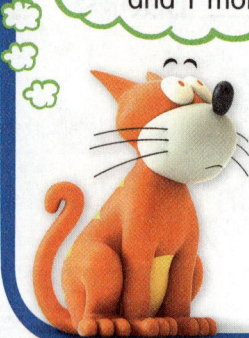

Step 2: Find the sum of your acorns and your friend's acorns.

17 + 32 = ?

17 + 30 + 2

47 + 2 = 49

49 acorns

Show and Grow *I can do it!*

1. You have 7 cherries. You pick 6 more. Your friend has 45 cherries. How many cherries do you and your friend have in all?

_____ cherries

Name ______

Apply and Grow: Practice

2. You have 15 blueberries. You pick 12 more. Your friend picks 32 blueberries. How many blueberries do you and your friend pick in all?

______ blueberries

3. You have 26 green crayons. You find 10 more. You have 16 red crayons. How many crayons do you have in all?

______ crayons

4. DIG DEEPER! You take 24 pictures on Friday. You take 20 more on Saturday. You and your friend take 50 pictures in all. How many pictures does your friend take?

______ pictures

Think and Grow: Modeling Real Life

There are 31 children at a craft fair. There are 20 more adults than children at the craft fair. How many people are at the craft fair in all?

Circle what you know.

Underline what you need to find.

Solve:

______ people

Show and Grow *I can think deeper!*

5. Your friend has 40 pens. You have 16 more than your friend. How many pens do you and your friend have in all?

______ pens

6. You plant 28 seeds. Your friend plants 13 more than you. How many seeds do you and your friend plant in all?

______ seeds

Name ____________________

Practice 3.7

Learning Target: Solve two-step addition problems.

You have 5 stamps and collect 12 more. Your friend has 21 stamps. How many stamps do you and your friend have in all?

Circle what you know. Underline what you need to find.

Solve:

Step 1: Find how many stamps you have.

5 + 12 = 17

Step 2: Find the sum of your stamps and your friend's stamps.

17 + 21 = ?

⊕ 1 ⊖ 1

18 + 20 = 38

38 stamps

1. You see 14 zebras and 4 elephants at the zoo. Then you see 20 snakes. How many animals do you see in all?

_____ animals

2. You win 14 tokens at one game and 15 at another. You and your friend have 40 tokens in all. How many tokens does your friend have?

______ tokens

3. Your class sells 40 raffle tickets. Your friend's class sells 15 more than your class. How many raffle tickets do your class and your friend's class sell in all?

______ raffle tickets

4. **MP Modeling Real Life** Your friend picks 33 apples. You pick 11 more than your friend. How many apples do you and your friend pick in all?

______ apples

5. **DIG DEEPER!** Your read 10 haiku poems and 5 rhyming poems. Your friend reads 28 more poems than you. How many poems do you and your friend read in all?

______ poems

Review & Refresh

6. $7 + 7 + 3 =$ ______

7. $6 + 8 + 5 =$ ______

Name ___________________________________

Performance Task 3

I. You go to an amusement park. The wait times and ride times for the rides are shown below.

a. Find the total number of minutes it takes to wait and ride each ride.

Ride	Wait Time (minutes)	Ride Time (minutes)	Total Time (minutes)
Ferris wheel	28	14	
Log ride	58	10	
Train	34	20	
Bumper cars	39	5	

b. How many more minutes do you spend at the log ride than at the bumper cars?

______ minutes

c. You want to ride 2 different rides in less than 90 minutes. Which rides can you ride?

________________ and ________________

2. At 12:30, you spend 25 minutes eating lunch and 30 minutes playing games. How many more minutes are there until the show starts?

______ more minutes

Three in a Row: Addition

To Play: Players take turns. On your turn, spin both spinners. Add the two numbers and cover the sum. Continue playing until a player gets three in a row.

Name ____________________

Chapter 3 Practice

3.1 Add Tens Using a Number Line

1. 30 + 40 = ____

2. 26 + 50 = ____

3.2 Add Tens and Ones Using a Number Line

3. 46 + 33 = ____

4. **MP Modeling Real Life** You find 57 bugs. Your friend finds 12 more than you. How many bugs does your friend find?

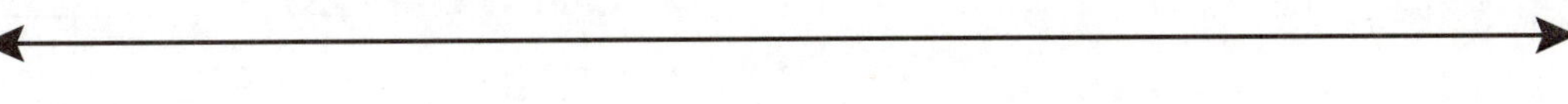

____ bugs

3.3 Use Place Value to Add

Use place value to break apart the addends. Then find the sum.

5. 36 → ____ + ____
+51 → ____ + ____
____ + ____
= ____

6. 62 → ____ + ____
+24 → ____ + ____
____ + ____
= ____

7. 80 → ____ + ____
+16 → ____ + ____
____ + ____
= ____

8. 47 → ____ + ____
+34 → ____ + ____
____ + ____
= ____

3.4 Decompose to Add Tens and Ones

Use place value to break apart an addend. Then find the sum.

9. 37 + 42 = ?

____ + ____ + ____

____ + ____ = ____

So, 37 + 42 = ____.

10. 51 + 26 = ?

____ + ____ + ____

____ + ____ = ____

So, 51 + 26 = ____.

11. MP **Maintain Accuracy** Which expressions have a sum of 95?

43 + 52   31 + 64   71 + 12

25 + 30   73 + 22

3.5 Use Compensation to Add

Use compensation to add.

12. 66 + 25 = ____

○ ____   ○ ____

____ + ____ = ____

13. 53 + 39 = ____

○ ____   ○ ____

____ + ____ = ____

14. MP **Modeling Real Life** You and your friend want to find 90 seashells. You find 45. Your friend finds 51. Do you and your friend reach your goal?

Yes   No

3.6 Practice Addition Strategies

15. 47 + 36 = ____

16. 50 + 19 = ____

17. 32 + 55 = ______

18. 54 + 26 = ______

3.7 Problem Solving: Addition

19. Newton has 23 rocks. He finds 7 more. Descartes has 51 rocks. How many rocks do Newton and Descartes have in all?

______ rocks

20. Your friend has 22 bracelets. You have 16 more. How many bracelets do you and your friend have in all?

______ bracelets

Fluently Add within 100

- Do you like to swim?
- It takes you 34 seconds to swim from one end of a pool to the other. It takes you 38 seconds to swim back. How many seconds do you swim in all?

Chapter Learning Target:
Understand addition.

Chapter Success Criteria:
- I can identify addition patterns.
- I can explain which strategy I used to write a sum.
- I can write a sum.
- I can solve addition problems.

Name ______________________________

Vocabulary

Review Words
array
column
row

Organize It

Use the review words to complete the graphic organizer.

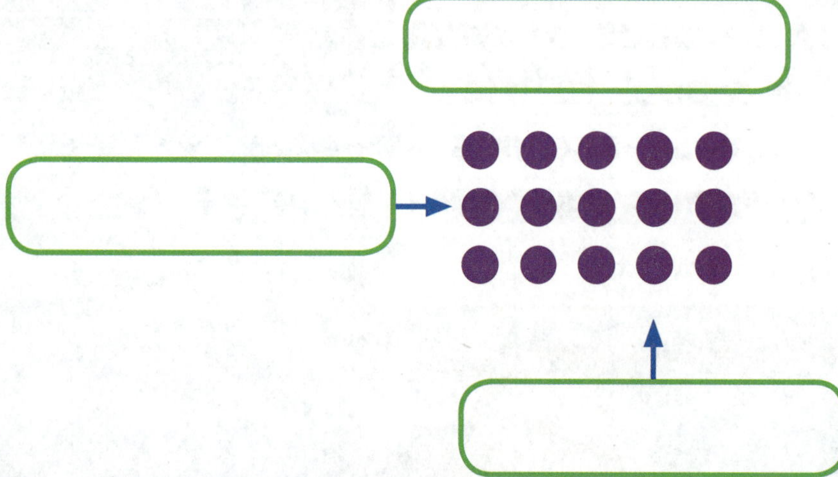

Define It

Use your vocabulary cards to match.

1. partial sums

	Tens	Ones
	1	9
+	2	4
10 + 20 =	3	0
9 + 4 =	1	3
	4	3

2. regroup

Tens	Ones

	Tens	Ones
	1	
	1	9
+	2	4
	4	3

Chapter 4 Vocabulary Cards

partial sums

regroup

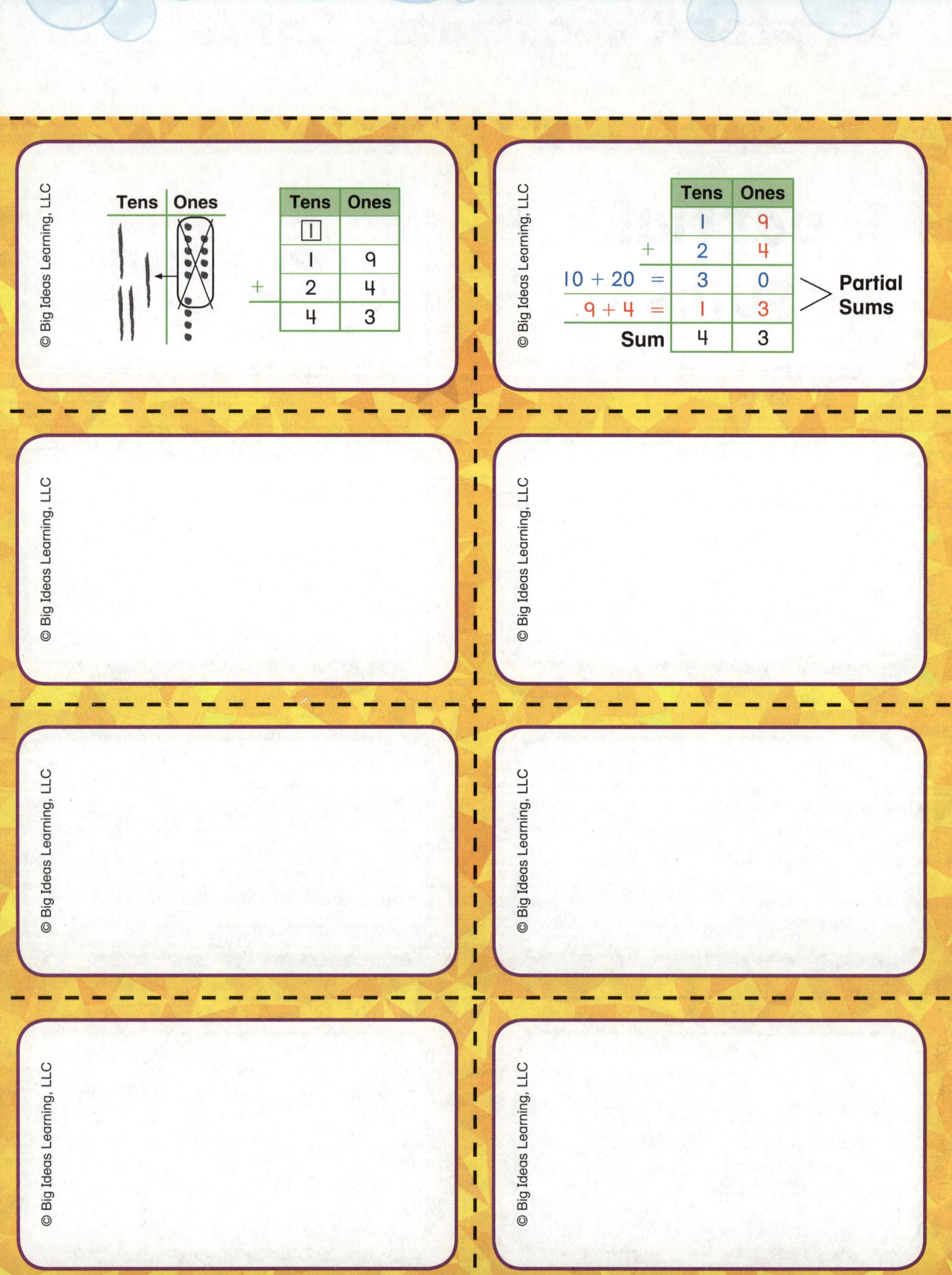

© Big Ideas Learning, LLC
Tens
Ones
1
1 9
+ 2 4
4 3
Tens
Ones
1 9
+ 2 4
10 + 20 = 3 0
9 + 4 = 1 3
Sum 4 3
Partial Sums

Name ______________________________

Learning Target: Use partial sums to add.

Model the problem. Make a quick sketch to show how you solved.

$32 + 27 =$ ______

Think and Grow

$51 + 36 = ?$

	Tens	Ones
	5	1
+	3	6
50 + 30 =	8	0
1 + 6 =		7
Sum	8	7

partial sums

Add the tens; add the ones. Then add the partial sums to find the whole sum: 80 + 7 = 87.

Show and Grow *I can do it!*

1. $73 + 12 = ?$

	Tens	Ones
	7	3
+	1	2
____ + ____ =		
____ + ____ =		
Sum		

2. $32 + 24 = ?$

	Tens	Ones
	3	2
+	2	4
____ + ____ =		
____ + ____ =		
Sum		

3. $37 + 42 = ?$

	Tens	Ones
	3	7
+	4	2
____ + ____ =		
____ + ____ =		
Sum		

4. $63 + 5 = ?$

	Tens	Ones
	6	3
+		5
____ + ____ =		
____ + ____ =		
Sum		

Name ____________________

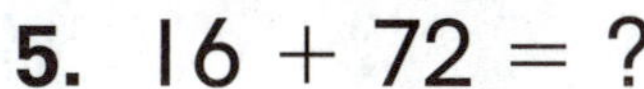

Apply and Grow: Practice

5. 16 + 72 = ?

	Tens	Ones
	1	6
+	7	2
___ + ___ =		
___ + ___ =		
Sum		

6. 33 + 43 = ?

	Tens	Ones
	3	3
+	4	3
___ + ___ =		
___ + ___ =		
Sum		

7. 91 + 7 = ?

	Tens	Ones
	9	1
+		7
___ + ___ =		
___ + ___ =		
Sum		

8. 25 + 64 = ?

	Tens	Ones
	2	5
+	6	4
___ + ___ =		
___ + ___ =		
Sum		

9. DIG DEEPER! Find the missing digits.

$$\begin{array}{r} 1\ 4 \\ +\ 3\ \square \\ \hline 4\ 6 \end{array} \qquad \begin{array}{r} 4\ 5 \\ +\ 2\ \square \\ \hline 6\ 9 \end{array} \qquad \begin{array}{r} 6\ 1 \\ +\ \square\ 6 \\ \hline 8\ 7 \end{array}$$

Think and Grow: Modeling Real Life

You read 34 pages one day and 23 the next day. How many pages do you read in all?

Model:

	Tens	Ones
+		
Sum		

______ pages

Show and Grow *I can think deeper!*

10. You have 57 common trading cards and 11 rare trading cards. How many trading cards do you have in all?

______ trading cards

11. A florist has 7 roses, 6 daisies, and 15 tulips. How many flowers are there in all?

______ flowers

Name ______________________________

Learning Target: Use partial sums to add.

Add the tens; add the ones. Then add the partial sums to find the whole sum: 60 + 7 = 67.

46 + 21 = ?

	Tens	Ones
	4	6
+	2	1
40 + 20 =	6	0
6 + 1 =		7
Sum	6	7

1. 55 + 14 = ?

	Tens	Ones
	5	5
+	1	4
____ + ____ =		
____ + ____ =		
Sum		

2. 62 + 13 = ?

	Tens	Ones
	6	2
+	1	3
____ + ____ =		
____ + ____ =		
Sum		

3. 71 + 8 = ?

	Tens	Ones
	7	1
+		8
____ + ____ =		
____ + ____ =		
Sum		

4. 22 + 26 = ?

	Tens	Ones
	2	2
+	2	6
____ + ____ =		
____ + ____ =		
Sum		

5. **DIG DEEPER!** Find the missing digits. Then find the sum.

	Tens	Ones
	____	4
+	1	____
20 + 10 =	3	0
4 + 5 =	____	9
Sum		

6. **Modeling Real Life** You have 45 balloons. Your friend has 31. How many balloons do you and your friend have in all?

_____ balloons

7. **Modeling Real Life** You have 8 toy trains, 4 bouncy balls, and 36 toy soldiers. How many toys do you have in all?

_____ toys

Review & Refresh

8. 16 + 10 = _____

9. 45 − 10 = _____

10. 50 − 10 = _____

11. 63 + 10 = _____

Name ______________________________

More Partial Sums 4.2

Learning Target: Use partial sums to add.

Make a quick sketch to find 38 + 19.

	Tens	Ones
+		
___ + ___ =		
___ + ___ =		
Sum		

38 + 19 = ____

Repeated Reasoning How can you write each number as tens plus ones? How does that help you solve?

Think and Grow

$38 + 27 = ?$

	Tens	Ones
	3	8
+	2	7
Tens:	5	0
Ones:	1	5
Sum	6	5

Add the partial sums to find the whole sum.

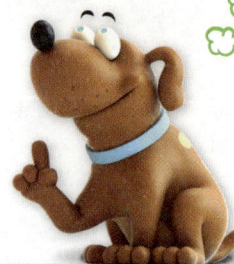

Show and Grow *I can do it!*

1. $25 + 19 = ?$

	Tens	Ones
	2	5
+	1	9
Tens:		
Ones:		
Sum		

2. $48 + 33 = ?$

	Tens	Ones
	4	8
+	3	3
Tens:		
Ones:		
Sum		

3. $57 + 35 = ?$

	Tens	Ones
	5	7
+	3	5
Tens:		
Ones:		
Sum		

Name ______________________________

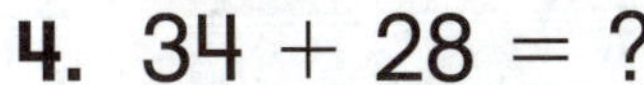

Apply and Grow: Practice

4. 34 + 28 = ?

	Tens	Ones
	3	4
+	2	8
Tens:		
Ones:		
Sum		

5. 15 + 76 = ?

	Tens	Ones
	1	5
+	7	6
Tens:		
Ones:		
Sum		

6. 29 + 62 = ?

	Tens	Ones
	2	9
+	6	2
Tens:		
Ones:		
Sum		

7. MP **Number Sense** Which choices are equal to 35 + 27?

30 + 20 + 5 + 7   80 + 9   62

30 + 50 + 2 + 7   50 + 12   89

8. A giraffe eats 37 pounds of food in the morning and 38 pounds of food in the afternoon. How many pounds of food does the giraffe eat in all?

	Tens	Ones
+		
Tens:		
Ones:		
Sum		

_____ pounds of food

Think and Grow: Modeling Real Life

You find 29 items on a scavenger hunt. Your friend finds 17 more than you. How many items does your friend find?

Model:

	Tens	Ones
+		
Tens:		
Ones:		
Sum		

_____ items

Show and Grow *I can think deeper!*

9. Your friend climbs 48 stairs. You climb 36 more than your friend. How many stairs do you climb?

_____ stairs

10. You write 13 fewer words than your friend. You write 39 words. How many words does your friend write?

_____ words

Name ______________________________

Practice 4.2

Learning Target: Use partial sums to add.

43 + 39 = ?

	Tens	Ones
	4	3
+	3	9
Tens:	7	0
Ones:	1	2
Sum	8	2

Add the partial sums to find the whole sum.

1. 27 + 46 = ?

	Tens	Ones
	2	7
+	4	6
Tens:		
Ones:		
Sum		

2. 54 + 28 = ?

	Tens	Ones
	5	4
+	2	8
Tens:		
Ones:		
Sum		

3. 18 + 72 = ?

	Tens	Ones
+		
Tens:		
Ones:		
Sum		

4. **DIG DEEPER!** Write the missing digits.

	Tens	Ones
	3	___
+	___	8
Tens:	6	0
Ones:	___	5
Sum	7	5

	Tens	Ones
	___	9
+	5	___
Tens:	___	0
Ones:	1	6
Sum	9	6

5. You recycle 42 cans and 29 jars. How many items do you recycle in all?

_____ items

6. **Modeling Real Life** Newton plants 63 seeds. Descartes plants 18 more than Newton. How many seeds does Descartes plant?

_____ seeds

Review & Refresh

7.

Favorite Instrument								
Drum	☺	☺	☺	☺	☺	☺		
Triangle	☺	☺	☺	☺				

Each ☺ = 1 student.

Which instrument is the most favorite?  

Name ___________________________

Learning Target: Use regrouping to add.

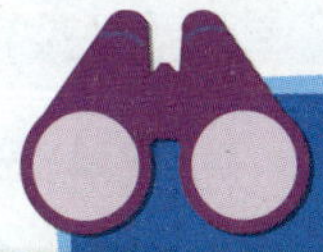

Explore and Grow

Model the problem. Make a quick sketch to show how you solved.

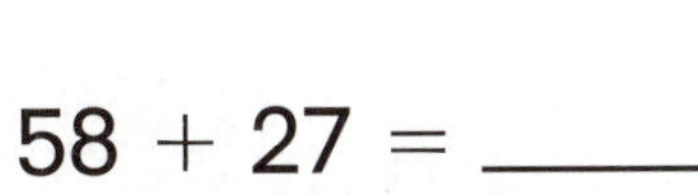

58 + 27 = _____

Think and Grow

$29 + 34 = ?$

Model the numbers.

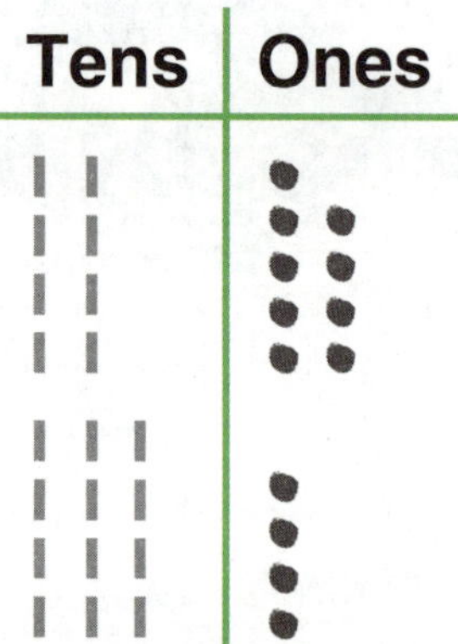

	Tens	Ones
	☐	
	2	9
+	3	4

Add the ones. **Regroup**.

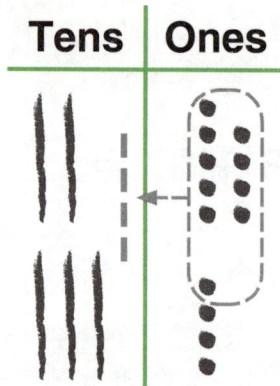

	Tens	Ones
	1	
	2	9
+	3	4
		3

Add the tens.

	Tens	Ones
	1	
	2	9
+	3	4
	6	3

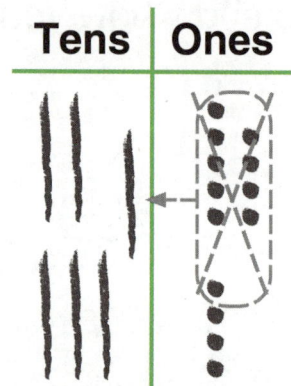

Show and Grow *I can do it!*

1. $46 + 26 = ?$

Tens	Ones

	Tens	Ones
	☐	
	4	6
+	2	6

Name ______________________________

Apply and Grow: Practice

2. $15 + 37 = ?$

Tens	Ones

	Tens	Ones
	☐	
	1	5
+	3	7

3. $39 + 32 = ?$

Tens	Ones

	Tens	Ones
	☐	
	3	9
+	3	2

4. DIG DEEPER! When do you need to regroup to add two numbers?

____

____

____

____

Think and Grow: Modeling Real Life

You must spell 60 words correctly to win a spelling game. You spell 19 words correctly in Round 1 and 36 in Round 2. Do you win?

Model:

Tens	Ones

Addition problem:

	Tens	Ones
	☐	
+		

Communicate Clearly
Explain how you found the sum.

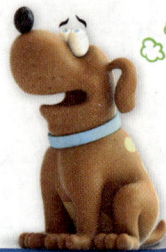

Yes No

Show and Grow *I can think deeper!*

5. You want to do 80 jumping jacks. You do 45 in the morning and 39 in the evening. Do you reach your goal?

Yes No

6. You raise $38 selling ham sandwiches and $43 selling turkey sandwiches. Your friend raises $72. Who raises more money?

You Friend

Name ______________________

Learning Target: Use regrouping to add.

Add the ones. Regroup 11 ones as 1 ten and 1 one. Then add the tens.

55 + 26 = ?

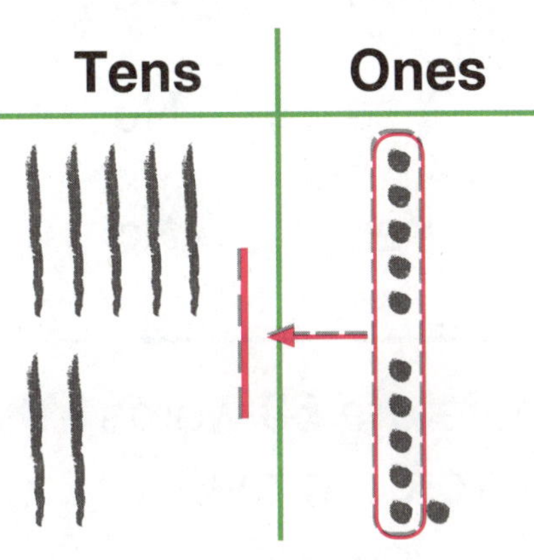

	Tens	Ones
	1	
	5	5
+	2	6
	8	1

1. 36 + 16 = ?

Tens	Ones

	Tens	Ones
	□	
	3	6
+	1	6

2. 47 + 39 = ?

Tens	Ones

	Tens	Ones
	□	
	4	7
+	3	9

3. DIG DEEPER! Do you have to regroup to add?

43 + 29 = ? Yes No

54 + 32 = ? Yes No

33 + 64 = ? Yes No

17 + 25 = ? Yes No

4. MP **Modeling Real Life** There are 50 words in a word search. You find 25 words in rows and 18 words in columns. Did you find all of the words?

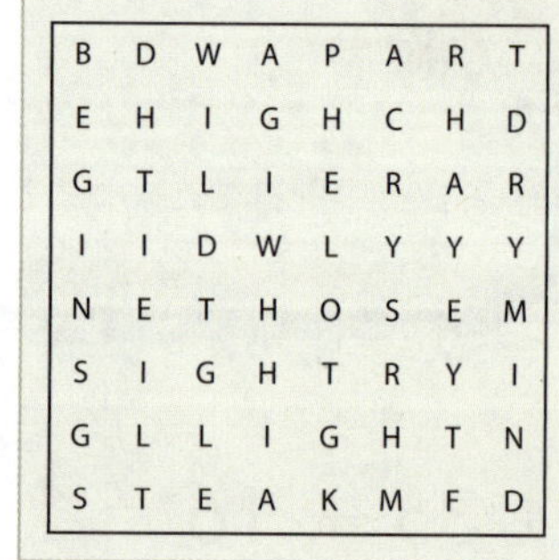

B	D	W	A	P	A	R	T
E	H	I	G	H	C	H	D
G	T	L	I	E	R	A	R
I	I	D	W	L	Y	Y	Y
N	E	T	H	O	S	E	M
S	I	G	H	T	R	Y	I
G	L	L	I	G	H	T	N
S	T	E	A	K	M	F	D

Yes No

5. MP **Modeling Real Life** You find 15 white shells and 17 spotted shells. Your friend finds 34 shells. Who finds more shells?

You Friend

Review & Refresh

Compare.

6. 34 ◯ 80

7. 15 ◯ 8

8. 67 ◯ 67

Name ______________________

Learning Target: Use regrouping when needed to add.

Make a quick sketch to find 38 + 24.

	Tens	Ones
	□	
	3	8
+	2	4

38 + 24 = ______

MP Structure
What step did you use to find 38 + 24 that you would not use to find 31 + 24? Why?

Think and Grow

Add the ones.
5 ones aren't enough to regroup.
Regroup 14 ones as 1 ten and 4 ones.
Then add the tens.

58 + 16 = ?

	Tens	Ones
	1	
	5	8
+	1	6
	7	4

44 + 21 = ?

	Tens	Ones
	4	4
+	2	1
	6	5

Show and Grow *I can do it!*

1. 69 + 22 = ?

	Tens	Ones
+		

2. 25 + 37 = ?

	Tens	Ones
+		

3. 31 + 26 = ?

	Tens	Ones
+		

4. 15 + 38 = ?

5. 62 + 13 = ?

6. 46 + 49 = ?

Name ______________________________

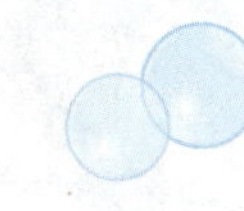

Apply and Grow: Practice

7. 33 + 39 = ?

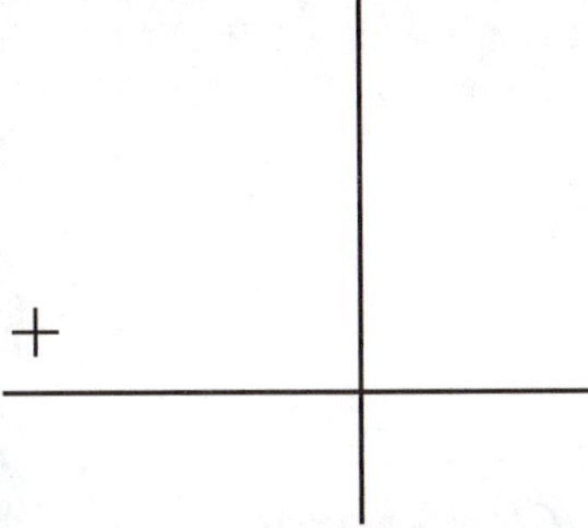

8. 23 + 71 = ?

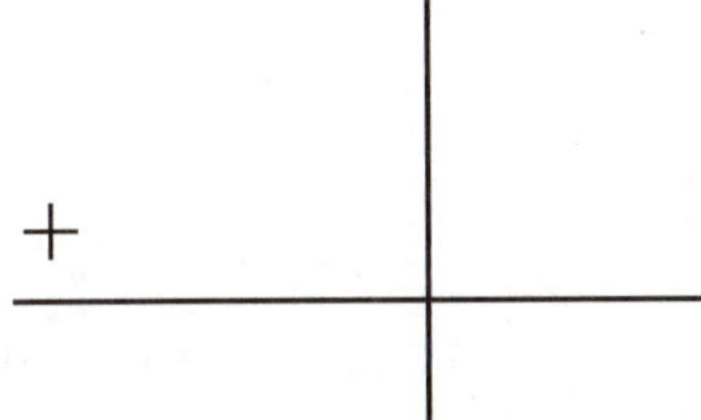

9. 17 + 64 = ?

10. 54 + 25 = ?

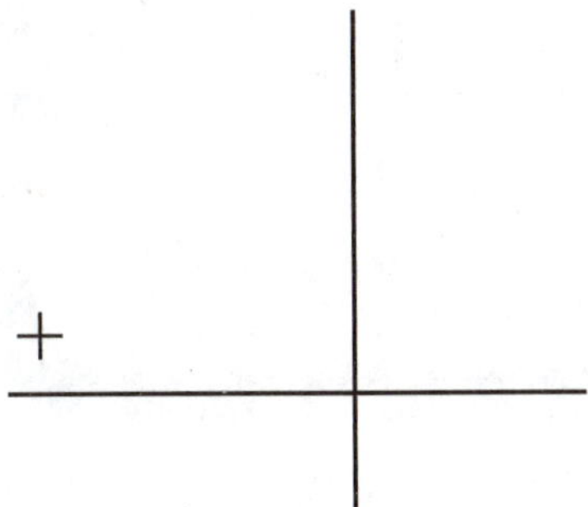

11. 47 + 39 = ?

12. 28 + 26 = ?

13. MP **YOU BE THE TEACHER** Newton finds 26 + 36. Is he correct? Explain.

____

____

____

Think and Grow: Modeling Real Life

You have 24 gel pens and you buy 36 more. Your friend has 48 and buys 18 more. Who has more gel pens?

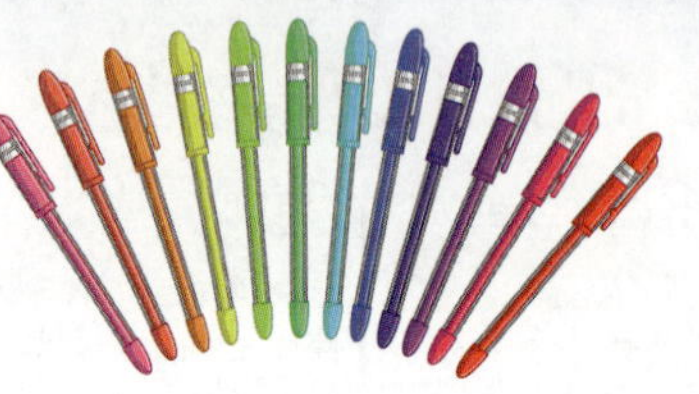

You:

	Tens	Ones
+		

Friend:

	Tens	Ones
+		

Compare:

___ ◯ ___

You Friend

Show and Grow *I can think deeper!*

14. You have 32 stencils and you buy 16 more. Your friend has 14 and buys 28 more. Who has more stencils?

You Friend

15. You have 22 green stars and 17 orange stars. Your friend has 26 blue stars and 12 pink stars. How many stars do you and your friend have in all?

______ stars

Name ___________________________

Learning Target: Use regrouping when needed to add.

Add the ones. Regroup 15 ones as 1 ten and 5 ones. Then add the tens.

$76 + 19 = ?$

	Tens	Ones
	1	
	7	6
+	1	9
	9	5

1. $47 + 36 = ?$

	Tens	Ones
	☐	
+		

2. $51 + 28 = ?$

	Tens	Ones
	☐	
+		

3. $13 + 79 = ?$

	Tens	Ones
	☐	
+		

4. $54 + 42 = ?$

5. $38 + 23 = ?$

6. $45 + 44 = ?$

7. **Writing** Find the sum. Write an addition story to match.

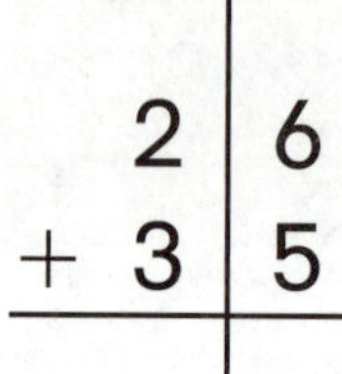

$$\begin{array}{r|l} 2 & 6 \\ + \ 3 & 5 \\ \hline & \end{array}$$

____

____

____

8. **Modeling Real Life** You have 35 dimes and you find 17 more. Your friend has 42 and finds 11 more. Who has more dimes?

You Friend

9. **Modeling Real Life** Newton plants 14 red flowers and 14 purple flowers. Descartes plants 26 pink flowers and 26 yellow flowers. How many flowers do Newton and Descartes plant in all?

_____ flowers

Review & Refresh

10. Model 56 two ways.

Tens	Ones

_____ tens and _____ ones is 56.

Tens	Ones

_____ tens and _____ ones is 56.

Name ______________________________

Practice Adding Two-Digit Numbers

4.5

Learning Target: Add two-digit numbers.

Use any strategy to find 17 + 23.

Choose Math Tools
What tools can you use
to check your answer?

Compare your strategy to your partner's strategy.
Are they the same or different? Explain.

____

____

Think and Grow

$27 + 35 = ?$

One Way: Use partial sums.

$$\begin{array}{r} 27 \\ +\ 35 \\ \hline 50 \\ 12 \\ \hline 62 \end{array}$$

Another Way: Regroup.

$$\begin{array}{r} 1 \\ 27 \\ +\ 35 \\ \hline 62 \end{array}$$

Show and Grow *I can do it!*

1. $\begin{array}{r} 43 \\ +\ 17 \\ \hline \end{array}$

2. $\begin{array}{r} 56 \\ +\ 25 \\ \hline \end{array}$

3. $\begin{array}{r} 19 \\ +\ 55 \\ \hline \end{array}$

4. $\begin{array}{r} 41 \\ +\ 52 \\ \hline \end{array}$

5. $\begin{array}{r} 47 \\ +\ 26 \\ \hline \end{array}$

6. $\begin{array}{r} 33 \\ +\ 49 \\ \hline \end{array}$

7. $\begin{array}{r} 29 \\ +\ 22 \\ \hline \end{array}$

8. $\begin{array}{r} 54 \\ +\ 44 \\ \hline \end{array}$

9. $\begin{array}{r} 36 \\ +\ 45 \\ \hline \end{array}$

Name ___________

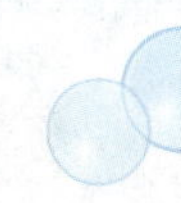

Apply and Grow: Practice

10.

$$\begin{array}{r} 24 \\ +\ 16 \\ \hline \end{array}$$

11.

$$\begin{array}{r} 37 \\ +\ 46 \\ \hline \end{array}$$

12.

$$\begin{array}{r} 18 \\ +\ 59 \\ \hline \end{array}$$

13.

$$\begin{array}{r} 61 \\ +\ 34 \\ \hline \end{array}$$

14.

$$\begin{array}{r} 23 \\ +\ 28 \\ \hline \end{array}$$

15.

$$\begin{array}{r} 42 \\ +\ 57 \\ \hline \end{array}$$

16. 73 + 17 = ?

+ ______

17. 82 + 12 = ?

+ ______

18. 15 + 77 = ?

+ ______

19. MP **YOU BE THE TEACHER** Descartes finds 38 + 53. Is he correct? Explain.

____

____

____

Think and Grow: Modeling Real Life

Are there more state parks in North Carolina and Kentucky or in Kentucky and South Carolina?

State Parks	
State	**Number of State Parks**
North Carolina	29
Kentucky	38
South Carolina	43

Addition equations:

Compare: ______ ◯ ______

There are more state parks in __________ and __________.

Show and Grow *I can think deeper!*

20. Are there more students in first and second grade or in first and third grade?

Students at School	
Grade	**Number of Students**
First	37
Second	53
Third	49

There are more students in __________ and __________ grade.

Name ______________________

Learning Target: Add two-digit numbers.

$46 + 37 = ?$

One Way: Use partial sums.

$$\begin{array}{r} 46 \\ +\ 37 \\ \hline 70 \\ 13 \\ \hline 83 \end{array}$$

Another Way: Regroup.

$$\begin{array}{r} {\scriptstyle 1} \\ 46 \\ +\ 37 \\ \hline 83 \end{array}$$

1. $\begin{array}{r} 63 \\ +\ 12 \\ \hline \end{array}$

2. $\begin{array}{r} 32 \\ +\ 58 \\ \hline \end{array}$

3. $\begin{array}{r} 53 \\ +\ 38 \\ \hline \end{array}$

4. $\begin{array}{r} 13 \\ +\ 39 \\ \hline \end{array}$

5. $\begin{array}{r} 62 \\ +\ 18 \\ \hline \end{array}$

6. $\begin{array}{r} 48 \\ +\ 16 \\ \hline \end{array}$

7. $11 + 66 = ?$

$+$ ______

8. $64 + 21 = ?$

$+$ ______

9. $79 + 14 = ?$

$+$ ______

10. **DIG DEEPER!** Find the missing digits.

$$\begin{array}{r} 3\ \square \\ +\ 4\ 5 \\ \hline \square\ 1 \end{array} \qquad \begin{array}{r} \square\ 5 \\ +\ 3\ \square \\ \hline 9\ 7 \end{array} \qquad \begin{array}{r} \square\ 4 \\ +\ 4\ 8 \\ \hline 7\ \square \end{array}$$

11. **MP Modeling Real Life** Do more people attend the show on Monday and Tuesday or on Tuesday and Wednesday?

People at the Show	
Day	**Number of People**
Monday	48
Tuesday	26
Wednesday	56

Monday and Tuesday   Tuesday and Wednesday

Review & Refresh

12. Order from shortest to longest.

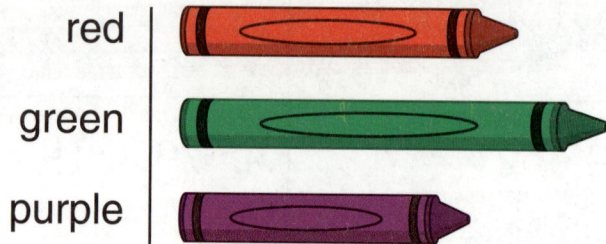

red

green

purple

______, ______, ______

Name ____________________

Add Up to 3 Two-Digit Numbers 4.6

Learning Target: Add up to 3 two-digit numbers.

Explore and Grow

Add the circled numbers first. Then find the sum of all three numbers.

(34) + (26) + 24 = ______

□

34 + (26) + (24) = ______

□

(34) + 26 + (24) = ______

□

What is the same? What is different?

____

____

____

Think and Grow

$37 + 14 + 23 = ?$

Remember, you can add in any order.

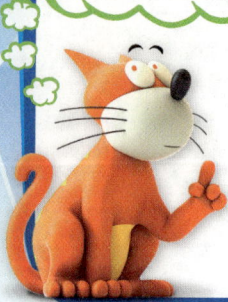

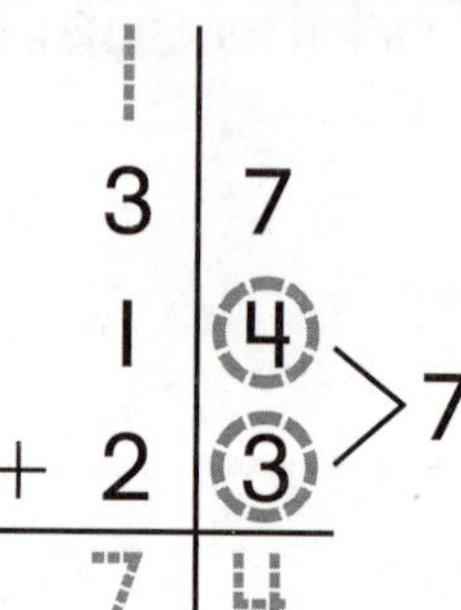

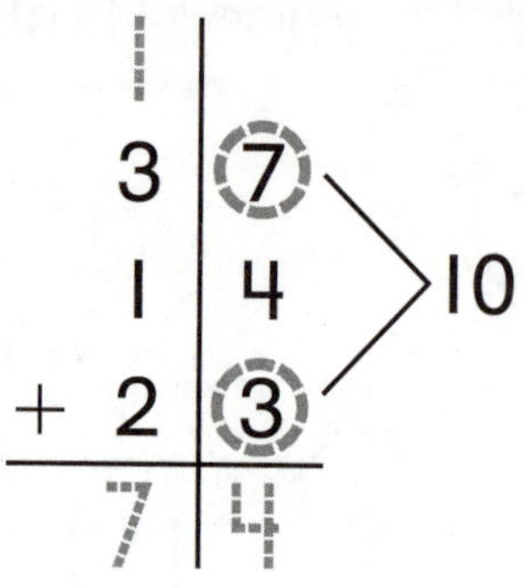

If you can, make a 10 to help you add.

Show and Grow *I can do it!*

1.
```
  16
  34
+ 21
```

2.
```
  33
  15
+ 17
```

3.
```
  31
  12
+ 24
```

4.
```
  25
  15
+ 13
```

5.
```
  29
  22
+ 23
```

6.
```
  19
  32
+ 11
```

7.
```
  18
  28
+ 42
```

8.
```
  53
  13
+ 19
```

9.
```
  27
  27
+ 25
```

Name ________________________________

Apply and Grow: Practice

10.

$$\begin{array}{r} 23 \\ 42 \\ +\ 17 \\ \hline \end{array}$$

11.

$$\begin{array}{r} 18 \\ 34 \\ +\ 26 \\ \hline \end{array}$$

12.

$$\begin{array}{r} 51 \\ 22 \\ +\ 26 \\ \hline \end{array}$$

13.

$$\begin{array}{r} 30 \\ 45 \\ +\ 19 \\ \hline \end{array}$$

14.

$$\begin{array}{r} 24 \\ 21 \\ +\ 28 \\ \hline \end{array}$$

15.

$$\begin{array}{r} 39 \\ 12 \\ +\ 31 \\ \hline \end{array}$$

16.

$$\begin{array}{r} 14 \\ 20 \\ +\ 35 \\ \hline \end{array}$$

17.

$$\begin{array}{r} 46 \\ 11 \\ +\ 32 \\ \hline \end{array}$$

18.

$$\begin{array}{r} 35 \\ 33 \\ +\ 29 \\ \hline \end{array}$$

19. MP **Reasoning** You make a 10 to add 16, 38, and 24. Which digits do you add first? Explain.

____

____

____

Think and Grow: Modeling Real Life

Newton buys the items shown. How much money does he spend?

Addition problem:

+ ______ $ ______

Show and Grow *I can think deeper!*

20. Descartes buys the items shown. How much money does he spend?

$ ______

21. Newton sells 2 large candles and 1 small candle. How much money does he earn?

$ ______

Name ______________________________

Practice 4.6

Learning Target: Add up to 3 two-digit numbers.

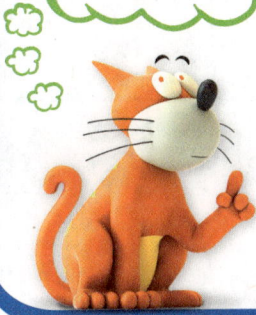

Remember, you can add in any order.

One Way:

```
  1
  2 | 6
  3 | 2 \
+ 1 | 4 / 6
  7 | 2
```

Another Way:

```
  1
  2 | 6 \
  3 | 2  > 10
+ 1 | 4 /
  7 | 2
```

1.

```
  1 | 1
  2 | 3
+ 4 | 7
```

2.

```
  3 | 2
  1 | 4
+ 2 | 8
```

3.

```
  1 | 6
  3 | 7
+ 3 | 3
```

4.

```
  4 3
  1 7
+ 3 7
```

5.

```
  1 5
  4 4
+ 1 1
```

6.

```
  1 6
  2 9
+ 3 8
```

7.

```
  3 1
  2 8
+ 1 2
```

8.

```
  5 6
  2 6
+ 1 3
```

9.

```
  3 5
  2 3
+ 3 9
```

10. **DIG DEEPER!** Solve two different ways.

$$\begin{array}{r} 38 \\ 36 \\ +\ 22 \\ \hline \end{array} \qquad \begin{array}{r} 38 \\ 36 \\ +\ 22 \\ \hline \end{array}$$

---

11. **Modeling Real Life** Descartes buys the items shown. How much money does he spend?

$ ______

---

12. **Modeling Real Life** Your cousin buys the items shown. How much money does she spend?

$ ______

Review & Refresh

Is the number even or odd?

13. 18

Even Odd

14. 17

Even Odd

Name ____________________

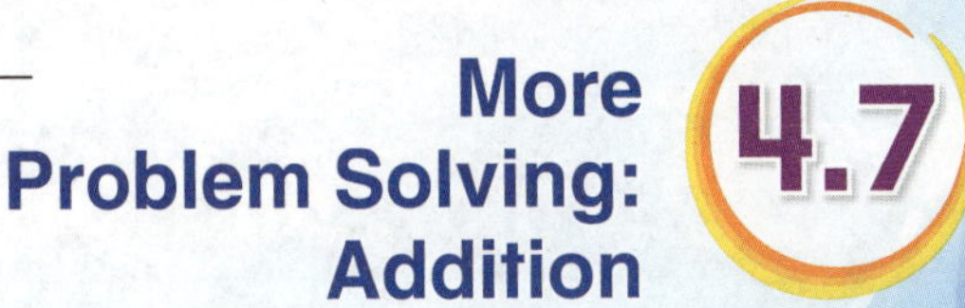

Learning Target: Solve one- and two-step addition problems.

Model the story.

There are 11 red ants and 14 black ants. 15 more black ants join them. How many ants are there now?

Analyze a Problem Are the colors of the ants important to solve the problem? Why or why not?

______ ants

Think and Grow

You find 19 objects in a scavenger hunt.

You find 13 fewer objects than your friend.

How many objects does your friend find?

Circle what you know.

Underline what you need to find.

Solve:

Use a model to help organize the information.

Friend: 32

You: 19 | 13

32 objects

Write and solve an addition problem.

$$\begin{array}{r} 19 \\ +\ 13 \\ \hline 32 \end{array}$$

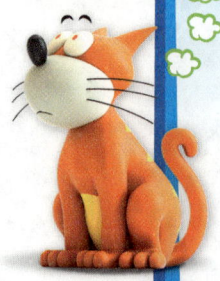

Show and Grow *I can do it!*

1. You have 66 marbles. You have 26 fewer marbles than your friend. How many marbles does your friend have?

_____ marbles

Name ______________________________

Apply and Grow: Practice

2. You collect 16 red leaves, 21 orange leaves, and 14 yellow leaves. How many leaves do you collect in all?

_____ leaves

3. A dentist has 41 toothbrushes. She buys some more. Now she has 85. How many toothbrushes did the dentist buy?

_____ toothbrushes

4. You make 17 origami dogs and 13 origami fish. Your friend makes 12 more origami animals than you. How many origami animals does your friend make?

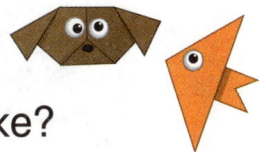

Step 1: How many origami animals do you make?

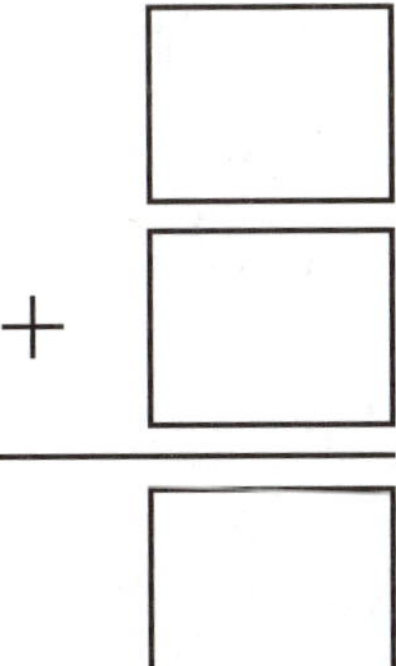

Step 2: How many origami animals does your friend make?

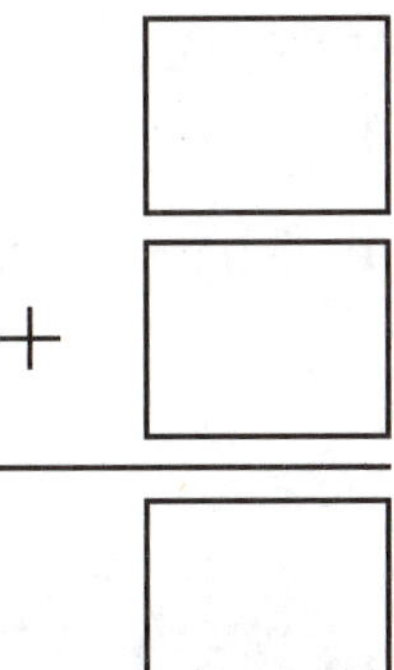

_____ origami animals

Think and Grow: Modeling Real Life

You make a paper chain. Your friend adds 24 links to your chain. Now there are 57. How many links were there to start?

_____ links

Show and Grow *I can think deeper!*

5. You have some stickers. Your friend gives you 32 more stickers. Now you have 58. How many stickers did you have to start?

_____ stickers

6. There are 3 buses. There are 29 students on each of the first 2 buses. There are 88 students in all. How many students are on the third bus?

_____ students

Name ______________________________

Practice 

Learning Target: Solve one- and two-step addition problems.

You see 22 orange butterflies and some yellow butterflies. You see 39 in all. How many yellow butterflies do you see?

Circle what you know. Underline what you need to find.

Solve:

$$\begin{array}{r} 22 \\ +\ 17 \\ \hline 39 \end{array}$$

17 yellow butterflies

1. You study for 31 minutes. You study 11 fewer minutes than your friend. How long does your friend study?

_____ minutes

2. You see 23 red cars, 25 black cars, and 15 blue cars. How many cars do you see in all?

_____ cars

3. **MP Number Sense** Your friend scores 29 points. You score 16 more points than your friend. Use the given numbers to find how many points you and your friend score in all.

16 74 29 45

Step 1:

29

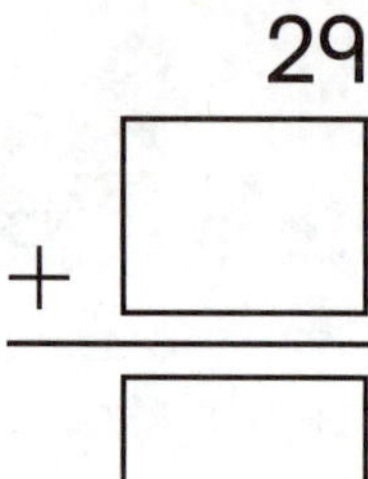

Step 2:

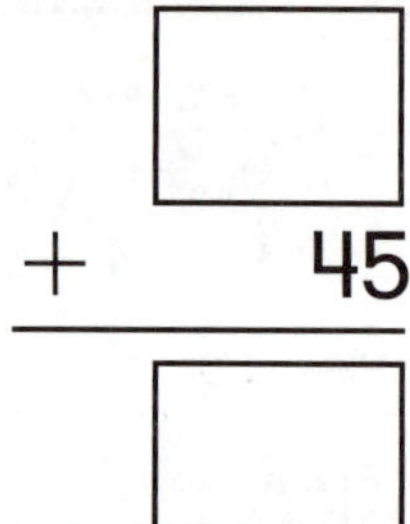

+ 45

_____ points

---

4. **DIG DEEPER!** In Exercise 3, Newton scores 4 three-point shots. How many points do you, your friend, and Newton score in all?

_____ points

---

5. **MP Modeling Real Life** There are 3 subway cars. There are 36 people on each of the first 2 subway cars. There are 92 people in all. How many people are on the third subway car?

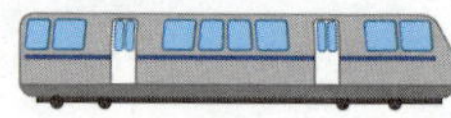

_____ people

Review & Refresh

6. 50 − 10 = _____

7. 90 − 40 = _____

Name ___________________________

Performance Task 4

1. a. You swim for 37 minutes on Monday. You swim 12 more minutes on Tuesday than on Monday. How many minutes do you swim in all?

_____ minutes

b. Do you swim an even or odd number of minutes in all?

Even Odd

2. a. There are 35 girls and some boys signed up for swim lessons this year. There are 83 kids signed up in all. Then some more boys sign up. Now there are 56 boys signed up. How many more boys signed up for swim lessons?

_____ more boys

b. Last year there were 95 kids signed up for swim lessons. 45 were girls. Are there more boys signed up for swim lessons this year or last year?

This year Last year

Solve and Cover: Addition

To Play: Place a Solve and Cover: Addition Sum Card on each box. Players take turns. On your turn, flip over a Solve and Cover: Addition Problem Card. Solve the problem. Place the problem card on the sum. Play until all sums are covered.

Name ___________________________

Chapter Practice

4.1 Use Partial Sums to Add

1. 35 + 22 = ?

	Tens	Ones
	3	5
+	2	2
___ + ___ =		
___ + ___ =		
Sum		

2. 81 + 8 = ?

	Tens	Ones
	8	1
+		8
___ + ___ =		
___ + ___ =		
Sum		

4.2 More Partial Sums

3. 26 + 43 = ?

	Tens	Ones
	2	6
+	4	3
Tens:		
Ones:		
Sum		

4. 64 + 19 = ?

	Tens	Ones
+		
Tens:		
Ones:		
Sum		

4.3 Regroup to Add

5. **Modeling Real Life** You want to complete 40 hours of volunteer work this year. You complete 28 hours during the school year and 13 during the summer. Do you reach your goal?

Model:

Tens	Ones

Addition Problem:

	Tens	Ones
	□	
+		

Yes No

4.4 Add Two-Digit Numbers

6. 14 + 77 = ?

	Tens	Ones
	□	
+		

7. 35 + 35 = ?

	Tens	Ones
	□	
+		

8. 43 + 49 = ?

	Tens	Ones
	□	
+		

4.5 Practice Adding Two-Digit Numbers

9. $\begin{array}{r} 36 \\ +\ 38 \\ \hline \end{array}$

10. $\begin{array}{r} 62 \\ +\ 29 \\ \hline \end{array}$

11. $\begin{array}{r} 25 \\ +\ 45 \\ \hline \end{array}$

12. MP **Number Sense** Find the missing digits.

$\begin{array}{r} \square\ 5 \\ +\ 3\ \square \\ \hline 4\ 9 \end{array}$

$\begin{array}{r} 4\ \square \\ +\ 2\ 8 \\ \hline \square\ 6 \end{array}$

$\begin{array}{r} \square\ 6 \\ +\ 1\ 4 \\ \hline 7\ \square \end{array}$

4.6 Add Up to 3 Two-Digit Numbers

13. $\begin{array}{r|l} 1 & 2 \\ 3 & 2 \\ +\ 1 & 8 \\ \hline & \end{array}$

14. $\begin{array}{r|l} 5 & 0 \\ 2 & 8 \\ +\ 1 & 8 \\ \hline & \end{array}$

15. $\begin{array}{r|l} 2 & 5 \\ 3 & 7 \\ +\ 2 & 5 \\ \hline & \end{array}$

16. $\begin{array}{r} 17 \\ 26 \\ +\ 12 \\ \hline \end{array}$

17. $\begin{array}{r} 27 \\ 33 \\ +\ 18 \\ \hline \end{array}$

18. $\begin{array}{r} 15 \\ 18 \\ +\ 16 \\ \hline \end{array}$

19. **Modeling Real Life** You, Newton, and Descartes play paddle ball. You record how many times each of you hits the ball in a row. How many times is the ball hit in all?

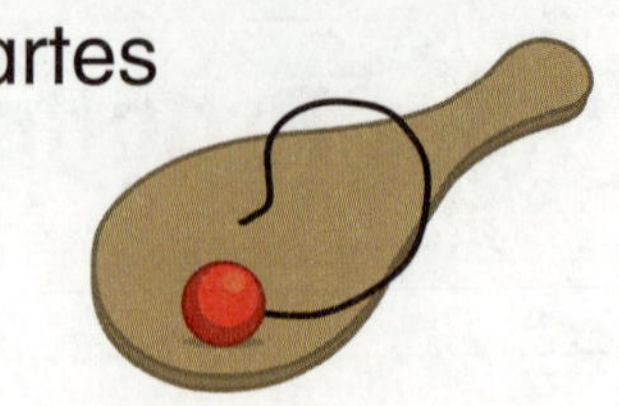

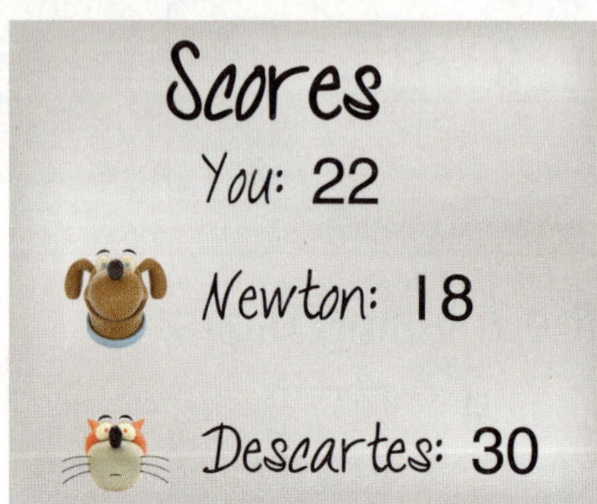

_____ times

4.7 More Problem Solving: Addition

20. **Modeling Real Life** You pick 11 berries and 23 apples. Your friend picks 18 more pieces of fruit than you. How many pieces does your friend pick?

Step 1: How many pieces of fruit do you pick?

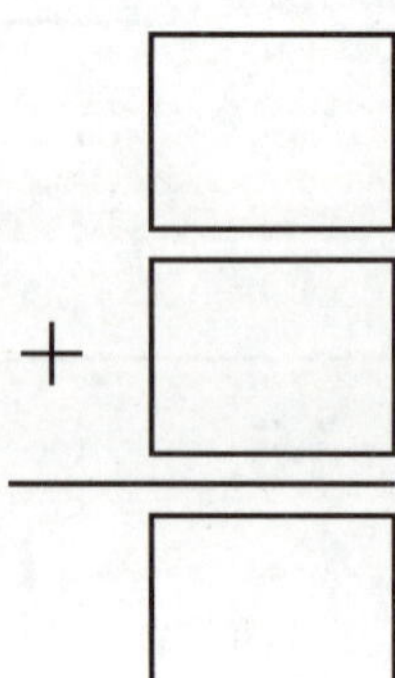

Step 2: How many pieces of fruit does your friend pick?

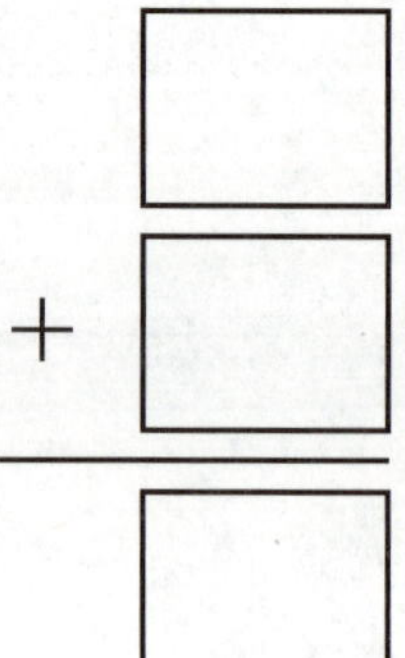

_____ pieces of fruit

Name ______________________________

1. Which equation represents the array?

- ◯ $4 + 4 = 8$
- ◯ $4 + 3 = 7$
- ◯ $3 + 3 + 3 + 3 = 12$
- ◯ $3 + 3 + 3 = 9$

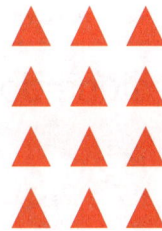

2. Which expressions are equal to $62 + 24$?

- ◯ $60 + 20 + 2 + 4$
- ◯ $50 + 16$
- ◯ $60 + 26$
- ◯ $80 + 6$

---

3. Is each sum equal to $7 + 4$?

$10 + 2$	Yes	No
$10 + 1$	Yes	No
$8 + 4$	Yes	No
$10 + 4$	Yes	No

4. Write an equation that matches the number line.

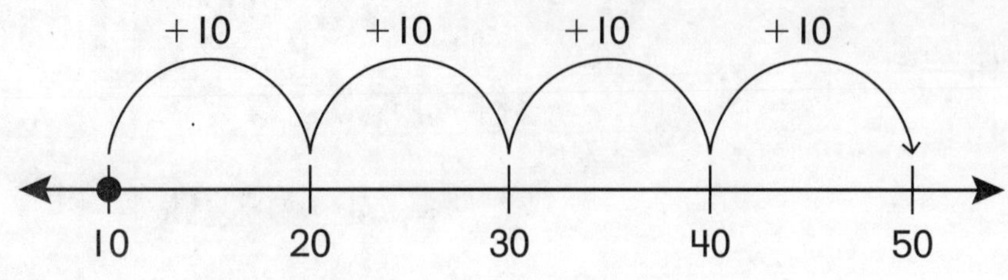

_____ + _____ = _____

---

5. Which expressions do you need to regroup to solve?

○ 30 + 29

○ 54 + 38

○ 43 + 44

○ 62 + 28

---

6. Which equation has an even sum greater than 14?

○ 6 + 6 = ?

○ 7 + 8 = ?

○ 8 + 8 = ?

○ 6 + 7 = ?

7. There are 4 rows of trees. Each row has 5 trees. How many trees are there in all?

_____ + _____ + _____ + _____ = _____

---

8. You have 16 oranges. You give 7 away. How many oranges do you have left?

_____ oranges

---

9. Find the sum.

2 4
1 2
+ 3 5

3 1
1 4
+ 4 2

10. Find the sum. Write the double you used.

7 + 8 = _____   _____ + _____ = _____

---

11. Break apart the addends to find 42 + 37.

42 + 37 = _____

---

12. You have 64 craft sticks for a project. 22 are red. The rest are yellow. You buy 39 more yellow craft sticks. How many yellow craft sticks do you have now?

_____ yellow craft sticks

5 Subtraction to 100 Strategies

- What is an incubator? How are they used?
- There are 48 eggs in an incubator. 32 eggs hatch. How many eggs did *not* hatch yet?

Chapter Learning Target:
Understand subtraction.

Chapter Success Criteria:
- I can identify subtraction patterns.
- I can explain which strategy I used to find a difference.
- I can write a difference.
- I can solve subtraction problems.

Name ______________________________

Vocabulary

Review Words

difference
halves
minus
quarters
subtraction equation
unequal shares

Organize It

Use the review words to complete the graphic organizer.

$9 - 6 = 3$

Define It

Match.

1. halves

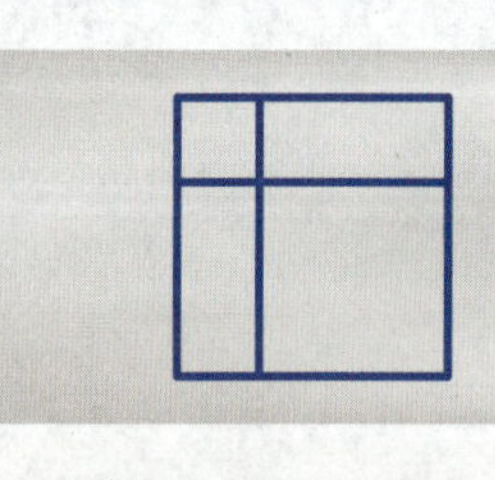

2. quarters

3. unequal shares

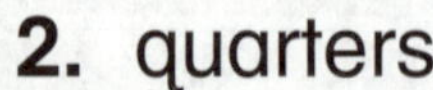

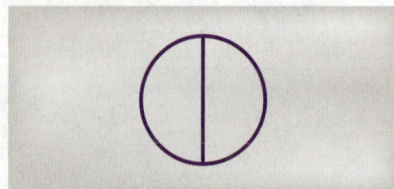

Name ______________________________

Subtract Tens Using a Number Line

5.1

Learning Target: Use an open number line to subtract tens.

Explore and Grow

Color to show how you can use the hundred chart to solve.

20 − 10 = _____

75 − 40 = _____

1	2	3	4	5	6	7	8	9	10
11	12	13	14	15	16	17	18	19	20
21	22	23	24	25	26	27	28	29	30
31	32	33	34	35	36	37	38	39	40
41	42	43	44	45	46	47	48	49	50
51	52	53	54	55	56	57	58	59	60
61	62	63	64	65	66	67	68	69	70
71	72	73	74	75	76	77	78	79	80
81	82	83	84	85	86	87	88	89	90
91	92	93	94	95	96	97	98	99	100

Think and Grow

$58 - 30 = ?$

Start at 58. 30 is the same as 3 tens. So, count back 3 tens.

One Way:

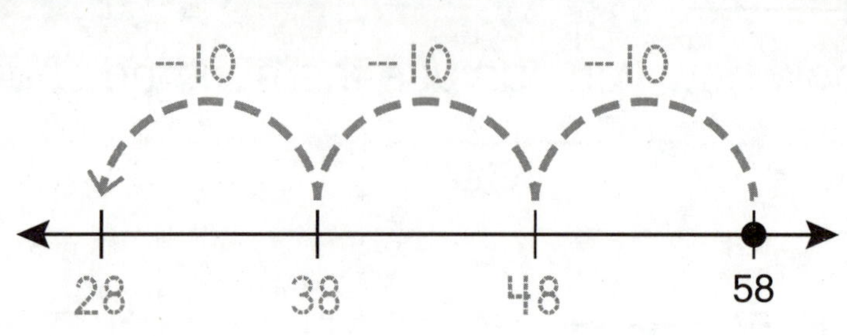

Make a larger jump. Counting back 3 tens is the same as counting back 30.

Another Way:

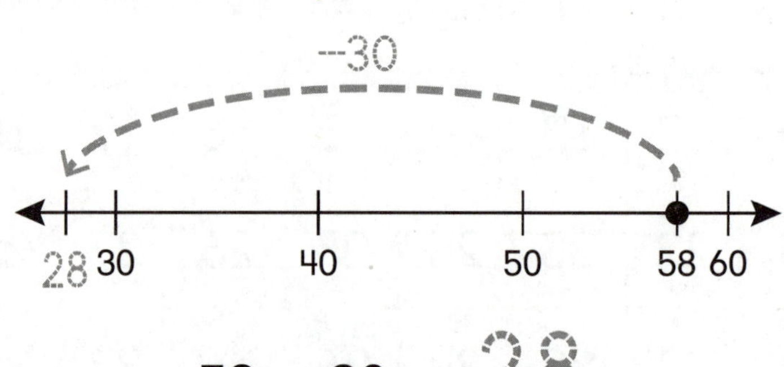

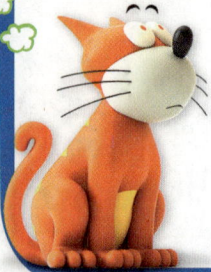

$58 - 30 = \underline{28}$

Show and Grow *I can do it!*

1. $70 - 50 =$ ______

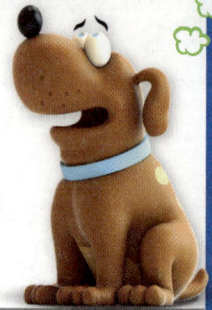

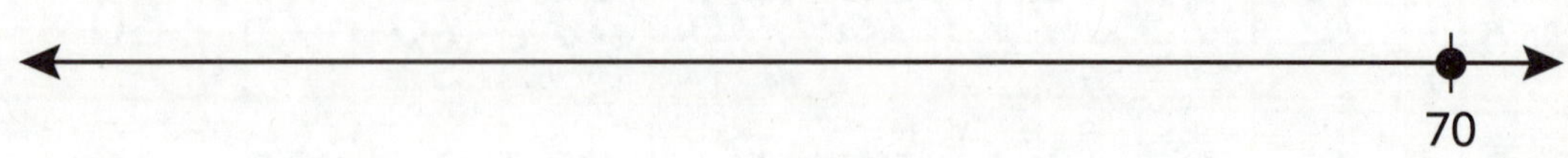

2. $33 - 20 =$ ______

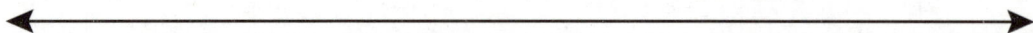

Name ______________________________

Apply and Grow: Practice

3. 60 − 40 = _____

4. 71 − 20 = _____

5. 46 − 30 = _____

6. MP **YOU BE THE TEACHER** Your friend shows 79 − 40 on a number line. Is your friend correct? Explain.

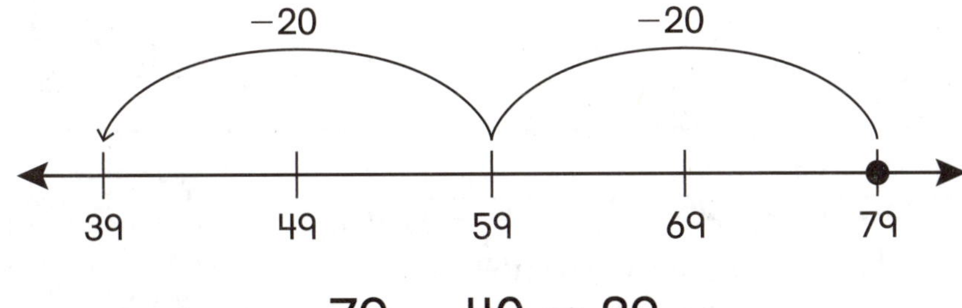

79 − 40 = 39

____

____

Think and Grow: Modeling Real Life

You have a 74-piece set of magnetic tiles. You use 60 of them to make buildings. How many pieces are left?

Subtraction equation:

Model:

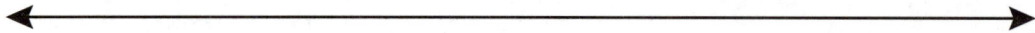

_____ pieces

Show and Grow *I can think deeper!*

7. A clown has 62 balloons. She uses 40 of them to make balloon animals. How many balloons are left?

_____ balloons

8. **DIG DEEPER!** There are 35 people at a park. 20 of them leave. Then 10 more arrive at the park. How many people are at the park now?

_____ people

Name ______________________

Learning Target: Use an open number line to subtract tens.

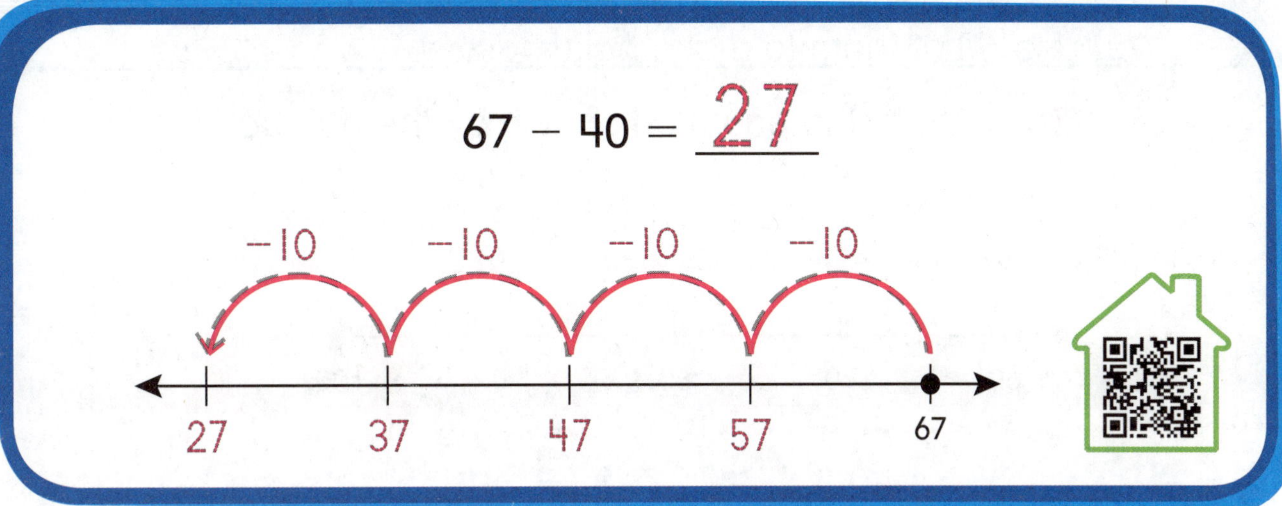

1. 90 − 50 = ______

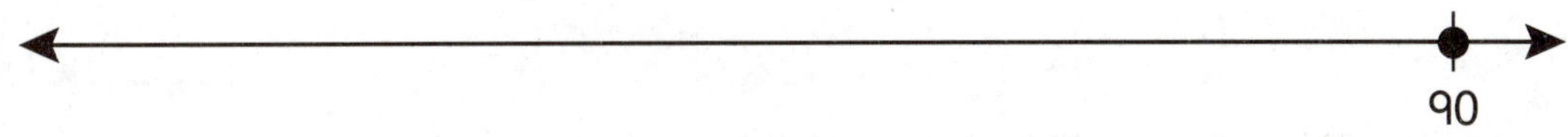

2. 84 − 60 = ______

3. 22 − 10 = ______

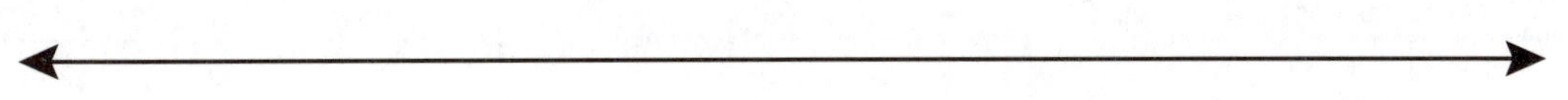

4. 54 − 50 = ______

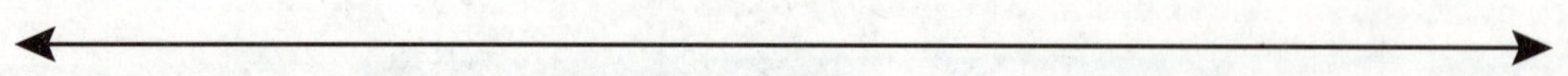

5. **Structure** Write the equation shown by the number line.

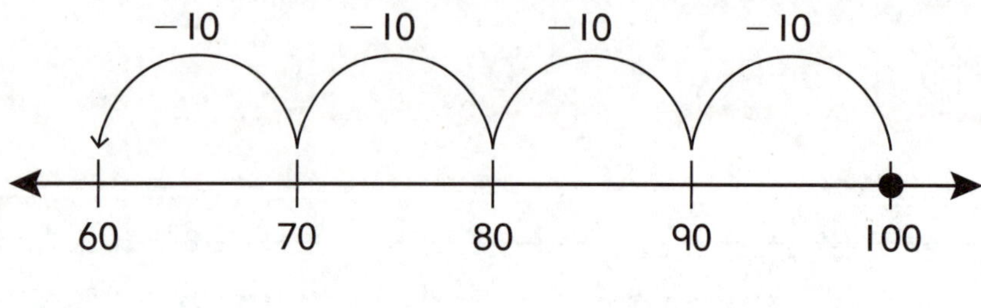

______ − ______ = ______

6. **Modeling Real Life** There are 52 cards in a deck. You pass out 20 of them. How many cards are left in the deck?

______ cards

7. **Does It Make Sense?** There are 48 chicks. 38 are yellow. The rest are either black or brown. Can 20 chicks be brown? Explain.

____

____

Review & Refresh

8.

2	6
+ 2	5

9.

6	4
+ 2	9

10.

3	7
+ 1	7

Name ______________________

Subtract Tens and Ones Using a Number Line

5.2

Learning Target: Use an open number line to subtract tens and ones.

Explore and Grow

Color to show how you can use the hundred chart to solve.

50 − 24 = _____ 78 − 26 = _____

1	2	3	4	5	6	7	8	9	10
11	12	13	14	15	16	17	18	19	20
21	22	23	24	25	26	27	28	29	30
31	32	33	34	35	36	37	38	39	40
41	42	43	44	45	46	47	48	49	50
51	52	53	54	55	56	57	58	59	60
61	62	63	64	65	66	67	68	69	70
71	72	73	74	75	76	77	78	79	80
81	82	83	84	85	86	87	88	89	90
91	92	93	94	95	96	97	98	99	100

Think and Grow

$67 - 42 = ?$

One Way:

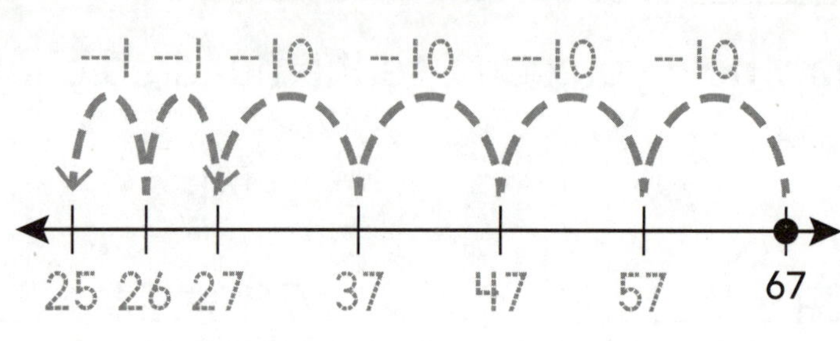

Start at 67.
Count back by tens,
then by ones.

Another Way:

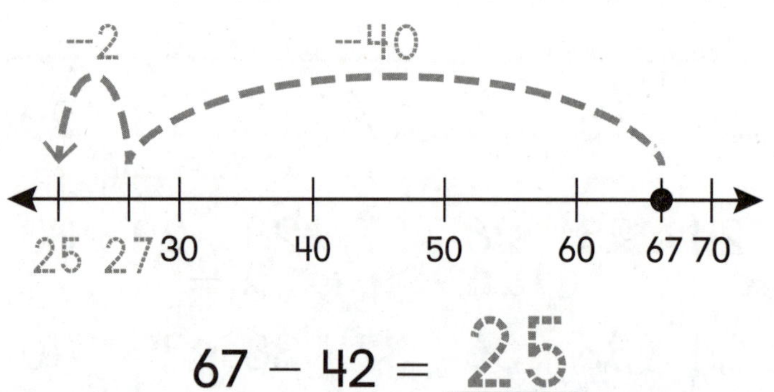

$67 - 42 = \underline{25}$

Show and Grow *I can do it!*

1. $80 - 34 =$ ______

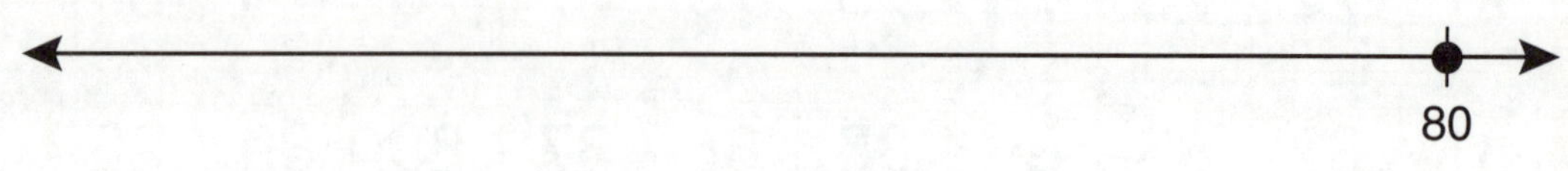

2. $56 - 23 =$ ______

Name ______________________________

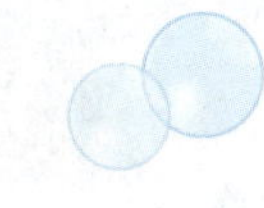

Apply and Grow: Practice

3. $74 - 51 =$ ____

4. $86 - 44 =$ ____

5. $97 - 61 =$ ____

6. $46 - 15 =$ ____

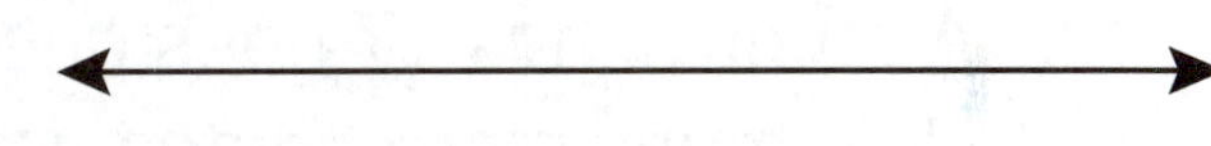

7. $69 - 35 =$ ____

8. $38 - 22 =$ ____

9. **Reasoning** Complete the number line and the equation.

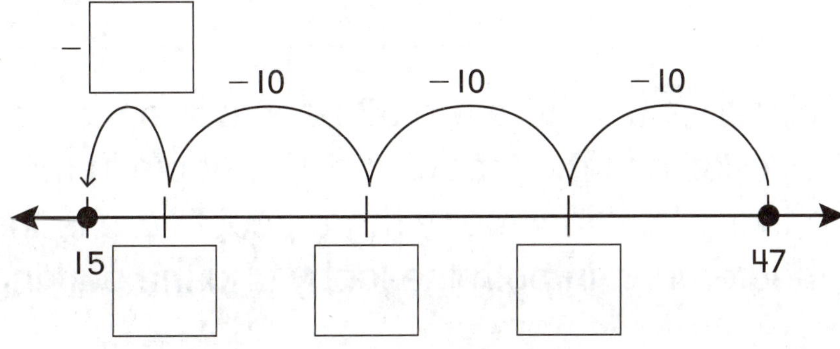

____ − ____ = ____

Think and Grow: Modeling Real Life

You have 85 baseball cards and 54 football cards. How many more baseball cards do you have?

Subtraction equation:

Model:

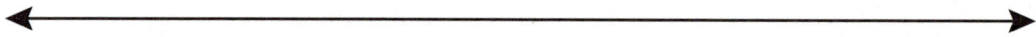

_____ more baseball cards

Show and Grow *I can think deeper!*

10. A carnival has 17 rides and 48 games. How many more games are there?

_____ more games

Use Math Tools How can you use a drawing to help organize the information given?

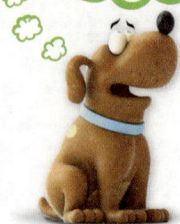

11. **DIG DEEPER!** There are 63 people in a theater, 21 people in the lobby, and 10 people in the parking lot. How many more people are in the theater than in both the lobby and the parking lot?

_____ more people

Name ______________________

Practice 5.2

Learning Target: Use an open number line to subtract tens and ones.

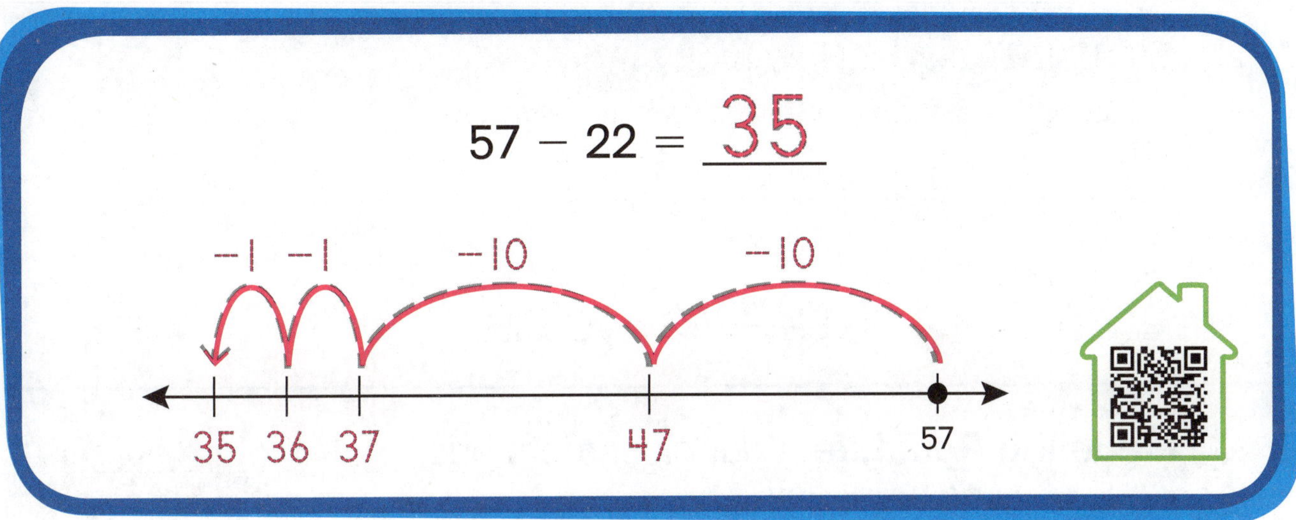

1. 95 − 40 = ____

95

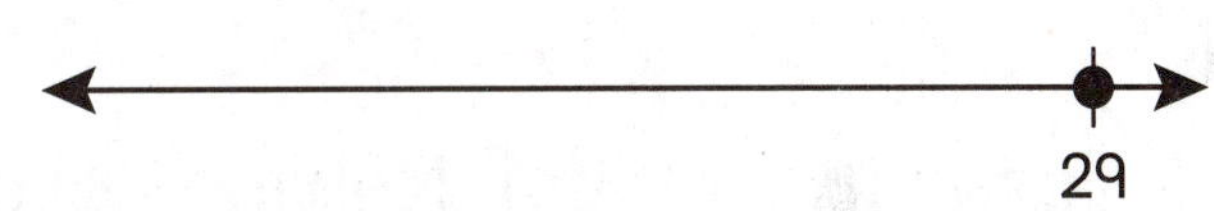

2. 29 − 12 = ____

3. 58 − 14 = ____

4. 77 − 31 = ____

5. 86 − 26 = ____

6. 70 − 18 = ____

7. **Structure** Use the number lines to show 84 − 62 in two ways.

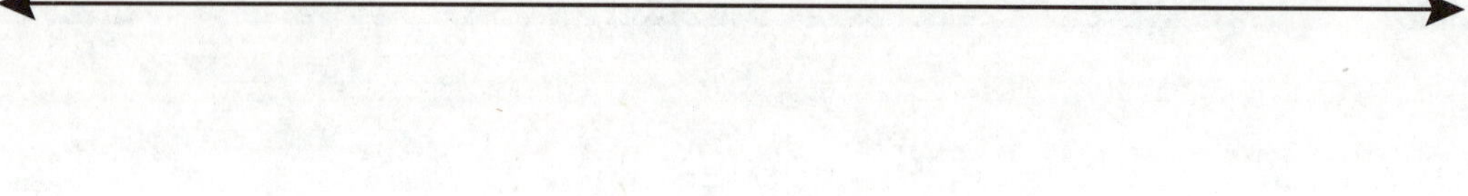

84 − 62 = ______

8. **Modeling Real Life** Your classroom has 26 desks and 38 chairs. How many more chairs are there?

______ chairs

9. **Does It Make Sense?** Descartes collects 63 clams. He loses 21 of them. Newton collects 58 clams, and then loses some. Newton now has more clams than Descartes. Could Newton have lost 25 clams? Explain.

____

____

Review & Refresh

Is the number even or odd?

10. 8

Even Odd

11. 13

Even Odd

Name ______________________

Use Addition to Subtract 5.3

Learning Target: Use addition to subtract on an open number line.

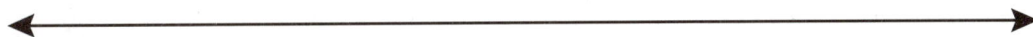

Explore and Grow

Show how you can use a number line to solve.

52 − 29 = ____

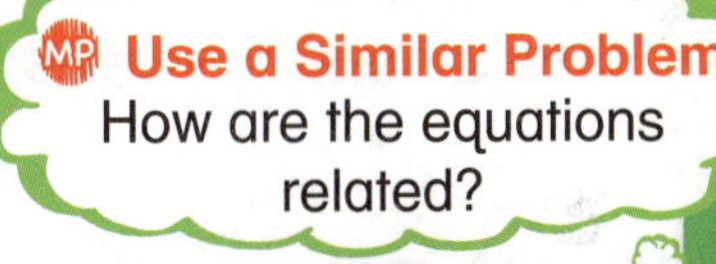

Use a Similar Problem
How are the equations related?

29 + ____ = 52

Think and Grow

You can use addition to subtract. Start at 38. Add 2 to get to 40. Then add 10, and 10 again to get to 60. Then add 4 to get to 64.

64 − 38 = ?

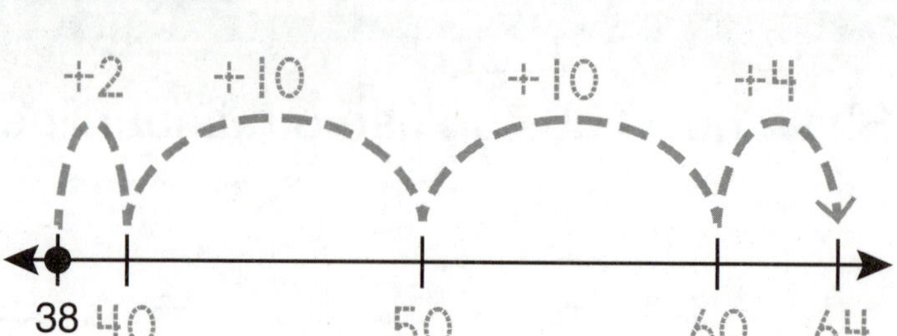
+2
+10
+10
+4
38
40
50
60
64

Add your jumps to find the difference.

2 + 10 + 10 + 4 = 26

64 − 38 = 26

Show and Grow *I can do it!*

Add to find the difference.

1. 43 − 15 = _____

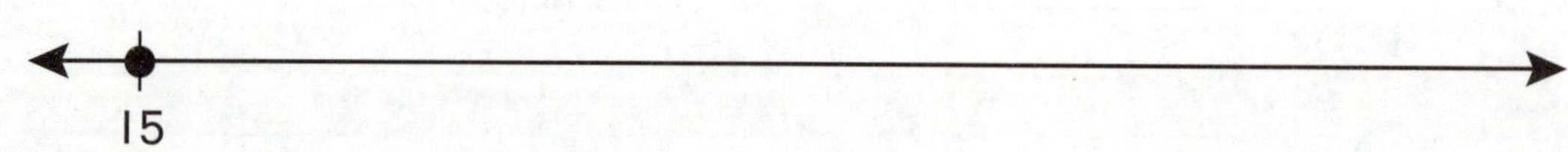
15

2. 76 − 59 = _____

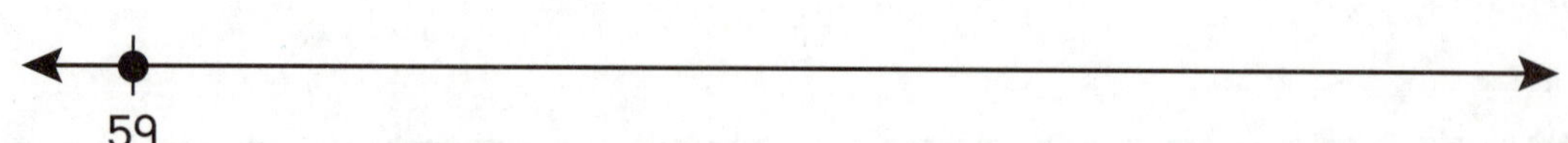
59

Name ________________________________

Apply and Grow: Practice

Add to find the difference.

3. 56 − 27 = _____

4. 21 − 13 = _____

5. 72 − 57 = _____

6. 33 − 15 = _____

7. 45 − 36 = _____

8. 61 − 46 = _____

9. MP **Structure** Use addition and the number lines to show 64 − 35 in two ways.

64 − 35 = _____

Think and Grow: Modeling Real Life

A ship has a crew of 52 pirates. Some of them leave. There are 27 left. How many pirates got off the ship?

Model:

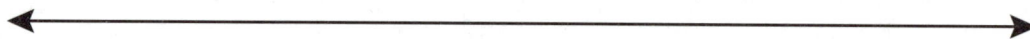

Equations:

______ pirates

Show and Grow *I can think deeper!*

10. A pumpkin patch has 85 pumpkins. Some of them are picked. There are 48 left. How many pumpkins were picked?

______ pumpkins

11. **DIG DEEPER!** There are 96 treats in a bowl. Newton takes 15 treats. Descartes takes some treats. There are 68 treats left. How many treats did Descartes take?

______ treats

Name ______________________________

Learning Target: Use addition to subtract on an open number line.

Add your jumps to find the difference.

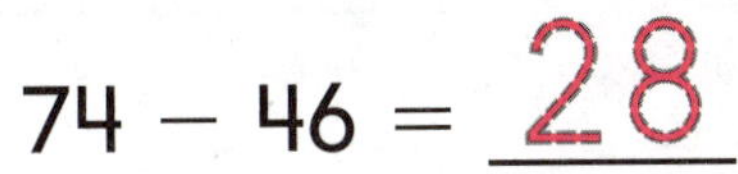

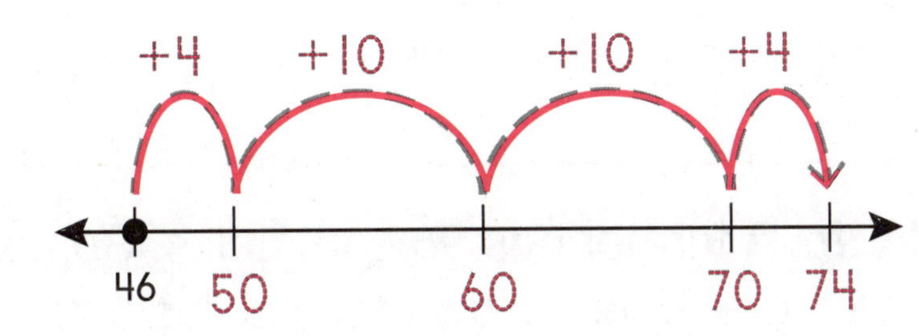

$4 + 10 + 10 + 4 = 28$

Add to find the difference.

1. $92 - 67 =$ ______

67

2. $43 - 24 =$ ______

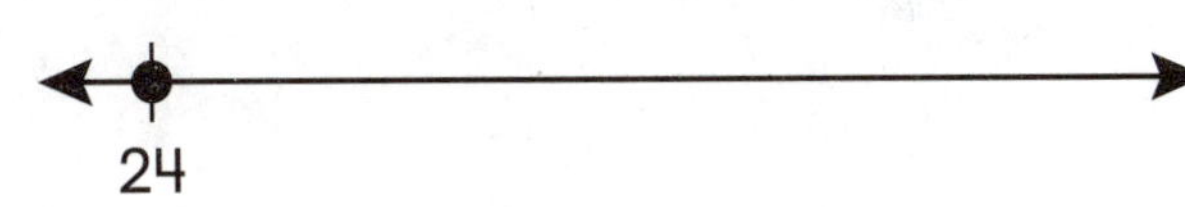

3. $71 - 42 =$ ______

4. $63 - 58 =$ ______

5. $55 - 19 =$ ______

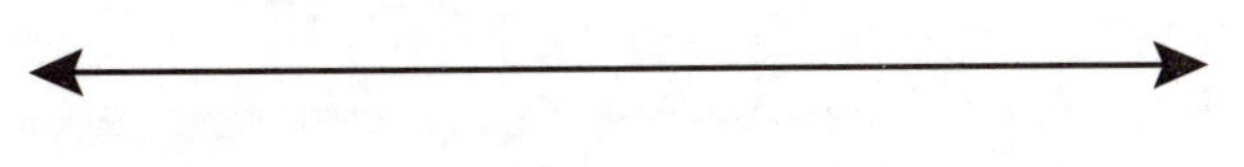

6. $86 - 29 =$ ______

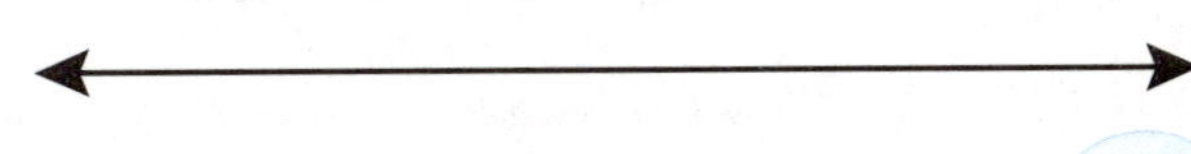

7. YOU BE THE TEACHER Descartes adds to find 35 − 12. Is he correct? Explain.

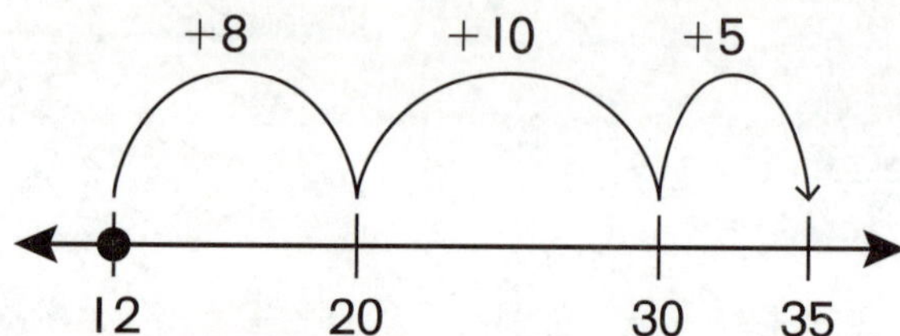

____

____

____

____

8. Modeling Real Life A farmer has 96 cornstalks. Some of them are sold. There are 38 left. How many cornstalks were sold?

_____ cornstalks

9. DIG DEEPER! There are 56 bouncy balls in a pack. Your friend takes some. You take 23. There are 23 bouncy balls left. How many did your friend take?

_____ bouncy balls

Review & Refresh

Draw to show the time.

10. 2:30

11. 11 o'clock

Name ______________________________

Decompose to Subtract 5.4

Learning Target: Break apart one-digit numbers to subtract.

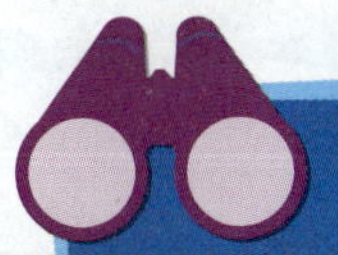

Explore and Grow

Color to show how you can get to a decade number by subtracting.

36 − _____ = 30

1	2	3	4	5	6	7	8	9	10
11	12	13	14	15	16	17	18	19	20
21	22	23	24	25	26	27	28	29	30
31	32	33	34	35	36	37	38	39	40
41	42	43	44	45	46	47	48	49	50

How can the equation above help you find 36 − 9?

____

____

____

Think and Grow

$53 - 7 = ?$

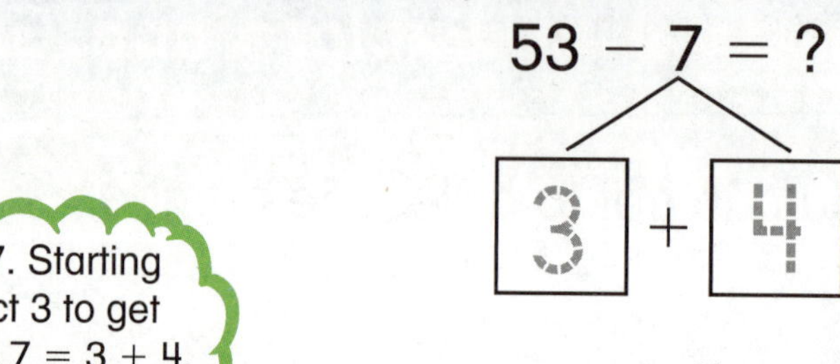

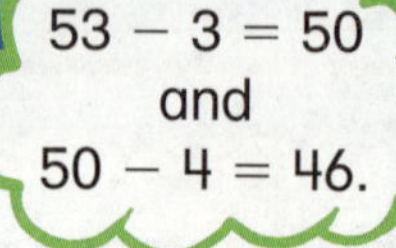

53 − 3 = 50 and 50 − 4 = 46.

Break apart 7. Starting at 53, subtract 3 to get to 50. Because 7 = 3 + 4, subtract 4 more.

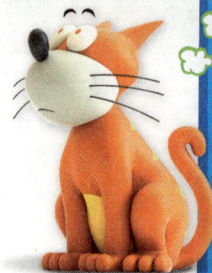

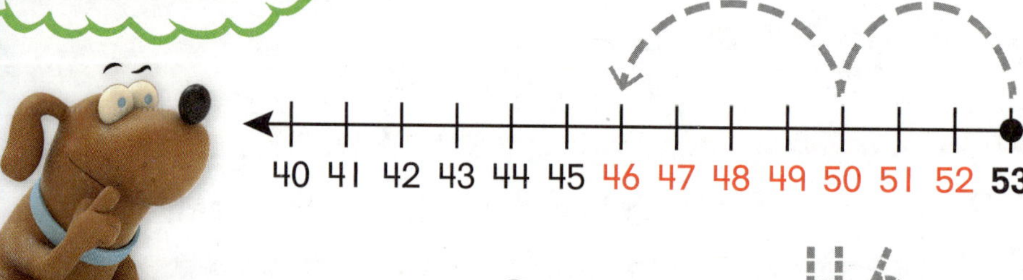

So, $53 - 7 = $ 46.

Show and Grow *I can do it!*

Break apart the number being subtracted. Then find the difference. Use the number line to help.

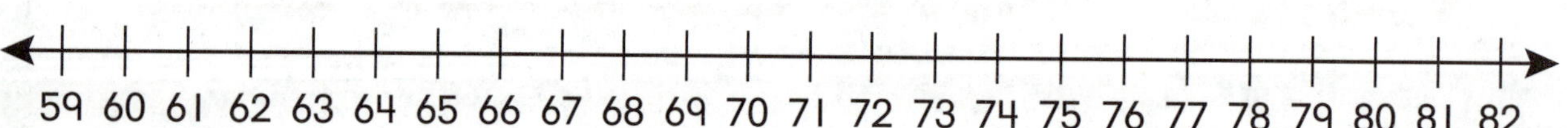

1. $64 - 5 =$ _____

2. $77 - 8 =$ _____

3. $75 - 7 =$ _____

4. $82 - 6 =$ _____

Name ______________________________

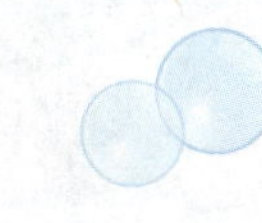

Apply and Grow: Practice

Break apart the number being subtracted. Then find the difference.

5. $47 - 8 =$ ______

6. $56 - 9 =$ ______

7. $43 - 5 =$ ______

8. $62 - 6 =$ ______

9. ______ $= 41 - 4$

10. ______ $= 44 - 7$

11. **Reasoning** Which equation is shown by the number line?

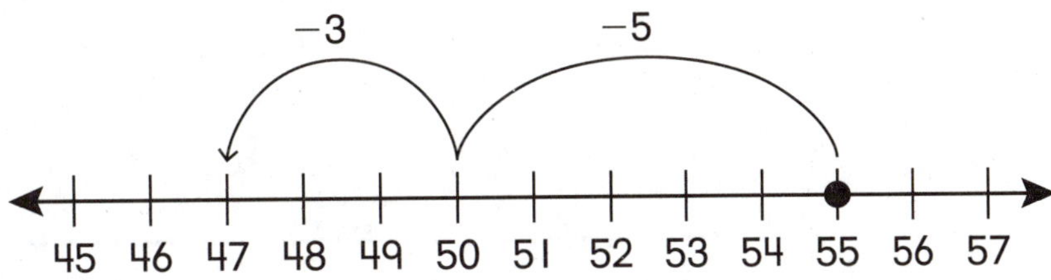

$50 + 5 = 55$ $\qquad$ $55 - 8 = 47$ $\qquad$ $47 + 3 = 50$

Think and Grow: Modeling Real Life

Your friend has 45 comic books. You have 8 fewer. How many comic books do you have?

Subtraction equation:

_____ comic books

Show and Grow *I can think deeper!*

12. Your friend can do 33 tricks on a yo-yo. You can do 9 fewer. How many tricks can you do?

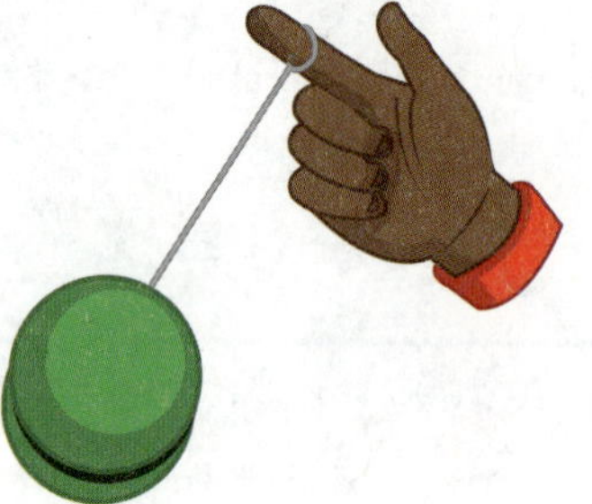

_____ tricks

13. Descartes's walk was 8 minutes longer than Newton's. Descartes's walk was 56 minutes. How long was Newton's walk?

_____ minutes

Name ______________________

Learning Target: Break apart one-digit numbers to subtract.

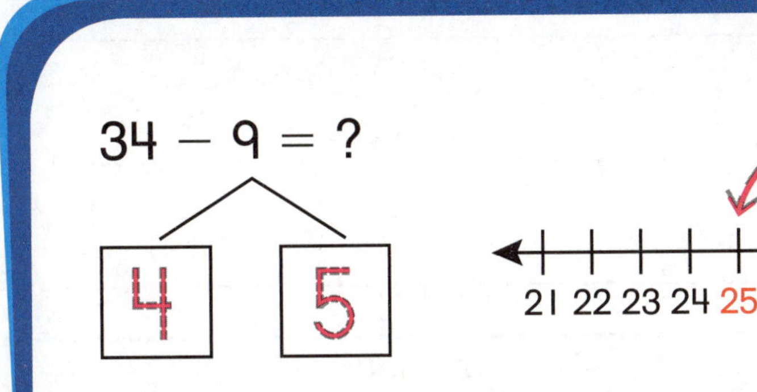

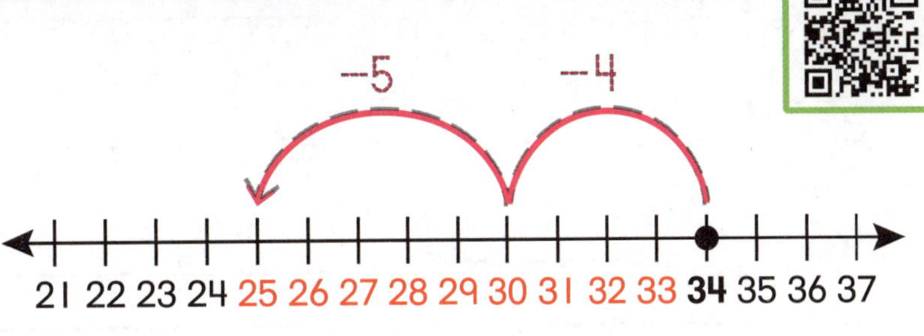

So, 34 − 9 = 25.

Break apart the number being subtracted. Then find the difference. Use the number line to help.

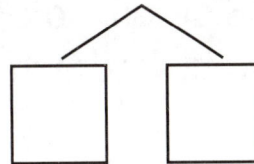

1. 95 − 6 = ______

2. 86 − 8 = ______

3. 89 − 9 = ______

4. 82 − 7 = ______

5. ______ = 83 − 5

6. ______ = 98 − 9

7. **Number Sense** Which way would you break apart 9 to find 25 − 9? Explain. Then find the difference.

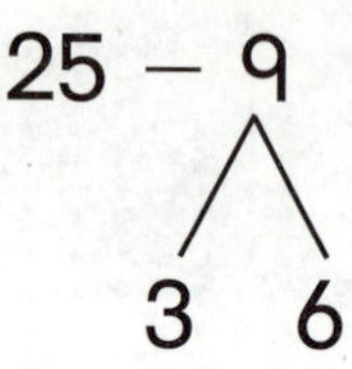

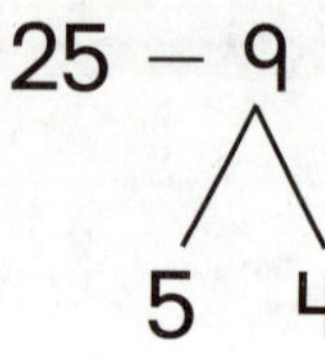

____

____

25 − 9 = ______ ______________________

---

8. **Modeling Real Life** You build a train track with 32 pieces. You remove 6 pieces. How many pieces does the train track have now?

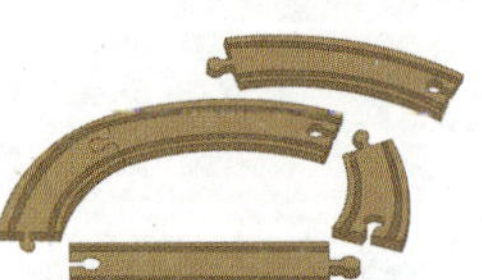

______ pieces

---

9. **Modeling Real Life** A vendor has 41 dream catchers with feathers and 35 dream catchers with beads. She sells all but 8 of them. How many dream catchers does she sell?

______ dream catchers

Review & Refresh

10. 

______ rows of ______

______ + ______ + ______ = ______

Name ______________________________

Decompose to Subtract Tens and Ones

5.5

Learning Target: Break apart two-digit numbers to subtract.

Explore and Grow

Color to show how you can break apart 16 to find the difference.

$43 - 16 =$ ______

1	2	3	4	5	6	7	8	9	10
11	12	13	14	15	16	17	18	19	20
21	22	23	24	25	26	27	28	29	30
31	32	33	34	35	36	37	38	39	40
41	42	43	44	45	46	47	48	49	50

Explain your strategy.

____

____

____

Think and Grow

Break apart 25 into tens and ones. Starting at 84, subtract 20 to get to 64.

84 − 25 = ?

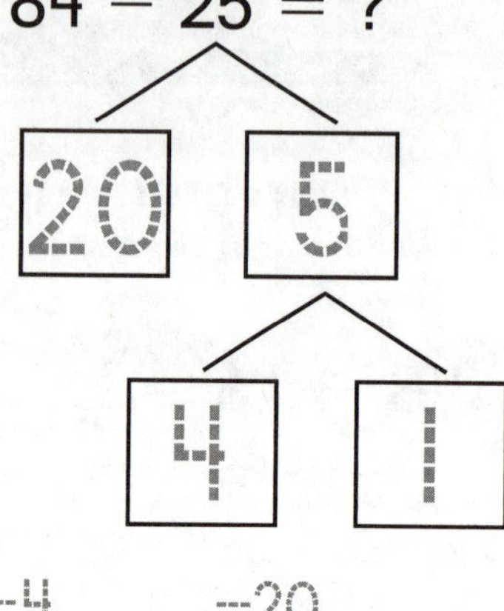

Break apart 5. Subtract 4 to get to 60. Then subtract 1 to get to 59.

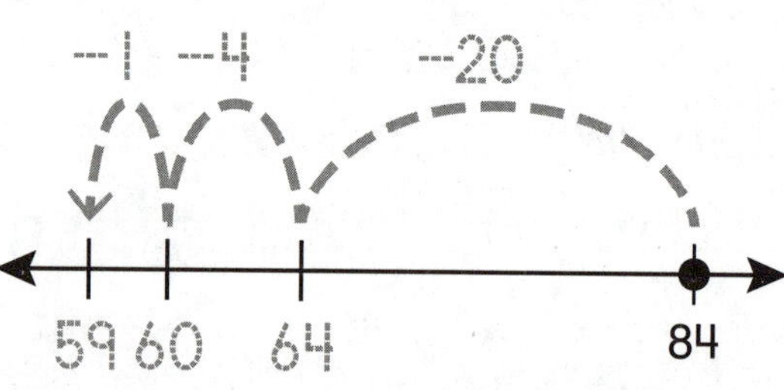

So, 84 − 25 = 59.

Show and Grow *I can do it!*

Break apart the number being subtracted. Then find the difference.

1. 41 − 17 = _____

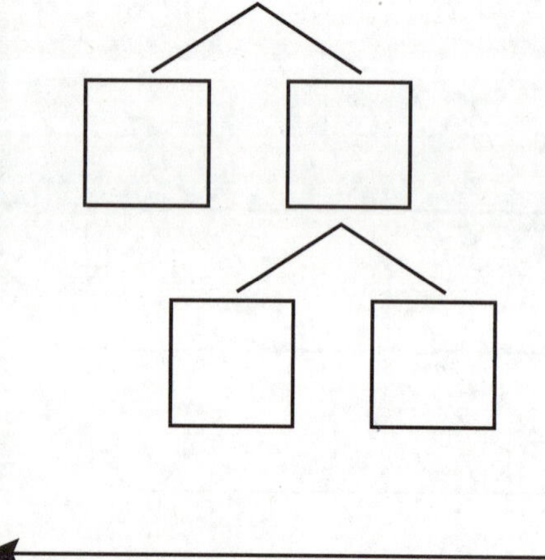

41

2. 63 − 26 = _____

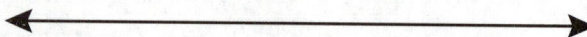

Name ____

Apply and Grow: Practice

Break apart the number being subtracted. Then find the difference.

3. 32 − 13 = ______

4. 46 − 17 = ______

5. 93 − 45 = ______

6. 71 − 24 = ______

7. **Structure** Can you use the equations to find 87 − 29?

87 − 20 = 67 67 − 9 = 58	87 − 10 = 77 77 − 7 = 70	87 − 20 = 67 67 − 7 = 60 60 − 2 = 58
Yes No	Yes No	Yes No

Think and Grow: Modeling Real Life

How many more pizzas do you sell than Newton?

Equation:

Number of Pizzas Sold	
You	72
Descartes	57
Newton	38

_____ more pizzas

How many fewer pizzas does Newton sell than Descartes?

_____ fewer pizzas

Show and Grow *I can think deeper!*

8. How many more tickets does Newton sell than Descartes?

Number of Tickets Sold	
You	59
Descartes	47
Newton	85

_____ more tickets

9. **DIG DEEPER!** Your friend picks 49 apples. 11 apples are green and 14 apples are red. The rest are yellow. How many apples are yellow?

_____ yellow apples

Name ______________________

Learning Target: Break apart two-digit numbers to subtract.

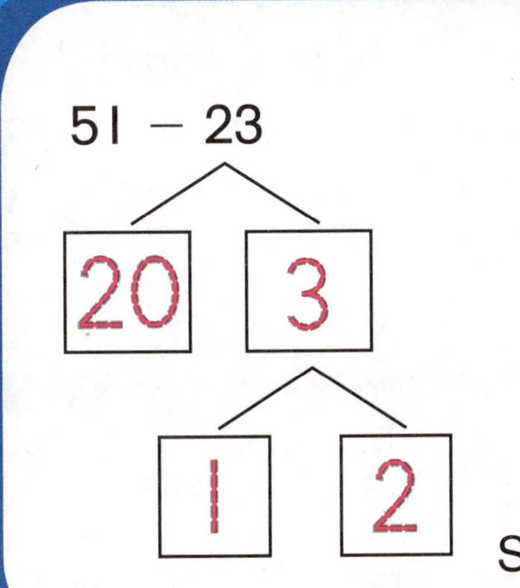

51 − 23 = ?

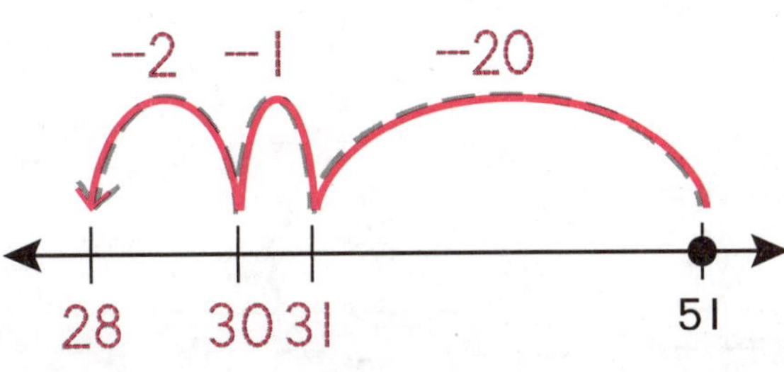

So, 51 − 23 = 28.

Break apart the number being subtracted. Then find the difference.

1. 45 − 16 = ______

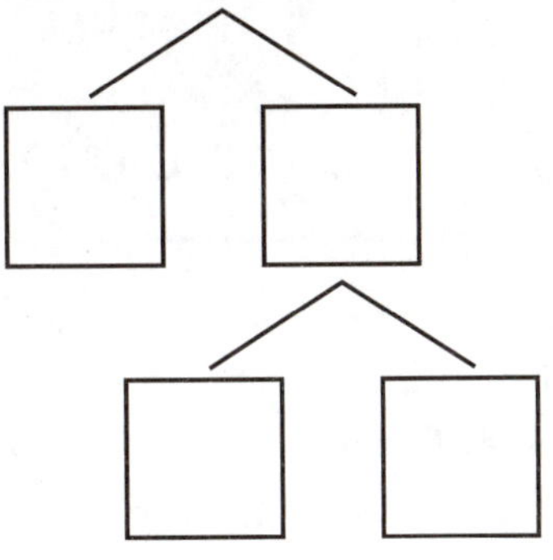

45

2. 52 − 27 = ______

3. 84 − 55 = ______

4. 76 − 29 = ______

5. _____ = 23 − 14

6. _____ = 68 − 49

7. MP **Reasoning** Complete the number line and the equation.

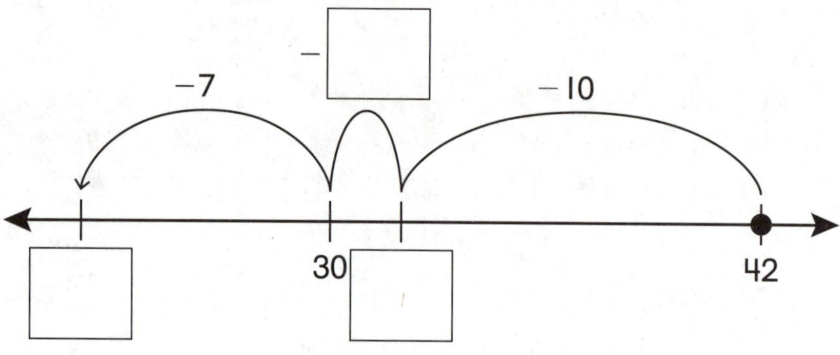

_____ − _____ = _____

8. MP **Modeling Real Life** How many more cups does Descartes sell than Newton?

Number of Cups Sold	
Descartes	62
Newton	21

_____ more cups

9. DIG DEEPER! In Exercise 8, 100 cups are sold for the day. Newton sold the rest. How many cups did Newton sell?

_____ cups

Review & Refresh

10. 47 + 32 = _____

11. 74 + 15 = _____

Name ______________________

Use Compensation to Subtract 5.6

Learning Target: Use compensation to subtract.

Explore and Grow

Use mental math to find each difference.

$41 - 20 =$ ______ $41 - 20 =$ ______

$41 - 19 =$ ______ $41 - 21 =$ ______

$41 - 20 =$ ______ $41 - 20 =$ ______

$41 - 18 =$ ______ $41 - 22 =$ ______

$41 - 20 =$ ______ $41 - 20 =$ ______

$41 - 17 =$ ______ $41 - 23 =$ ______

MP Repeated Reasoning How did you use mental math and $41 - 20$ to find each difference?

____

____

____

Think and Grow

73 − 28 = ?
↓ + 2
73 − 30 = 43
↓ + 2
73 − 28 = 45

You subtract 3 *less* than 43, so you must *subtract* 3 from 39 to find the answer.

79 − 43 = ?
↓ − 3
79 − 40 = 39
↓ − 3
79 − 43 = 36

Show and Grow *I can do it!*

Use compensation to subtract.

1. 46 − 9 = ?
↓ + 1
46 − ____ = ____
46 − 9 = ____ ↓ + 1

2. 88 − 41 = ?
↓ − 1
88 − ____ = ____
88 − 41 = ____ ↓ − 1

3. 62 − 37 = ?
↓ ☐
62 − ____ = ____
62 − 37 = ____ ↓ ☐

4. 51 − 26 = ?
↓ ☐
51 − ____ = ____
51 − 26 = ____ ↓ ☐

Name ___________________________________

Apply and Grow: Practice

Use compensation to subtract.

5. 49 − 31 = ?

↓ ☐

49 − ____ = ____

49 − 31 = ____ ↓ ☐

6. 88 − 56 = ?

↓ ☐

88 − ____ = ____

88 − 56 = ____ ↓ ☐

7. 75 − 18 = ?

↓ ☐

75 − ____ = ____

75 − 18 = ____ ↓ ☐

8. 64 − 24 = ?

↓ ☐

64 − ____ = ____

64 − 24 = ____ ↓ ☐

9. 35 − 7 = ____

10. 53 − 37 = ____

11. MP **Maintain Accuracy** Match the expressions that have the same difference.

81 − 42   76 − 33   78 − 54

74 − 50   79 − 40   73 − 30

Think and Grow: Modeling Real Life

You blow up 57 balloons for a carnival game. Some of them pop. There are 29 left. How many balloons popped?

Subtraction equation:

_____ balloons

Show and Grow *I can think deeper!*

12. There are 66 cars in a parking lot. Some of them leave. There are 31 left. How many cars leave the parking lot?

_____ cars

13. You have 78 pictures on your tablet. You take 4 more pictures. Then you delete 17. How many pictures are on your tablet now?

_____ pictures

14. You pick 59 strawberries. You eat 5 of them. Then you give 22 to your friend. How many strawberries do you have left?

_____ strawberries

Name ______________________

Practice 5.6

Learning Target: Use compensation to subtract.

55 − 37 = ?
↓ + 3
55 − 40 = 15
↓ + 3
55 − 37 = 18

Use compensation to subtract.

1. 42 − 21 = ?
↓ − 1
42 − ____ = ____
42 − 21 = ____ ↓ − 1

2. 94 − 48 = ?
↓ + 2
94 − ____ = ____
94 − 48 = ____ ↓ + 2

3. 84 − 71 = ?
↓ ☐
84 − ____ = ____
84 − 71 = ____ ↓ ☐

4. 59 − 33 = ?
↓ ☐
59 − ____ = ____
59 − 33 = ____ ↓ ☐

5. 27 − 6 = ____

6. 67 − 14 = ____

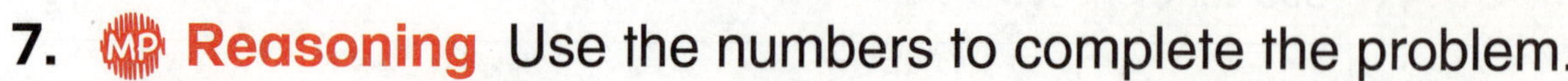

7. **Reasoning** Use the numbers to complete the problem.

50 2 13

15 2

63 − 48 = ?

↓ + ____

63 − ____ = ____

63 − 48 = ____ ↓ + ____

8. **Modeling Real Life** There are 36 boats on a lake. Some of them leave. There are 21 boats left. How many boats leave the lake?

____ boats

9. **Modeling Real Life** A city bus has 56 seats. There are 23 children and 18 adults sitting in seats. The rest of the seats are empty. How many seats are empty?

____ seats

Review & Refresh

10. Circle groups of 3. Write a repeated addition equation to match.

____ groups of 3   ____ + ____ + ____ + ____ = ____

Name ______________________________

Practice Subtraction Strategies 5.7

Learning Target: Choose a strategy to subtract.

Use any strategy to find the difference.

76 − 34 = ____

Compare Arguments Compare your strategy to your partner's strategy. Which strategy makes the most sense to use with these numbers?

____

____

____

Think and Grow

$93 - 57 = ?$

One Way:

Use addition.

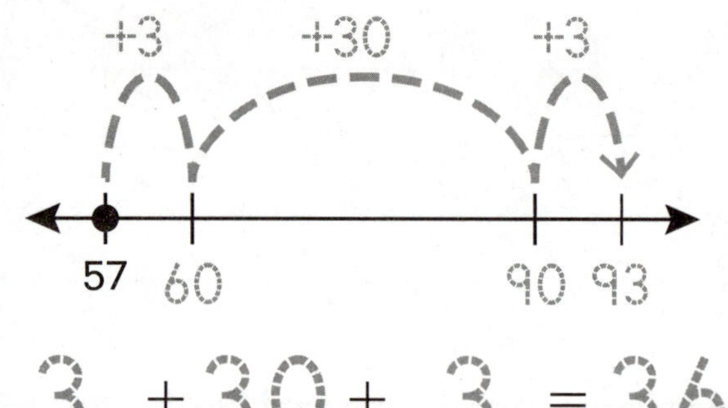

3 + 30 + 3 = 36

So, $93 - 57 = 36$.

Another Way:

Use compensation.

$93 - 57 = ?$

↓ + 3

$93 - 60 = 33$

↓ + 3

$93 - 57 = 36$

Show and Grow *I can do it!*

1. $81 - 50 =$ _____

2. $94 - 8 =$ _____

3. $58 - 49 =$ _____

4. $77 - 35 =$ _____

Name ___

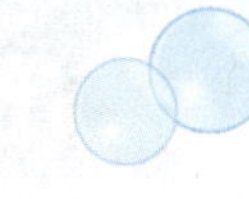

Apply and Grow: Practice

5. 97 − 71 = ___

6. 68 − 9 = ___

7. 52 − 28 = ___

8. 83 − 60 = ___

9. ___ = 75 − 11

10. ___ = 46 − 35

11. **YOU BE THE TEACHER** Your friend uses compensation to subtract. Is your friend correct? Explain.

35 − 29 = ?

↓ + 1

35 − 30 = 5

___

___

___

12. A store has 38 hats. 17 of them are sold. How many hats are left?

___ hats

Think and Grow: Modeling Real Life

You have 41 toys. You put some away. There are 22 toys left. How many toys did you put away?

Subtraction equation:

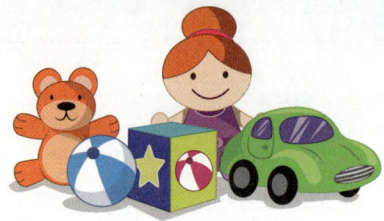

_____ toys

Show and Grow *I can think deeper!*

13. A teacher has 62 prizes. He gives some away. There are 26 left. How many prizes did the teacher give away?

_____ prizes

14. A roller-skating rink rents 28 pairs of skates. There are 52 pairs left. How many pairs of skates were there to start?

_____ pairs of skates

15. A baker has 16 loaves of french bread and 31 loaves of wheat bread. She sells 18 loaves. How many loaves does the baker have left?

_____ loaves

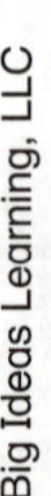

Name ______________________

Practice 5.7

Learning Target: Choose a strategy to subtract.

33 − 16 = ?

One Way:

Use a number line.

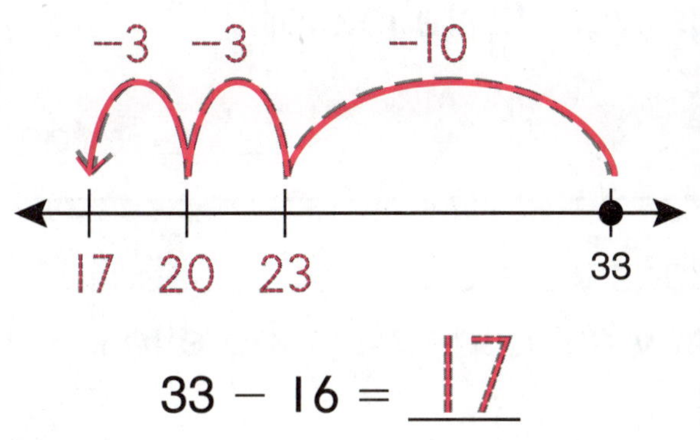

33 − 16 = 17

Another Way:

Use compensation.

33 − 16 = ?
↓ + 4
33 − 20 = 13
↓ + 4
33 − 16 = 17

1. 50 − 20 = ______

2. 62 − 30 = ______

3. 88 − 64 = ______

4. 42 − 17 = ______

5. ______ = 97 − 56

6. ______ = 71 − 18

7. MP **Maintain Accuracy** Which expressions have a difference of 24?

44 − 20   24 − 10

32 − 8   76 − 50 − 2   40 − 22

8. MP **Modeling Real Life** 27 dogs were adopted from a shelter. There are 14 left. How many dogs were there to start?

_____ dogs

9. MP **Modeling Real Life** 86 hot dogs were sold at a baseball game. There are 14 left. How many hot dogs were there to start?

_____ hot dogs

10. **DIG DEEPER!** Complete the equation. Write a subtraction story to match.

25 − _____ = 12

____

____

Review & Refresh

11. Circle the shapes that show halves.

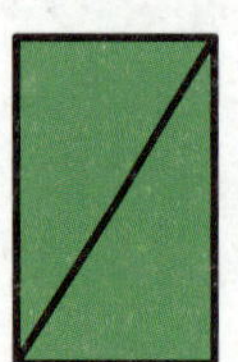
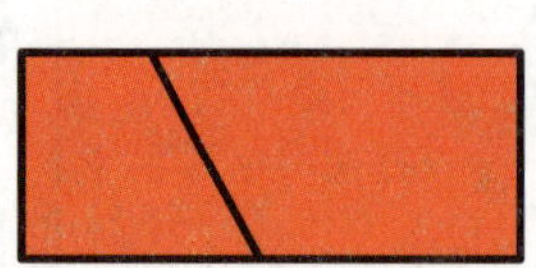
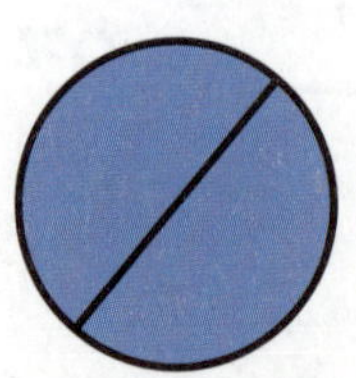

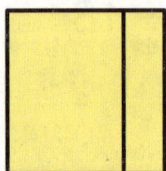

Name ______________________________

Learning Target: Solve two-step subtraction problems.

Model the story.

Newton collects 58 flowers. He gives 27 away. How many flowers does Newton have left?

_____ flowers

Newton gives 11 more flowers away. How many flowers does Newton have now?

_____ flowers

Think and Grow

There are 53 people on a bus. 9 exit at the first stop. 17 exit at the second stop. How many people are still on the bus?

Circle what you know. Underline what you need to find.

Solve:

Step 1: Find the number of people on the bus after the first stop.

53 − 9 = ?

+ 1

53 − 10 = 43

+ 1

53 − 9 = 44

Step 2: Subtract the number of people who exit at the second stop from your result in Step 1.

44 − 17 = ?

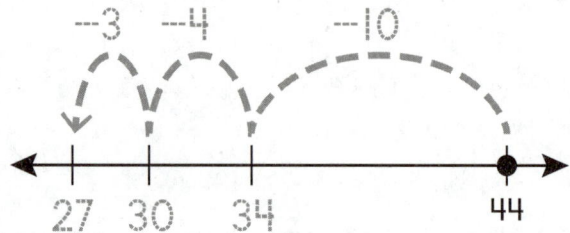

−3 −4 −10

27 30 34 44

44 − 17 = 27

27 people

Show and Grow *I can do it!*

1. There are 60 kids at a summer camp. 26 are swimming. 15 are playing soccer. The rest are hiking. How many kids are hiking?

_____ kids

Name ____

Apply and Grow: Practice

2. Your class recycles 72 cans. You collected 18 of them. Your friend collected 9. The other students collected the rest. How many cans did the other students collect?

_______ cans

3. 98 people visit the library in a week. 34 visit on Monday. 14 visit on Tuesday. How many people visit the library the rest of the week?

_______ people

4. You have 61 stickers. You give 24 stickers to your friend. Then you get 6 more stickers. How many stickers do you have now?

_______ stickers

Think and Grow: Modeling Real Life

You collect 47 pine cones. Your friend collects 21 fewer than you. How many pine cones do you and your friend collect in all?

Circle what you know.

Underline what you need to find.

Solve:

_____ pine cones

Show and Grow *I can think deeper!*

5. A garbage truck collects trash from 68 trash cans. Another truck collects trash from 39 fewer cans. How many cans of trash do the trucks collect from in all?

_____ trash cans

Communicate Clearly Explain the steps you used to solve the problem.

____

____

Name ___________________________

Practice **5.8**

Learning Target: Solve two-step subtraction problems.

You have 43 toys. 15 are in your bedroom. 12 are in the living room. The rest are in your toy box. How many toys are left in your toy box?

Circle what you know. Underline what you need to find.

Solve:

Step 1: Find the number of toys that are not in your room.

43 − 15 = ?

⊕ 5

43 − 20 = 23

⊕ 5

43 − 15 = 28

Step 2: Subtract the number of toys in the living room from your result in Step 1.

28 − 12 = ?

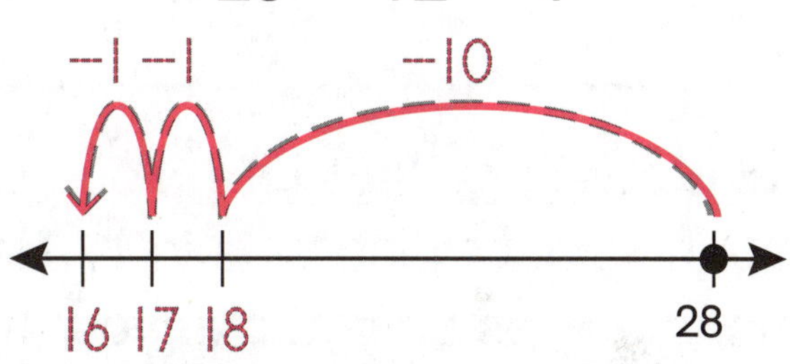

28 − 12 = 16

16 toys

1. There are 39 people in a pool. 8 are floating on rafts. 11 are playing a game. The rest are swimming laps. How many people are swimming laps?

______ people

2. DIG DEEPER! Find each difference. Write a subtraction story to match.

65 − 19 = ______   46 − 12 = ______

____

____

3. MP **Modeling Real Life** You use 76 craft sticks. Your friend uses 62 fewer than you. How many craft sticks do you and your friend use in all?

______ craft sticks

4. MP **Modeling Real Life** You put 52 photos in an album. Your friend puts in 17 fewer than you. How many photos do you and your friend put in the album in all?

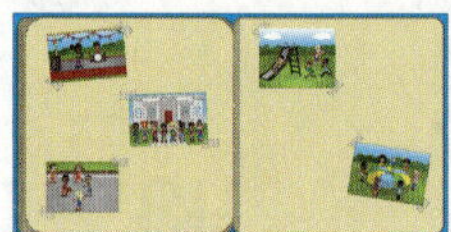

______ photos

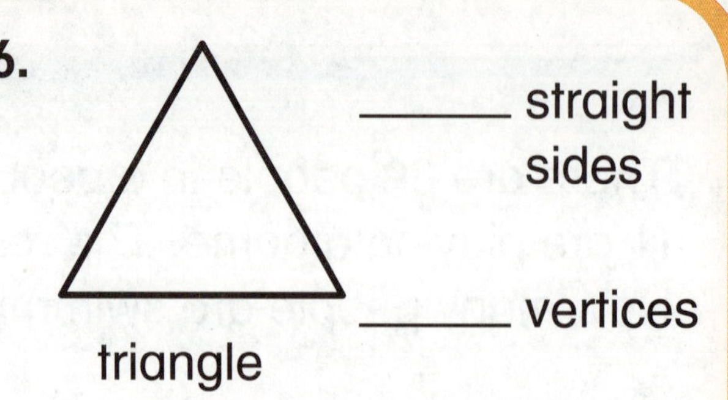

Review & Refresh

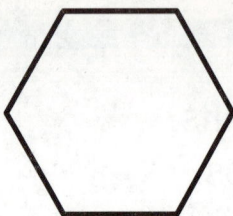

5. hexagon

______ straight sides

______ vertices

6. triangle

______ straight sides

______ vertices

Name ____________________

Performance Task 5

A science class uses an incubator to hatch chicken eggs.

1. The temperature of the incubator must be 99°F. The current temperature is 25°F less than the correct temperature. What is the current temperature?

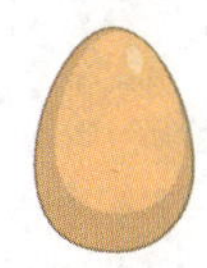

_____ °F

2. a. The school has 4 incubators. Each one has 8 eggs. Each egg must be rotated 3 times every day. How many total rotations must be made to all of the eggs in all 4 incubators?

_____ rotations

b. Two of your friends each complete 25 rotations. How many rotations are left?

_____ rotations

3. a. The first egg hatches at 11:00. The second egg hatches a half hour later. What time does the second egg hatch?

____

b. The third egg hatches an hour after the second egg. What time does the third egg hatch?

____

Three in a Row: Subtraction

To Play: Players take turns. On your turn, spin both spinners. Subtract the numbers, and cover the difference on the game board. Continue until someone gets three in a row.

Name ______________________________

Chapter Practice 5

5.1 Subtract Tens Using a Number Line

1. 90 − 40 = _____

2. 66 − 20 = _____

5.2 Subtract Tens and Ones Using a Number Line

3. 78 − 32 = _____

4. 49 − 16 = _____

5. **MP Modeling Real Life** You have 54 stickers and 21 key chains. How many more stickers do you have than key chains?

_____ stickers

5.3 Use Addition to Subtract

Add to find the difference.

6. 44 − 28 = _____

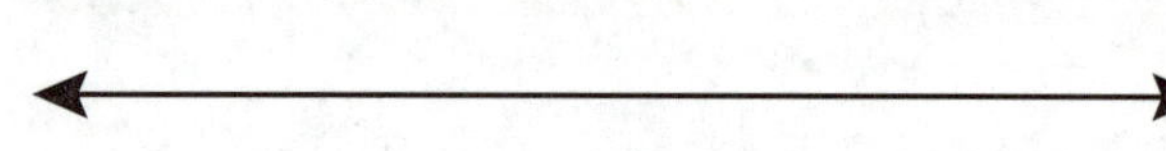

7. 84 − 56 = _____

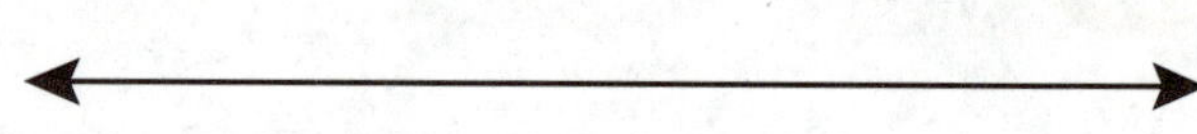

5.4 Decompose to Subtract

Break apart the number being subtracted. Then find the difference.

8. 44 − 5 = _____

9. 82 − 7 = _____

10. 67 − 9 = _____

11. 32 − 4 = _____

12. **Number Sense** Which way would you break apart 8 to find 56 − 8? Explain.

56 − 8
6 2

56 − 8
4 4

____

____

____

____

5.5 Decompose to Subtract Tens and Ones

Break apart the number being subtracted. Then find the difference.

13. 51 − 19 = ____

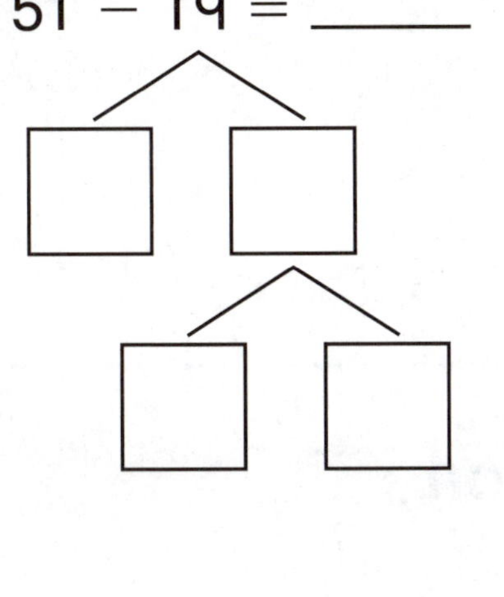

51

14. 43 − 25 = ____

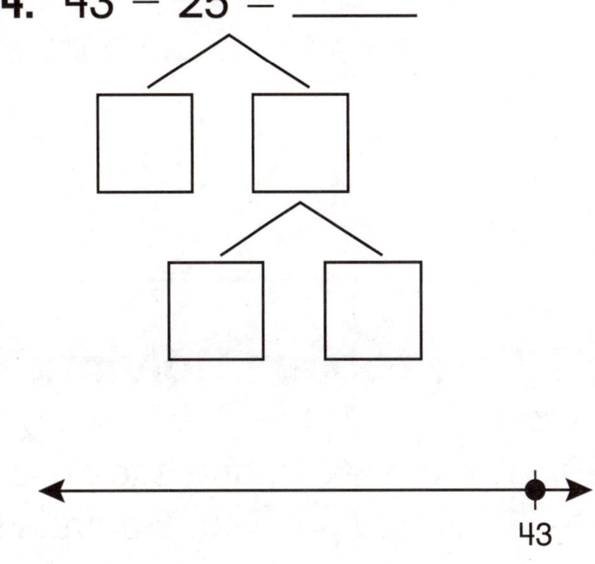

43

5.6 Use Compensation to Subtract

Use compensation to subtract.

15. 42 − 21 = ?

42 − ____ = ____

42 − 21 = ____

16. 99 − 35 = ?

99 − ____ = ____

99 − 35 = ____

17. **Maintain Accuracy** Match the expressions that have the same difference.

47 − 22   48 − 15   46 − 34

43 − 10   45 − 20   42 − 30

5.7 Practice Subtraction Strategies

18. 58 − 36 = ______

19. 67 − 52 = ______

5.8 Problem Solving: Subtraction

20. There are 31 papers to pass out. You pass out 12 papers. Then you pass out 8 more. How many papers do you have left?

______ papers

21. 47 students are on the playground. 23 fewer students are playing soccer than on the playground. How many students are on the playground and playing soccer in all?

______ students

6 Fluently Subtract within 100

- Does it snow where you live?
- You build a snowman that is 23 inches tall. Your friend builds a snowman that is 30 inches tall. How many inches taller is your friend's snowman?

Chapter Learning Target:
Understand subtraction fluently.

Chapter Success Criteria:
- I can identify subtraction patterns.
- I can explain which strategy I used to find a difference.
- I can show regrouping.
- I can model subtraction problems.

Name ______________________________

6 Vocabulary

Review Words
equal groups
even
odd
repeated addition

Organize It

Use the review words to complete the graphic organizer.

[ ]	[ ]
45	72
127	388
91	4
3	60

Define It

Match.

1. equal groups

$2 + 2 + 2 + 2$

2. repeated addition

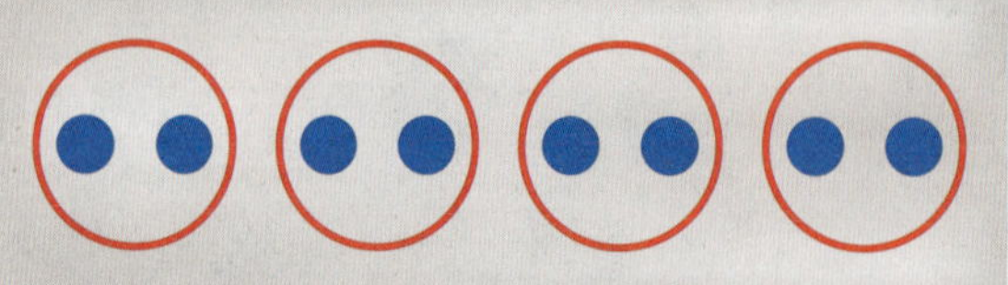

Name ______________________________

Model and Regroup to Subtract 6.1

Learning Target: Use models and regrouping to subtract a one-digit number from a two-digit number.

Explore and Grow

Model each problem. Make quick sketches to show how you found the difference.

19 − 6

19 − 6 = _____

21 − 6

21 − 6 = _____

MP Structure Compare your quick sketches. What step did you use to find 21 − 6 that you did not use to find 19 − 6?

____

____

____

Think and Grow

Model 34. There are not enough ones to subtract 8. So, *regroup* 1 ten as 10 ones.

34 − 8 = ?

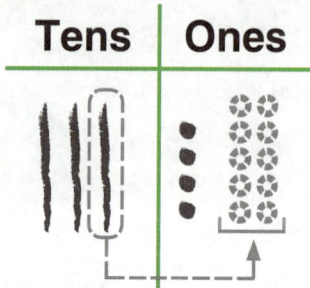

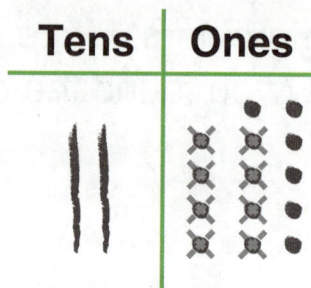

Tens	Ones

Regroup?

Yes No

Now there are 2 tens and 14 ones. Subtract 8. Count the tens and ones that are left. That is the difference!

Tens	Ones

2 tens 6 ones

34 − 8 = 26

Show and Grow *I can do it!*

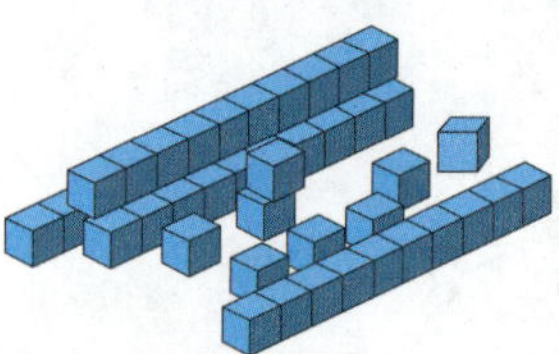

Use models to subtract. Draw to show your work.

1. 23 − 9 = ?

Regroup?

Yes No

Tens	Ones

Tens	Ones

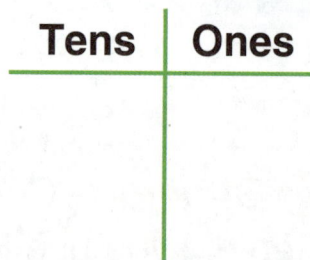

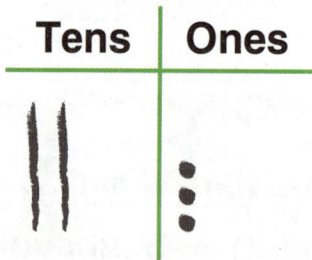

_____ tens _____ ones 23 − 9 = _____

Name ____

Apply and Grow: Practice

Use models to subtract. Draw to show your work.

2. 26 − 4 = ?

Regroup?

Yes   No

Tens	Ones

Tens	Ones

_____ tens _____ ones   26 − 4 = _____

3. 41 − 5 = ?

Regroup?

Yes   No

Tens	Ones

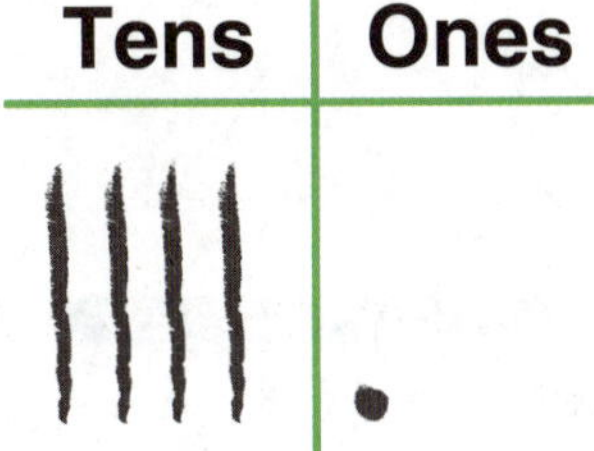

Tens	Ones

_____ tens _____ ones   41 − 5 = _____

4. 57 − 3 = ?

Regroup?

Yes   No

Tens	Ones

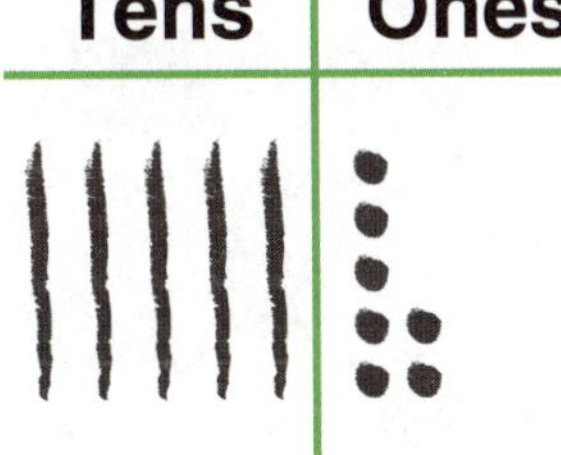

Tens	Ones

_____ tens _____ ones   57 − 3 = _____

5. MP **Number Sense** Which numbers can you subtract from 44 without regrouping?

5   3   4   6

Think and Grow: Modeling Real Life

You have 42 craft sticks. You use 8 of them. How many craft sticks are *not* used?

Subtraction equation:

Model:

Tens	Ones

Find a Rule Look at the ones digit in each number. Will you have to regroup? How do you know?

_____ craft sticks

Show and Grow *I can think deeper!*

6. There are 74 people in a theater. 7 of them leave. How many people are left?

_____ people

7. DIG DEEPER! You have 50 straws. You use some of them for a project. There are 44 left. How many straws did you use?

_____ straws

Name ______________________________

Practice 6.1

Learning Target: Use models and regrouping to subtract a one-digit number from a two-digit number.

42 − 6 = ?

Tens	Ones

Tens	Ones

Regroup?

Yes   No

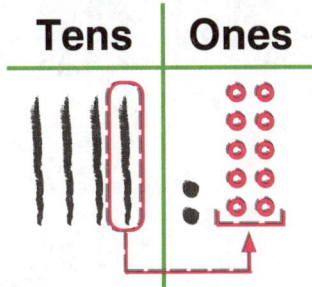

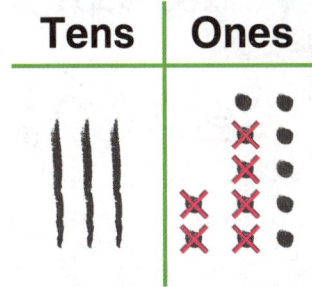

3 tens 6 ones   42 − 6 = 36

Use models to subtract. Draw to show your work.

1. 65 − 8 = ?

Tens	Ones

Tens	Ones

Regroup?

Yes   No

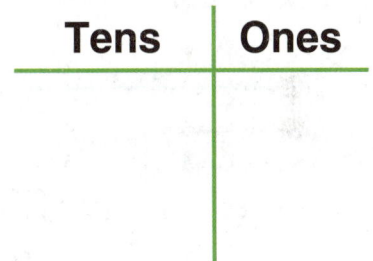

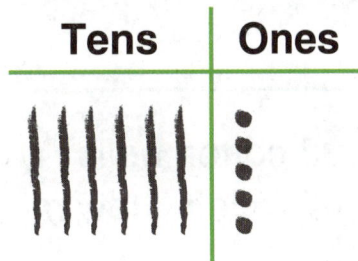

_____ tens _____ ones   65 − 8 = _____

2. 78 − 5 = ?

Tens	Ones

Tens	Ones

Regroup?

Yes   No

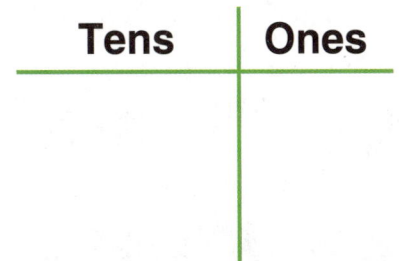

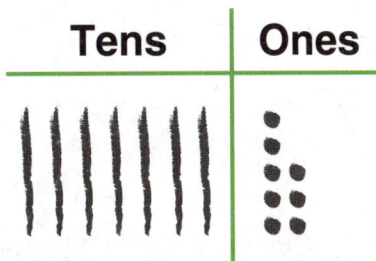

_____ tens _____ ones   78 − 5 = _____

3.  **YOU BE THE TEACHER** Is Newton correct? Explain.

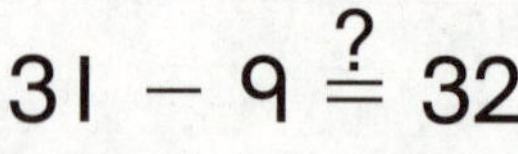

$31 - 9 \stackrel{?}{=} 32$

Regroup?

Yes   No

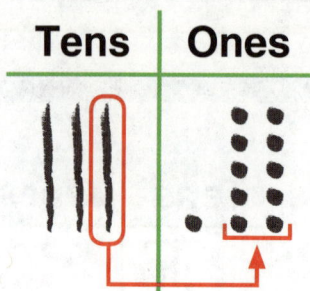

Tens	Ones

Tens	Ones

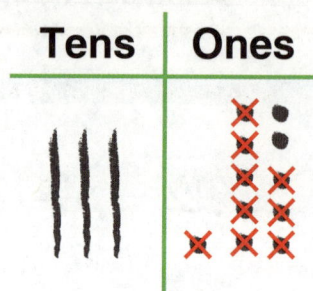

3 tens 2 ones

____

____

---

4. **Modeling Real Life** You have 26 magnets. You put 9 of them on your refrigerator. How many magnets are *not* on the refrigerator?

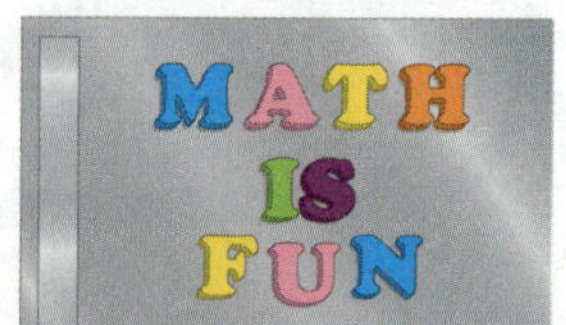

_____ magnets

---

5. **DIG DEEPER!** You have 83 cotton balls. You use some of them. There are 76 left. How many cotton balls do you use?

_____ cotton balls

Review & Refresh

6. $44 + 46 = ?$

$+$ ______

7. $28 + 34 = ?$

$+$ ______

8. $75 + 13 = ?$

$+$ ______

Name ____________________

Use Models to Subtract a One-Digit Number from a Two-Digit Number

6.2

Learning Target: Use models to subtract a one-digit number from a two-digit number.

Make a quick sketch to find 41 − 3.

41 − 3 = ______

Communicate Clearly How do you regroup 4 tens and 1 one to subtract 3?

____

____

____

Think and Grow

Model the number 23. There are not enough ones to subtract 5. So, regroup 1 ten as 10 ones.

Now there are 1 ten and 13 ones. Subtract the ones, then subtract the tens.

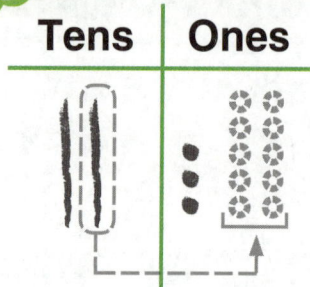

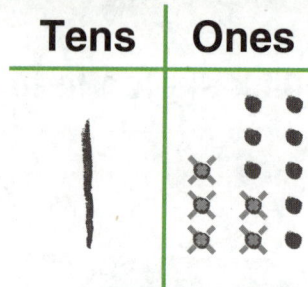

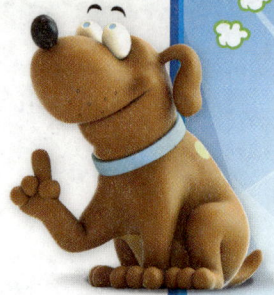

23 − 5 = ?

Tens	Ones
1	13
~~2~~	~~3~~
−	5

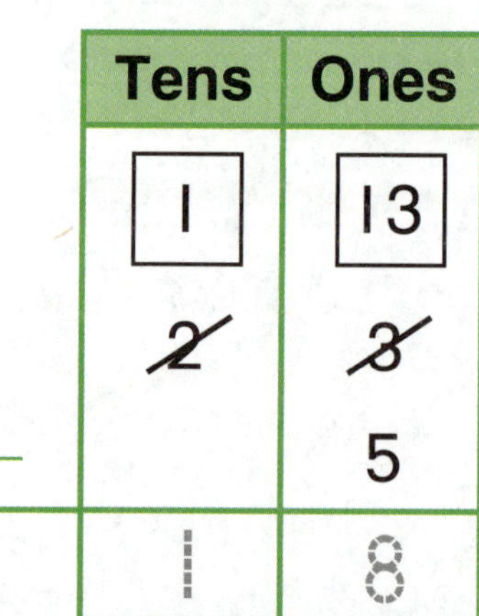

Tens	Ones
1	13
~~2~~	~~3~~
−	5
1	8

Show and Grow *I can do it!*

1. 31 − 4 = ?

Tens	Ones

Tens	Ones
☐	☐
3	1
−	4

Name ______________________________

Apply and Grow: Practice

2. 72 − 5 = ?

Tens	Ones

	Tens	Ones
	☐	☐
	7	2
−		5

3. 88 − 9 = ?

Tens	Ones

	Tens	Ones
	☐	☐
	8	8
−		9

4. 63 − 2 = ?

Tens	Ones

	Tens	Ones
	☐	☐
	6	3
−		2

5. 90 − 8 = ?

Tens	Ones

	Tens	Ones
	☐	☐
	9	0
−		8

6. MP **Number Sense** What one-digit numbers can you subtract from 24 without regrouping? Explain.

____

____

____

____

Think and Grow: Modeling Real Life

You catch 33 fish. You keep the state limit of 25. How many fish do you release?

Subtraction problem:

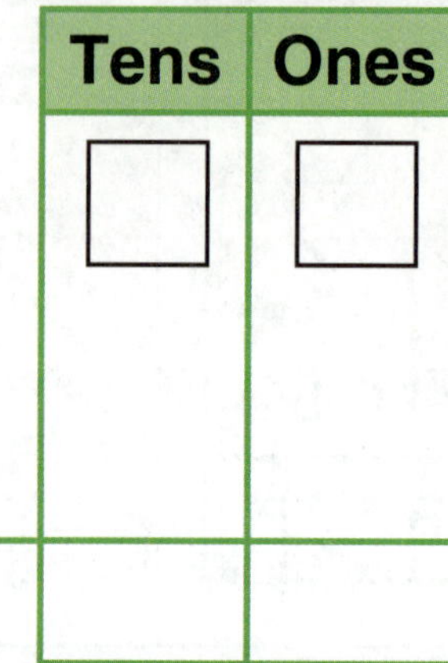

_____ fish

Show and Grow *I can think deeper!*

7. The temperature this morning was 72 degrees. This afternoon, it is 67 degrees. How much did the temperature drop?

_____ degrees

8. **DIG DEEPER!** You have a bowl of strawberries. You eat 7 of them. There are 19 left. How many strawberries were in the bowl to start?

_____ strawberries

Name ___________________________

Practice 6.2

Learning Target: Use models to subtract a one-digit number from a two-digit number.

Model the number 35. There are not enough ones to subtract 7. So, regroup 1 ten as 10 ones.

$35 - 7 = ?$

Now there are 2 tens and 15 ones. Subtract the ones, then subtract the tens.

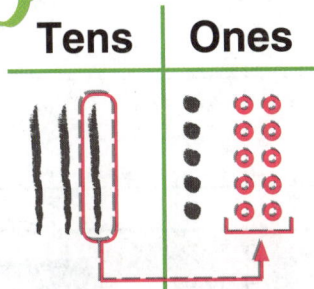

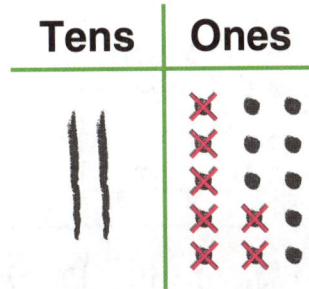

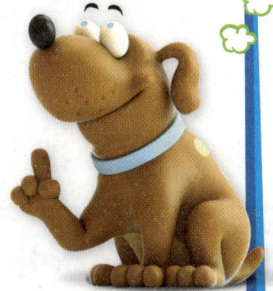

	Tens	Ones
	2	15
	~~3~~	~~5~~
−		7

	Tens	Ones
	2	15
	~~3~~	~~5~~
−		7
	2	8

1. $52 - 6 = ?$

	Tens	Ones
	☐	☐
	5	2
−		6

2. $78 - 5 = ?$

	Tens	Ones
	☐	☐
	7	8
−		5

3. **MP YOU BE THE TEACHER** Is Descartes correct? Explain.

	Tens	Ones
	☐	☐
	8	6
−		8
	8	2

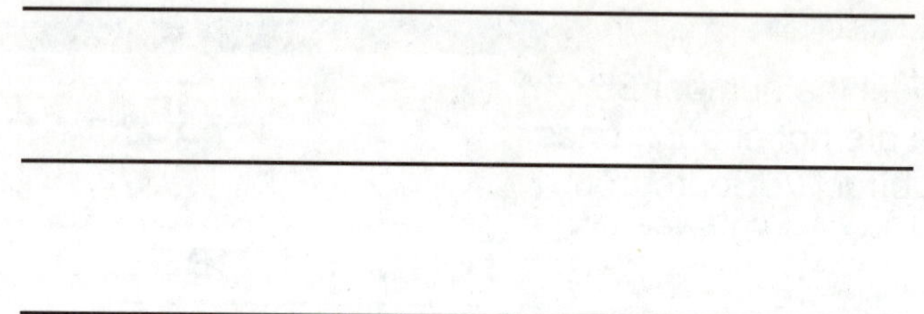

4. **MP Modeling Real Life** Descartes scores 8 more points than Newton. How many points did Newton score?

_____ points

5. **DIG DEEPER!** There are some piñata toys on the ground. 6 of your friends each pick 1 up. There are 17 left. How many toys were there to start?

_____ toys

Review & Refresh

Break apart an addend to find the sum.

6. $43 + 15 =$ _____

_____ + _____ + _____

_____ + _____ = _____

7. $22 + 77 =$ _____

_____ + _____ + _____

_____ + _____ = _____

Name ______________________________

Use Models to Subtract Two-Digit Numbers

6.3

Learning Target: Use models to subtract a two-digit number from a two-digit number.

Explore and Grow

Model the problem. Make a quick sketch to find 33 − 17.

33 − 17 = ______

Think and Grow

Model the number 32. There are not enough ones to subtract 3. So, regroup 1 ten as 10 ones.

32 − 13 = ?

Subtract 3 ones from 12 ones. Then subtract 1 ten from 2 tens.

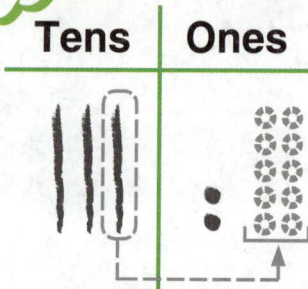

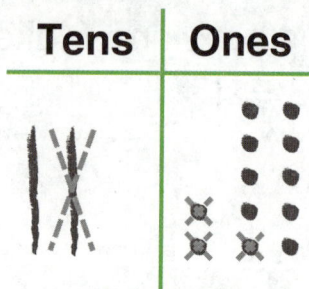

Tens	Ones
2	12
~~3~~	~~2~~
− 1	3

Tens	Ones
2	12
~~3~~	~~2~~
− 1	3
1	9

Show and Grow *I can do it!*

1. 55 − 18 = ?

Tens	Ones

Tens	Ones
☐	☐
5	5
− 1	8

Name ______________________________

Apply and Grow: Practice

2. 21 − 18 = ?

Tens	Ones

	Tens	Ones
	□	□
	2	1
−	1	8

3. 44 − 29 = ?

Tens	Ones

	Tens	Ones
	□	□
	4	4
−	2	9

4. 60 − 32 = ?

Tens	Ones

	Tens	Ones
	□	□
	6	0
−	3	2

5. 75 − 21 = ?

Tens	Ones

	Tens	Ones
	□	□
	7	5
−	2	1

6. MP **Number Sense** Use two of the numbers to write and solve a subtraction problem that requires regrouping.

68 56 37 25

	Tens	Ones
	□	□
−		

Think and Grow: Modeling Real Life

You have 68 flowers. You give 17 to Newton. Then you give 14 to Descartes. How many flowers do you have left?

Subtraction problems:

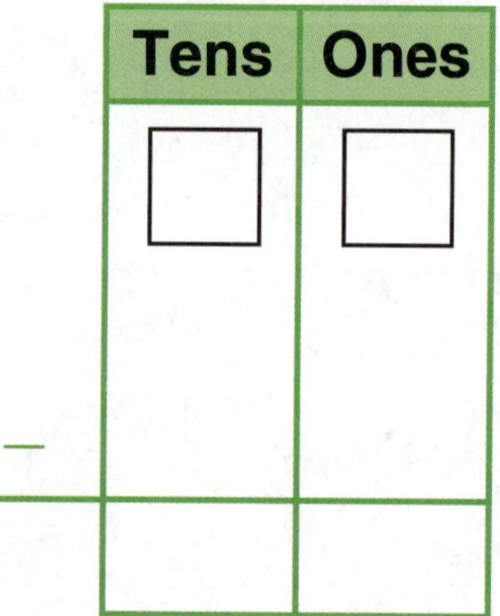

Tens	Ones
−	

_____ flowers

Show and Grow *I can think deeper!*

7. There are 32 pretzels. You eat 11 of them. Your friend eats 12 of them. How many pretzels are left?

_____ pretzels

8. Can you solve the problems on this page using addition and subtraction? Think: How do you know?

Yes No

Name ______________________________

Learning Target: Use models to subtract a two-digit number from a two-digit number.

68 − 49 = ?

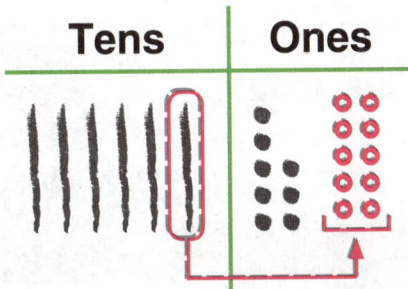

Tens	Ones
5	18
~~6~~	~~8~~
− 4	9

Tens	Ones
5	18
~~6~~	~~8~~
− 4	9
1	9

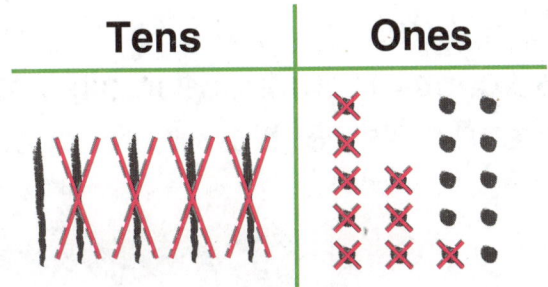

1. 84 − 60 = ?

Tens	Ones
8	4
− 6	0

2. 40 − 15 = ?

Tens	Ones
4	0
− 1	5

3. **Number Sense** Which numbers can you subtract from 55 without regrouping?

15 49 33 24

---

4. **Modeling Real Life** You and your friend have 38 cups of lemonade in all. You sell 14 cups. Your friend sells 16. How many cups are left?

_____ cups

---

5. **DIG DEEPER!** Write the missing numbers.

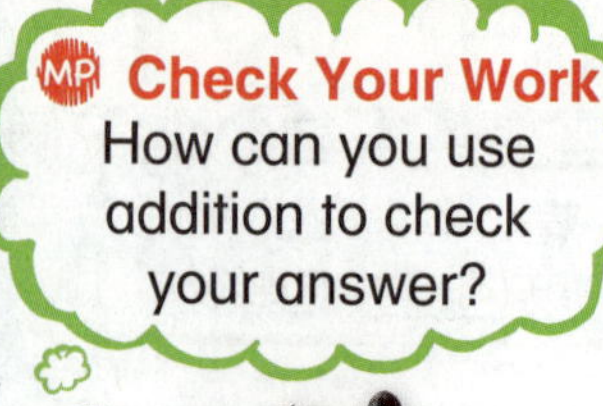

Check Your Work
How can you use addition to check your answer?

	Tens	Ones
	☐	☐
−	5	3
	3	4

Review & Refresh

6. A bookcase has 5 shelves. There are 3 plants on each shelf. How many plants are there in all?

_____ + _____ + _____ + _____ + _____ = _____ _____ plants

Name ______________________________

Subtract from a Two-Digit Number

6.4

Learning Target: Subtract a one- or two-digit number from a two-digit number.

Explore and Grow

Make quick sketches to find each difference.

$31 - 3 = ?$

	Tens	Ones
	☐	☐
	3	1
−		3

$31 - 3 =$ ______

$31 - 23 = ?$

	Tens	Ones
	☐	☐
	3	1
−	2	3

$31 - 23 =$ ______

Use a Similar Problem How are the problems the same? How are they different?

____

____

____

Think and Grow

There are not enough ones to subtract. So, regroup 1 ten as 10 ones.

41 − 16 = ?

	Tens	Ones
	3	11
	~~4~~	~~1~~
−	1	6
	2	5

Subtract the ones, then subtract the tens.

Show and Grow *I can do it!*

1. 52 − 19 = ?

	Tens	Ones
−		

2. 46 − 9 = ?

	Tens	Ones
−		

3. 60 − 21 = ?

	Tens	Ones
−		

4. 66 − 8 = ?

5. 84 − 2 = ?

6. 65 − 38 = ?

Name ___________________________

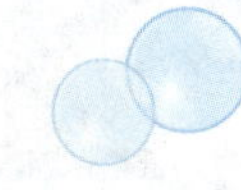

Apply and Grow: Practice

7. 58 − 22 = ?

8. 33 − 4 = ?

9. 22 − 15 = ?

10. 70 − 6 = ?

11. 43 − 26 = ?

12. 95 − 4 = ?

13. MP **Number Sense** Use the given numbers to complete the problem.

7

12

1

	Tens	Ones
	2	☐
	~~3~~	2
−	1	5

14. **DIG DEEPER!** Subtract a one-digit number from a two-digit number to complete the problem.

	Tens	Ones
	☐	☐
−		
	3	7

Think and Grow: Modeling Real Life

You pick 19 yellow flowers and 24 purple flowers. You give 8 flowers away. How many flowers do you have left?

Step 1: Find the total number of flowers you picked.

Step 2: Subtract the number of flowers you give away from your result in Step 1.

+ ______   − ______

______ flowers

Show and Grow *I can think deeper!*

15. You bake 36 blueberry muffins and 36 banana nut muffins. You sell 47 muffins. How many muffins do you have left?

______ muffins

16. There are 54 ladybugs. 7 fly away. Then 25 join. How many ladybugs are there now?

______ ladybugs

Name ___________________________

Learning Target: Subtract a one- or two-digit number from a two-digit number.

$54 - 38 = ?$

There are not enough ones to subtract. So, regroup 1 ten as 10 ones.

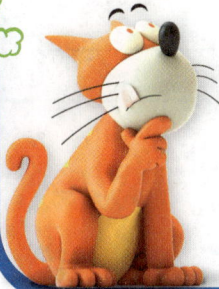

	Tens	Ones
	4	14
	~~5~~	~~4~~
−	3	8
	1	6

Subtract the ones, then subtract the tens.

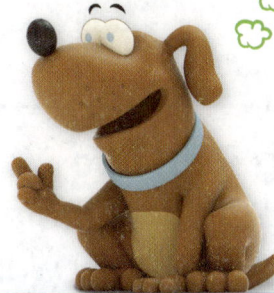

1. $25 - 7 = ?$

	Tens	Ones
	☐	☐
−		

2. $65 - 35 = ?$

	Tens	Ones
	☐	☐
−		

3. $33 - 29 = ?$

	Tens	Ones
	☐	☐
−		

4. $80 - 53 = ?$

5. $92 - 47 = ?$

6. $56 - 4 = ?$

7. **Writing** Write and solve a subtraction problem using 2 two-digit numbers. Write a story to match.

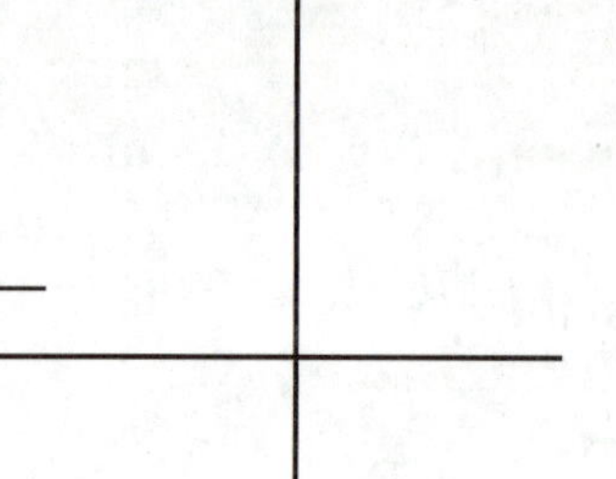

____

____

____

____

8. **MP Modeling Real Life** You fill up 17 large water balloons and 24 small water balloons. You break 26 balloons. How many water balloons do you have left?

_____ water balloons

9. **MP Modeling Real Life** You have 45 rings. You throw 28 of them. You earn a bonus and get 15 more rings to throw. How many rings do you have now?

_____ rings

Review & Refresh

10. How can you make a 10 to find $5 + 8$?

$10 + 3$ $\quad$ $10 + 8$ $\quad$ $10 + 4$ $\quad$ $10 + 5$

Name ______________________________

Use Addition to Check Subtraction 6.5

Learning Target: Use addition to check subtraction.

Explore and Grow

Write the equation shown by each model.

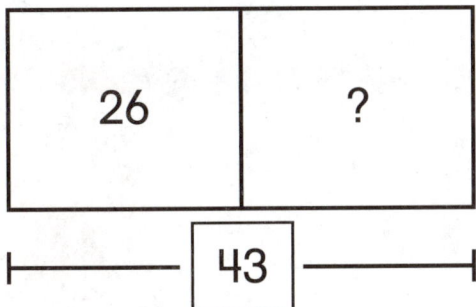

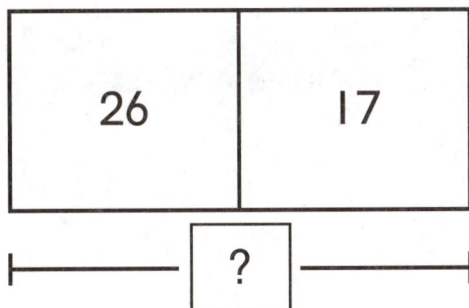

26	?
43	

26	17
?	

_____ − _____ = _____

_____ + _____ = _____

Analyze a Problem How are the equations related?

____

____

Explain how you can check whether 24 − 13 = 11 is correct.

____

____

Think and Grow

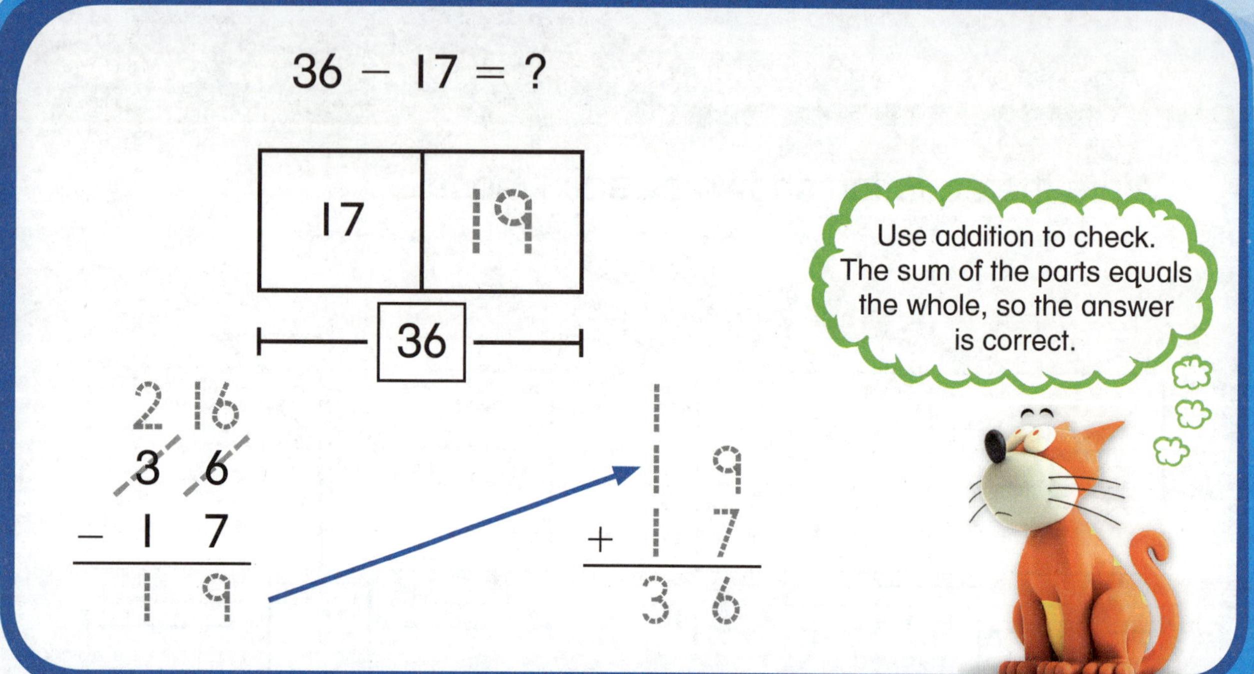

36 − 17 = ?
17
19
36
2 16
3 6
− 1 7
1 9
1
1 9
+ 1 7
3 6
Use addition to check. The sum of the parts equals the whole, so the answer is correct.

Show and Grow *I can do it!*

Find the difference. Use addition to check your answer.

1. 51 − 28 = ?

28	

51

$$\begin{array}{r} 51 \\ -\ 28 \\ \hline \end{array} \qquad + \underline{\qquad\qquad}$$

2. 75 − 37 = ?

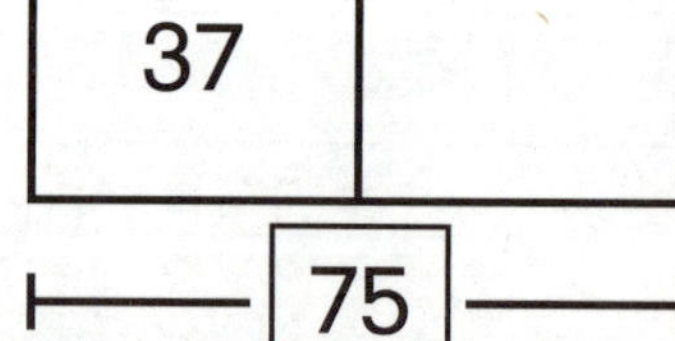

$$\begin{array}{r} 75 \\ -\ 37 \\ \hline \end{array} \qquad + \underline{\qquad\qquad}$$

Name ____________________

Apply and Grow: Practice

Find the difference. Use addition to check your answer.

3. $52 - 27 = ?$

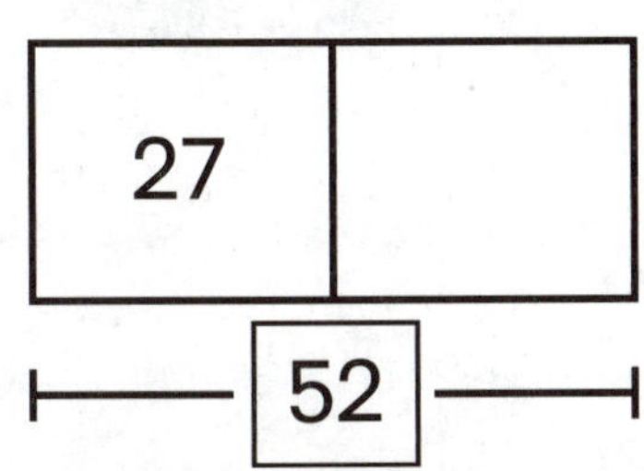

$$\begin{array}{r} 52 \\ -\ 27 \\ \hline \end{array} \qquad \begin{array}{r} \\ +\ \_\_ \\ \hline \end{array}$$

4. $76 - 58 = ?$

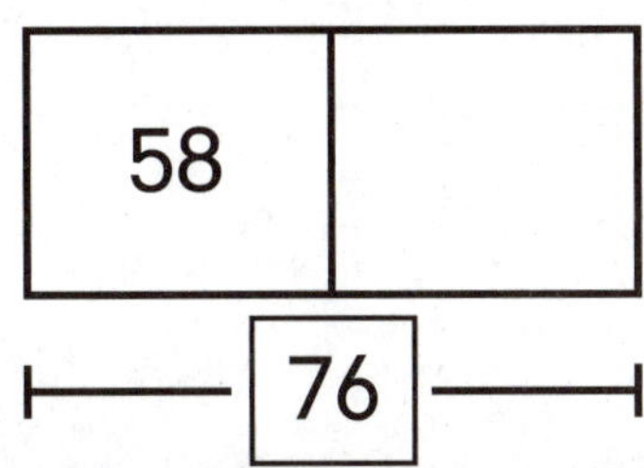

$$\begin{array}{r} 76 \\ -\ 58 \\ \hline \end{array} \qquad \begin{array}{r} \\ +\ \_\_ \\ \hline \end{array}$$

5.

$$\begin{array}{r} 30 \\ -\ 14 \\ \hline \end{array} \qquad \begin{array}{r} \\ +\ \_\_ \\ \hline \end{array}$$

6.

$$\begin{array}{r} 63 \\ -\ 6 \\ \hline \end{array} \qquad \begin{array}{r} \\ +\ \_\_ \\ \hline \end{array}$$

7.

$$\begin{array}{r} 90 \\ -\ 40 \\ \hline \end{array} \qquad \begin{array}{r} \\ +\ \_\_ \\ \hline \end{array}$$

8.

$$\begin{array}{r} 47 \\ -\ 39 \\ \hline \end{array} \qquad \begin{array}{r} \\ +\ \_\_ \\ \hline \end{array}$$

9. MP **Reasoning** Newton uses $16 + 37$ to check his answer to a subtraction problem. What two subtraction problems could he have solved?

_____ − _____ = _____

_____ − _____ = _____

Think and Grow: Modeling Real Life

A joke book has 96 jokes. 58 are knock-knock jokes. The rest are riddles. How many riddles are there?

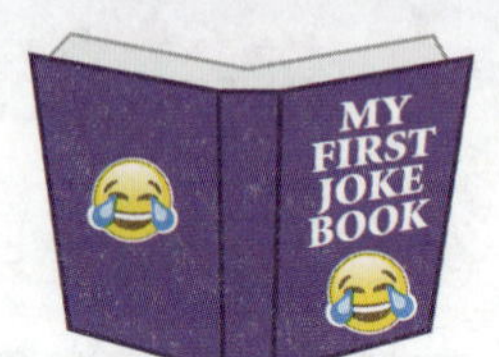

Subtraction problem:

−

Check:

\+

______ riddles

Show and Grow *I can think deeper!*

10. A museum has 71 fossils. 47 are dinosaur fossils. The rest are fish fossils. How many fish fossils are there?

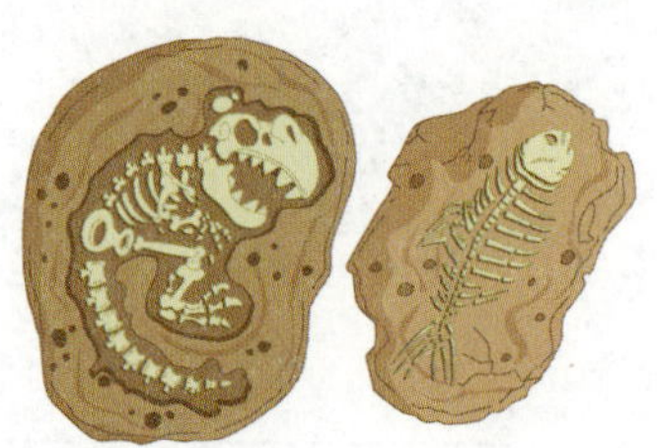

______ fish fossils

11. There are 27 more countries in Europe than in North America. There are 50 countries in Europe. How many countries are there in North America?

______ countries

Name ______________________________

Practice 6.5

Learning Target: Use addition to check subtraction.

Subtract to find the missing part.

$73 - 38 = ?$

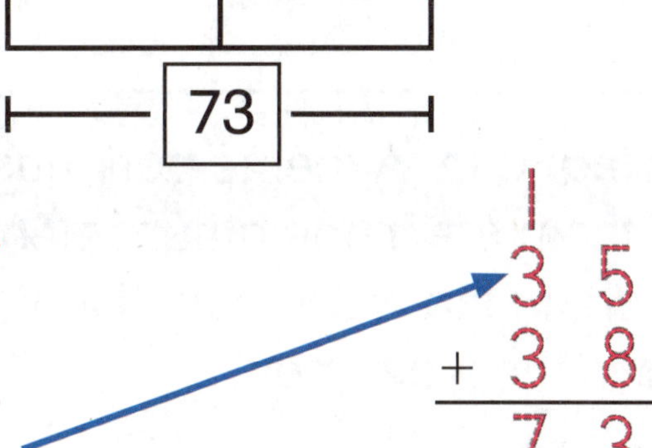

Use addition to check. The sum of the parts equals the whole, so the answer is correct.

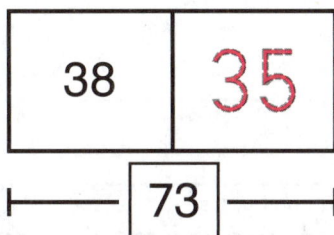

$$\begin{array}{r} \overset{6}{\cancel{7}}\,\overset{13}{\cancel{3}} \\ -\;3\;8 \\ \hline 3\;5 \end{array} \qquad \begin{array}{r} \overset{1}{3}\;5 \\ +\;3\;8 \\ \hline 7\;3 \end{array}$$

Find the difference. Use addition to check your answer.

1. $44 - 21 = ?$

21	
44	

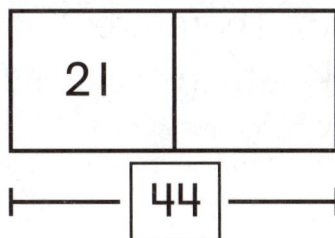

$$\begin{array}{r} 4\;4 \\ -\;2\;1 \\ \hline \end{array} \qquad + \underline{\qquad}$$

2.
$$\begin{array}{r} 2\;3 \\ -\;1\;4 \\ \hline \end{array} \qquad + \underline{\qquad}$$

3.
$$\begin{array}{r} 5\;9 \\ -\;2\;9 \\ \hline \end{array} \qquad + \underline{\qquad}$$

4.
$$\begin{array}{r} 7\;0 \\ -\;\;\;8 \\ \hline \end{array} \qquad + \underline{\qquad}$$

5.
$$\begin{array}{r} 8\;2 \\ -\;4\;7 \\ \hline \end{array} \qquad + \underline{\qquad}$$

6. **Compare Arguments** Your friend subtracts to find 44 − 18 = 26. He uses 26 + 18 to check his work. Your cousin tells him he should use 18 + 26. Who is correct? Explain how you know.

____

____

7. **Modeling Real Life** A theme park has 62 rides. 45 of them are in the amusement park. The rest are in the water park. How many rides are in the water park?

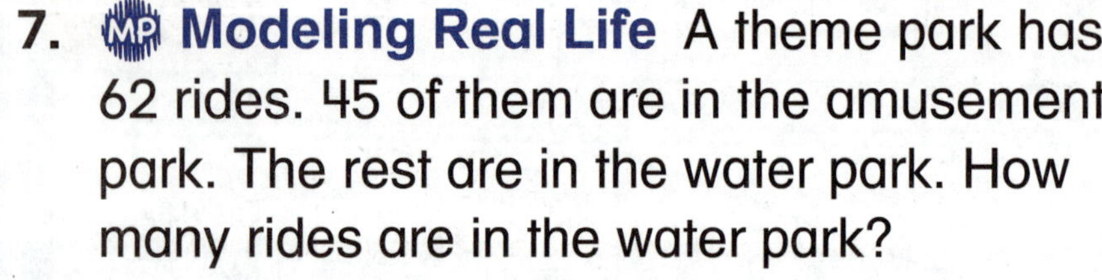

_____ rides

8. **Modeling Real Life** There are 58 more books in a library than in a classroom. There are 94 books in the library. How many books are in the classroom?

_____ books

Review & Refresh

Use compensation to solve.

9. 18 + 44 = ____

○____ ○____

____ + ____ = ____

10. 63 + 27 = ____

○____ ○____

____ + ____ = ____

Name ______________________

Practice Two-Digit Subtraction

6.6

Learning Target: Subtract two-digit numbers.

Explore and Grow

Work with a partner. Choose different strategies to find 76 − 29.

Subtraction Strategies
Subtract on an Open Number Line
Add On to Subtract
Break Apart
Compensation
Model and Regroup to Subtract

Compare your strategy to your partner's. Are your answers the same? Which strategy do you prefer? Why?

____

____

____

Think and Grow

$63 - 24 = ?$

One Way: Break apart 24.

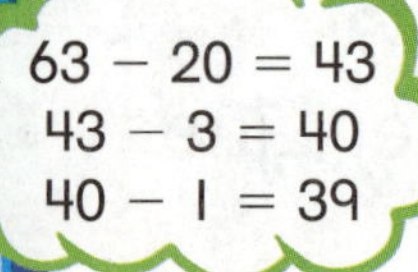

$63 - 24 = \underline{39}$

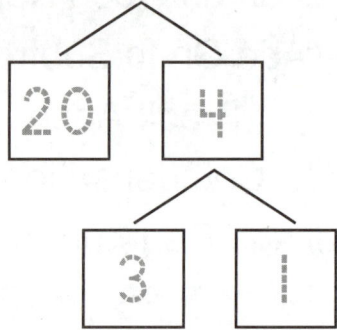

24 → 20 and 4

4 → 3 and 1

Another Way: Use place value.

5	13
~~6~~	~~3~~
− 2	4
3	9

Regroup 6 tens and 3 ones as 5 tens and 13 ones.

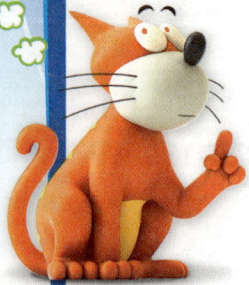

Show and Grow *I can do it!*

Use any strategy to find the difference.

1. $52 - 25 =$ ____
2. $78 - 56 =$ ____
3. $61 - 33 =$ ____
4. $83 - 37 =$ ____
5. $72 - 49 =$ ____
6. $45 - 39 =$ ____
7. $69 - 58 =$ ____
8. $94 - 45 =$ ____
9. $86 - 48 =$ ____

Name ______________________________

Apply and Grow: Practice

Use any strategy to find the difference.

10. 95 − 38 = ____

11. 66 − 47 = ____

12. 58 − 6 = ____

13. 81 − 35 = ____

14. 43 − 17 = ____

15. 37 − 18 = ____

16. 28 − 19 = ____

17. 72 − 30 = ____

18. 82 − 4 = ____

19. DIG DEEPER! Fill in the missing digits.

$$\begin{array}{rr} 6 & 16 \\ \square & \square \\ - \square & \square \\ \hline 4 & 7 \end{array}$$

20. MP YOU BE THE TEACHER Is Descartes correct? Explain.

____

____

____

____

Think and Grow: Modeling Real Life

Is there a greater difference between the number of guests on Saturday and Sunday or on Sunday and Monday?

Aquarium Attendance	
Day	**Number of Guests**
Saturday	92
Sunday	77
Monday	59

Subtraction problems:

− ______   − ______

Compare: _____ ◯ _____

Saturday and Sunday   Sunday and Monday

Show and Grow *I can think deeper!*

21. Is there a greater difference between the number of bagels sold on Sunday and Monday or on Monday and Tuesday?

Bagel Shop Sales	
Day	**Number of Bagels Sold**
Sunday	81
Monday	47
Tuesday	68

Sunday and Monday   Monday and Tuesday

Name ______________________________

Practice 6.6

Learning Target: Subtract two-digit numbers.

42 − 35 = ?

One Way: Break apart 35.

42 − 30 = 12
12 − 2 = 10
10 − 3 = 7

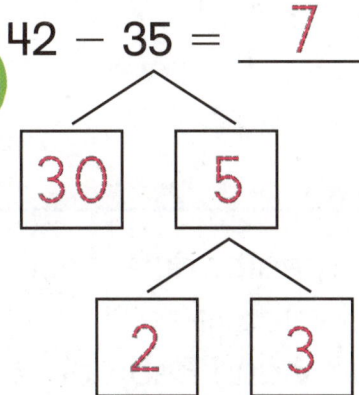

42 − 35 = 7

30 5

2 3

Another Way: Regroup.

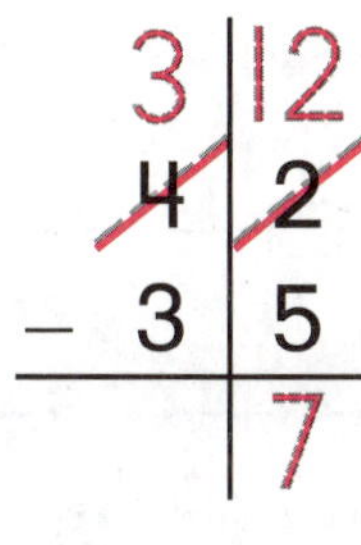

Regroup 4 tens and 2 ones as 3 tens and 12 ones.

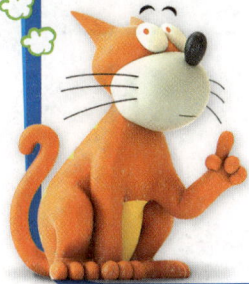

Use any strategy to find the difference.

1. 34 − 26 = ____

2. 75 − 47 = ____

3. 96 − 48 = ____

4. 51 − 21 = ____

5. 23 − 16 = ____

6. 47 − 8 = ____

7. 25 − 3 = ____

8. 87 − 69 = ____

9. 48 − 29 = ____

10. **Number Sense** Find each missing number.

26 − 18 = 27 − ____

15 − 7 = 16 − ____

57 − 35 = 58 − ____

11. **DIG DEEPER!** Descartes swims 5 fewer laps than Newton. Descartes swims a total of 18 laps. Your friend swims 17 laps. How many more laps does Newton swim than your friend?

____ laps

12. **Modeling Real Life** Is there a greater difference between the number of animals adopted in December and January or in January and February?

Animal Rescue Center	
Month	**Number of Animals Adopted**
December	61
January	54
February	46

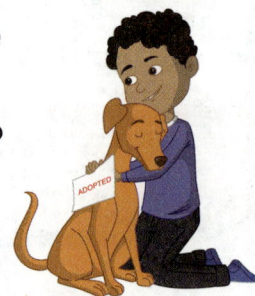

December and January   January and February

Review & Refresh

13.

2 + 8 = ____

10 − 8 = ____

14.

5 + 6 = ____

11 − 6 = ____

15.

9 + 8 = ____

17 − 8 = ____

Name ______________________________

More Problem Solving: Subtraction 6.7

Learning Target: Solve one- and two-step problems.

Explore and Grow

Model the story.

Newton has 34 balloons. 18 fly away. How many balloons does Newton have left?

Choose Tools Which tool did you use to help solve? Why?

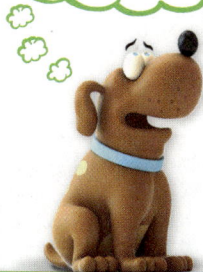

_____ balloons

Think and Grow

Some birds are on a wire. 9 fly away. There are 18 left.
How many birds were there to start?

Circle what you know. Underline what you need to find.

Solve:

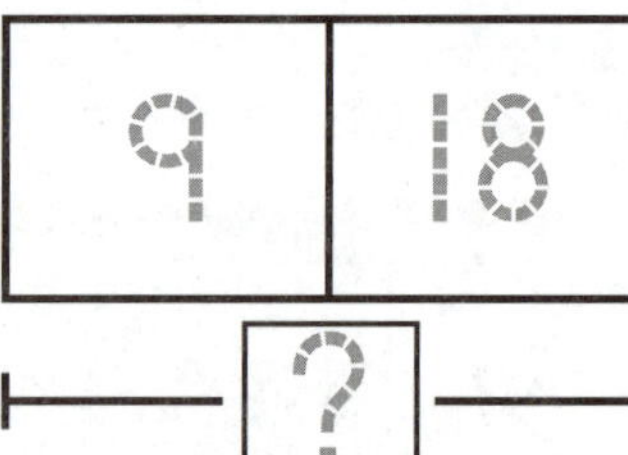

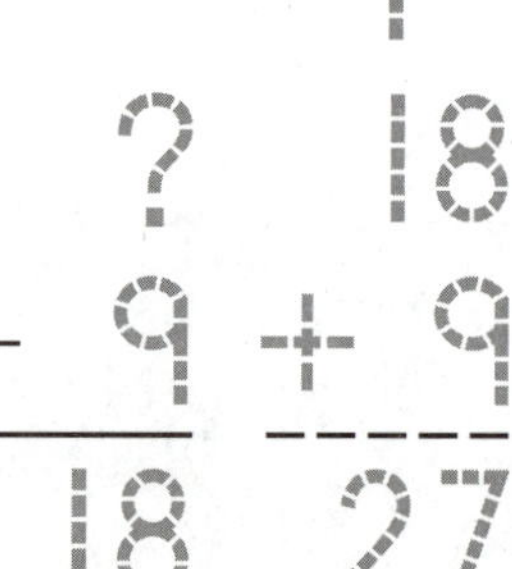

Add the parts to find the whole.

Use a model to help organize the information.

27 birds

Show and Grow *I can do it!*

1. There are 27 more harmonicas than drums in a music room. There are 55 harmonicas. How many drums are there?

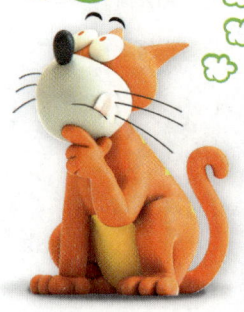

Harmonicas: ______

Drums: ______

−
______

______ drums

Name ______________________________

Apply and Grow: Practice

2. There are 71 fish crackers. You eat 29 of them. Your friend eats 28. How many fish crackers are left?

______ fish crackers

3. Newton solves 16 more math problems than Descartes. Newton solves 34 math problems. How many math problems does Descartes solve?

______ math problems

4. **Number Sense** You have 78 tokens. Your friend gives you 14 more. You use 35 tokens. Use the given numbers to find how many tokens you have now.

14	35
57	92

Step 1:

$$\begin{array}{r} 78 \\ + \square \\ \hline \square \end{array}$$

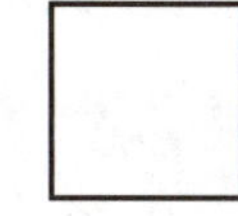

Step 2:

$$\begin{array}{r} 92 \\ - \square \\ \hline \square \end{array}$$

______ tokens

Think and Grow: Modeling Real Life

You see 20 elephants on a safari. You see 7 fewer giraffes than elephants. Then 5 of the giraffes leave the group. How many giraffes are left?

Step 1: $-$ ______

Step 2: $-$ ______

Check:

______ giraffes

Show and Grow *I can think deeper!*

5. Your friend has 54 blocks. You have 18 fewer blocks than your friend. You use 29 blocks to make a tower. How many blocks do you have left?

______ blocks

6. DIG DEEPER! You had 19 almonds. You ate some. There are 11 left. Your friend ate 3 fewer almonds than you. How many almonds did your friend eat?

______ almonds

Name ______________________________

Practice 6.7

Learning Target: Solve one- and two-step problems.

Descartes wins 25 more games of limbo than Newton. Descartes wins 43 games. How many games does Newton win?

Circle what you know. Underline what you need to find.

Solve:

Descartes:	43	
Newton:	18	25

$$\begin{array}{r} \overset{3}{\cancel{4}}\,\overset{13}{\cancel{3}} \\ -\ 2\ 5 \\ \hline 1\ 8 \end{array}$$

18 games

1. Some kids are at a trampoline park. 24 leave. There are 57 left. How many kids were there to start?

______ kids

2. MP **Modeling Real Life** You have 62 dollars saved. You spend 37 dollars on a video game. Then you give 16 dollars to your friend. How many dollars do you have left?

______ dollars

3. **MP Structure** You have 50 toothpicks. Your friend has 30 fewer toothpicks than you. Which picture shows how many toothpicks you and your friend have in all?

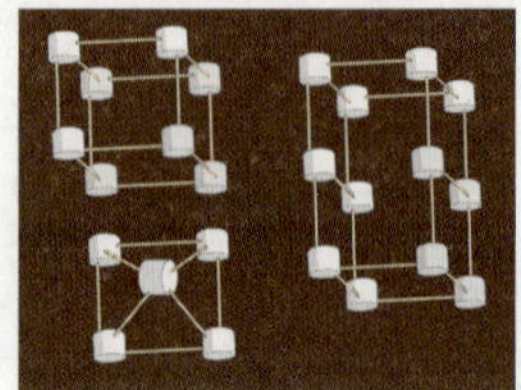

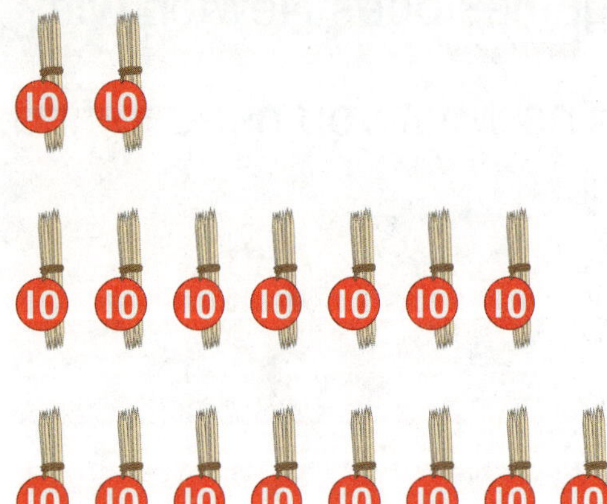

4. **DIG DEEPER!** A museum has 12 dinosaur exhibits and some art exhibits. There are 34 exhibits in all. Then 3 more art exhibits are added. How many art exhibits are there now?

_____ art exhibits

Review & Refresh

Break apart the addends to find the sum.

5. 74 → _____ + _____
+21 → _____ + _____
_____ + _____
= _____

6. 38 → _____ + _____
+59 → _____ + _____
_____ + _____
= _____

Name ______________________________

Performance Task 6

1. Your class makes 53 paper snowflakes to decorate your classroom.

a. Your group makes 16 of them. How many snowflakes does the other group make?

_____ snowflakes

b. Your teacher hangs 49 of the snowflakes from the ceiling in an array with 7 equal rows. How many columns of snowflakes are there?

_____ columns

c. Your teacher wants to hang one more equal row of snowflakes. Are there enough snowflakes? If so, how many extra snowflakes are there? If not, how many more snowflakes are needed?

Yes No

_____ extra snowflakes _____ more snowflakes

2. Another class makes 75 paper snowflakes. 29 are white and some are blue. They make some more blue snowflakes. Now they have 61 blue snowflakes. How many more blue snowflakes did they make?

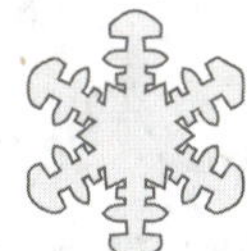

_____ more blue snowflakes

Solve and Cover: Subtraction

To Play: Use Solve and Cover: Subtraction Cards. Place a Difference Card face up on each box. Place the stack of Problem Cards face down. Players take turns. On your turn, flip over a card from the stack. Solve the problem. Place the card on the difference. Play until all of the differences are covered.

Name ______________________________________

Chapter Practice

6.1 Model and Regroup to Subtract

1. Use models to subtract. Draw to show your work.

22 − 4 = ?

Regroup?

Yes No

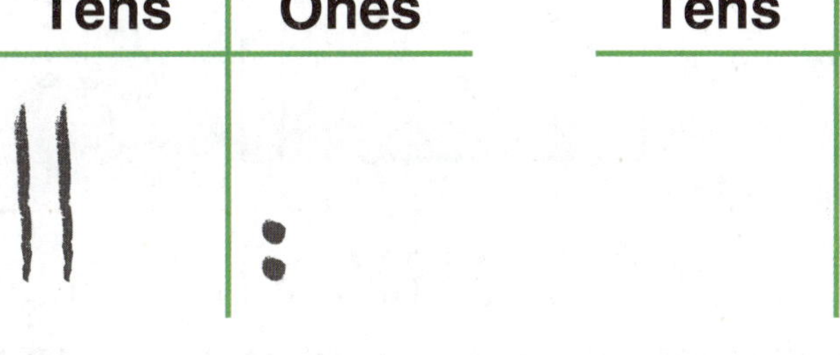

Tens	Ones

Tens	Ones

_____ tens _____ ones 22 − 4 = _____

6.2 Use Models to Subtract a One-Digit Number from a Two-Digit Number

2. 60 − 8 = ?

Tens	Ones

	Tens	Ones
	☐	☐
	6	0
−		8

3. 74 − 3 = ?

Tens	Ones

	Tens	Ones
	☐	☐
	7	4
−		3

6.3 Use Models to Subtract Two-Digit Numbers

4. 45 − 38 = ?

Tens	Ones

	Tens	Ones
	☐	☐
	4	5
−	3	8

5. 74 − 27 = ?

Tens	Ones

	Tens	Ones
	☐	☐
	7	4
−	2	7

6. MP **Number Sense** Use two of the numbers to write and solve a subtraction problem that requires regrouping.

21 45

63 87

	Tens	Ones
	☐	☐
−		

6.4 Subtract from a Two-Digit Number

7. 93 − 50 = ?

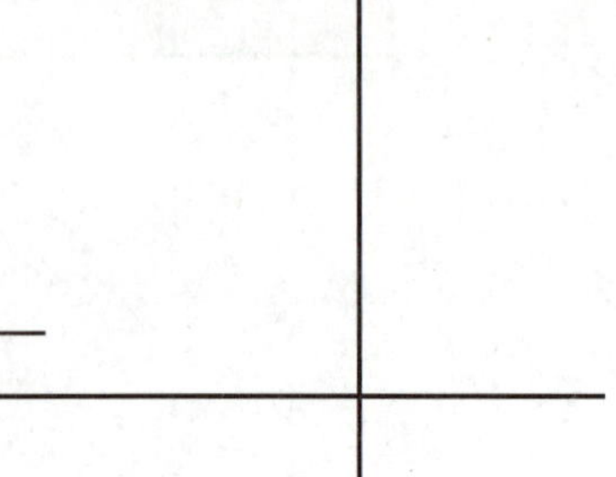

8. 57 − 28 = ?

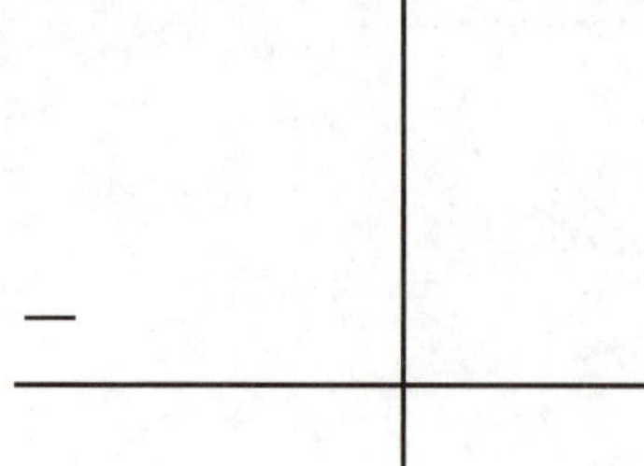

9. 67 − 9 = ?

6.5 Use Addition to Check Subtraction

Find the difference. Use addition to check your answer.

10. $64 - 27 = ?$

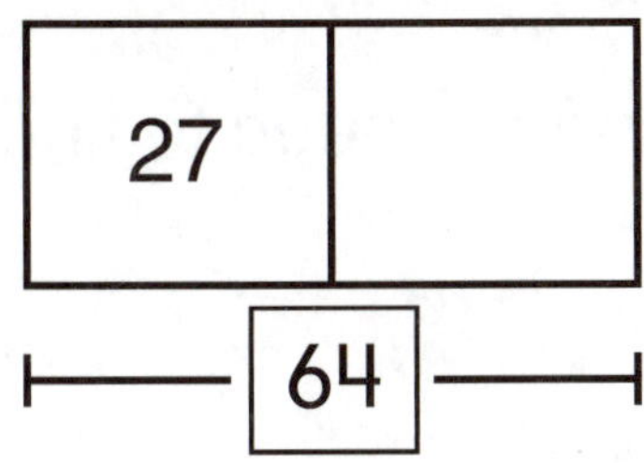

$$\begin{array}{r} 64 \\ -\ 27 \\ \hline \end{array} \qquad + \underline{\qquad}$$

11. $86 - 36 = ?$

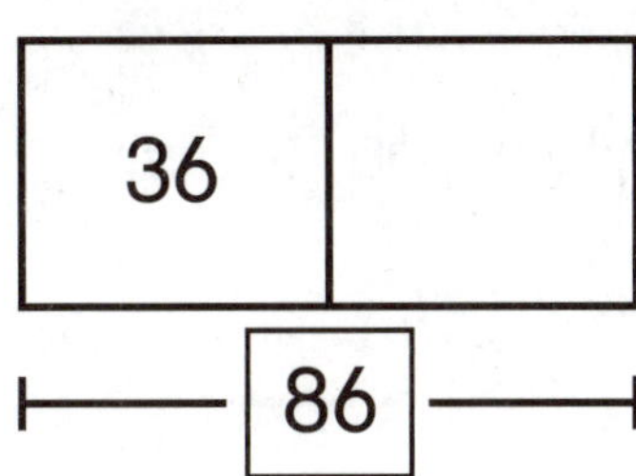

$$\begin{array}{r} 86 \\ -\ 36 \\ \hline \end{array} \qquad + \underline{\qquad}$$

12.

$$\begin{array}{r} 50 \\ -\ 46 \\ \hline \end{array} \qquad + \underline{\qquad}$$

13.

$$\begin{array}{r} 32 \\ -\ \ 7 \\ \hline \end{array} \qquad + \underline{\qquad}$$

6.6 Practice Two-Digit Subtraction

Use any strategy to find the difference.

14. $55 - 37 =$ ____

15. $60 - 20 =$ ____

16. $39 - 3 =$ ____

6.7 More Problem Solving: Subtraction

17. Newton has some BINGO chips. He gives 25 of them away. He has 28 left. How many chips did he have to start?

Circle what you know.

Underline what you need to find.

Solve:

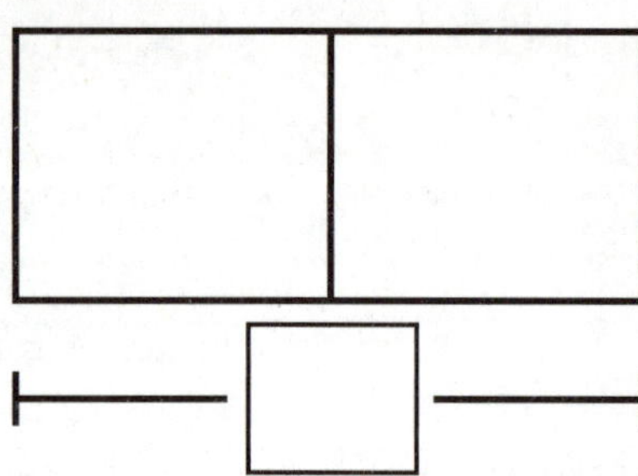

−

______ chips

18. Number Sense You have 35 balls. You use 18 of them. You win a bonus and get 10 more balls. Use the given numbers to find how many balls you have now.

10	17
18	27

Step 1:

35
− ☐
☐

Step 2:

17
+ ☐
☐

______ balls

19. Modeling Real Life A petting zoo has 27 sheep and some goats. There are 41 animals in all. Then 16 more goats are added. How many goats are there now?

______ goats

7 Understand Place Value to 1,000

Chapter Learning Target:
Understand place value.

Chapter Success Criteria:

- I can identify different numbers.
- I can explain the values of numbers.
- I can model and write numbers.
- I can represent numbers in different ways.

- What is your favorite snack?
- One package of trail mix contains about 225 nuts and 50 raisins. What is the value of the digit 5 in 225? in 50? Are the values the same?

Name ___

7 Vocabulary

Review Words
digits
ones place
tens place

Organize It

Use the review words to complete the graphic organizer.

The [ ] of 58 are 5 and 8.

58

[ ] → 5   [ ] → 8

Define It

Use your vocabulary cards to identify the word.

1. 300 + 20 + 9 [ ]

2. three hundred twenty-nine [ ]

3. 329 [ ]

Chapter 7 Vocabulary Cards

expanded form

hundred

hundreds place

standard form

thousand

word form

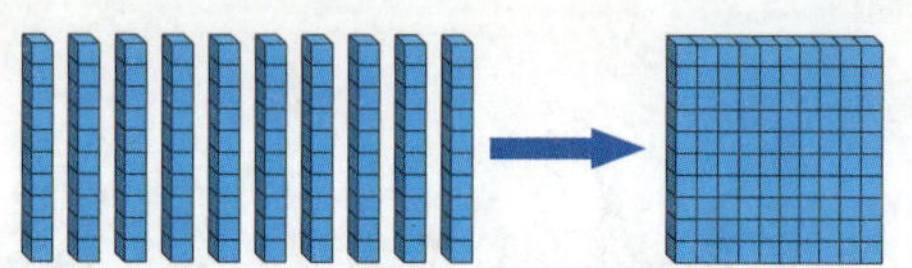

There are 10 tens in 1 hundred.

300 + 20 + 9

329

329

three hundred twenty-nine

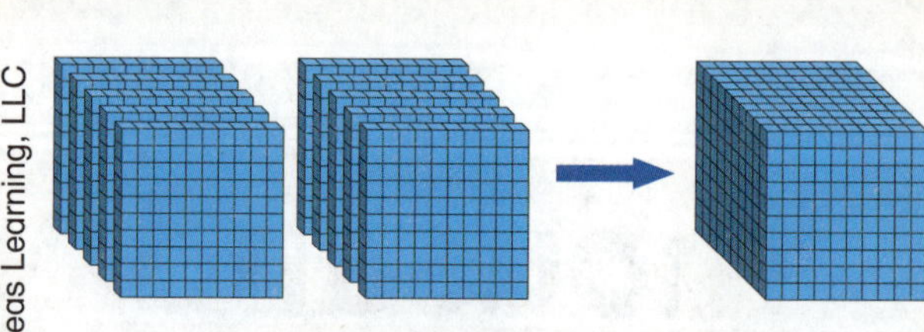

There are 10 hundreds in 1 thousand.

Name ______________________________

Hundreds 7.1

Learning Target: Identify groups of tens as hundreds.

How many unit cubes and rods are in a flat?

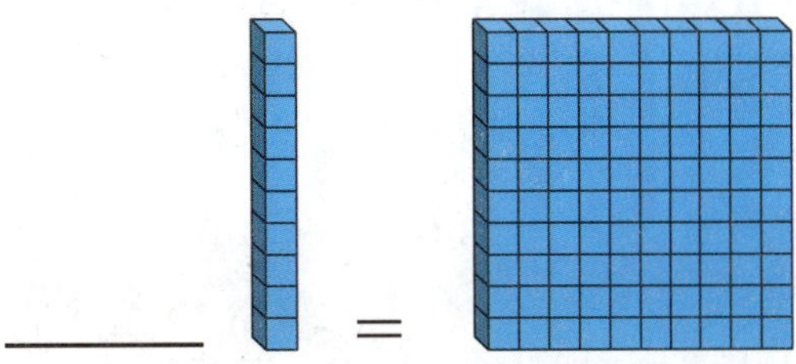

_____ [unit cube] = [flat]

_____ [rod] = [flat]

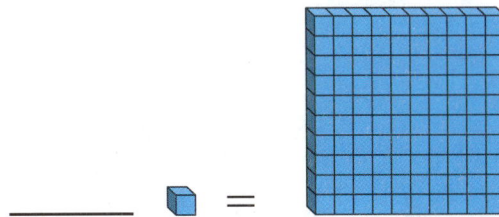

Think and Grow

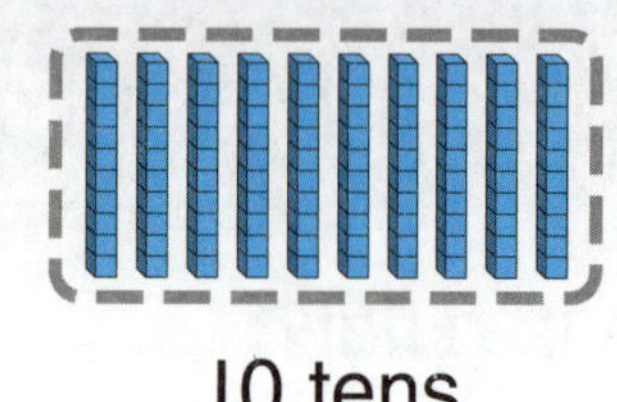

10 tens

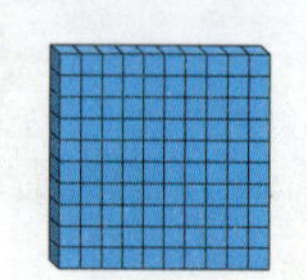

1 **hundred** or 100

10 tens

1 hundred

100

Show and Grow *I can do it!*

Write how many tens. Circle groups of 10 tens. Write how many hundreds. Then write the number.

1.

_____ tens

_____ hundreds

_____

2.

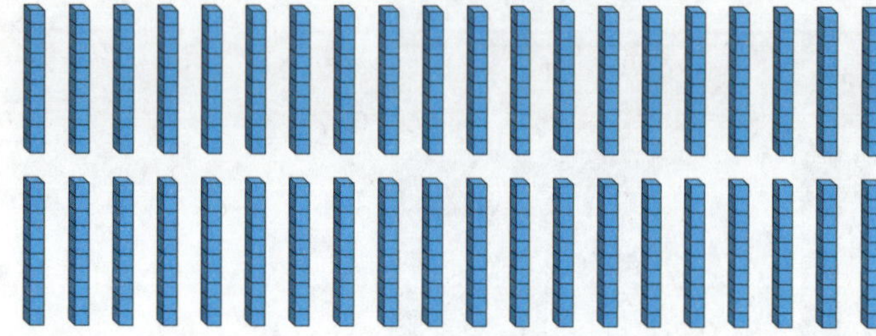

_____ tens

_____ hundreds

_____

Name ______________________________

Apply and Grow: Practice

Write how many tens. Circle groups of 10 tens. Write how many hundreds. Then write the number.

3. 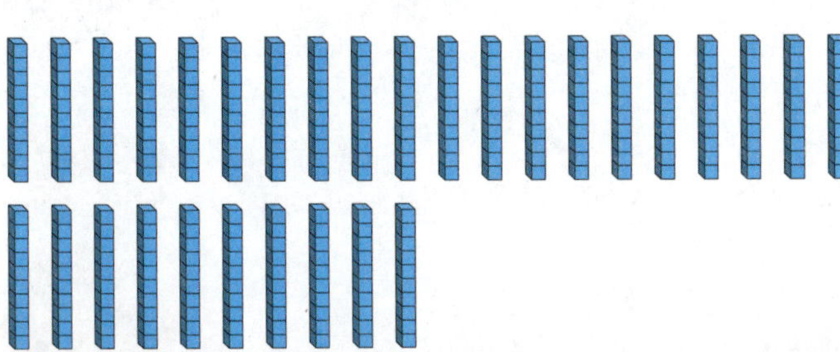

_____ tens

_____ hundreds

_____

4. 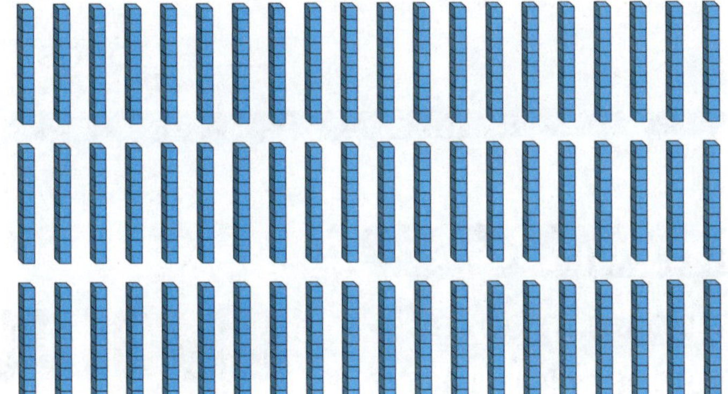

_____ tens

_____ hundreds

_____

5. **DIG DEEPER!** How many hundreds are in 700? How many tens?

_____ hundreds

_____ tens

6. You have 80 bags of crayons. There are 10 crayons in each bag. How many crayons do you have in all?

_____ crayons

Think and Grow: Modeling Real Life

A store sells oranges in bags of 10. The store sells 500 oranges. How many bags do they sell?

Make a quick sketch:

Make a Plan
Will you draw rods or flats to solve? Explain.

______ bags

Show and Grow *I can think deeper!*

7. A store sells bottles of glitter glue in boxes of 10. The store sells 600 bottles. How many boxes do they sell?

______ boxes

8. **DIG DEEPER!** You have 10 packages of invitations. Each package has 10 invitations. You need 300 invitations. How many more packages do you need?

______ more packages

Name ______________________

Practice 7.1

Learning Target: Identify groups of tens as hundreds.

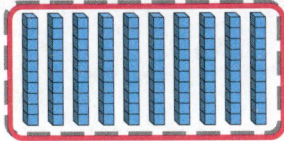

20 tens

2 hundreds

200

Write how many tens. Circle groups of 10 tens. Write how many hundreds. Then write the number.

1. 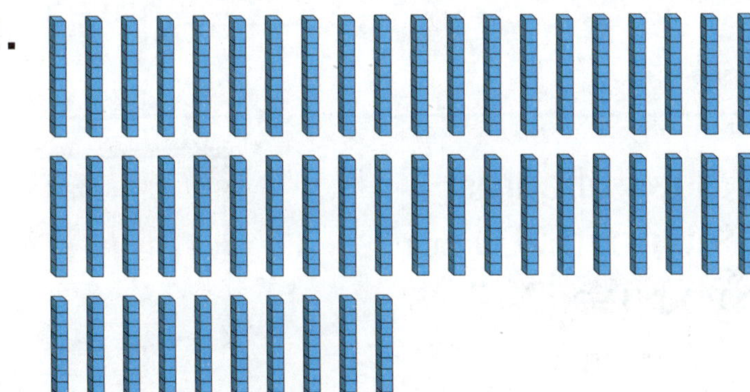

_____ tens

_____ hundreds

_____

2. 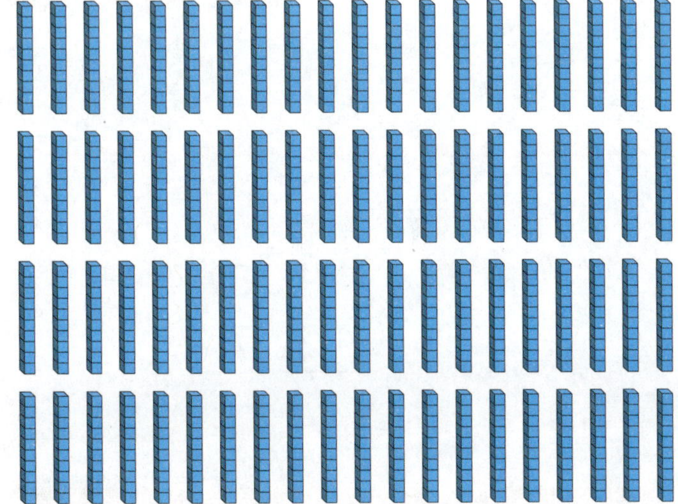

_____ tens

_____ hundreds

_____

3. Which One Doesn't Belong? Which does *not* belong with the other three?

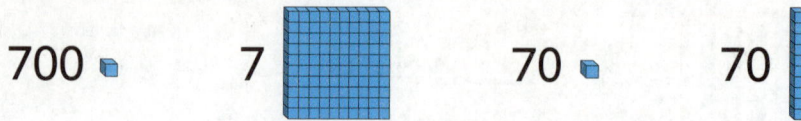

700  7 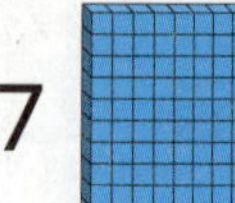 70 ▪ 70 ▮

---

4. Modeling Real Life A class has 30 boxes of pencils. Each box has 10 pencils. The class needs 600 pencils. How many more boxes does the class need?

_____ boxes

---

5. DIG DEEPER! You have 10 packages of cards. Each package has 10 cards. You need 200 cards. How many more packages do you need?

_____ more packages

Review & Refresh

6.

$$\begin{array}{r} 65 \\ +\ 34 \\ \hline \end{array}$$

7.

$$\begin{array}{r} 48 \\ +\ 27 \\ \hline \end{array}$$

Name ____________________

Model Numbers to 1,000 7.2

Learning Target: Model and write numbers to 1,000.

Explore and Grow

Model the number. Make a quick sketch to match.

138

Think and Grow

The 2 is in the **hundreds place**. The 3 is in the tens place. The 1 is in the ones place.

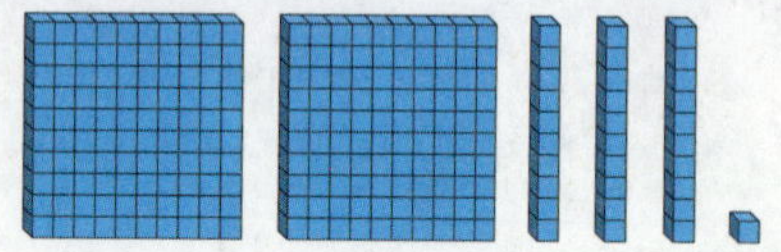

Hundreds	Tens	Ones
2	3	1

2 hundreds, 3 tens, and 1 ones is 231.

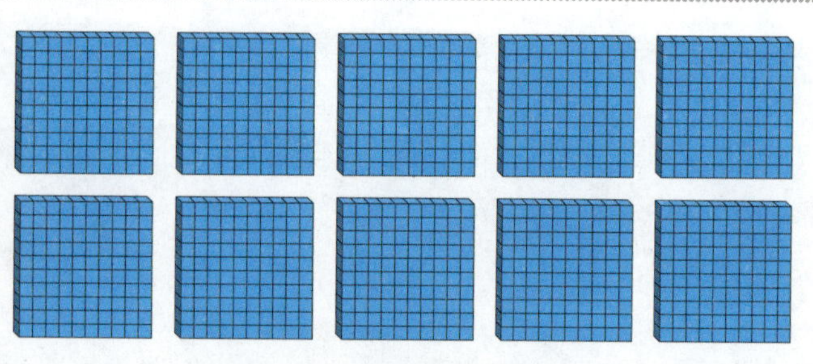

10 hundreds

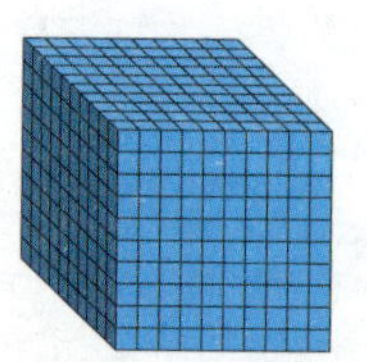

1 **thousand**

Show and Grow *I can do it!*

1. 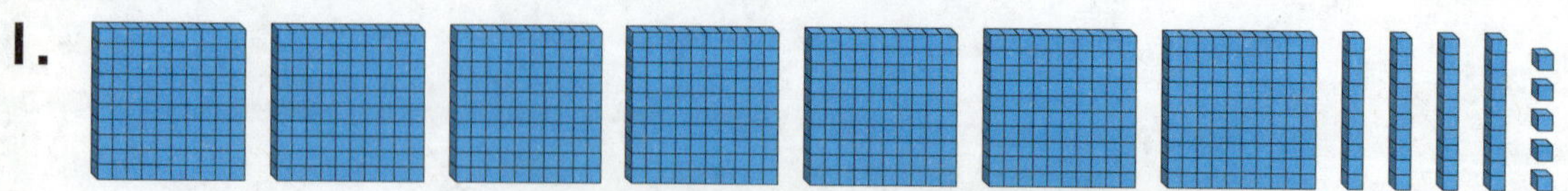

Hundreds	Tens	Ones
_____	_____	_____

_____ hundreds, _____ tens, and _____ ones is _____.

Name ______________________________

Apply and Grow: Practice

2. 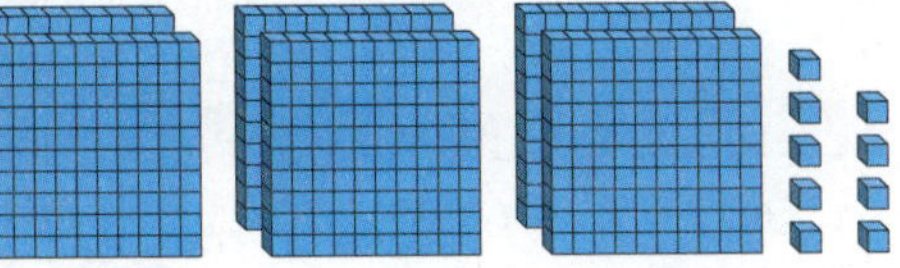

Hundreds	Tens	Ones
____	____	____

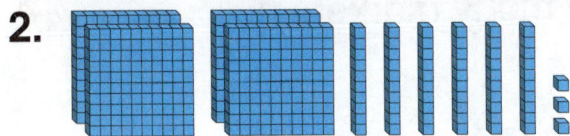

____ hundreds, ____ tens, and ____ ones is ____.

3. 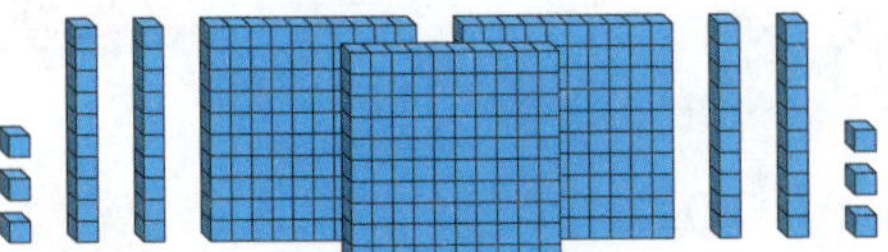

Hundreds	Tens	Ones
____	____	____

____ hundreds, ____ tens, and ____ ones is ____.

4.

____ hundreds, ____ tens, and ____ ones is ____.

5. DIG DEEPER! What number is Newton thinking about?

It has 5 hundreds. The digit in the tens place is between 7 and 9. The ones digit is 2 more than the hundreds digit.

____

Think and Grow: Modeling Real Life

You buy the markers shown. How many markers do you buy?

Write the missing numbers:

_____ hundreds, _____ tens, and _____ ones

_____ markers

Choose Tools What tools can you use to represent each pack of markers?

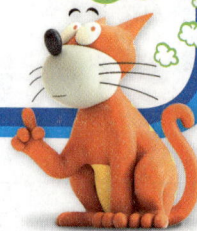

Show and Grow *I can think deeper!*

6. You buy the balloons shown. How many balloons do you buy?

_____ balloons

Name ____________________

Practice 7.2

Learning Target: Model and write numbers to 1,000.

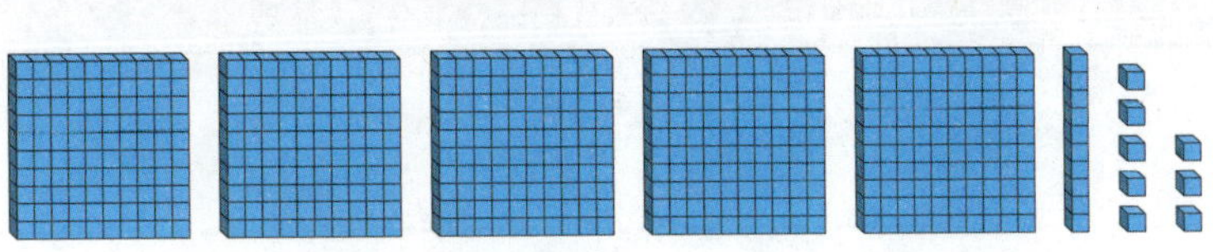

Hundreds	Tens	Ones
5	1	8

5 hundreds, 1 tens, and 8 ones is 518.

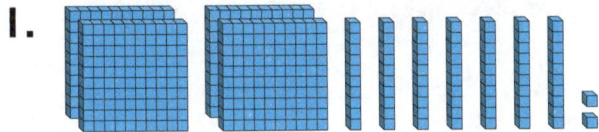

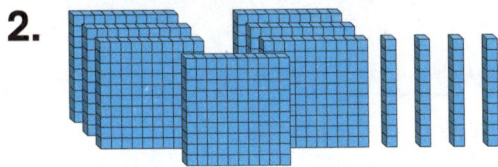

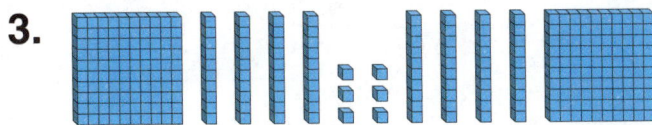

1.

Hundreds	Tens	Ones
____	____	____

____ hundreds, ____ tens, and ____ ones is ____.

2.

Hundreds	Tens	Ones
____	____	____

____ hundreds, ____ tens, and ____ ones is ____.

3.

____ hundreds, ____ tens, and ____ ones is ____.

4. **YOU BE THE TEACHER** Your friend writes 8 hundreds and 3 ones as 83. Is your friend correct? Explain.

____

____

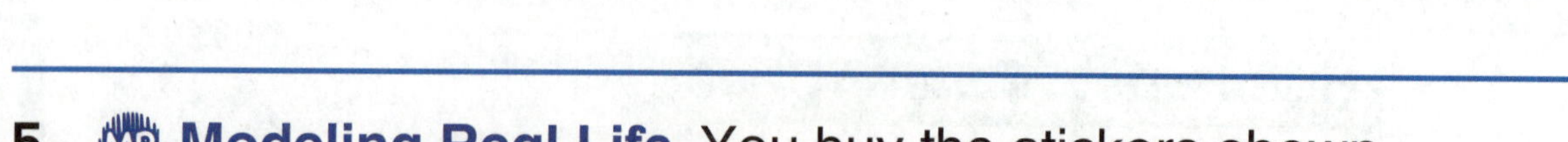

5. **Modeling Real Life** You buy the stickers shown. How many stickers do you buy?

______ stickers

6. **DIG DEEPER!** What is the greatest number you can make using three different digits from 0 to 9? What is the least number?

greatest: ______ least: ______

Review & Refresh

7.
$$\begin{array}{r} 39 \\ 12 \\ +\ 31 \\ \hline \end{array}$$

8.
$$\begin{array}{r} 28 \\ 22 \\ +\ 33 \\ \hline \end{array}$$

9.
$$\begin{array}{r} 34 \\ 16 \\ +\ 21 \\ \hline \end{array}$$

Name ___________________________

Understand Place Value 7.3

Learning Target: Understand the values of digits in a number.

Make quick sketches to model each number.

	Hundreds	Tens	Ones
324			
432			
243			

Structure What do you notice about the numbers?

____

____

Think and Grow

Circle the value of the underlined digit.

> The place of a digit in a number tells its value.

<u>8</u>64	(8 hundreds 800)	8 tens 80	8 ones 8
9<u>5</u>7	5 hundreds 500	(5 tens 50)	5 ones 5
17<u>2</u>	2 hundreds 200	2 tens 20	(2 ones 2)

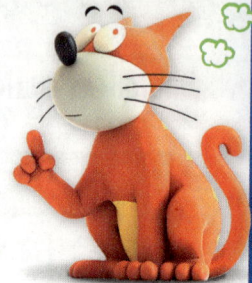

Show and Grow *I can do it!*

Circle the value of the underlined digit.

1.	48<u>3</u>	300	30	3
2.	7<u>9</u>1	9 hundreds	9 tens	9 ones
3.	<u>6</u>12	6	60	600
4.	5<u>7</u>8	7 hundreds	7 tens	7 ones

Name ______________________________

Apply and Grow: Practice

Circle the value of the underlined digit.

5.	<u>3</u>54	300	30	3
6.	7<u>2</u>6	2 hundreds	2 tens	2 ones
7.	59<u>4</u>	4	40	400
8.	47<u>5</u>	5 hundreds	50	5 ones

Circle the values of the underlined digit.

9.	6<u>3</u>9	3 tens	300	30
10.	<u>8</u>72	8 hundreds	80	800

11. MP **Number Sense** Write the number that has the following values.

The tens digit has a value of 40.

The ones digit has a value of 2.

The hundreds digit has a value of 600. ________

Think and Grow: Modeling Real Life

How many points is one ball worth in each bucket?

Score: 354

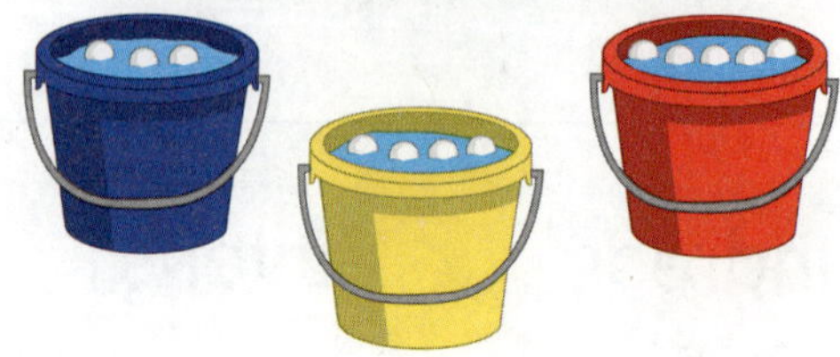

Write the score:

_____ hundreds, _____ tens, and _____ ones

Blue bucket: _____ points

Yellow bucket: _____ point

Red bucket: _____ points

Show and Grow *I can think deeper!*

12. How many points is one ring worth on each peg?

Score: 213

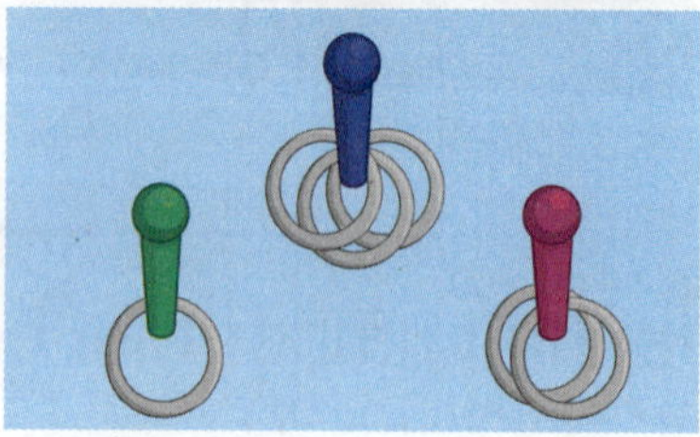

Green peg: _____ points

Blue peg: _____ point

Purple peg: _____ points

Name ______________________________

Practice 

Learning Target: Understand the values of digits in a number.

Circle the value of the underlined digit.

195	9 hundreds	9 tens	9 ones
	900	90	9

Circle the value of the underlined digit.

1.	523	500	50	5
2.	738	8 hundreds	8 ones	8 tens
3.	364	60	6 ones	6 hundreds

Circle the values of the underlined digit.

4.	434	4	4 ones	4 hundreds
5.	920	2	2 tens	20

6. **DIG DEEPER!** Write the number that matches the clues.

The value of the hundreds digit is 800.

The value of the tens digit is 10 less than 70.

The value of the ones digit is an even number greater than 7.

____

7. **Structure** Write each number in the correct circle.

152

215

452

205

650

5 in the tens place

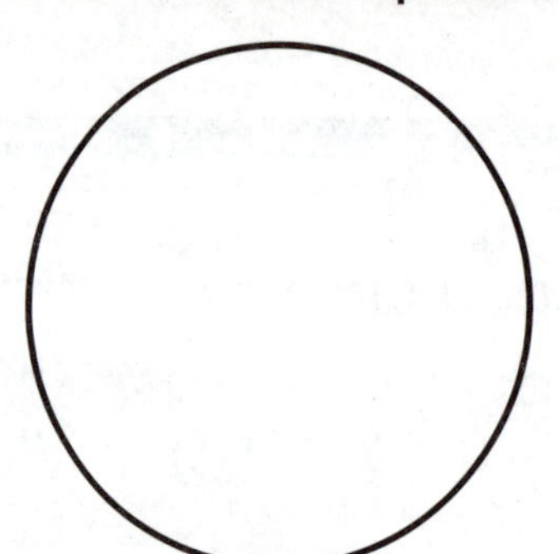

2 in the hundreds place

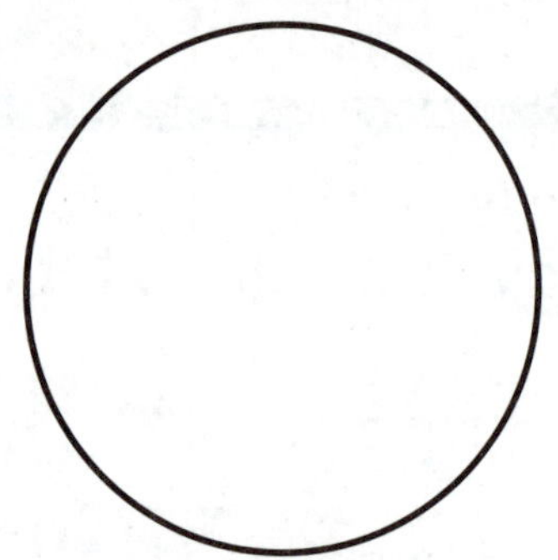

8. **Modeling Real Life** How many points is one ball worth in each hoop?

Score: 425 points

Blue hoop: _____ points

Orange hoop: _____ points

Red hoop: _____ point

Review & Refresh

9.
$$\begin{array}{r} 37 \\ -\ 18 \\ \hline \end{array}$$

10.
$$\begin{array}{r} 64 \\ -\ 22 \\ \hline \end{array}$$

11.
$$\begin{array}{r} 91 \\ -\ 53 \\ \hline \end{array}$$

Name ______________________________

Write Three-Digit Numbers 7.4

Learning Target: Write numbers in standard form, expanded form, and word form.

Explore and Grow

Identify the value of the base ten blocks.

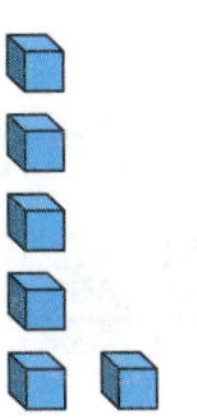

______________ ______________ ______________

What is the total value of the base ten blocks? ______________

How can you write the value of the base ten blocks as an equation?

_____ ◯ _____ ◯ _____ = _____

Think and Grow

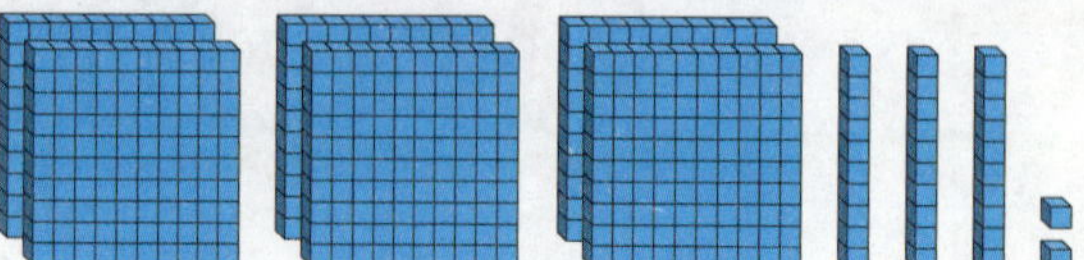

632 Standard form

600 + 30 + 2 Expanded form

six hundred thirty-two Word form

Show and Grow I can do it!

Write the number in standard form, expanded form, and word form.

1\.

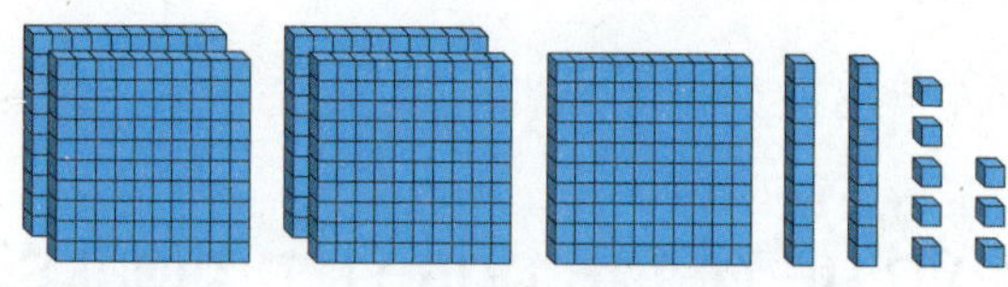

_____

_____ + _____ + _____

____

2\.

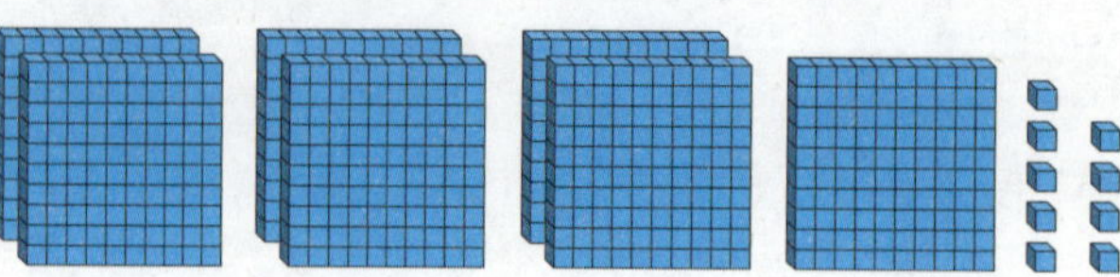

_____

_____ + _____ + _____

____

Name ______________________________

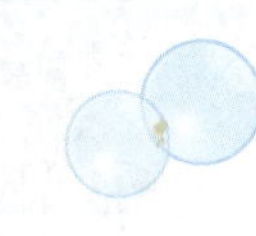

Apply and Grow: Practice

Write the number in expanded form and word form.

3. 837

_____ + _____ + _____

____

4. 954

_____ + _____ + _____

____

Write the number in standard form and word form.

5. 500 + 60

_____

____

6. 700 + 20 + 1

_____

____

Write the number in expanded form and standard form.

7. six hundred seventy-four

_____ + _____ + _____

_____

8. four hundred seven

_____ + _____ + _____

_____

9. **Structure** Which number did Newton model?

 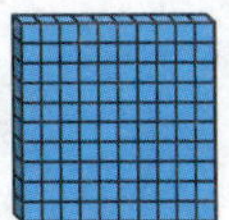 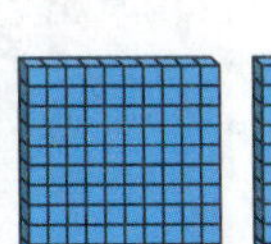 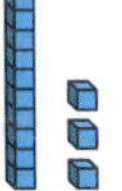

331

three hundred thirteen

300 + 30 + 1

Think and Grow: Modeling Real Life

There are 819 pets in a pet store. 800 are fish. 9 are cats. The rest are birds. How many birds are there?

Expanded form:

_____ + _____ + _____

_____ birds

Show and Grow *I can think deeper!*

10. There are 217 flowers at a flower stand. 200 are roses. 7 are sunflowers. The rest are tulips. How many tulips are there?

_____ tulips

11. There are 185 books at a book fair. 80 are chapter books. 5 are comic books. The rest are picture books. How many picture books are there?

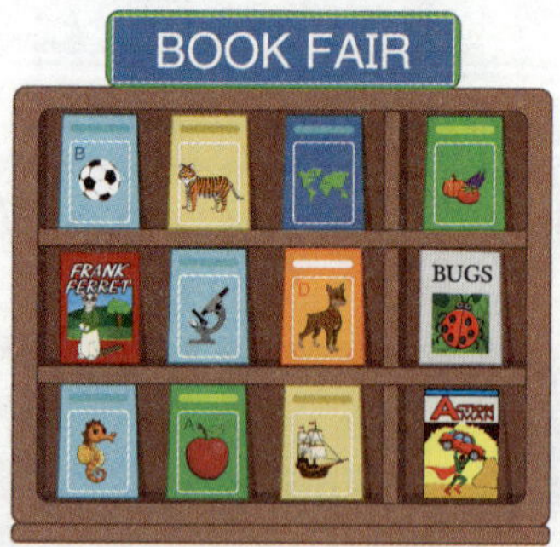

_____ picture books

12. You sell 326 candles. You sell 6 small candles. You sell 20 medium candles. The rest are large candles. How many large candles did you sell?

_____ large candles

Name ______________________

Learning Target: Write numbers in standard form, expanded form, and word form.

Write the number in standard form, expanded form, and word form.

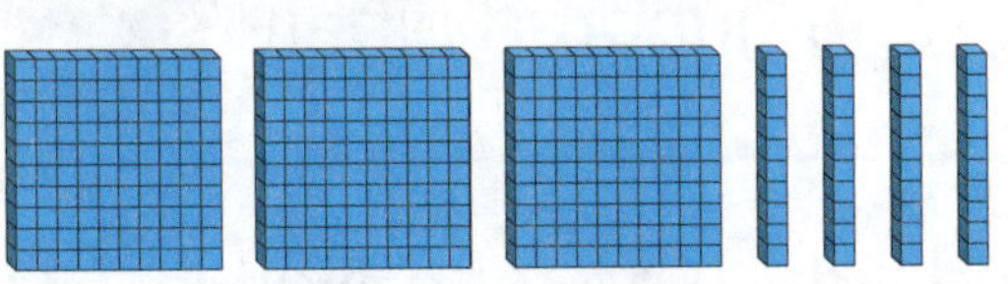

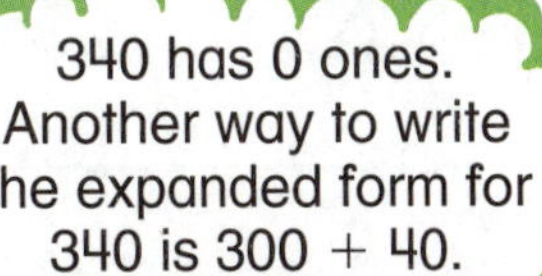

340 has 0 ones.
Another way to write the expanded form for 340 is 300 + 40.

340

300 + 40 + 0

three hundred forty

Write the number in expanded form and word form.

1. 137

_____ + _____ + _____

____

2. 280

_____ + _____ + _____

____

Write the number in standard form and word form.

3. 600 + 10 + 5 _____

____

4. 900 + 70 + 6 _____

____

Write the number in expanded form and standard form.

5. three hundred nine

_____ + _____ + _____

_____

6. eight hundred sixty-two

_____ + _____ + _____

_____

7. **Which One Doesn't Belong?** Which does *not* belong with the other three?

196

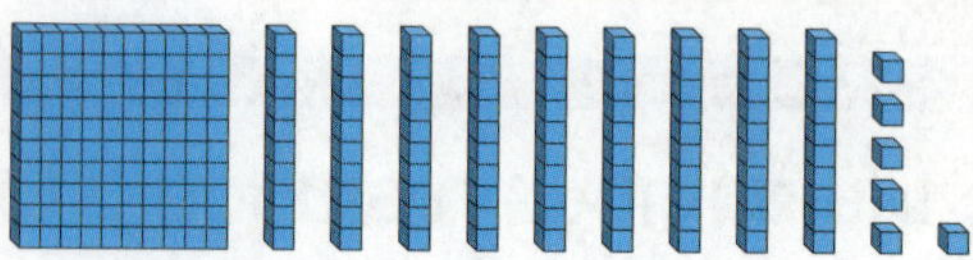

one hundred ninety-six

---

8. **DIG DEEPER!** A number has 7 hundreds. The tens digit is 5 less than the hundreds digit. The ones digit is 2 more than the hundreds digit. What is the number?

_____

---

9. **Modeling Real Life** There are 438 vegetables planted. 400 are carrots. 8 are beets. The rest are onions. How many onions are there?

_____ onions

---

10. **Modeling Real Life** There are 593 students in after-school programs. 3 students take dance class. 90 students take art class. The rest take karate class. How many students take karate class?

_____ students

Review & Refresh

11. Find the sum. Then change the order of the addends. Write the new equation.

$4 + 7 =$ _____ | _____ + _____ = _____

Name ______________________________

Represent Numbers in Different Ways

7.5

Learning Target: Represent numbers in different ways.

Explore and Grow

Circle the models that show each number.

100

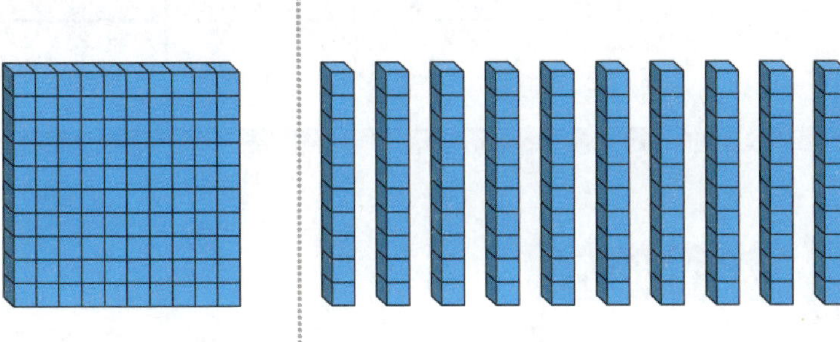

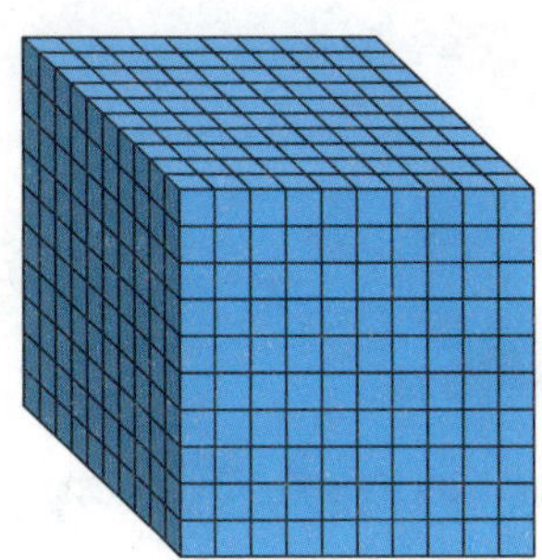

132

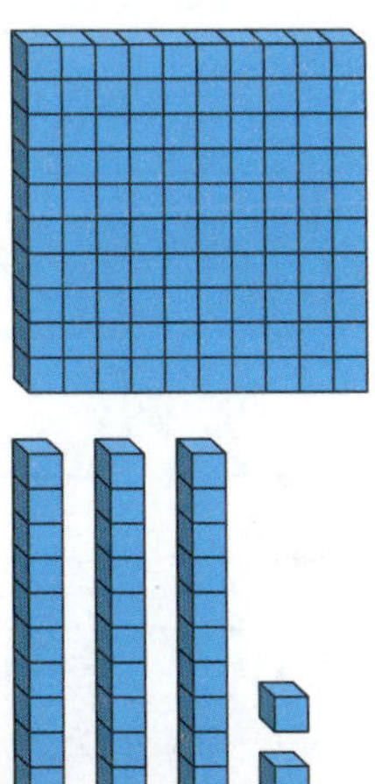

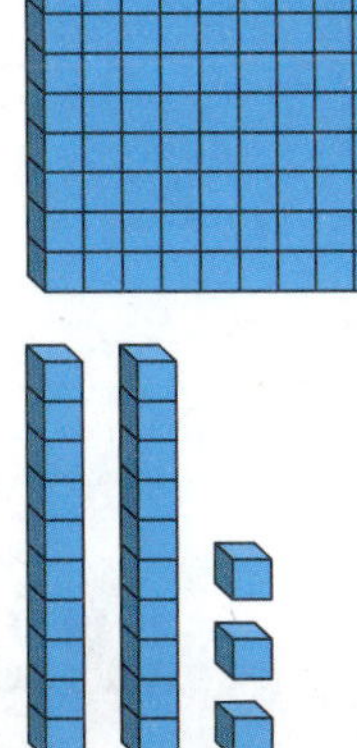

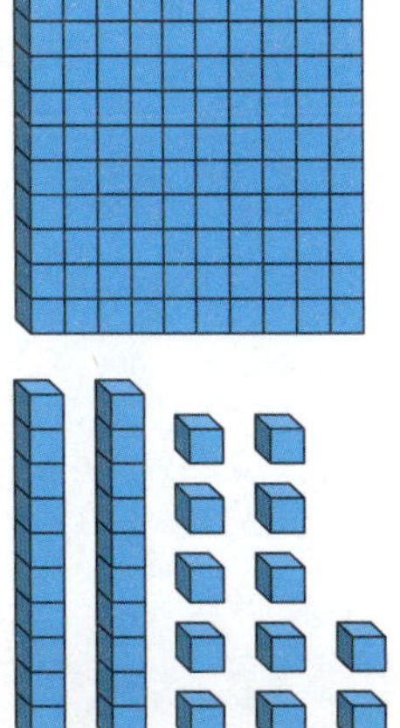

Think and Grow

Show 123 two ways.

Hundreds	Tens	Ones
1	2	3

Hundreds	Tens	Ones
0	12	3

MP Communicate Clearly
Explain why 1 hundred, 2 tens, and 3 ones has the same value as 12 tens and 3 ones.

Show and Grow *I can do it!*

1. Show 261 two ways.

Hundreds	Tens	Ones
____	____	____

Hundreds	Tens	Ones
____	____	____

2. Show 345 two ways.

Hundreds	Tens	Ones
____	____	____

Hundreds	Tens	Ones
____	____	____

Name ________________________________

Apply and Grow: Practice

3. Show 432 two ways.

Hundreds	Tens	Ones
____	____	____

Hundreds	Tens	Ones
____	____	____

4. Show 527 two ways.

Hundreds	Tens	Ones
____	____	____

Hundreds	Tens	Ones
____	____	____

5. MP **Repeated Reasoning** Complete the statements. What do you notice?

____ ones equal 1 ten.

____ tens equal 1 hundred.

____ hundreds equal 1 thousand.

Think and Grow: Modeling Real Life

The models show how many dinosaur toys you and your friend have. Does your friend have the same number of dinosaur toys as you? Explain.

You

Friend

Yes No

____

____

Show and Grow *I can think deeper!*

6. The models show how many trading cards you and your friend have. Does your friend have the same number of trading cards as you? Explain.

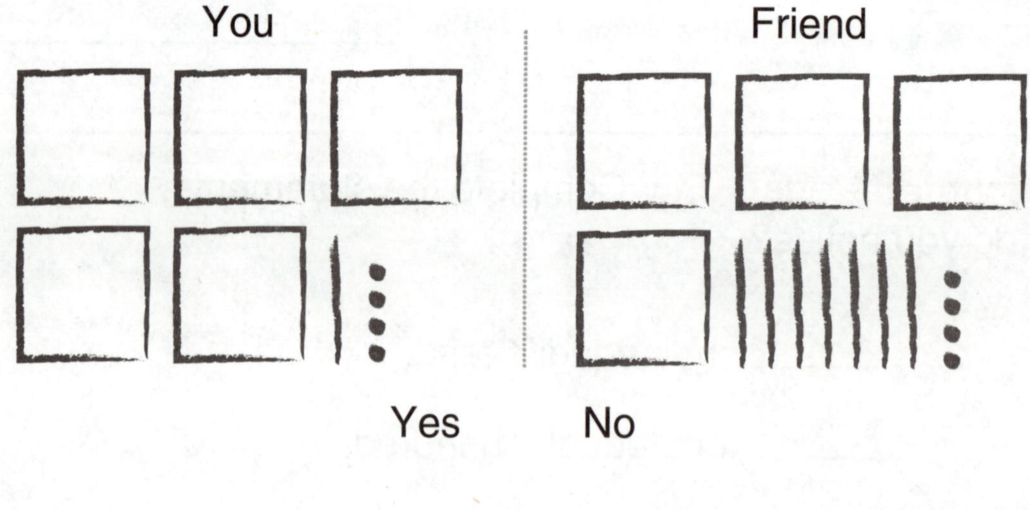

____

____

Name ____________________

Practice 

Learning Target: Represent numbers in different ways.

Show 285 two ways.

Hundreds	Tens	Ones
2	8	5

Hundreds	Tens	Ones
1	18	5

1. Show 134 two ways.

Hundreds	Tens	Ones
____	____	____

Hundreds	Tens	Ones
____	____	____

2. Show 319 two ways.

Hundreds	Tens	Ones
____	____	____

Hundreds	Tens	Ones
____	____	____

3. **Number Sense** Which ways show 948?

8 hundreds, 4 tens, and 8 ones

9 hundreds, 4 tens, and 8 ones

8 hundreds, 4 tens, and 9 ones

8 hundreds, 14 tens, and 9 ones

94 tens and 8 ones

948 ones

4. **Modeling Real Life** The models show how many bouncy balls you and your friend have. Does your friend have the same number of bouncy balls as you? Explain.

You

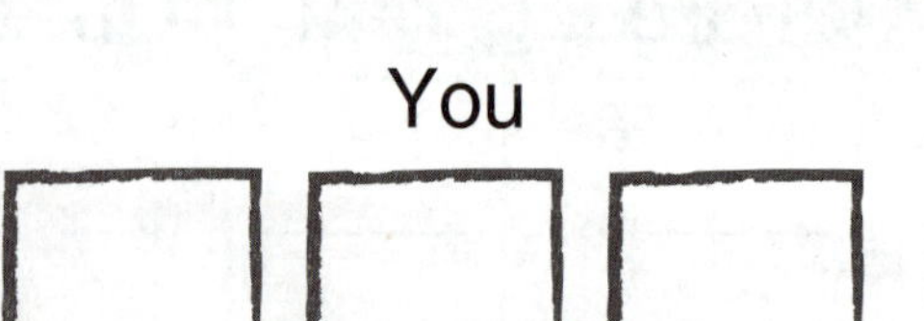

Friend

Yes No

____

____

Review & Refresh

5. $70 + 30 =$ _____

6. $53 + 19 =$ _____

7. $90 - 50 =$ _____

8. $64 - 40 =$ _____

Name ______________________________

Performance Task 7

You make trail mix using the sunflower seeds, almonds, and raisins shown.

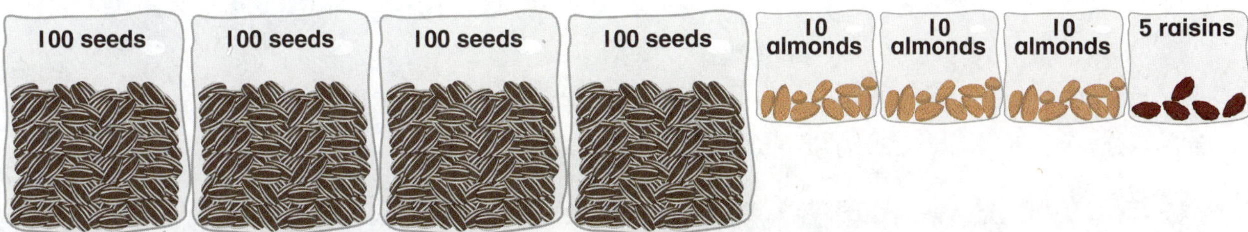

1. How many sunflower seeds, almonds, and raisins do you use?

_____ + _____ + _____

_____

2. You add another bag of almonds and another bag of raisins to your trail mix. How many sunflower seeds, almonds, and raisins are there now?

_____ + _____ + _____

_____

3. Your friend makes trail mix with 3 bags of sunflower seeds, 13 bags of almonds, and 4 bags of raisins. Does your friend use the same number of ingredients as you? Explain.

Yes No

____

____

Naming Numbers Flip and Find

To Play: Place the Naming Numbers Flip and Find Cards face down in the boxes. Take turns flipping 2 cards. If your cards show the same number, keep the cards. If your cards show different numbers, flip the cards back over. Play until all matches are made.

Name ______________________________

Chapter Practice 7

7.1 Hundreds

Write how many tens. Circle groups of 10 tens. Write how many hundreds. Then write the number.

1. 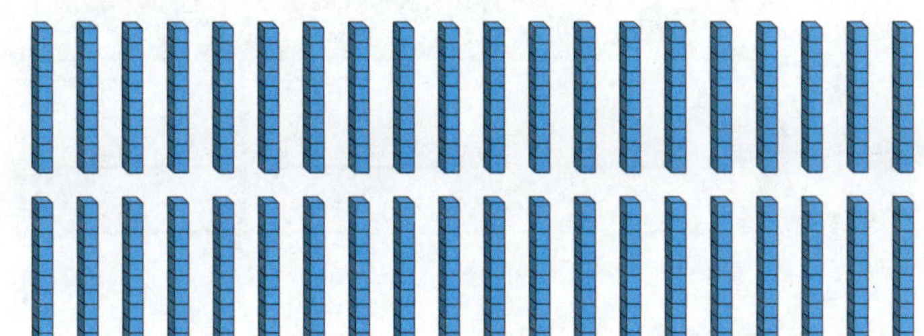

_____ tens

_____ hundreds

_____

2. 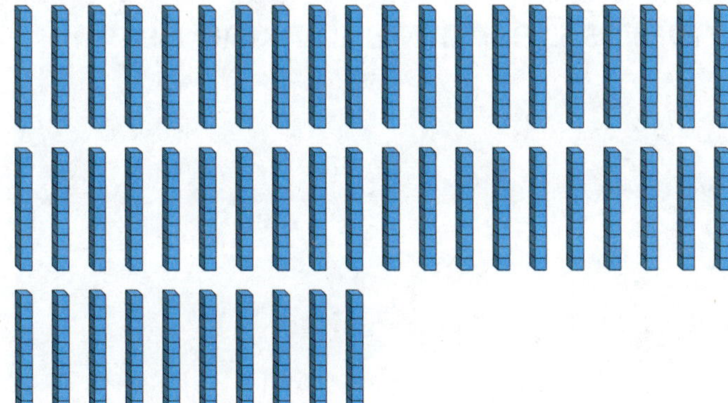

_____ tens

_____ hundreds

_____

3. **Modeling Real Life** A cafeteria has 80 bags of pretzels. Each bag has 10 pretzels. The cafeteria needs 900 pretzels. How many more bags does the cafeteria need?

_____ more bags

7.2 Model Numbers to 1,000

4. 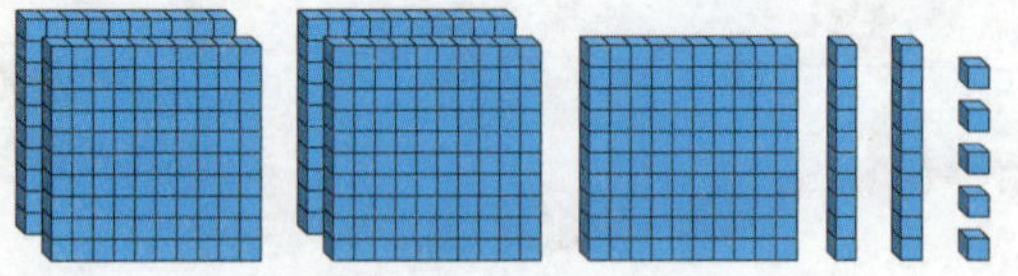

Hundreds	Tens	Ones
_____	_____	_____

_____ hundreds, _____ tens, and _____ ones is _____.

5. 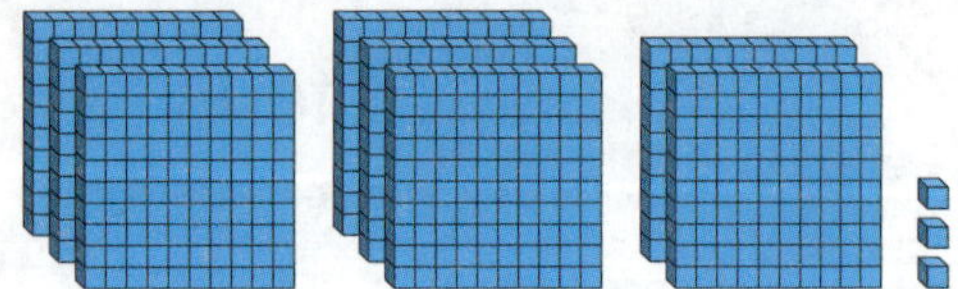

Hundreds	Tens	Ones
_____	_____	_____

_____ hundreds, _____ tens, and _____ ones is _____.

6. MP **Number Sense** What number is Descartes thinking about?

It has 4 hundreds. The digit in the tens place is between 1 and 3. The ones digit is 5 more than the hundreds digit.

_____

7.3 Understand Place Value

Circle the value of the underlined digit.

7. 4<u>2</u>9 | 200 | 2 | 2 tens

8. <u>7</u>51 | 70 | 700 | 7 tens

9. **MP Number Sense** Write the number that has the following values.

The tens digit has a value of 60.

The ones digit has a value of 3.

The hundreds digit has a value of 900. 

7.4 Write Three-Digit Numbers

Write the number in expanded form and word form.

10. 605

_____ + _____ + _____

____

11. 541

_____ + _____ + _____

____

Write the number in standard form and word form.

12. 100 + 20 + 4

_____

____

13. 700 + 8

_____

____

Write the number in expanded form and standard form.

14. three hundred thirty

_____ + _____ + _____

_____

15. two hundred fifty-six

_____ + _____ + _____

_____

7.5 Represent Numbers in Different Ways

16. Show 345 two ways.

Hundreds	Tens	Ones
____	____	____

Hundreds	Tens	Ones
____	____	____

17. Show 562 two ways.

Hundreds	Tens	Ones
____	____	____

Hundreds	Tens	Ones
____	____	____

18. MP **Number Sense** Which ways show 564?

4 hundreds, 6 tens, and 5 ones

4 hundreds, 16 tens, and 5 ones

564 ones

5 hundreds, 6 tens, and 4 ones

56 tens and 4 ones

4 hundreds, 16 tens, and 4 ones

8 Count and Compare Numbers to 1,000

- What types of living things are in an aquarium?
- There are 568 fish in an aquarium. What is 10 less than 568? What is 100 more than 568?

Chapter Learning Target:
Understand counting.

Chapter Success Criteria:
- I can identify patterns.
- I can skip count.
- I can compare numbers and their values.
- I can represent numbers in different ways.

Name ______________________________

8 Vocabulary

Review Words
addends
equation
sum

Organize It

Use the review words to complete the graphic organizer.

28 + 33 = 61

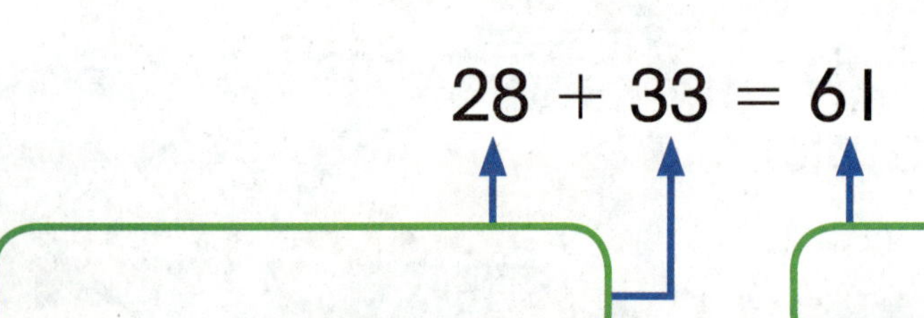

Define It

Use your vocabulary cards to complete the puzzle.

Across

1. 542 → 532 → 522

Down

2. 732 > 399 399 < 732

399 = 399

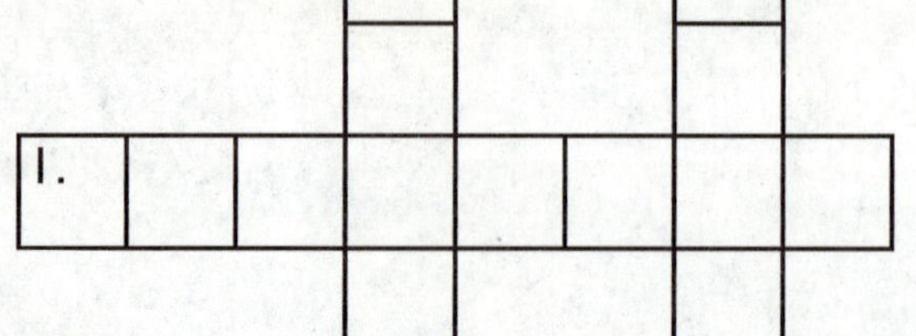

3. 522 → 532 → 542

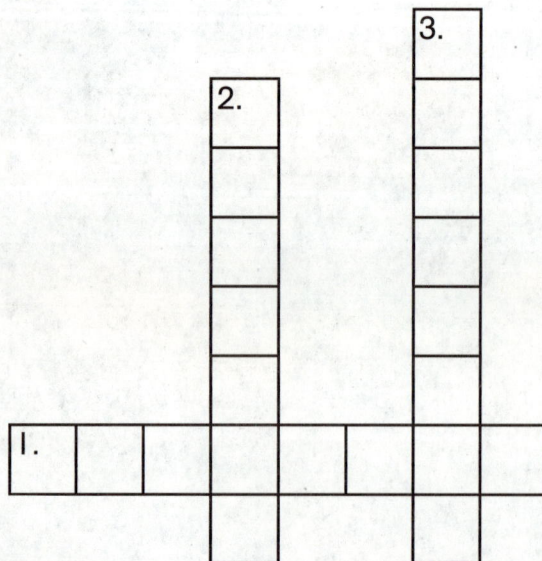

Chapter 8 Vocabulary Cards

compare	decrease
equal to (=)	greater than (>)
increase	less than (<)

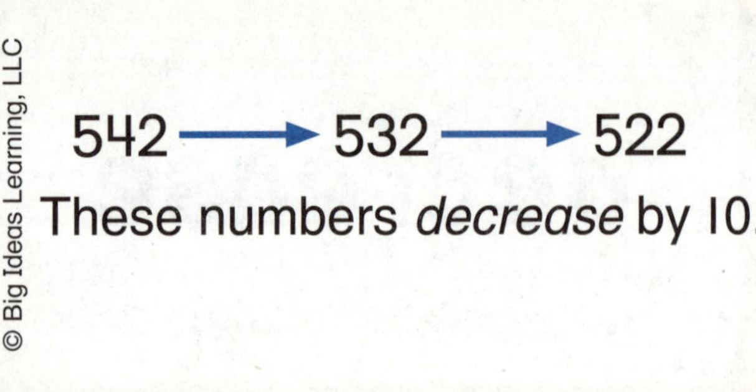

542 → 532 → 522

These numbers *decrease* by 10.

The symbols used to *compare* numbers are <, >, and =.

732 > 399 399 < 732

399 = 399

732 > 399

732 is greater than 399.

399 = 399

399 is equal to 399.

399 < 732

399 is less than 732.

522 → 532 → 542

These numbers *increase* by 10.

Name ______________________________

Learning Target: Skip count within 120 in different ways.

Explore and Grow

Start at 5. Skip count by fives. Circle the numbers you count.
Start at 10. Skip count by tens. Color the numbers you count.

1	2	3	4	5	6	7	8	9	10
11	12	13	14	15	16	17	18	19	20
21	22	23	24	25	26	27	28	29	30
31	32	33	34	35	36	37	38	39	40
41	42	43	44	45	46	47	48	49	50
51	52	53	54	55	56	57	58	59	60
61	62	63	64	65	66	67	68	69	70
71	72	73	74	75	76	77	78	79	80
81	82	83	84	85	86	87	88	89	90
91	92	93	94	95	96	97	98	99	100
101	102	103	104	105	106	107	108	109	110
111	112	113	114	115	116	117	118	119	120

MP **Patterns** What patterns do you notice?

____

____

Think and Grow

You can count on by ones, fives, or tens from any number.

Count by ones.

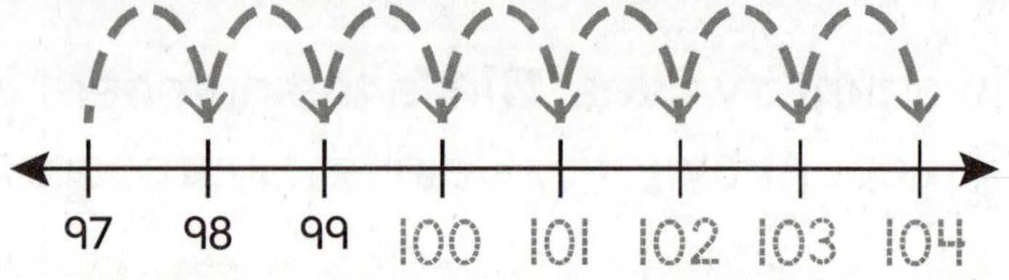

Do you see any patterns in the digits?

Count by fives.

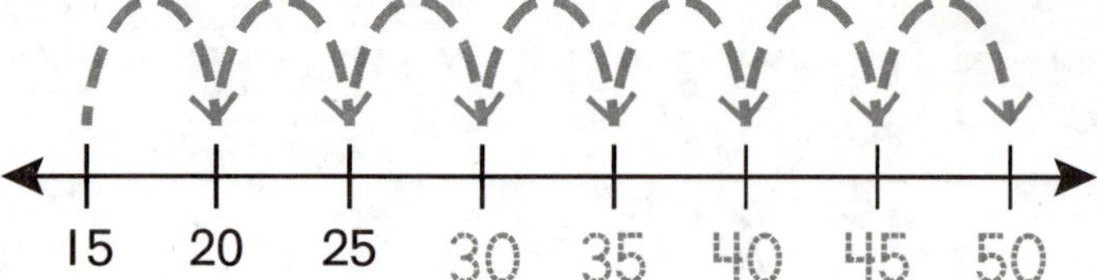

Count by tens.

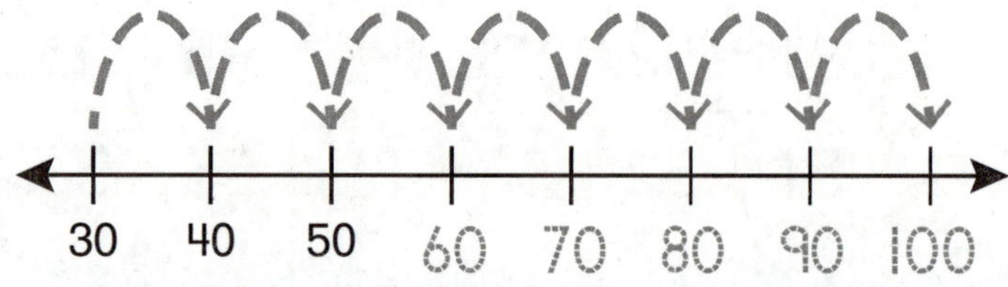

Show and Grow *I can do it!*

1. Count by ones.

   35, 36, 37, _____, _____, _____, _____, _____

2. Count by fives.

   55, 60, 65, _____, _____, _____, _____, _____

3. Count by tens.

   21, 31, 41, _____, _____, _____, _____, _____

Name ___________________________________

Apply and Grow: Practice

Count by ones.

4. 57, 58, 59, ______, ______, ______, ______, ______

5. ______, 106, ______, 108, ______, ______, ______

Count by fives.

6. 35, 40, 45, ______, ______, ______, ______, ______

7. ______, 80, ______, 90, ______, ______, ______

Count by tens.

8. 12, 22, 32, ______, ______, ______, ______, ______

9. ______, 50, ______, 70, ______, ______, ______

10. MP **Number Sense** Newton counts by ones from 47 to 53. Which numbers does he count?

49 | 55 | 40 | 52

11. MP **Number Sense** Descartes counts by fives from 90 to 115. Which numbers does he count?

120 | 105 | 110 | 92

Think and Grow: Modeling Real Life

Newton has 65 points. He captures small aliens worth 5 points. Descartes has 25 points. He captures large aliens worth 10 points. Who needs to capture more aliens to reach 100 points?

Models:

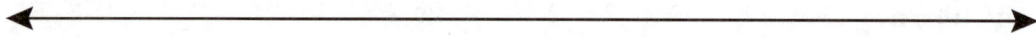

Who needs more aliens? Newton Descartes

Show and Grow *I can think deeper!*

12. Newton has 55 points. He collects gold coins worth 10 points. Descartes has 70 points. He collects silver coins worth 5 points. Who needs to collect more coins to reach 100 points?

Newton Descartes

13. You and your friend count from 30 to 70. You count by fives. Your friend counts by tens. Who says more numbers? Explain.

Name ______________________

Practice 8.1

Learning Target: Skip count within 120 in different ways.

Count by fives.

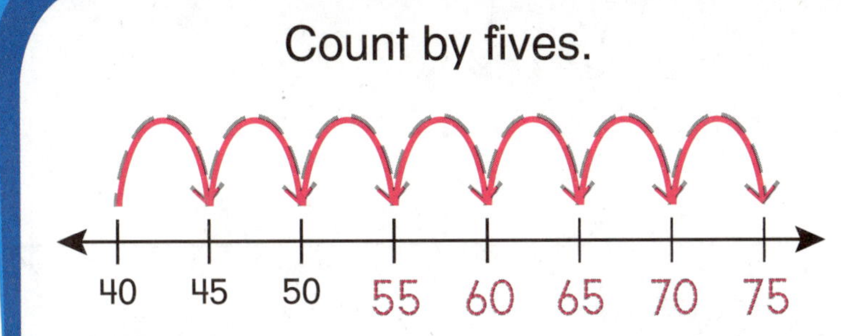

You can also count by ones or tens.

Count by ones.

1. 63, 64, 65, ______, ______, ______, ______, ______

2. ______, 112, ______, 114, ______, ______, ______

Count by fives.

3. 10, 15, 20, ______, ______, ______, ______, ______

4. ______, 95, ______, 105, ______, ______, ______

Count by tens.

5. 44, 54, 64, ______, ______, ______, ______, ______

6. ______, 20, ______, 40, ______, ______, ______

7. **DIG DEEPER!** Write a three-digit number. Increase the tens digit by 1 for each following number. Describe how you would skip count with your numbers.

______, ______, ______, ______, ______

8. **MP Modeling Real Life** Who needs to make more shots to earn 50 points?

Who needs to make more shots?

 Newton

 Descartes

Review & Refresh

9. $34 - 16 = ?$

Tens	Ones
☐	☐
−	

10. $75 - 32 = ?$

Tens	Ones
☐	☐
−	

11. $93 - 28 = ?$

Tens	Ones
☐	☐
−	

Name ___________________________

Count to 1,000 in Different Ways 8.2

Learning Target: Skip count within 1,000 in different ways.

Explore and Grow

Count by hundreds to 1,000.

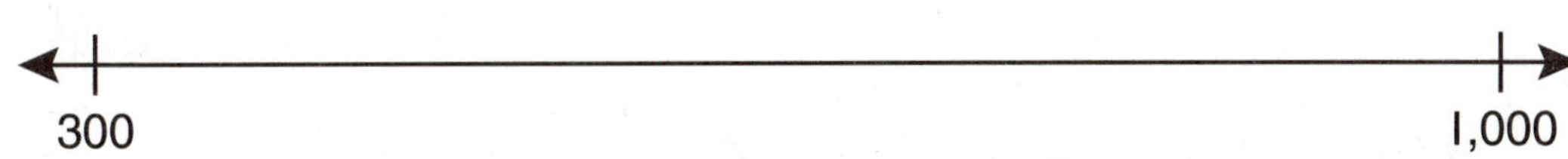

Count by tens to 1,000.

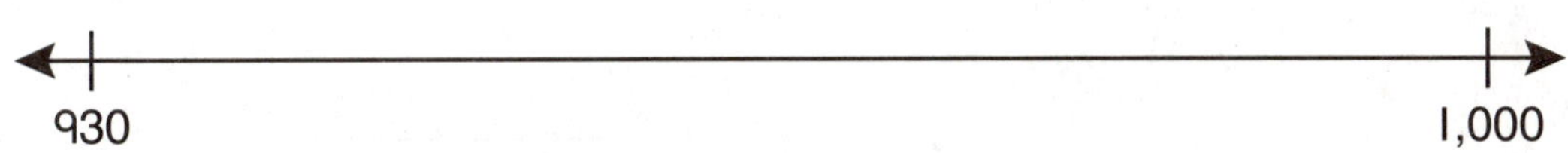

Count by fives to 1,000.

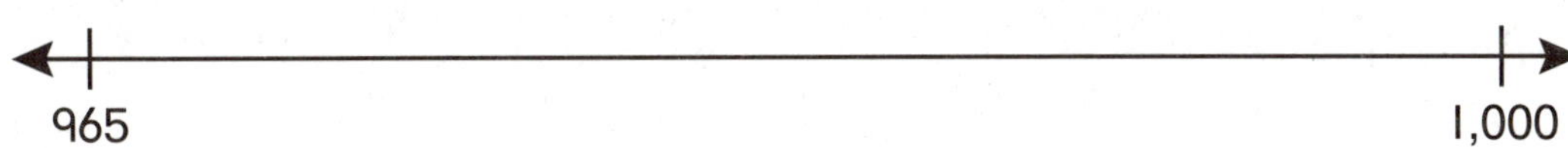

Count by ones to 1,000.

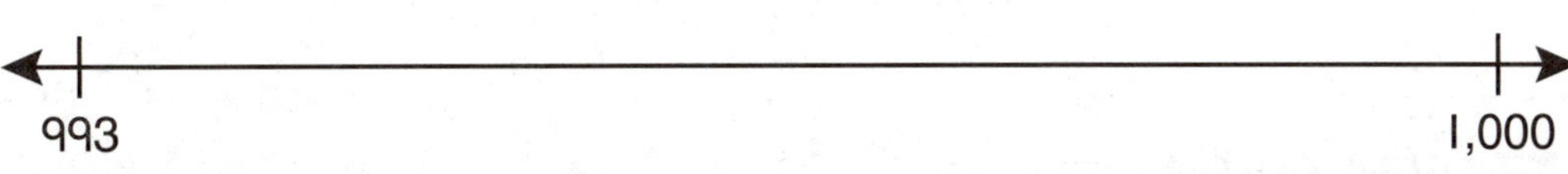

Think and Grow

Think of the counting patterns with lesser numbers.

Count by fives.

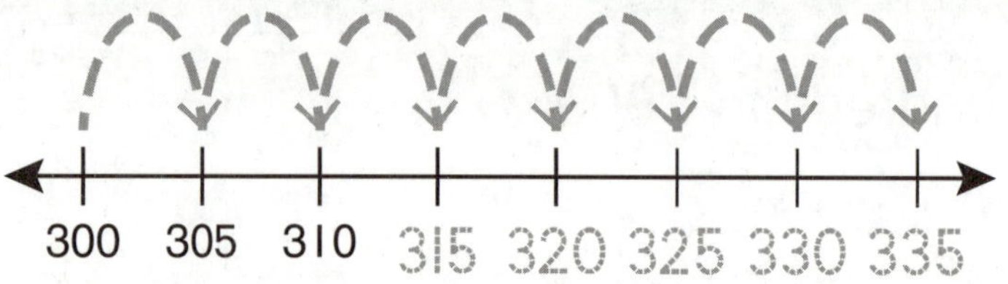

Count by tens.

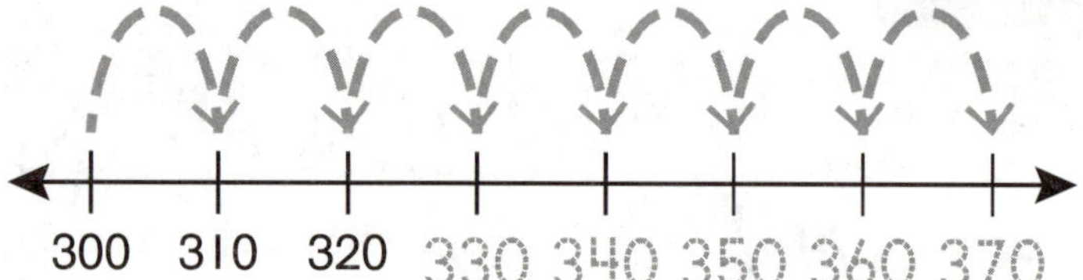

Count by hundreds.

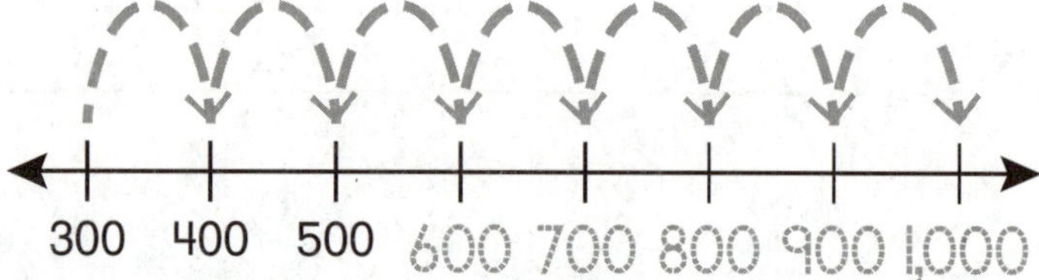

Show and Grow *I can do it!*

1. Count by fives.

675, 680, 685, ______, ______, ______, ______, ______

2. Count by tens.

850, 860, 870, ______, ______, ______, ______, ______

3. Count by hundreds.

100, 200, 300, ______, ______, ______, ______, ______

Name ______________________________

Apply and Grow: Practice

Count by fives.

4. 520, 525, 530, ____, ____, ____, ____, ____

5. 875, 880, ____, ____, ____, ____, ____

Count by tens.

6. 600, 610, 620, ____, ____, ____, ____, ____

7. 460, 470, ____, ____, ____, ____, ____

Count by hundreds.

8. 200, 300, 400, ____, ____, ____, ____, ____

9. 400, 500, ____, ____, ____, ____, ____

10. DIG DEEPER! Newton counts by hundreds. Find the missing number. Think: How do you know?

11. MP **Structure** Did Descartes count by tens or by hundreds? Think: How do you know?

Think and Grow: Modeling Real Life

A summer camp leader has 240 T-shirts. He buys 6 more colors with 10 shirts in each color. How many T-shirts does he have now?

Model:

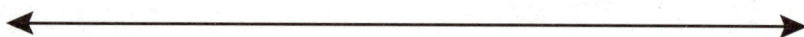

_____ T-shirts

Show and Grow *I can think deeper!*

12. You have 100 bracelets. You buy 5 more boxes with 100 bracelets in each box. How many bracelets do you have now?

_____ bracelets

13. You and your friend count from 370 to 420. You count by tens. Your friend counts by fives. Who says more numbers? Explain.

____

____

Name ______________________

Practice 8.2

Learning Target: Skip count within 1,000 in different ways.

Count by hundreds.

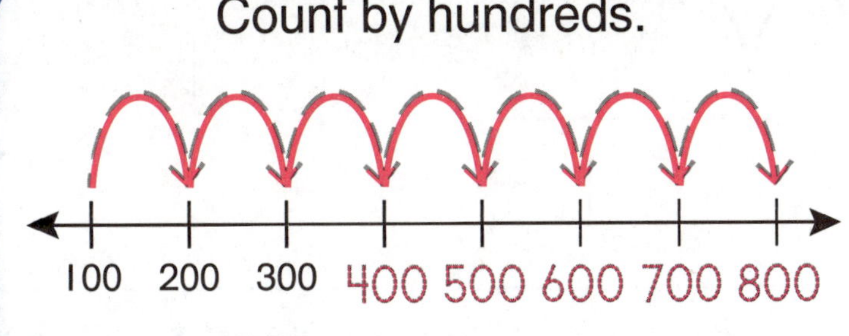

You can also count by fives or tens.

Count by fives.

1. 445, 450, 455, ____, ____, ____, ____, ____

2. 770, 775, ____, ____, ____, ____, ____

Count by tens.

3. 520, 530, 540, ____, ____, ____, ____, ____

4. 660, 670, ____, ____, ____, ____, ____

Count by hundreds.

5. 300, 400, 500, ____, ____, ____, ____, ____

6. 200, 300, ____, ____, ____, ____, ____

7. DIG DEEPER! Newton starts at 950 and counts to 1,000 by fives. Complete the number line to show the last 6 numbers he counts.

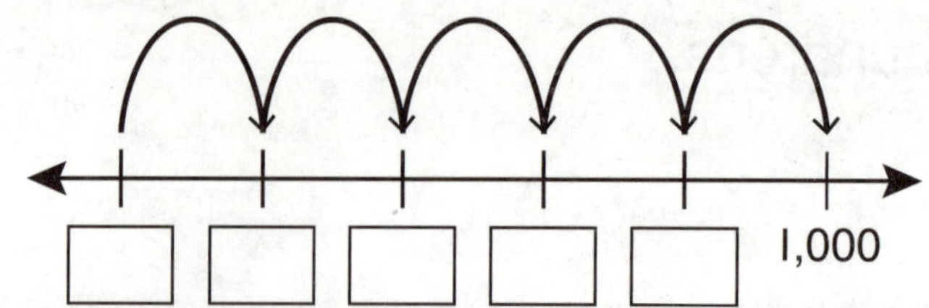

8. Modeling Real Life A carnival worker has 380 stuffed animals. She buys 6 more boxes with 5 stuffed animals in each box. How many stuffed animals does she have now?

_____ stuffed animals

9. Modeling Real Life A water park shop owner has 100 goggles. He buys 4 more colors with 100 goggles in each color. How many goggles does the shop owner have now?

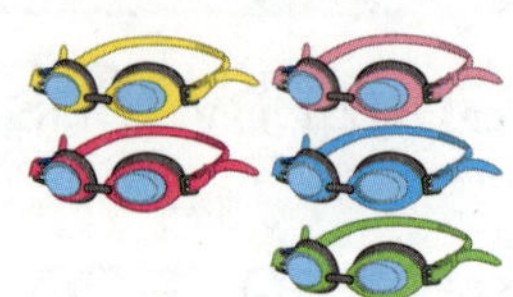

_____ goggles

Review & Refresh

10. You see 14 geese in a pond. 17 more join them. Then you see 11 more fly to the pond. How many geese do you see in all?

_____ geese

Name ____________________

Learning Target: Identify patterns to find missing numbers.

Explore and Grow

What patterns do you see in the shaded row and column? Use the patterns to complete the chart.

601	602	603	604	605	606	607	608	609	610
611	612	613	614	615	616	617	618	619	620
621	622	623	624	625	626	627		629	630
631	632	633	634	635	636	637	638	639	
641	642	643	644	645		647	648	649	
651	652		654	655	656	657	658	659	660
661	662		664	665	666				670
671	672		674	675	676	677	678	679	680
681	682	683	684		686	687		689	690
691	692			695	696	697	698	699	

Think and Grow

The tens digit **increases** by 1.

Use place value to find the next two numbers.

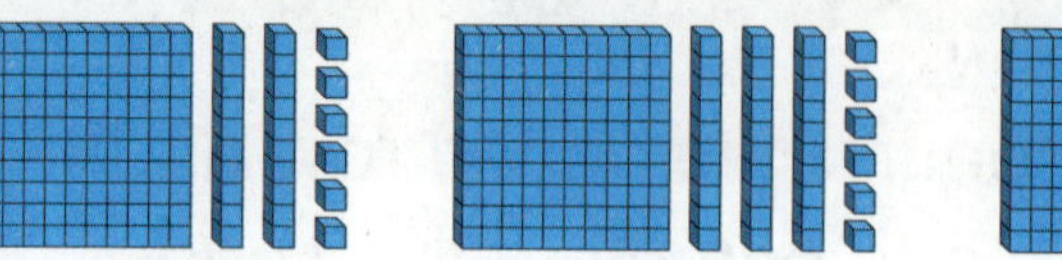

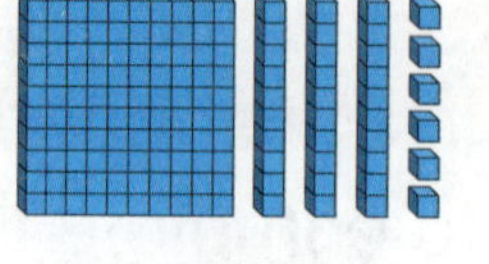

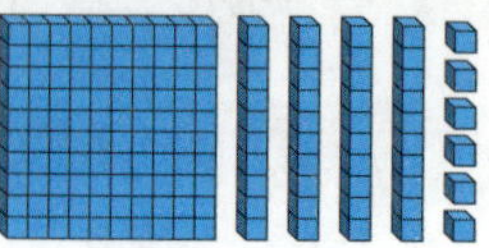

126, 136, 146, ?, ?

The next two numbers are 156 and 166.

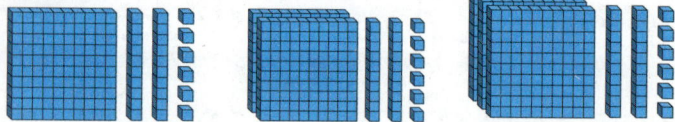

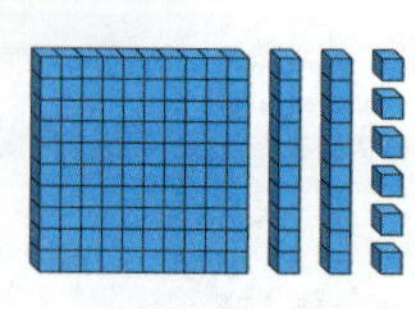

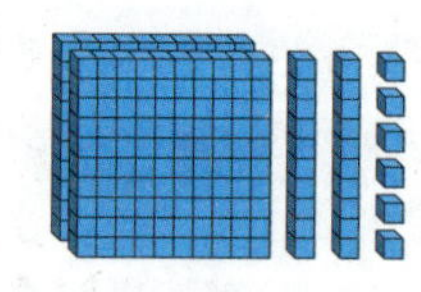

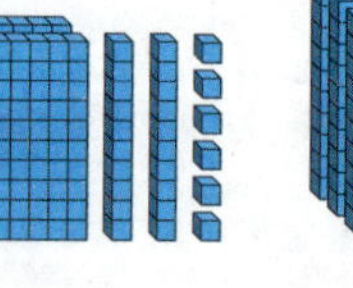

126, 226, 326, ?, ?

The next two numbers are 426 and 526.

The hundreds digit increases by 1.

Show and Grow *I can do it!*

Use place value to find the missing numbers.

1. 485, 486, 487, ______, ______, ______, ______

2. 612, 622, 632, ______, ______, ______, ______

3. 267, 277, ______, 297, ______, 317, ______

4. 101, 201, ______, 401, ______, ______, ______

Name ______________________________

Apply and Grow: Practice

Use place value to find the missing numbers.

5. 324, 325, _____, 327, _____, _____, _____

6. 194, 294, _____, 494, _____, _____, _____

7. 463, 473, _____, 493, _____, _____, _____

8. 232, 332, _____, 532, _____, _____, _____

9. 985, 986, _____, 988, _____, _____, _____

10. 751, 761, _____, 781, _____, _____, _____

11. 606, 607, _____, 609, _____, _____, _____

12. **MP Repeated Reasoning** Use place value to describe each pattern.

540, 640, 740, 840, 940

____

____

310, 320, 330, 340, 350

____

____

Think and Grow: Modeling Real Life

There are 273 tickets in a bin. Some more are put in the bin. Now there are 973. How many groups of 100 tickets were put in the bin?

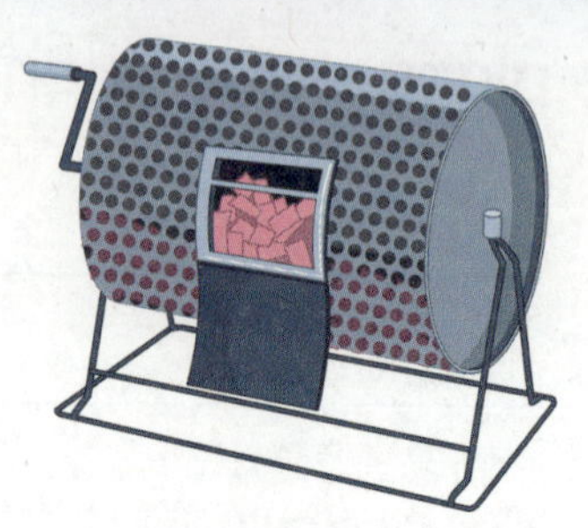

Model:

_____ groups of 100 tickets

Show and Grow *I can think deeper!*

13. You have 338 pennies in a jar. You put more in the jar. Now there are 388. How many groups of 10 pennies were put in the jar?

_____ groups of 10 pennies

14. DIG DEEPER! There are 410 people at a show. 8 more rows of seats get filled. Now there are 490 people. How many people can sit in each row?

_____ people

MP **Communicate Clearly** Explain how you solved.

____

____

Name ______________________

Practice 8.3

Learning Target: Identify patterns to find missing numbers.

The ones
digit increases
by 1.

Use place value to find the next two numbers.

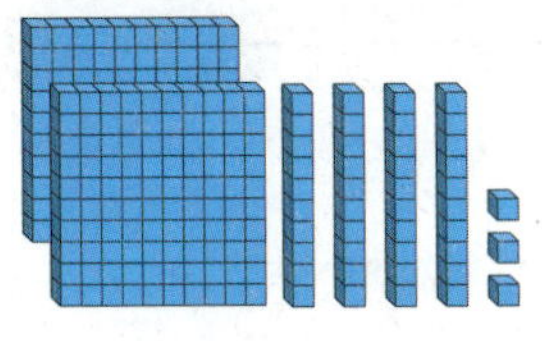
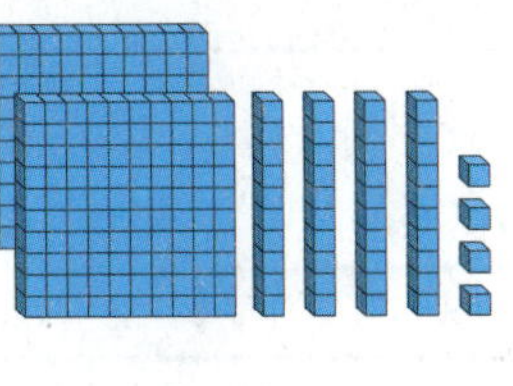
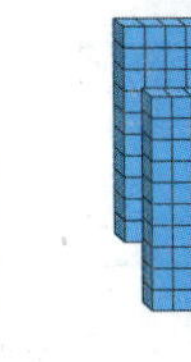
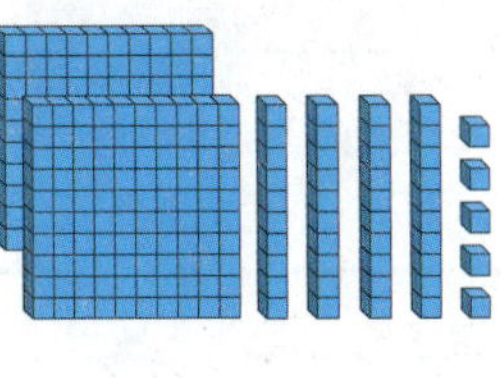

243, 244, 245, ?, ?

The next two numbers are 246 and 247.

Use place value to find the missing numbers.

1. 710, 711, 712, _____, _____, _____, _____

2. 822, 832, 842, _____, _____, _____, _____

3. 325, 425, 525, _____, _____, _____, _____

4. 669, 679, _____, 699, _____, _____, _____

5. 534, 535, _____, 537, _____, _____, _____

6. 368, 468, _____, 668, _____, _____, _____

7. MP YOU BE THE TEACHER Newton says the hundreds digit in the numbers shown increases by 1. Is he correct? Explain.

540, 550, 560, 570, 580, 590

____

____

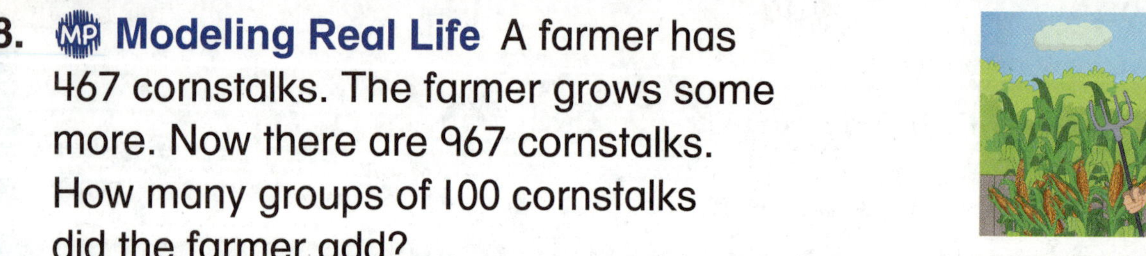

8. MP **Modeling Real Life** A farmer has 467 cornstalks. The farmer grows some more. Now there are 967 cornstalks. How many groups of 100 cornstalks did the farmer add?

_____ groups of 100 cornstalks

9. DIG DEEPER! There are 250 people at a party. 3 more tables get filled. Now there are 280 people. How many people can sit at each table?

_____ people

Review & Refresh

10. $8 + 4 =$ _____

11. $15 - 8 =$ _____

12. $\begin{array}{r} 5 \\ +\ 5 \\ \hline \square \end{array}$

13. $\begin{array}{r} 14 \\ -\ 8 \\ \hline \square \end{array}$

14. $\begin{array}{r} 7 \\ +\ 6 \\ \hline \square \end{array}$

15. $\begin{array}{r} 18 \\ -\ 9 \\ \hline \square \end{array}$

Name ______________________________

Learning Target: Identify numbers that are 1, 10, or 100 more and less than a number.

Model 253. Use your model to complete the sentences.

1 more than 253 is ______.

1 less than 253 is ______.

10 more than 253 is ______.

10 less than 253 is ______.

100 more than 253 is ______.

100 less than 253 is ______.

Use Math Tools How should you change your model for each sentence?

Think and Grow

247

Hundreds	Tens	Ones
2	5	7

10 more than 247 is 257.

Hundreds	Tens	Ones
2	3	7

10 less than 247 is 237.

Increase or **decrease** the digit in the tens place to find 10 more or 10 less. Increase or decrease the digit in the hundreds place to find 100 more or 100 less.

Hundreds	Tens	Ones
3	4	7

100 more than 247 is 347.

Hundreds	Tens	Ones
1	4	7

100 less than 247 is 147.

Show and Grow *I can do it!*

1. 10 more than 452 is ______.

2. 10 less than 813 is ______.

3. 100 less than 729 is ______.

4. 100 more than 386 is ______.

Name ______________________

Apply and Grow: Practice

5. 10 more than 571 is ______.

6. 10 less than 333 is ______.

7. 100 more than 604 is ______.

8. 100 less than 592 is ______.

9. 1 more than 934 is ______.

10. 1 less than 101 is ______.

11. 10 less than 286 is ______.

12. 1 more than 467 is ______.

13. 10 more than 763 is ______.

14. 100 less than 846 is ______.

15. 1 less than 999 is ______.

16. 100 more than 28 is ______.

17. 100 less than 135 is ______.

18. 100 more than 900 is ______.

19. MP **Number Sense** Complete each sentence.

336 is ______ more than 326.

542 is ______ less than 543.

937 is ______ more than 837.

681 is ______ less than 691.

276 is ______ more than 275.

315 is ______ less than 415.

Think and Grow: Modeling Real Life

An orange tree has 639 oranges. A lemon tree has 100 fewer lemons. How many lemons does the tree have?

Model:

_____ lemons

Show and Grow *I can think deeper!*

20. A history book has 197 pictures. A science book has 10 more pictures. How many pictures are in the science book?

_____ pictures

21. **DIG DEEPER!** A boat puzzle has 525 pieces. A bird puzzle has 100 more than the boat puzzle. A space puzzle has 10 fewer than the bird puzzle. How many puzzle pieces does the space puzzle have?

_____ puzzle pieces

22. **DIG DEEPER!** You have 398 points. Newton has 100 fewer than you. Descartes has 10 more than Newton. How many points does Descartes have?

_____ points

Name ___________________________

Learning Target: Identify numbers that are 1, 10, or 100 more and less than a number.

318

Hundreds	Tens	Ones
3	1	9

1 more than 318 is 319.

Hundreds	Tens	Ones
3	1	7

1 less than 318 is 317.

1. 10 more than 106 is ______.

2. 10 less than 467 is ______.

3. 100 more than 321 is ______.

4. 100 less than 945 is ______.

5. 1 more than 513 is ______.

6. 1 less than 899 is ______.

7. 1 less than 264 is ______.

8. 100 more than 555 is ______.

9. 1 more than 852 is ______.

10. 100 less than 573 is ______.

11. 10 less than 314 is ______.

12. 10 more than 687 is ______.

13. MP **Structure** Complete the table.

	1 more	1 less	10 more	10 less	100 more	100 less
438						
751						

14. MP **Number Sense** Complete the sentence.

_____ is 10 less than 546 and 10 more than _____.

15. MP **Modeling Real Life** Your magic book has 163 tricks. Your friend's magic book has 100 more tricks than yours. How many tricks does your friend's magic book have?

_____ tricks

16. DIG DEEPER! You have 624 songs. Newton has 100 fewer than you. Descartes has 10 more than Newton. How many songs does Descartes have?

_____ songs

Review & Refresh

17. A bookcase has 5 shelves. There are 2 stuffed animals on each shelf. How many stuffed animals are there in all?

_____ + _____ + _____ + _____ + _____ = _____

Name ______________________________

Compare Numbers Using Symbols 8.5

Learning Target: Use symbols to compare two numbers up to 1,000.

Make a quick sketch of each number. Circle the greater number.

472

439

MP Analyze a Problem Look at your quick sketches. What is the same? What is different?

MP Justify a Result How do you know which number is greater?

____

____

Think and Grow

To **compare** numbers, look at the digits that have the greatest place value. Compare the hundreds first.

Compare 563 and 490.

Hundreds	Tens	Ones
5	6	3
4	9	0

5 hundreds is **greater than** 4 hundreds.

So, 563  490.

Compare 786 and 798.

Hundreds	Tens	Ones
7	8	6
7	9	8

8 tens is **less than** 9 tens.

So, 786  798.

When each place value is the same, the numbers are **equal to** each other. Use = for *equal to*.

Show and Grow *I can do it!*

1. Compare.

Hundreds	Tens	Ones
6	5	2
6	1	4

652 ◯ 614

Name ______________________________

Apply and Grow: Practice

Compare.

2. 324 ◯ 317	**3.** 26 ◯ 206
4. 546 ◯ 564	**5.** 931 ◯ 842
6. 735 ◯ 700 + 30 + 5	**7.** 412 ◯ 400 + 20

8. MP **Reasoning** Find the number that will make all three comparisons true.

_____ < 106 _____ > 104 _____ = 105

9. MP **YOU BE THE TEACHER** Is Newton correct? Explain.

____

____

____

10. There are 125 kids in a taekwondo club. There are 135 kids in a soccer club. Which club has fewer kids?

 taekwondo club  soccer club

Think and Grow: Modeling Real Life

Newton reads 200 pages on Monday, 70 on Tuesday, and 9 on Wednesday. Descartes reads 297 pages. Who reads more pages in all?

Models:

Compare: _____ ◯ _____

Who reads more pages in all? Newton Descartes

Show and Grow *I can think deeper!*

11. Newton counts train cars. The train has 100 boxcars, 40 tank cars, and 4 locomotives. Descartes counts a train with 142 cars. Who counts more cars in all?

Newton Descartes

12. You have 221 coins in your piggy bank. Your friend has 219 coins. Who has fewer coins?

You Friend

13. **DIG DEEPER!** 652 people go to a play on Friday. 625 people go on Saturday. 655 people go on Sunday. On which day are there fewer than 650 people at the play?

_____

Name ___________________________

Learning Target: Use symbols to compare two numbers up to 1,000.

The hundreds and tens are the same. So, compare the ones.

Compare 457 and 452.

Hundreds	Tens	Ones
4	5	7
4	5	2

457 (>) 452

Compare.

1.

Hundreds	Tens	Ones
9	2	3
8	5	4

923 ◯ 854

2.

Hundreds	Tens	Ones
3	8	6
3	8	9

386 ◯ 389

3. 406 ◯ 406

4. 621 ◯ 63

5. 746 ◯ 752

6. 235 ◯ 130

7. 562 ◯ 500 + 60 + 1

8. 110 ◯ 100 + 10

9. 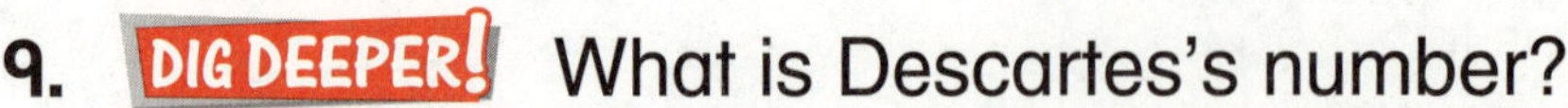 DIG DEEPER! What is Descartes's number?

- It is less than 300.
- It is greater than 200.
- The ones digit is 6 less than 10.
- The tens digit is 2 more than the ones digit.

______

---

10. There are 428 pages in a science book. There are 424 pages in a math book. Which book has more pages?

science book

math book

---

11. **MP Modeling Real Life** A concession stand sells 300 bags of popcorn on Saturday, 50 on Sunday, and 4 on Monday. They sell 345 drinks. Did they sell more bags of popcorn or drinks?

bags of popcorn   drinks

---

12. DIG DEEPER! Newton climbs 136 stairs on Friday. He climbs 132 on Saturday. He climbs 128 on Sunday. On which day does he climb more than 134 stairs?

______

Review & Refresh

Find the difference. Use addition to check your answer.

13.

$$\begin{array}{r} 52 \\ -\ 26 \\ \hline \end{array} \qquad + \underline{\qquad}$$

14.

$$\begin{array}{r} 67 \\ -\ 28 \\ \hline \end{array} \qquad + \underline{\qquad}$$

Name ______________________________

Compare Numbers Using a Number Line

8.6

Learning Target: Use a number line to compare two numbers up to 1,000.

Explore and Grow

Identify a number that is less than 538. Identify a number that is greater than 538. Model the numbers on the number line.

_____ < 538

_____ > 538

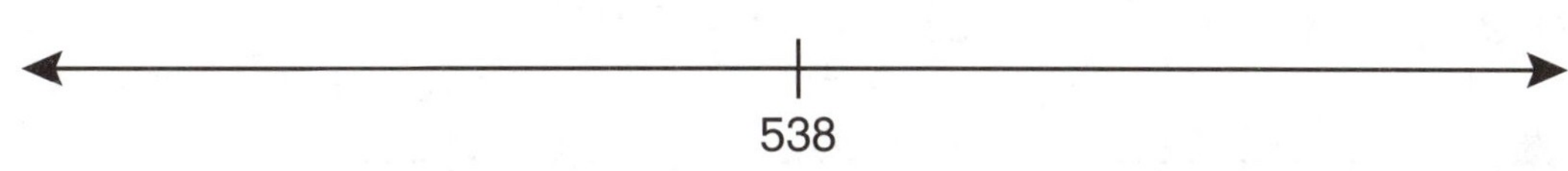

Communicate Clearly Explain how you know.

____

____

____

Think and Grow

Numbers to the left of 265 on a number line are less than 265.

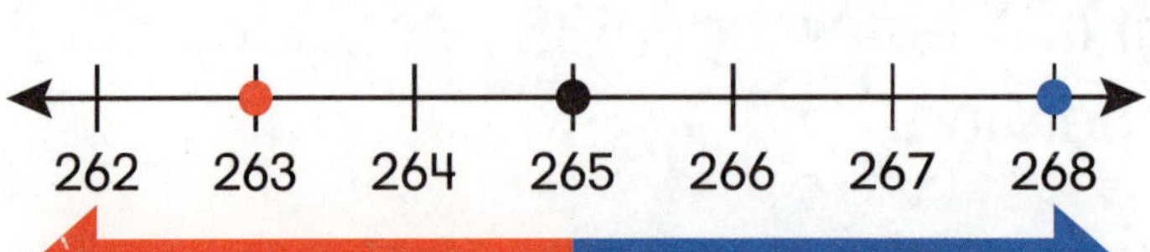

Numbers to the right are greater than 265.

263  265 265 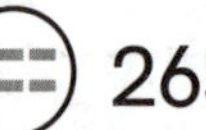 265 268  265

Show and Grow *I can do it!*

Compare.

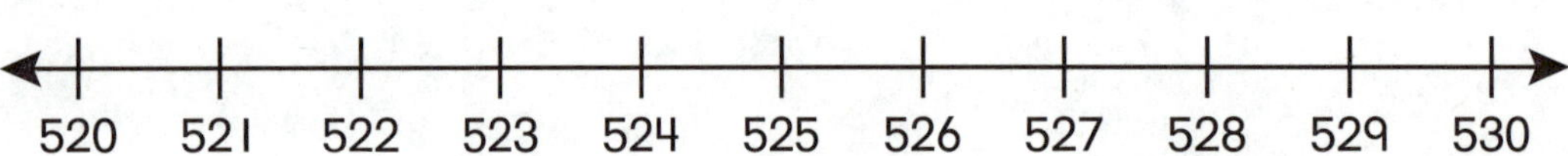

1. 527 ◯ 525
2. 521 ◯ 524
3. 528 ◯ 528
4. 530 ◯ 520
5. 522 ◯ 523
6. 529 ◯ 526

Write a number that makes the statement true.

7. 372 < ______
8. 195 > ______

Name ______________________________

Apply and Grow: Practice

Compare.

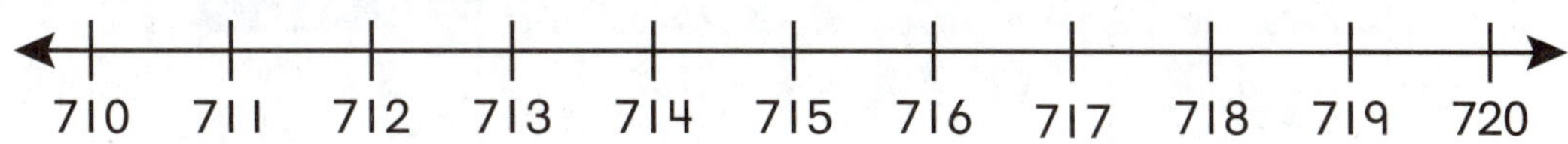

9. 714 ◯ 714

10. 720 ◯ 710

11. 718 ◯ 717

12. 711 ◯ 713

Write a number that makes the statement true.

13. 736 = ______

14. 461 > ______

15. ______ < 295

16. ______ > 573

17. **MP Logic** Is ★ greater than or less than ▼? Explain.

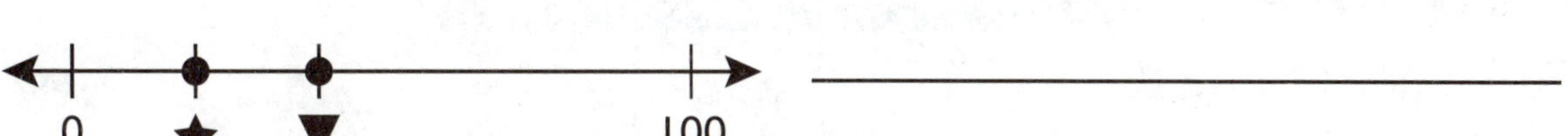

____

____

____

18. **DIG DEEPER!** What number might Newton be thinking?

350 342 365

My number is less than 356 and greater than 342.

Think and Grow: Modeling Real Life

Order the race numbers from least to greatest.

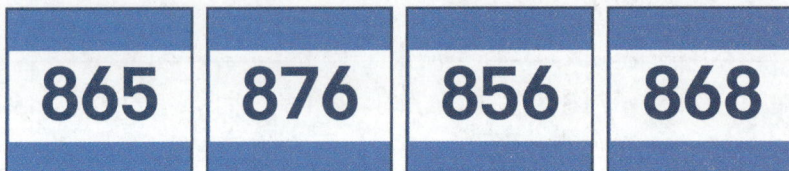

865	876	856	868

Model:

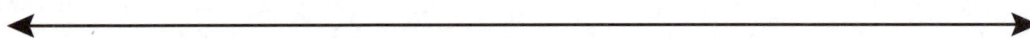

Order from least to greatest: _____, _____, _____, _____

Your race number is greater than all of the other numbers but less than 900. What is a possible race number for you?

_____

Show and Grow *I can think deeper!*

19. Order the race times from least to greatest.

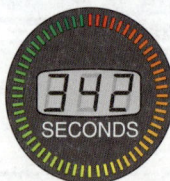

342 SECONDS

Order from least to greatest: _____, _____, _____, _____

DIG DEEPER! Your time is less than all of the other times but greater than 320 seconds. What is a possible time for you?

_____ seconds

Name ______________________________

Practice 8.6

Learning Target: Use a number line to compare two numbers up to 1,000.

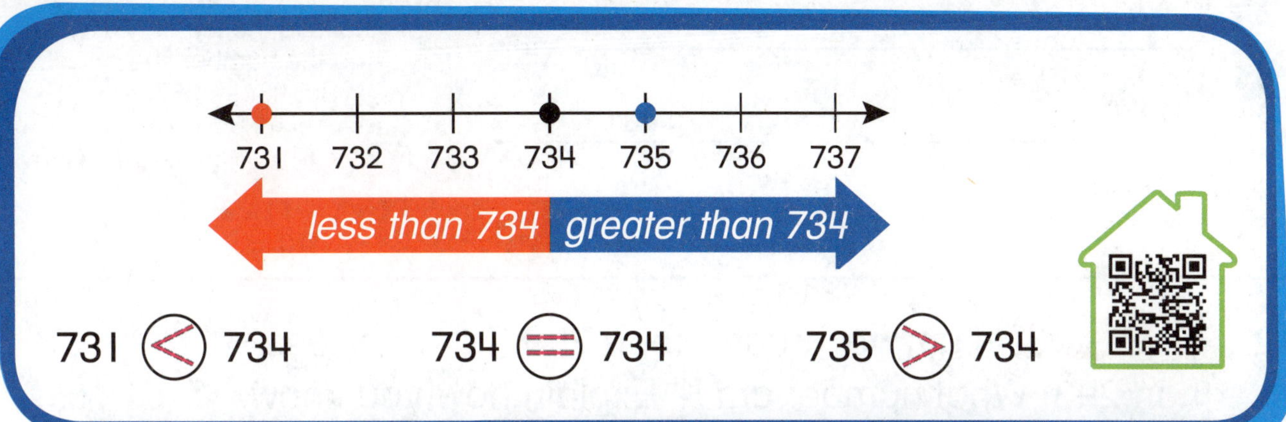

Compare.

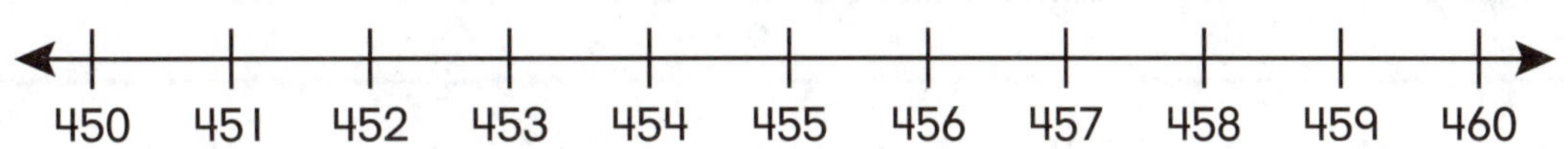

1. 450 ◯ 460

2. 459 ◯ 457

3. 455 ◯ 451

4. 456 ◯ 456

5. 455 ◯ 454

6. 452 ◯ 453

Write a number that makes the statement true.

7. 529 > _____

8. 815 < _____

9. _____ < 142

10. _____ = 364

11. MP **YOU BE THE TEACHER** Is Descartes correct? Explain.

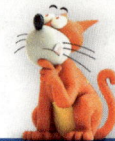

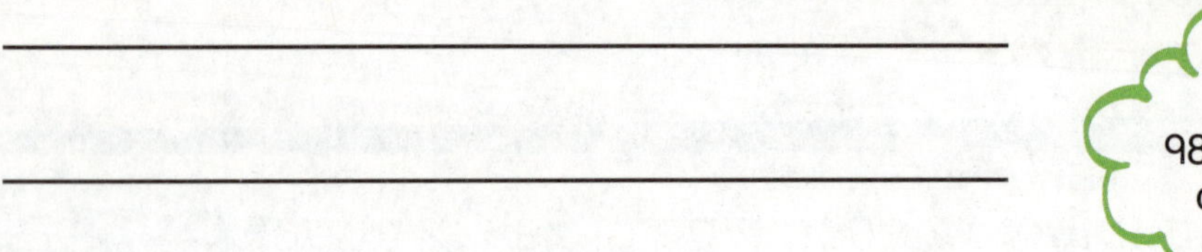

986 987
986 is to the left of 987 on the number line. So, 986 > 987.

12. **DIG DEEPER!** I am *not* greater than 243. I am *not* less than 243. What number am I? Explain how you know.

____

____

13. MP **Modeling Real Life** Order the numbers from least to greatest.

_____, _____, _____, _____

DIG DEEPER! Your car's number is greater than all of the others but less than 705. What is a possible number for your car?

_____

Review & Refresh

14. Circle the shapes with flat surfaces that are circles.

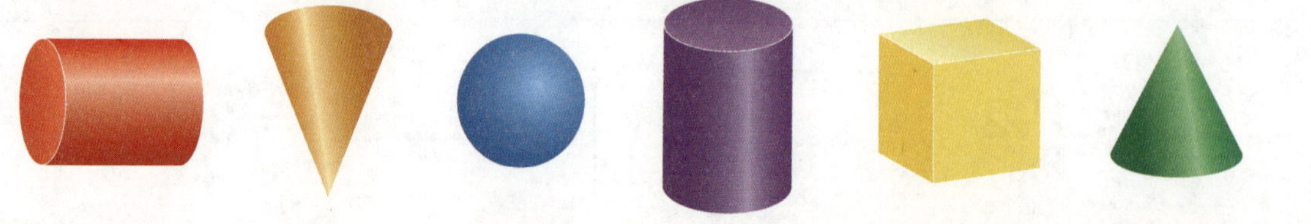

Name ____________________

Performance Task 8

The table shows the number of each type of fish in a tank.

1. Complete the table.

Type	Number of Fish	Standard Form
	Three hundred fifty-one	
	100 more than 429	
	100 + 100 + 100 + 10 + 2	
	100 less than 558	
	202 + 100 + 10	

2. Compare the numbers of fish.

a. 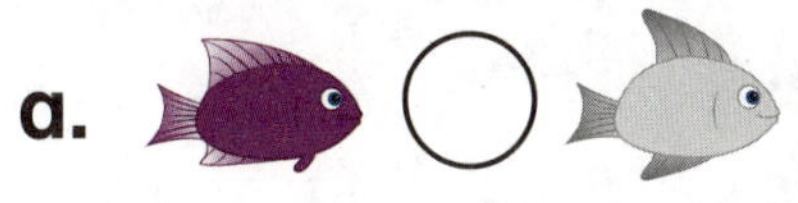

b. 

c. 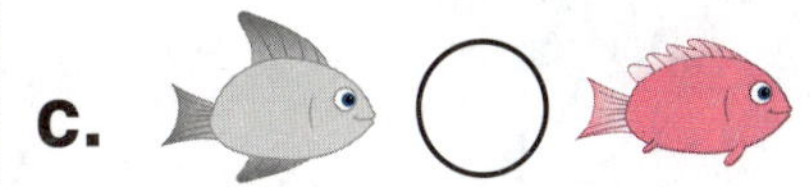

3. All of the purple, green, and pink fish are moved to a new exhibit. How many fish are left in the tank?

______ fish

4. A school of 24 fish swim in an array. Draw an array for the fish.

Number Boss

To Play: Place Number Cards 0–9 in a pile. Each player flips 3 cards and makes a three-digit number. Compare the numbers. The player with the greater number takes both sets of cards. If the numbers are equal, flip cards again. The person with the greater number takes all of the cards. Repeat until all of the cards have been used.

Hundreds	Tens	Ones

Name ______________________________

Chapter Practice 8

8.1 Count to 120 in Different Ways

1. Count by ones.

113, 114, 115, ____, ____, ____, ____, ____

2. Count by fives.

25, 30, 35, ____, ____, ____, ____, ____

3. Count by tens.

33, 43, 53, ____, ____, ____, ____, ____

8.2 Count to 1,000 in Different Ways

4. Count by fives.

210, 215, 220, ____, ____, ____, ____, ____

5. Count by tens.

740, 750, 760, ____, ____, ____, ____, ____

6. Count by hundreds.

300, 400, 500, ____, ____, ____, ____, ____

8.3 Place Value Patterns

Use place value to find the missing numbers.

7. 854, 855, 856, _____, _____, _____, _____

8. 940, 950, 960, _____, _____, _____, _____

9. 275, 375, 475, _____, _____, _____, _____

10. MP **Repeated Reasoning** Use place value to describe each pattern.

100, 101, 102, 103, 104

____

____

600, 700, 800, 900, 1,000

____

____

8.4 Find More or Less

11. 10 more than 813 is _____.

12. 10 less than 976 is _____.

13. 100 more than 254 is _____.

14. 100 less than 531 is _____.

15. 1 more than 444 is _____.

16. 1 less than 622 is _____.

17. **Modeling Real Life** Your craft book has 110 ideas. Your friend's craft book has 10 fewer ideas than yours. How many ideas does your friend's craft book have?

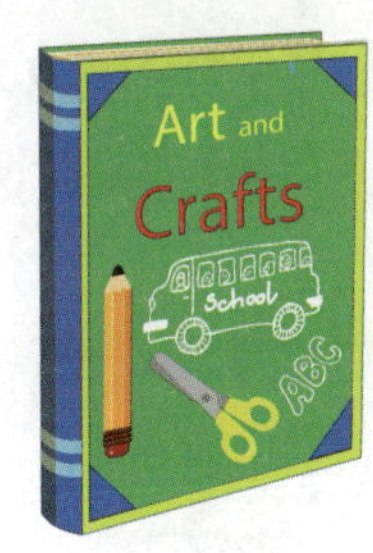

_____ ideas

18. **Modeling Real Life** You have 324 beads. Newton has 100 more than you. Descartes has 10 fewer than Newton. How many beads does Descartes have?

_____ beads

8.5 Compare Numbers Using Symbols

Compare.

19.

Hundreds	Tens	Ones
5	8	3
5	8	3

583 ◯ 583

20.

Hundreds	Tens	Ones
6	2	6
7	2	5

626 ◯ 725

21. 932 ◯ 910

22. 49 ◯ 411

23. 328 ◯ 300 + 40 + 6

24. 280 ◯ 200 + 10 + 8

25. There are 318 kids in a gymnastics club. There are 219 kids in a swim club. Which club has fewer kids?

 gymnastics club  swim club

8.6 Compare Numbers Using a Number Line

Compare.

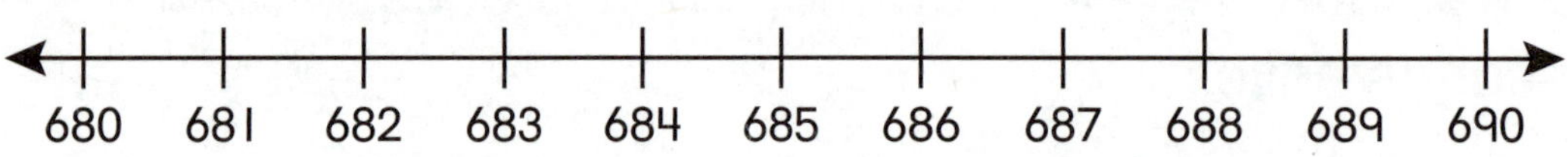

26. 683 ◯ 687

27. 689 ◯ 688

28. 681 ◯ 681

29. 690 ◯ 680

Write a number that makes the statement true.

30. 324 < ______

31. 136 > ______

32. ______ = 750

33. ______ < 871

34. **Number Sense** What number might Descartes be thinking?

326 238 315

My number is greater than 238 and less than 325.

Name ____________________

Cumulative Practice 1–8

1. Which equation can you use to check your answer to 32 − 18?

○ 32 + 14 = 46

○ 18 + 32 = 50

○ 18 + 14 = 32

○ 14 + 4 = 18

2. Which number does *not* belong?

324, 334, 344, ____, ____, ____

○ 345

○ 374

○ 364

○ 354

3. Find the missing digits.

$$\begin{array}{r} \square\ 4 \\ +\ 6\ 3 \\ \hline 8\ \square \end{array} \qquad \begin{array}{r} 4\ \square \\ +\ 1\ 6 \\ \hline \square\ 5 \end{array} \qquad \begin{array}{r} \square\ 6 \\ +\ 5\ \square \\ \hline 9\ 1 \end{array}$$

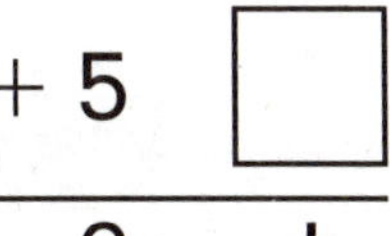

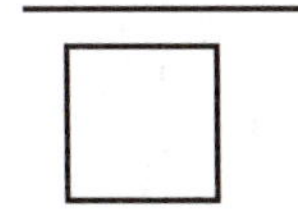

4. Use the number cards to decompose to subtract.

64 − 37 = ______

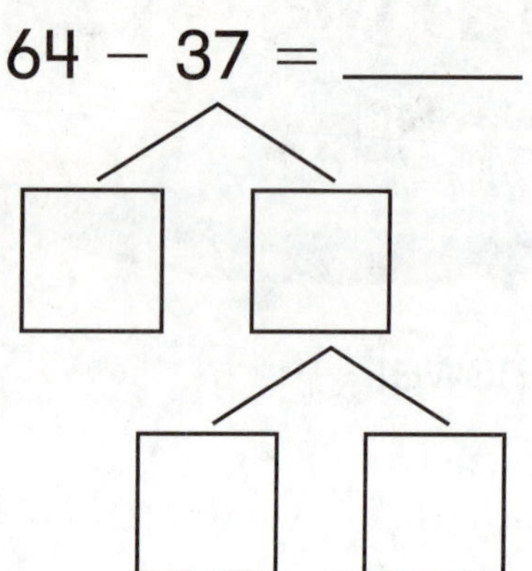

27 30 7

4 3

5. Which choice does *not* show 124?

○ 0 hundreds, 12 tens, and 4 ones

○ 

○ 1 hundred, 4 tens, and 2 ones

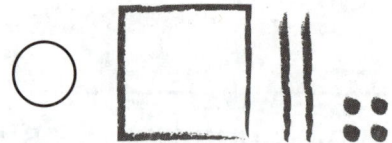

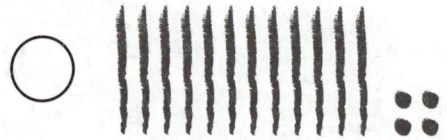

○

6. Which quick sketch shows 43 − 25?

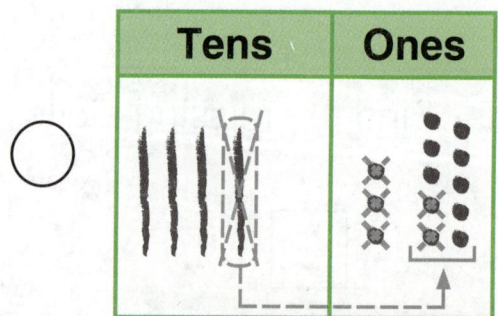

○ 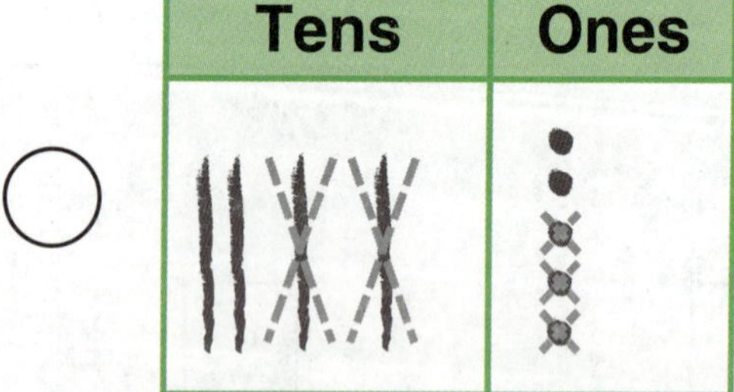

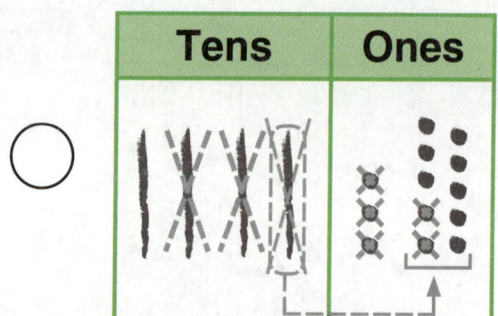

○

○ 

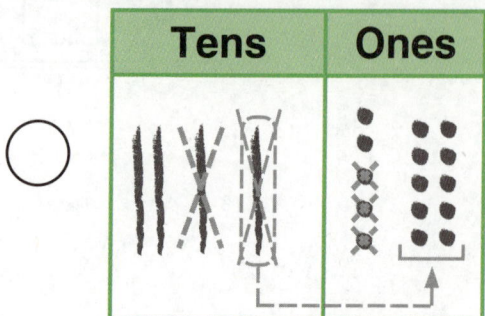

○

7. You have 4 fewer gel pens than your friend. You have 6 gel pens. Which picture shows how many gel pens your friend has?

○ 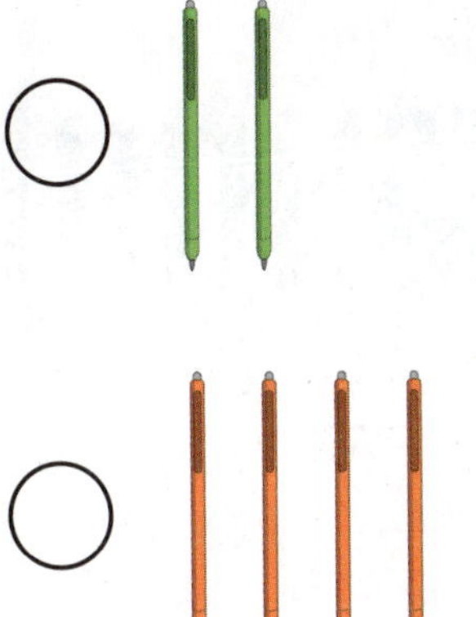

○ 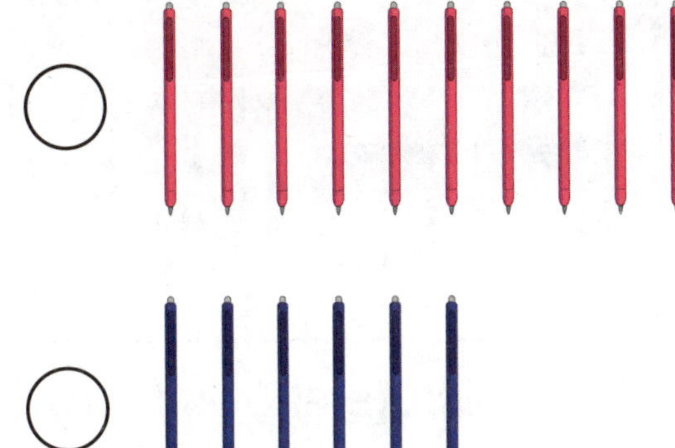

○ 

○ 

8. Which number does *not* belong?

My number is greater than 563 and less than 567.

○ 566

○ 563

○ 564

○ 565

9. Your friend uses compensation to add. Complete the equation to show what numbers he added after using compensation.

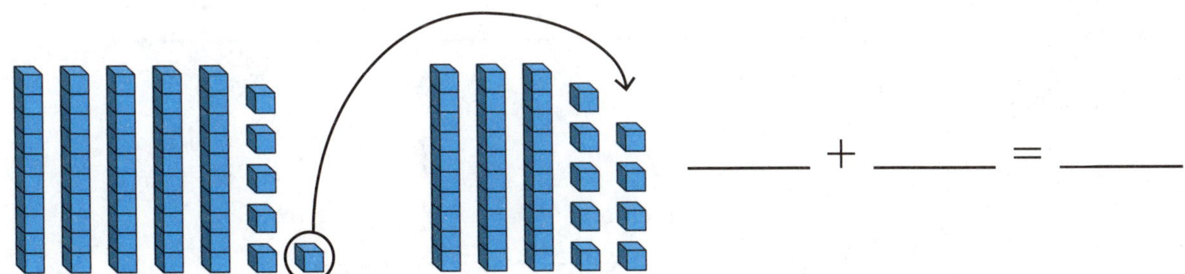

_____ + _____ = _____

10. Which choices show 238?

○ 200 + 80 + 3

○ two hundred thirty-eight

○

○

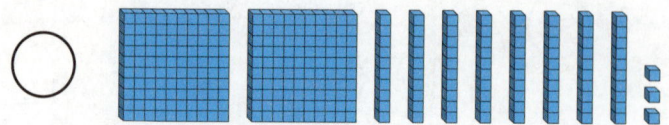

11. Which picture shows 2 groups of 3?

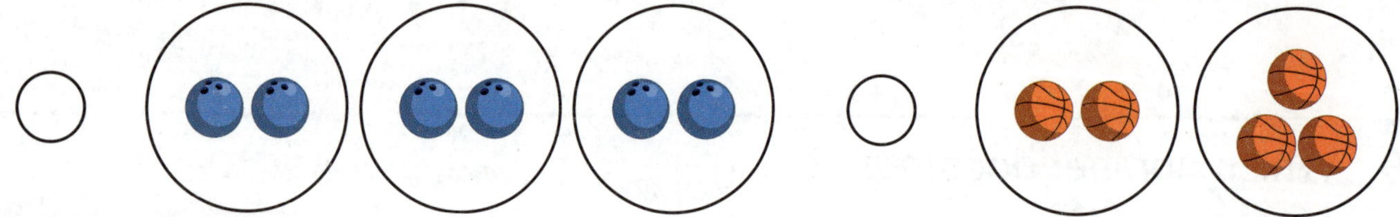

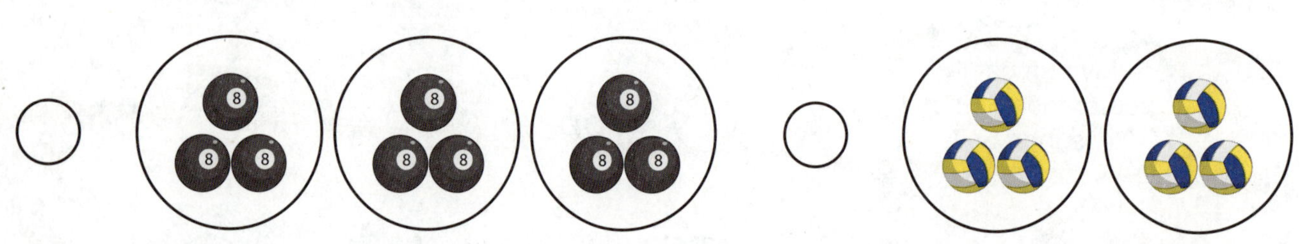

12. Descartes wants to use addition to subtract 51 − 25. Help him complete the number line and equations.

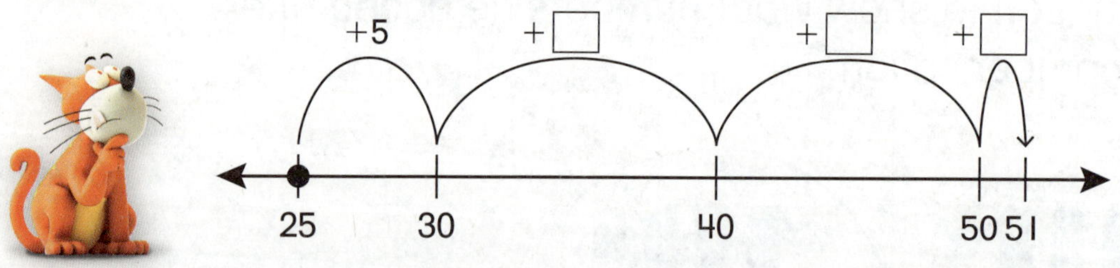

5 + ______ + ______ + ______ = ______

So, 51 − 25 = ______.

Glossary

a.m. [a.m.]

go to school

8:00 a.m.

addends [sumandos]

$4 + 3 = 7$

angle [ángulo]

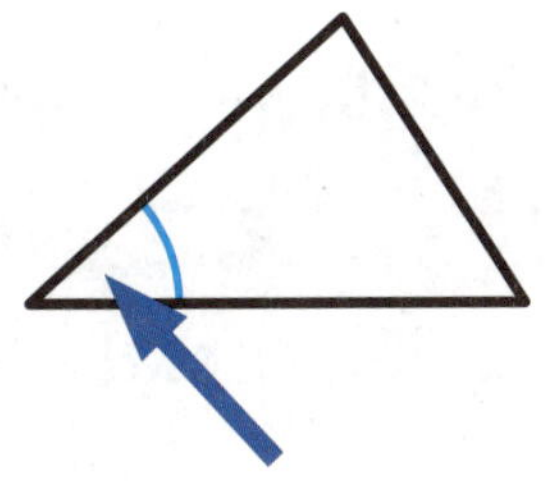

array [formación]

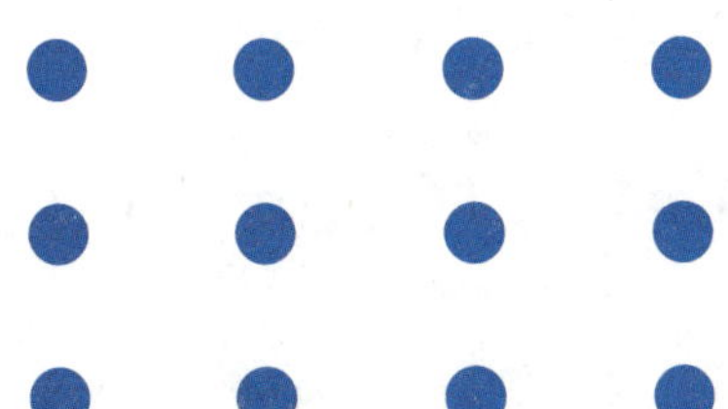

B

bar graph [gráfica de barras]

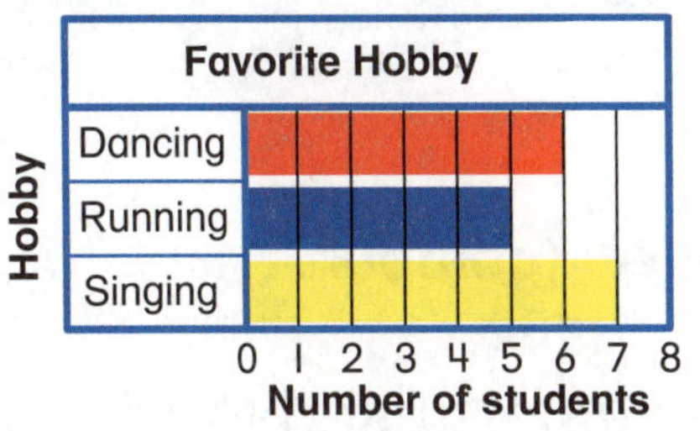

C

cent sign [signo de centavo]

centimeter [centímetro]

centimeter (cm)

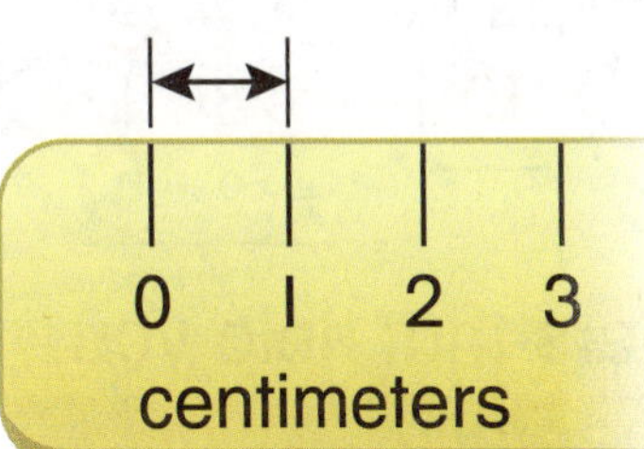

cents [centavos]

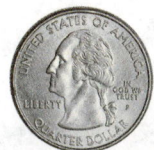

1 cent or 1¢

25 cents or 25¢

column [columna]

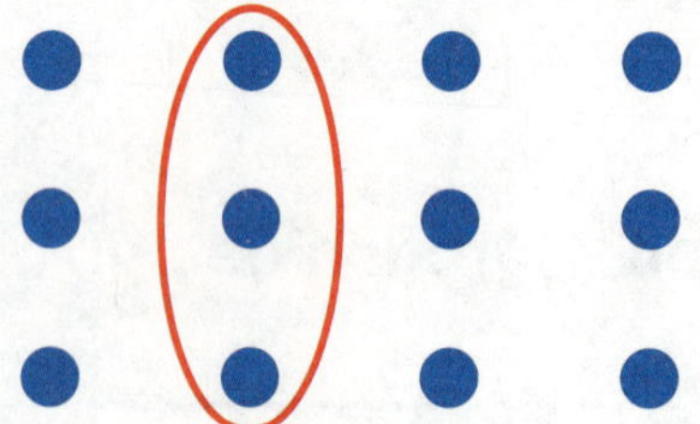

compare [comparar]

The symbols used to *compare* numbers are <, >, and =.

$732 > 399$ $399 < 732$

$399 = 399$

compatible numbers [números compatibles]

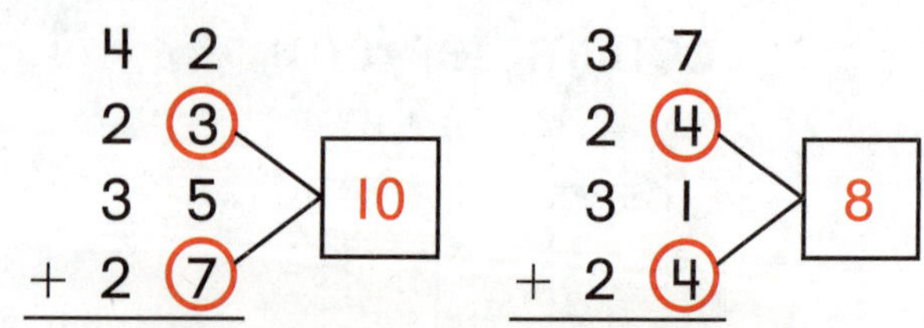

numbers that help you add mentally

compensation [compensación]

A strategy used to make a ten to help add and subtract numbers

cube [cubo]

D

data [datos]

Favorite Hobby

dancing	dancing	singing
running	dancing	running
running	running	singing
singing	singing	dancing
singing	dancing	dancing
singing	running	singing

decrease [disminución]

542 → 532 → 522

These numbers *decrease* by 10.

difference [diferencia]

$8 - 3 = 5$

dime [moneda de diez centavos]

A **dime** is 10 cents or 10¢.

dollar [dólar]

A **dollar** is $1 or 100¢.

dollar sign [signo de dólar]

doubles minus 1
[dobles menos 1]

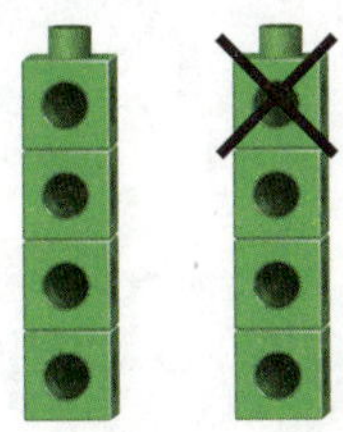

$4 + 4 = 8$, so $4 + 3 = 7$.

doubles plus 1
[dobles más 1]

$4 + 4 = 8$, so $4 + 5 = 9$.

edge [arista]

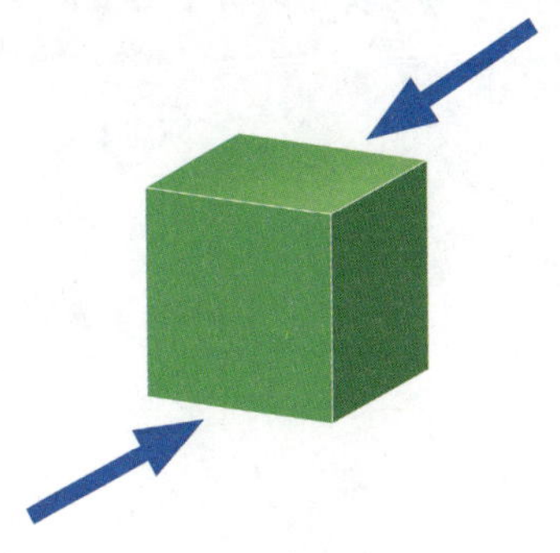

equal groups [grupos iguales]

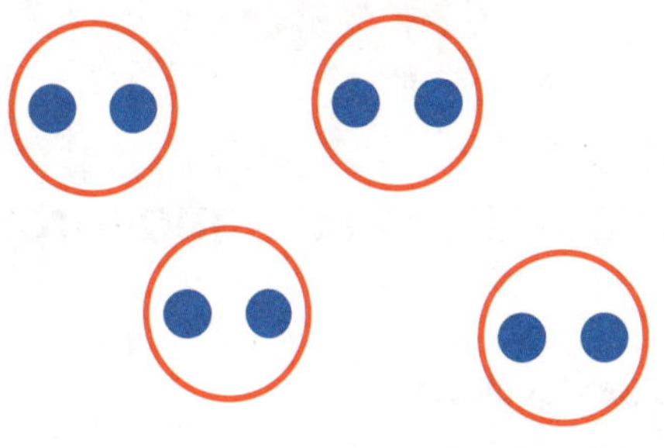

equal to (=) [igual a]

$399 = 399$

399 is equal to 399.

equation [ecuación]

$10 - 4 = 6$

$5 + 5 = 10$

Glossary

estimate [estimación]

even [par]

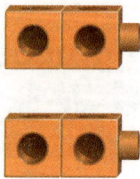

can be shown as equal groups

expanded form
[forma expandida]

300 + 20 + 9

expression [expresión]

4 + 7   7 − 4

face [cara]

$5 bill [billete de $5]

$5 bill

foot [pie]

foot (ft)

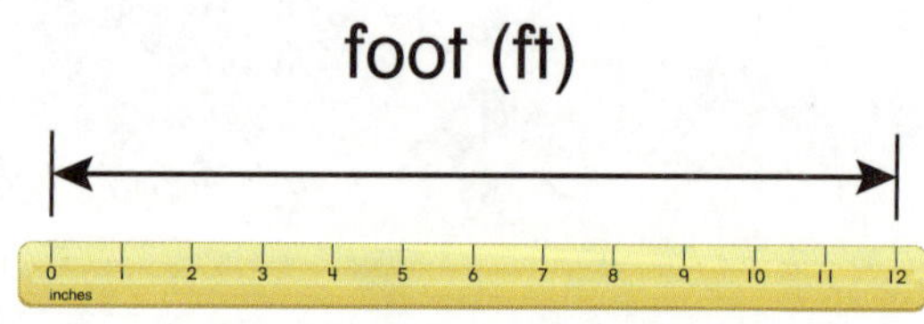

There are 12 inches in 1 foot.

fourths [cuartos]

The rectangle is divided into **fourths**.

greater than (>) [mayor que]

732 > 399

732 is greater than 399.

half past [y media]

half past 3

halves [mitades]

The circle is divided into **halves**.

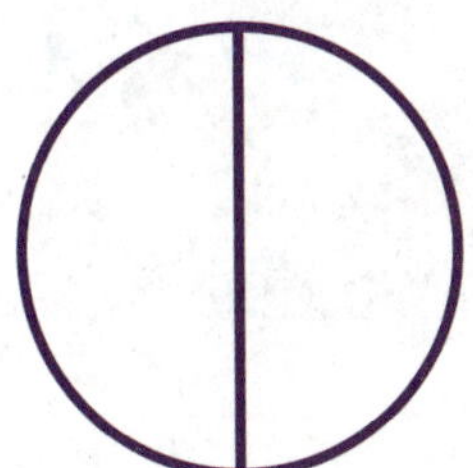

hexagon [hexágono]

6 sides
6 vertices

hundred [cien]

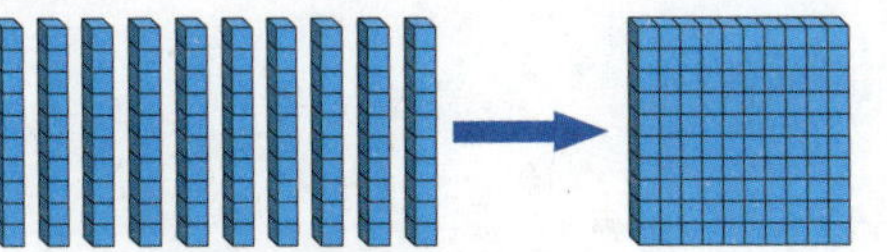

There are 10 tens in
1 hundred.

hundreds place
[lugar de cientos]

329

inch [pulgada]

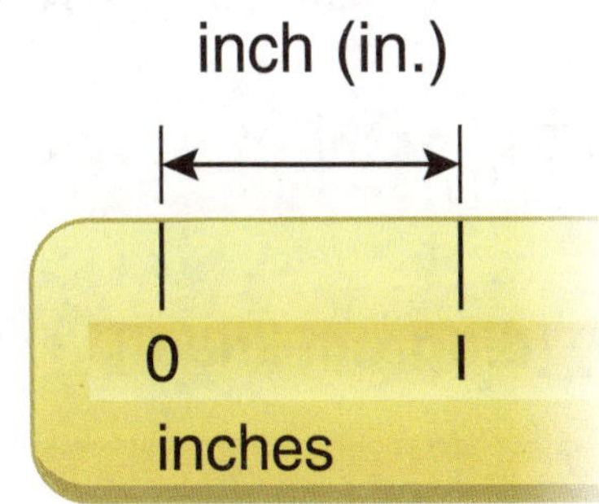

increase [incrementar]

522 → 532 → 542

These numbers *increase* by 10.

key [clave]

Favorite Color						
Blue	☺	☺				
Green	☺	☺	☺	☺		
Yellow	☺	☺	☺	☺	☺	

Each ☺ = 1 student.

less than (<) [menor que]

399 < 732

399 is less than 732.

line plot [diagram lineal]

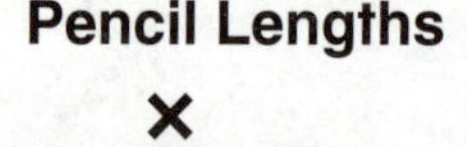

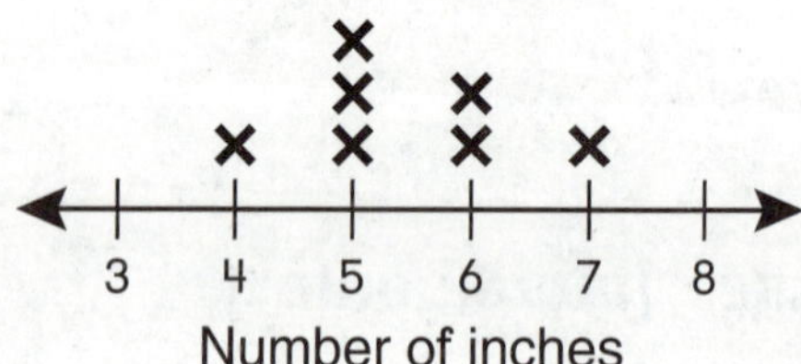

meter [metro]

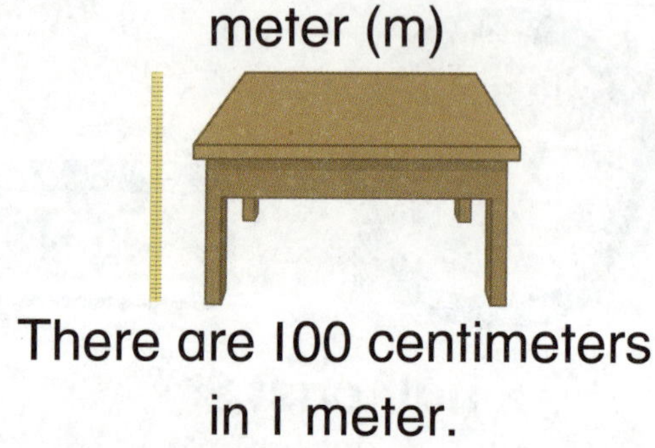

There are 100 centimeters in 1 meter.

midnight [medianoche]

Midnight is 12:00 at night.

nickel [moneda de 5¢]

A **nickel** is 5 cents or 5¢.

noon **[mediodía]**

Noon is 12:00 in the daytime.

octagon **[octágono]**

8 sides
8 vertices

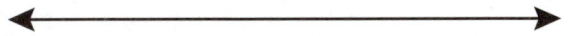

odd **[impar]**

cannot be shown as equal groups

$1 bill **[billete de $1]**

$1 bill

open number line
[abrir la línea numérica]

p.m. **[p.m.]**

go to sleep

8:00 p.m.

partial sums **[sumas parciales]**

	Tens	Ones	
	1	9	
+	2	4	
10 + 20 =	3	0	Partial Sums
9 + 4 =	1	3	
Sum	4	3	

penny [monedo de 1¢]

A **penny** is 1 cent or 1¢.

pentagon [pentágono]

5 sides
5 vertices

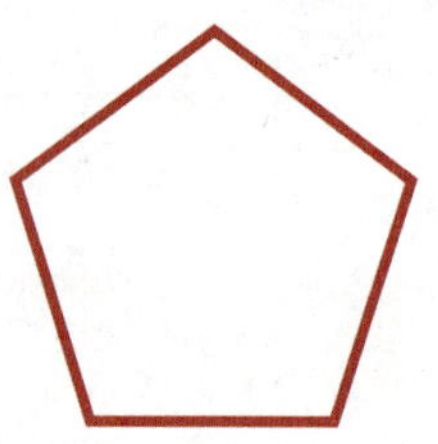

picture graph [gráfico de imagen]

Favorite Color						
Blue	🙂	🙂				
Green	🙂	🙂	🙂	🙂		
Yellow	🙂	🙂	🙂	🙂	🙂	

Each 🙂 = 1 student.

polygon [polígono]

A **polygon** is a closed two-dimensional shape with 3 or more sides.

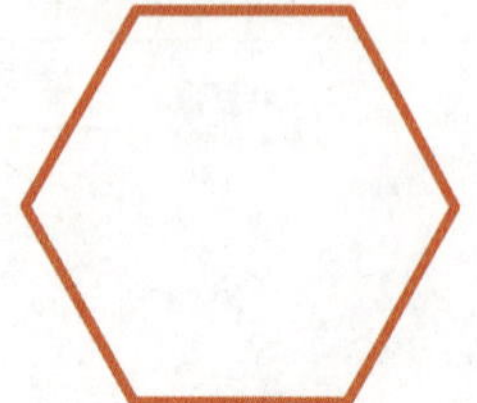

quadrilateral [cuadrilátero]

4 sides
4 vertices

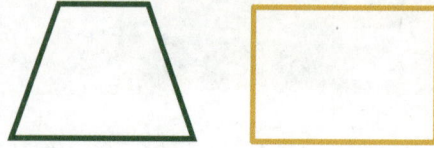

quarter [moneda de 25¢]

A **quarter** is 25 cents or 25¢.

quarter past [y cuarto]

15 minutes after 8 or **quarter past** 8

quarter to [menos cuarto]

15 minutes before 8 or
quarter to 8

R

regroup [reagrupar]

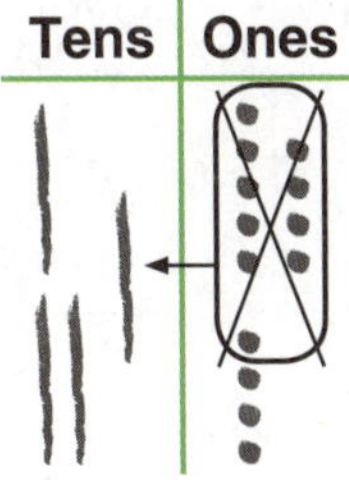

	Tens	Ones
	1	
	1	9
+	2	4
	4	3

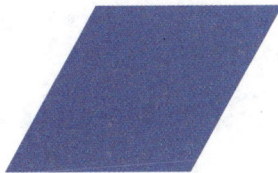

repeated addition
[adición repetida]

$$2 + 2 + 2 + 2$$

rhombus [rombo]

4 sides that are the same length

right angle [ángulo recto]

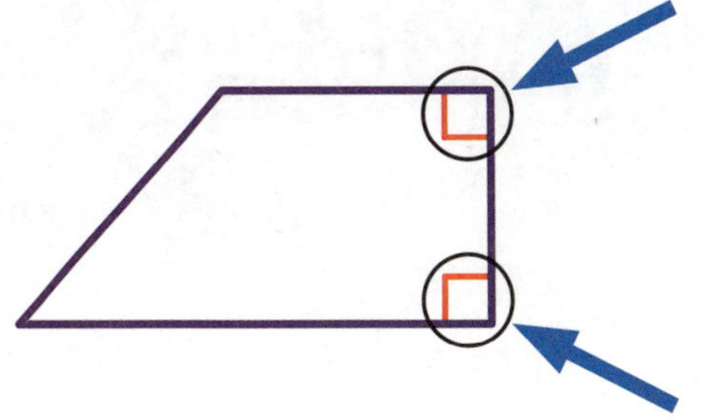

row [fila]

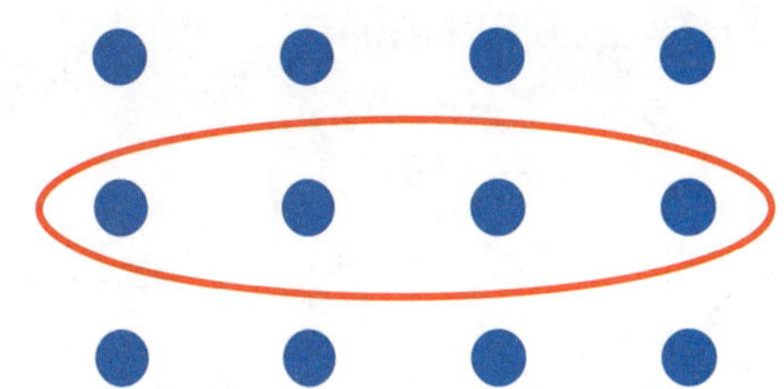

S

side [lado]

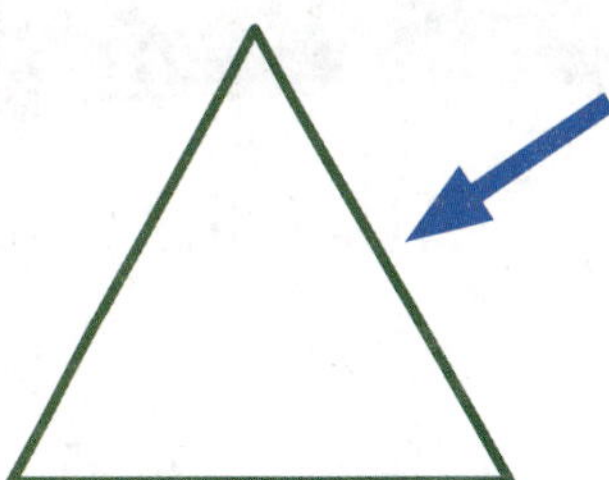

standard form [forma estándar]

329

sum [suma]

$5 + 3 = 8$

survey [encuesta]

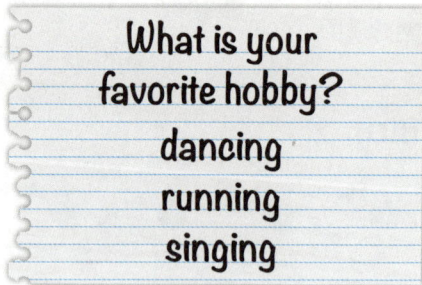

What is your
favorite hobby?
dancing
running
singing

$10 bill [billete de $10]

$10 bill

thirds [tercios]

The square is divided into **thirds**.

thousand [mil]

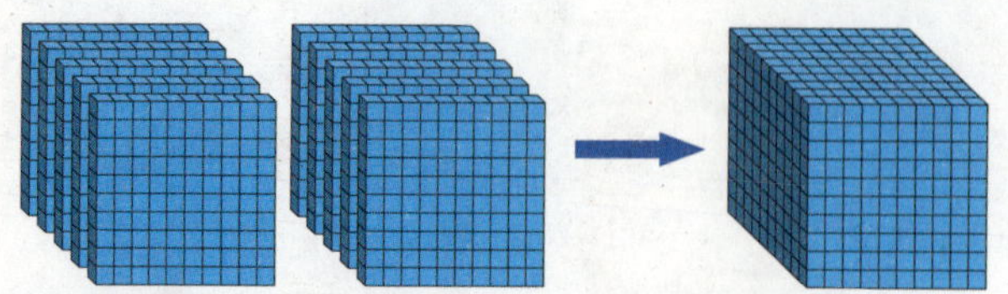

There are 10 hundreds in 1 thousand.

$20 bill [billete de $20]

$20 bill

vertex [vértice]

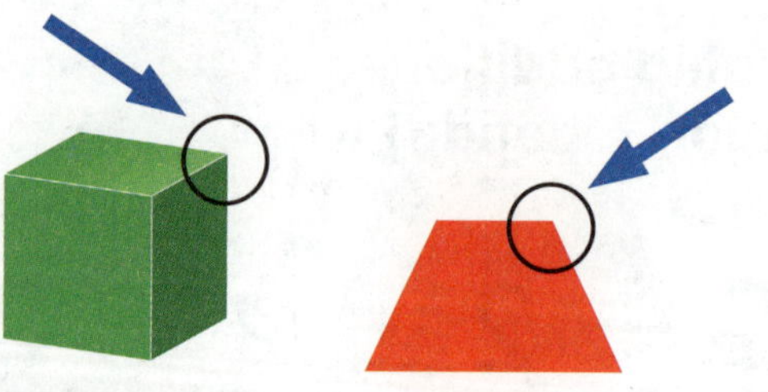

word form [forma de la palabra]

three hundred twenty-nine

yard **[yarda]**

yard (yd)

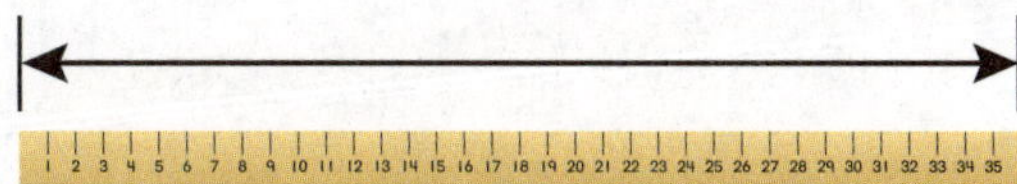

There are 36 inches, or
3 feet, in 1 yard.

Index

Addends, *See also* Addition
- breaking apart, 116–126
- changing order of, 41–46
- definition of, 42

Addition
- within 20, 83–88
- checking subtraction with, 287–292
- choosing strategies for, 133–138, 177–182, 447–452
- of compatible numbers, 442
- using compensation
  - with three-digit numbers, 417–422
  - with two-digit numbers, 127–132
- using decomposition (breaking addends apart), 116–126
- using doubles strategies, 47–52, 84
- of even and odd numbers, 9–14
- explaining strategies for, 447–452
- of four two-digit numbers, 441–446
- of lengths, 579–584
- using "make a 10" strategy, 59–64, 84
- using mental math, 399–404
- on number line (*See* Number line, adding on)
- order of addends in, 41–46
- using partial sums
  - with three-digit numbers, 423–428
  - with two-digit numbers, 153–164
- using place value, 115–126
- using regrouping, 165–176
- relationship between subtraction and, 71–76
- repeated, with equal groups, 16–18
- subtraction using, 219–224, 503–508
- summary of strategies for, 447
- of three one-digit numbers, 53–58
- of three two-digit numbers, 183–188
- of three-digit numbers, 411–440
  - using compensation, 417–422
  - using models, 429–434
  - using number line, 411–416
  - using partial sums, 423–428
- of two-digit numbers
  - using compensation, 127–132
  - four, 441–446
  - using partial sums, 153–164
  - three, 183–188
- word problems solved using
  - one-step, 89–94, 189–194
  - two-step, 139–144, 189–194

A.M., 717–722

Angles
- definition of, 738
- of polygons, identifying, 737–742
- right, 738–742

Another Way, *Throughout. For example, see:* 20, 60, 110, 178, 208, 294, 406, 468, 676

Apply and Grow: Practice, *In every lesson. For example, see:* 5, 43, 105, 209, 315, 401, 525, 581, 671

Arrays
- definition of, 152
- finding number of objects in, 21–26
- solving word problems using, 27–32

Bar graphs
- making, 637–642
- tally charts compared to, 631, 637
- understanding, 631–636

Bar model, 90

Base ten, 331

Bills, *See* Dollar bills

Breaking apart, *See* Decomposition

Centimeters
estimating lengths in, 535–540
measuring lengths in, 523–534
Challenge, *See* Dig Deeper
Chapter Practice, *In every chapter. For example, see:* 35–38, 97–100, 147–150, 257–260, 307–310, 455–458, 573–576, 657–660, 725–728, 781–784
Charts, tally
bar graphs compared to, 631, 637
organizing data in, 613–618
picture graphs compared to, 619, 625
Choose Tools, 531, 549
Clocks, *See* Time
Coins
combining
in different ways, 675–680
to make one dollar, 681–686
finding total value of, 663–674
grouping by type, 669–674
making change from one dollar, 687–692
Columns
definition of, 152
in rectangles, 756–760
Common Error, *Throughout. For example, see:* T-30, T-113, T-294, T-338, T-366, T-450, T-492, T-582, T-708, T-734
Common Misconception, T-4, T-190, T-300
Comparing lengths, 565–570
in word problems, 585–590
Comparing numbers
using number line, 381–386
using symbols, 375–380
Compatible numbers, adding, 442
Compensation
addition using
with three-digit numbers, 417–422
with two-digit numbers, 127–132
subtraction using
with numbers containing zeros, 498–502
with three-digit numbers, 479–484
with two-digit numbers, 237–242
"Count back" strategy
definition of, 40
subtraction using, 65–70
"Count on" strategy
definition of, 40
subtraction using, 65–70
Counting, skip
within 120, 351–356
within 1,000, 357–362, 405–410, 467–472
Cross-Curricular Connections, *In every lesson. For example, see:* T-7, T-81, T-119, T-273, T-329, T-403, T-527, T-601, T-679, T-759
Cubes
definition of, 750
drawing, 749–754
identifying, 749–754
Cumulative Practice, *Throughout. For example, see:* 201–204, 393–396, 607–610, 785–788
Customary units
estimating lengths in, 553–558
measuring lengths in, 547–552

Data
in bar graphs, 631–642
in line plots, 643–654
in picture graphs, 619–630
in tally charts, 613–618
Decade number, *See* Ten
Decomposition
addition using, 116–126
subtraction using, 225–236
Define It, *In every chapter. For example, see:* 2, 102, 152, 206, 312, 398, 460, 578, 612, 730

Difference, *See* Subtraction
Differentiation, *see* Scaffolding Instruction
Dig Deeper, *Throughout. For example, see:* 8, 43, 155, 210, 315, 366, 414, 532, 582, 666
Dimes, *See also* Coins
value of, 664
Dollar bills
five ($5), finding total value of, 693–698
one ($1)
coins equal to, 681–686
finding total value of, 693–698
making change from, 687–692
value of, 682
ten ($10), finding total value of, 693–698
Dollar sign ($), 682
Doubles minus 1, addition using, 47–52
Doubles plus 1, addition using, 47–52, 84

E

Edges, of cubes, 750
ELL Support, *In every lesson. For example, see:* T-2, T-41, T-104, T-156, T-296, T-364, T-485, T-522, T-664, T-730
Equal groups
definition of, 16
finding number of objects in, 15–20
Equal shares
drawing lines showing, 767–778
identifying lines showing, 761–766
Equal squares, rectangles composed of, 755–760
Equal to symbol (=), 376–380
Equations, definition of, 10
Error Analysis, *See* You Be the Teacher
Estimating lengths
in customary units, 553–558
in metric units, 535–540
Even numbers
adding, 9–14
identifying, 3–8
modeling, 9–14
Explain, *Throughout. For example, see:* 8, 91, 132, 230, 343, 366, 494, 591, 696, 770
Explore and Grow, *In every lesson. For example, see:* 41, 103, 153, 207, 263, 313, 461, 523, 579, 663
Expressions, definition of, 42
Extended form of numbers, 331–336

F

Faces, of cubes, 750
Feet
estimating lengths in, 553–558
measuring lengths in, 547–552
Five (5), counting by
within 120, 351–356
within 1,000, 357–362
Five dollar bills ($5), finding total value of, 693–698
Formative Assessment, *Throughout. For example, see:* T-6, T-92, T-168, T-240, T-272, T-314, T-372, T-482, T-556, T-628
Fourths
definition of, 762
drawing lines showing, 767–778
identifying lines showing, 761–766

G

Games, *In every chapter. For example, see:* 34, 96, 196, 256, 388, 454, 516, 572, 656, 780
"Get to 10" strategy, subtraction using, 77–82, 84
Graphs
bar
making, 637–642
tally charts compared to, 631, 637
understanding, 631–636
picture
making, 625–630

tally charts compared to, 619, 625
understanding, 619–624
Greater than symbol (>), 376–380
Groups, equal
definition of, 16
finding number of objects in, 15–20

H

Half past, 712–716
Halves
definition of, 762
drawing lines showing, 767–778
identifying lines showing, 761–766
Hexagons
drawing, 734, 736
identifying, 254, 732–736, 737
Higher Order Thinking, *See* Dig Deeper
Hour, telling time before and after the, 711–716
Hundred(s) (100), 313–318
adding
using mental math, 399–404
using models, 429–434
using number line, 405–410
in partial sums, 423–428
counting by, within 1,000, 357–362, 405–410, 467–472
definition of, 320
identifying groups of tens as, 313–318
identifying numbers 100 more or 100 less, 369–374
subtracting
using mental math, 461–466
using models, 485–490
using number line, 467–472
understanding place value of, 325–330
Hundred chart, 103, 109, 207, 213

Inches
estimating lengths in, 553–558
measuring lengths in, 541–552

L

Learning Target, *In every lesson. For example, see:* 7, 103, 207, 313, 417, 541, 583, 631, 711
Lengths
adding, on number line, 579–584
comparing, 565–570, 585–590
estimating
in centimeters, 535–540
in customary units, 553–558
in feet, 553–558
in inches, 553–558
in meters, 535–540
in metric units, 535–540
in yards, 553–558
measuring
in centimeters, 523–534
comparing after, 565–570
in customary units, 547–552
in feet, 547–552
in inches, 541–552
making line plots after, 649–654
in meters, 529–534
in metric units, 529–534
using two different units, 559–564
in yards, 547–552
subtracting, on number line, 579–584
in word problems, solving
comparing lengths, 585–590
for missing measurements, 591–596
on number line, 579–584
practicing, 597–602
Less than symbol (<), 376–380
Line plots, making, 643–654
Logic, 23, 540, 558, 772

"Make a 10" strategy, addition using, 59–64, 84

Mathematical Practices
Make sense of problems and persevere in solving them, *Throughout. For example, see:* 3, 89, 139, 219, 281, 316, 411, 628, 698
Reason abstractly and quantitatively, *Throughout. For example, see:* 117, 185, 230, 265, 377, 446, 599, 665, 755
Construct viable arguments and critique the reasoning of others, *Throughout. For example, see:* 8, 80, 133, 173, 292, 441, 538, 677, 772
Model with mathematics, *Throughout. For example, see:* 58, 114, 212, 280, 356, 484, 540, 716, 760
Use appropriate tools strategically, *Throughout. For example, see:* 6, 124, 177, 299, 322, 369, 464, 549, 637
Attend to precision, *Throughout. For example, see:* 62, 123, 269, 429, 481, 537, 621, 713, 769
Look for and make use of structure, *Throughout. For example, see:* 108, 171, 263, 351, 416, 487, 651, 707, 748
Look for and express regularity in repeated reasoning, *Throughout. For example, see:* 85, 127, 237, 266, 464, 561, 636, 696, 739
Measurement, of lengths, *See* Lengths
Mental math
addition using, 399–404
subtraction using, 237, 461–466
Meters
estimating lengths in, 535–540
measuring lengths in, 529–534
Metric units
estimating lengths in, 535–540
measuring lengths in, 529–534
Midnight, 718
Minus sign (−), 206
Minutes, telling time to nearest five, 705–710
Missing numbers
in length word problems, 591–596
using place value to find, 363–368
Model(s)
addition of three-digit numbers using, 429–434
bar, 90
of even and odd numbers, 9–14
of numbers up to 1,000, 319–324
part-part-whole, 71, 72
subtraction using
of one-digit number from two-digit number, 263–274, 281–286
of three-digit numbers, 485–490
of two-digit number from two-digit number, 275–286
Modeling Real Life, *In every lesson. For example, see:* 8, 46, 108, 212, 318, 404, 466, 584, 618, 668
Money, *See also* Coins; Dollar bills
in word problems, 687–692, 699–704
Multiple Representations, *Throughout. For example, see:* 16, 63, 128, 169, 270, 394, 489, 581, 619, 682

Nickels, *See also* Coins
value of, 664
Noon, 718
Number(s)
comparing
using number line, 381–386
using symbols, 375–380
compatible, 442
even and odd
identifying, 3–8
modeling, 9–14
extended form of, 331–336
one-digit (*See* One-digit numbers)

Index

representing in different ways, 337–342
standard form of, 331–336
three-digit (*See* Three-digit numbers)
two-digit (*See* Two-digit numbers)
word form of, 331–336
Number line
adding on
of lengths, 579–584
using "make a 10" strategy, 60, 63, 84
of tens, 103–108
of tens and hundreds, 405–410
of tens and ones, 109–114
of three-digit numbers, 411–416
comparing numbers using, 381–386
definition of, 40, 104
subtracting on
using addition, 219–224, 503–508
using "count on" and "count back" strategies, 65–70
using "get to 10" strategy, 77, 78, 84
of lengths, 579–584
of tens, 207–212
of tens and hundreds, 467–472
of tens and ones, 213–218
of three-digit numbers, 473–478
Number Sense, *Throughout. For example, see:* 5, 46, 161, 212, 353, 371, 401, 534, 621, 683

O

Octagons
drawing, 734
identifying, 732–736
Odd numbers
adding, 9–14
identifying, 3–8
modeling, 9–14
One(s) (1)
adding
breaking addends apart in, 116–126
using models, 429–434
using number line, 109–114
in partial sums, 153–164, 423–428
in regrouping, 165–176
counting by
within 120, 352–356
within 1,000, 357
definition of, 320
identifying numbers 1 more or 1 less, 369–374
subtracting, using models, 485–490
understanding place value of, 325–330
One dollar bills ($1)
coins equal to, 681–686
finding total value of, 693–698
making change from, 687–692
value of, 682
One thousand (1,000)
modeling and writing numbers up to, 319–324
skip counting within, 357–362, 405–410, 467–472
One-digit numbers
adding three, 53–58
subtracting, from two-digit number, 263–274, 281–286
Open number line, *See* Number line
Open-Ended, 434, 440, 674
Organize It, *In every chapter. For example, see:* 2, 40, 152, 206, 312, 460, 522, 578, 612, 730

P

Partial sums
with three-digit numbers, 423–428
with two-digit numbers, 153–164
Part-part-whole model, 71, 72
Patterns, 487, 707, 748, 766
Pennies, *See also* Coins
value of, 664
Pentagons
drawing, 734
identifying, 732–736, 737
Performance Task, *In every chapter. For example, see:* 33, 145, 255, 305, 387, 453, 515, 603, 723, 779

Picture graphs
making, 625–630
tally charts compared to, 619, 625
understanding, 619–624
Place value, *See also* Hundred; One; Ten
breaking apart addends using, 115–126
identifying patterns in, 363–368
representing numbers in different ways with, 337–342
understanding, 325–330
Plots, line, making, 643–654
P.M., 717–722
Polygons, *See also specific types*
definition of, 738
drawing, 743–748
identifying angles of, 737–742
Practice, *In every lesson. For example, see:* 7–8, 45–46, 157–158, 211–212, 373–374, 465–466, 527–528, 583–584, 617–618, 679–680
Precision, *Throughout. For example, see:* 70, 123, 149, 528, 537, 555, 564, 668, 707, 736
Problem solving, *See* Word problems
Problem Solving Strategy, *Throughout. For example, see:* 90, 142, 193, 250, 303, 586, 594, 700
Problem Types, *Throughout. For example, see:*
add to,
change unknown, 50, 92, 114, 191, 410, 422, 455, 630, 746
result unknown, 11, 88, 126, 284, 362, 432, 496, 579, 758
start unknown, 91, 192, 408, 426, 453, 593, 700
compare,
bigger unknown, 52, 124, 162, 200, 395, 426, 453, 576, 786
difference unknown, 70, 112, 218, 256, 446, 566, 615, 680, 740, 766
smaller unknown, 52, 255, 292, 470, 552, 599, 628, 684, 702, 727
put together,
addend unknown, 44, 56, 62, 118, 204, 290, 606
both addends unknown, 76, 453
total unknown, 18, 56, 138, 174, 284, 441, 515, 570, 700, 786
take apart,
addend unknown, 44, 56, 62, 204, 476, 606
both addends unknown, 76, 478
total unknown, 83, 243, 490, 514
take from,
change unknown, 94, 222, 266, 302, 464, 592, 690
result unknown, 68, 92, 210, 299, 464, 500, 597, 701, 736, 785
start unknown, 68, 91, 120, 246, 272, 300, 506, 701

Quadrilaterals
angles of, 738–742
drawing, 734, 736
identifying, 732–736, 737
Quarter past, 712–716
Quarter to, 712–716
Quarters, *See also* Coins
value of, 664

Reading, *Throughout. For example, see:* T-7, T-87, T-107, T-169, T-279, T-545, T-589, T-635, T-667, T-741
Real World, *See* Modeling Real Life
Reasoning, *Throughout. For example, see:* 14, 111, 215, 227, 407, 469, 511, 599, 615, 665
Rectangles, equal squares in, 755–760
Regrouping
addition using, 165–176

subtraction using, 263–268
with numbers containing zeros, 498–502
Repeated addition, of equal groups, 16–18
Repeated Reasoning, 85, 365
Response to Intervention, *Throughout. For example, see:* T-1B, T-43, T-107, T-245, T-317, T-377, T-397B, T-531, T-595, T-661B
Review & Refresh, *In every lesson. For example, see:* 158, 212, 268, 404, 466
Rhombus
definition of, 744
drawing, 744
Right angles
definition of, 738
identifying, 738–742
Rows
definition of, 152
in rectangles, 756–760

S

Scaffolding Instruction, *In every lesson. For example, see:* T-5, T-135, T-185, T-251, T-353, T-401, T-487, T-599, T-615, T-745
Shapes, two-dimensional. *See also specific shapes*
angles of, 737–742
drawing, 743–748
equal shares of
drawing lines showing, 767–778
identifying lines showing, 761–766
identifying types of, 731–736
Shares, *See* Equal shares
Show and Grow, *In every lesson. For example, see:* 4, 42, 154, 208, 264, 314, 400, 524, 580, 664
Sides
definition of, 732
identifying number of, 254, 732–736
Skip counting
within 120, 351–356
within 1,000, 357–362, 405–410, 467–472
Squares
definition of, 744
drawing, 744
rectangles composed of, 755–760
Standard form of numbers, 331–336
Structure, *Throughout. For example, see:* 20, 55, 114, 218, 330, 374, 416, 478, 584, 677
Subtraction
within 20, 83–88
using addition, 219–224, 503–508
checking with addition, 287–292
choosing strategies for, 243–248, 293–298, 509–514
using compensation
with numbers containing zeros, 498–502
with three-digit numbers, 479–484
with two-digit numbers, 237–242
using "count on" and "count back" strategies, 65–70
using decomposition (breaking numbers apart), 225–236
explaining strategies for, 509–514
using "get to 10" strategy, 77–82, 84
of lengths, 579–584
using mental math, 237, 461–466
using models
of one-digit number from two-digit number, 263–274, 281–286
of three-digit numbers, 485–490
of two-digit number from two-digit number, 275–286
on number line (*See* Number line, subtracting on)
using regrouping, 263–268
with numbers containing zeros, 498–502
relationship between addition and, 71–76
summary of strategies for, 293, 509

of three-digit numbers, 473–496
using compensation, 479–484
using models, 485–490
using number line, 473–478
from numbers containing zeros, 497–502
word problems solved using
one-step, 89–94, 299–304
two-step, 249–254, 299–304
Success Criteria, *In every lesson. For example, see:* T-3, T-171, T-219, T-293, T-375, T-447, T-509, T-585, T-631, T-755
Sums, *See also* Addition
definition of, 42
partial
with three-digit numbers, 423–428
with two-digit numbers, 153–164
Surveys, 614
Symbols
comparing numbers using, 375–380
dollar sign ($), 682
equal to (=), 376–380
greater than (>), 376–380
less than (<), 376–380
minus sign (−), 206
right angle, 738

T

Tally charts
bar graphs compared to, 631, 637
organizing data in, 613–618
picture graphs compared to, 619, 625
Ten(s) (10)
adding
using decomposition, 116–126
using mental math, 399–404
using models, 429–434
using number line, 103–114, 405–410
in partial sums, 153–164, 423–428
in regrouping, 165–176
counting by
within 120, 351–356
within 1,000, 357–362, 405–410, 467–472
definition of, 320
in "get to 10" strategy, 77–82, 84
groups of, as hundreds, 313–318
identifying numbers 10 more or 10 less, 369–374
in "make a 10" strategy, 59–64, 84
subtracting
using decomposition, 231–236
using mental math, 461–466
using models, 485–490
using number line, 467–472
understanding place value of, 325–330
Ten dollar bills ($10), finding total value of, 693–698
Think and Grow, *In every lesson. For example, see:* 4, 42, 154, 208, 314, 352, 462, 524, 614, 664
Think and Grow: Modeling Real Life, *In every lesson. For example, see:* 6, 44, 106, 210, 266, 366, 402, 464, 526, 666
Thirds
definition of, 762
drawing lines showing, 767–778
identifying lines showing, 761–766
Three-digit numbers
adding, 411–440
using compensation, 417–422
using models, 429–434
using number line, 411–416
using partial sums, 423–428
subtracting, 473–496
using compensation, 479–484
using models, 485–490
using number line, 473–478
from numbers containing zeros, 497–502
writing standard, expanded, and word forms of, 331–336
Time, telling
A.M. and P.M. in, 717–722
before and after the hour, 711–716

Index

to nearest five minutes, 705–710
Triangles
angles of, 738–742
drawing, 734, 736
identifying, 254, 732–736, 737
Two-digit numbers
adding
using compensation, 127–132
four, 441–446
using partial sums, 153–164
three, 183–188
subtracting
using compensation, 237–242
one-digit number from, 263–274, 281–286
two-digit number from, 275–286
Two-dimensional shapes, *See* Shapes

Vertex (vertices)
of cubes, 750
definition of, 732
identifying number of, 254, 732–736

W

Which One Doesn't Belong?, *Throughout. For example, see:* 318, 336, 425, 695, 713
Word form of numbers, 331–336
Word problems, solving
length
comparing lengths, 585–590
for missing measurements, 591–596
using number line, 579–584
practicing, 597–602
money, 699–704
making change from one dollar, 687–692
one-step
using addition, 89–94, 189–194
using arrays, 27–32
using subtraction, 89–94, 299–304
two-step
using addition, 139–144, 189–194
using subtraction, 249–254, 299–304
Writing, *Throughout. For example, see:* 132, 176, 286, 481, 502, 567, 602, 636, 733, 739

Yards
estimating lengths in, 553–558
measuring lengths in, 547–552
You Be the Teacher, *Throughout. For example, see:* 11, 91, 105, 209, 268, 324, 368, 466, 525, 677

Zero (0), subtraction from numbers containing, 497–502

Reference Sheet

Symbols

+	plus
−	minus
=	equals
>	greater than
<	less than
¢	cent sign
$	dollar sign

Place Value

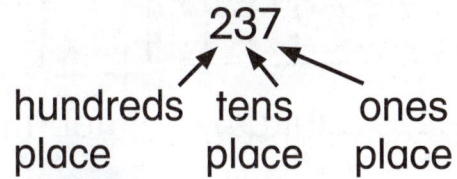

237

hundreds place — tens place — ones place

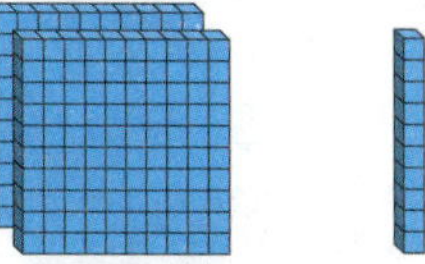
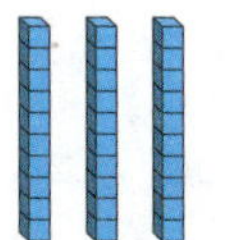
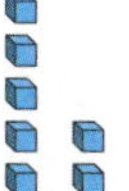

2 flats — 3 rods — 7 units

Hundreds	Tens	Ones
2	3	7

Money

penny 1¢

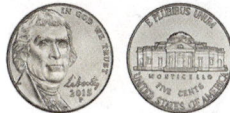

100 pennies = $1

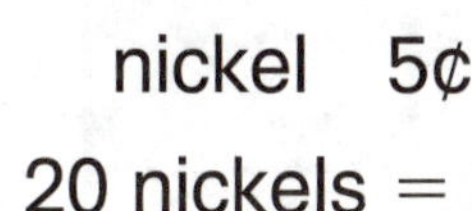

nickel 5¢

20 nickels = $1

dime 10¢

10 dimes = $1

quarter 25¢

4 quarters = $1

$1 bill

$5 bill

$10 bill

$20 bill

Time

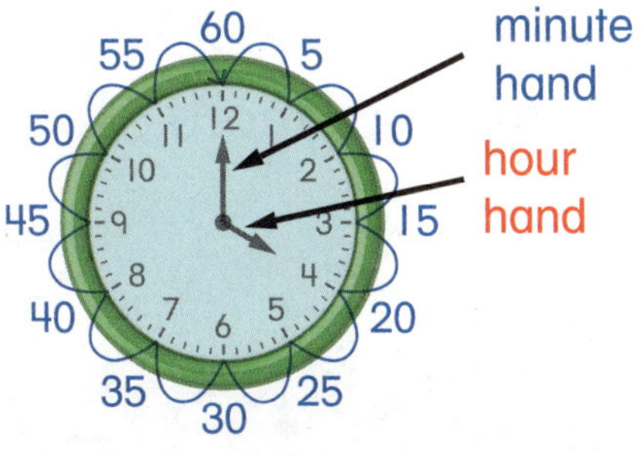

60 minutes = 1 hour

quarter to

quarter past

half past

Equal Shares

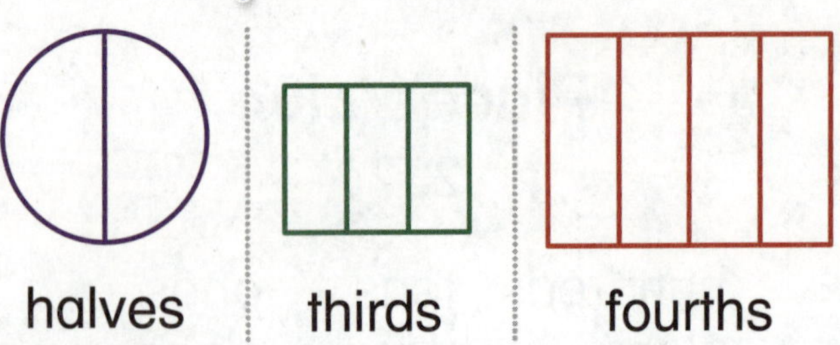

Length

1 meter = 100 centimeters

1 foot = 12 inches

1 yard = 36 inches

1 yard = 3 feet

Shapes

vertex

side

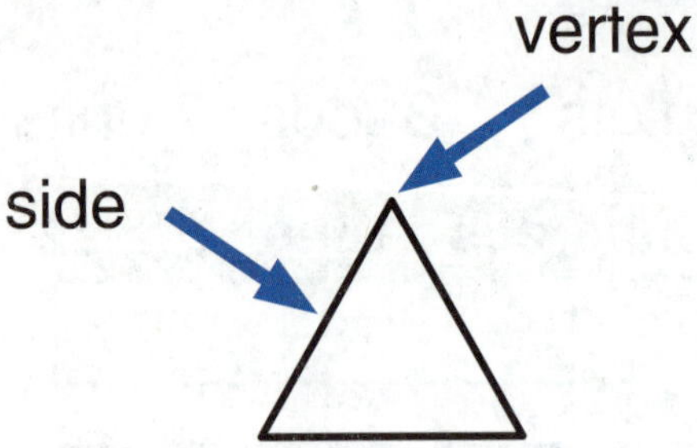

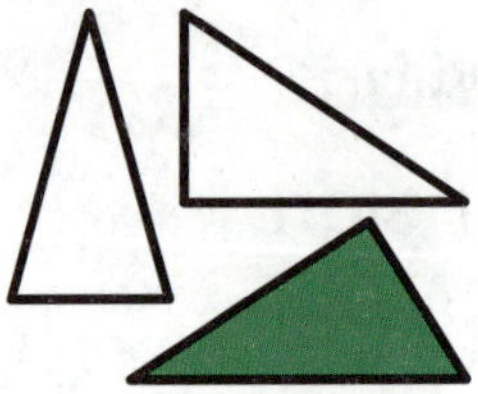

triangles

3 sides

3 vertices

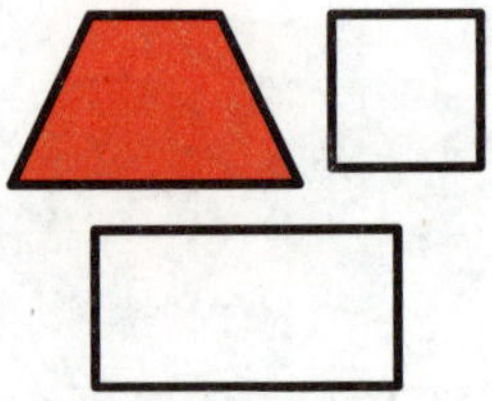

quadrilaterals

4 sides

4 vertices

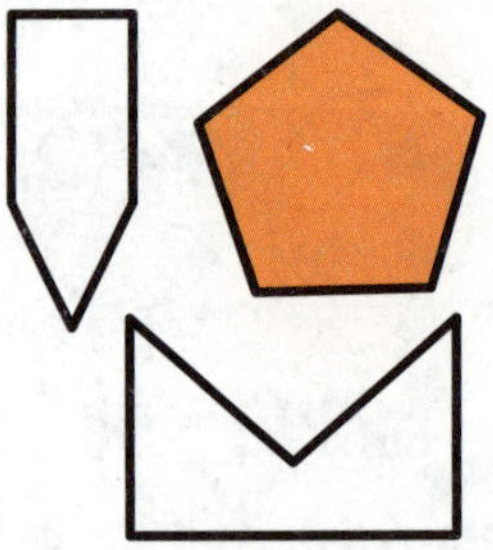

pentagons

5 sides

5 vertices

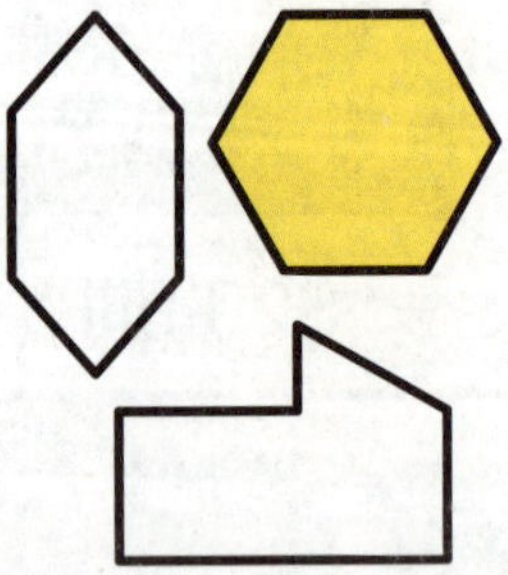

hexagons

6 sides

6 vertices

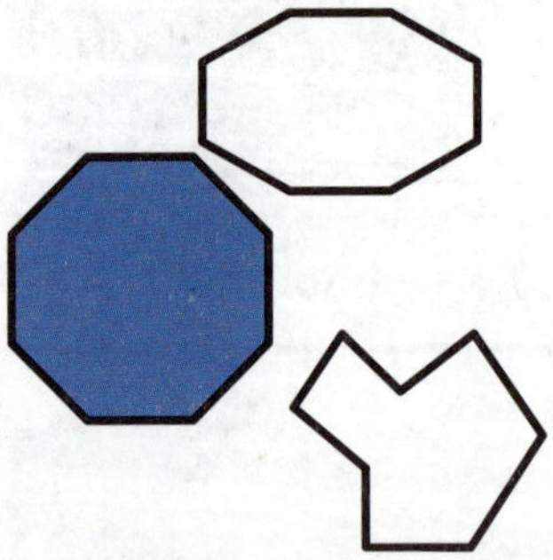

octagons

8 sides

8 vertices

A **polygon** is a closed two-dimensional shape with three or more sides. When two sides meet, they form an **angle**.

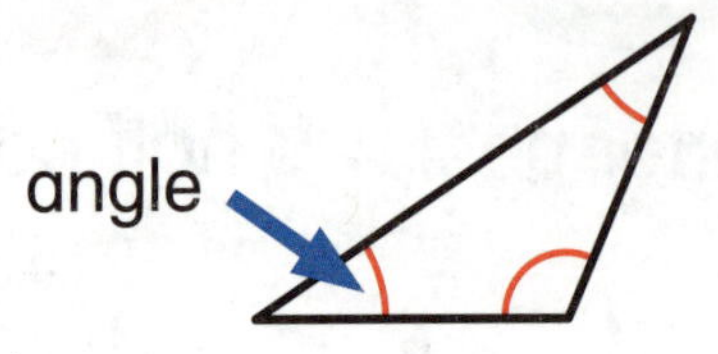

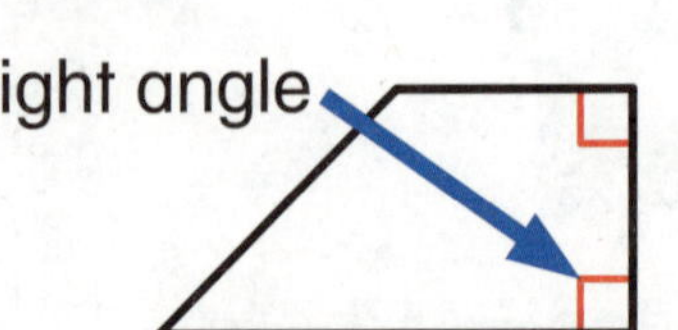

Credits

Chapter 1
1 GerhardvdS10/iStock/Getty Images Plus

Chapter 2
39 Wavebreakmeadia/iStock/Getty Images Plus

Chapter 3
101 LawrenceSawyer/E+/Getty Images

Chapter 4
151 phaitoons/iStock/Getty Images Plus

Chapter 5
205 Herhurricane/iStock/Getty Images Plus

Chapter 6
261 Blend Images/Shutterstock.com

Chapter 7
311 Brent Hofacker/Shutterstock.com

Chapter 8
349 aluxum/iStock/Getty Images Plus

Chapter 9
397 © highwaystarz - stock.adobe.com

Chapter 10
459 HodagMedia/Shutterstock.com

Chapter 11
521 kali9/E+/Getty Images; **547** paulprescott72/iStock/Getty Images Plus

Chapter 12
577 Itsra Sanprasert/Shutterstok.com; **604** Bullet_Chained/iStock/Getty Images Plus; filo/iStock/Getty Images Plus

Chapter 13
611 fstop123/iStock/Getty Images Plus

Chapter 14
661 querbeet/E+/Getty Images; **coins** TokenPhoto/E+/Getty Images; asafta/iStock/Getty Images Plus; Kuzmik_A/iStock/Getty Images Plus; Meral Hydaverdi/Shutterstock.com; **five dollar bill** Studio Araminta/Shutterstock.com

Chapter 15
729 akiyoko/iStock/Getty Images Plus

Cartoon Illustrations: MoreFrames Animation
Design Elements: oksanika/Shutterstock.com; icolourful/Shutterstock.com; Valdis Torms